Joe Cummings &
China Williams

Bangkok

The Top Five

1 **Bangkok River & Canal Trip**
Grab a ferry or long-tail boat ride up Mae Nam Chao Phraya (p72)

2 **Jim Thompson's House**
See a treasure trove of art amid traditional Thai architecture (p97)

3 **Wat Pho**
Discover beautiful Buddha images at Bangkok's oldest wat (p78)

4 **Wat Phra Kaew & Grand Palace**
Visit this shimmering temple fit for an 'Emerald Buddha' (p79)

5 **Vimanmek Teak Mansion**
Watch a traditional dance in this serene former royal palace (p90)

Contents

Published by Lonely Planet Publications Pty Ltd
ABN 36 005 607 983

Australia Head Office, Locked Bag 1, Footscray,
Victoria 3011, ☎ 03 8379 8000, fax 03 8379 8111,
talk2us@lonelyplanet.com.au

USA 150 Linden St, Oakland, CA 94607,
☎ 510 893 8555, toll free 800 275 8555,
fax 510 893 8572, info@lonelyplanet.com

UK 72–82 Rosebery Ave, Clerkenwell, London,
EC1R 4RW, ☎ 020 7841 9000, fax 020 7841 9001,
go@lonelyplanet.co.uk

The Authors

Joe Cummings

Born in New Orleans, Joe developed an attraction to seedy tropical ports at a young age. An interest in Southeast Asian politics first led him to Bangkok, where he took up residence for a year. Upon his return to the US, Joe completed a master's degree in Southeast Asian studies, then returned to Bangkok to begin writing Lonely Planet's first guidebook to Thailand. Joe later had plenty of time to delve more deeply into the city as Lonely Planet's Thailand and Bangkok author through the 1980s, '90s and '00s. Joe also scouts locations for international film and TV productions shooting in Thailand. Most recently he served as a production consultant and 'guitar wrangler' for *The Elephant King* (2006), in which he also had a small role. When he's not testing mattresses and slurping *tôm yam kûng* for Lonely Planet, Joe is playing with his band, The Tonic Rays, in clubs in Bangkok and Chiang Mai.

China Williams

China grew up in South Carolina, whose hot summers and easy-going chit-chat prepared her well for Thailand. She first arrived in the kingdom as an English teacher in the small provincial capital of Surin and made periodic trips to Bangkok for visa business, English bookstores and hamburgers. After a few years' absence, China returned to Bangkok to find a fully grown city that is quickly climbing to the top of the region's urban pedestal. China now lives in the US, where she works as a freelance writer. Home is most recently in Montana with her husband, Matt. China wrote the Sights, Walking Tours, Eating, Entertainment, Shopping, Sleeping and Excursions chapters.

PHOTOGRAPHER
Mick Elmore

When he was five Mick Elmore borrowed his older brother's camera and started taking pictures. His passion became his profession after university when Mick became a journalist on the Mexican border in Texas in 1984. Since then his cameras – mostly Nikon – have taken him around the world, with longer stays in Guatemala, Colombia, Australia, Cambodia and Thailand, where has been based for 10 years. Mick started selling photos to Lonely Planet in the early '90s and has been part of Lonely Planet Images team since its beginning.

China's Top Bangkok Day

Getting lost and eating my way towards a stomachache are two of my favourite things to do in Bangkok. Thankfully the two activities usually coincide. Chinatown reliably defies any map. I've accidentally stumbled into people's living rooms, been chased by junk-yard dogs through the machine shop district and practically fainted from heat exhaustion just before finding a stall with restorative duck noodles. I'm also that new generation of food snob that is suspicious of white tablecloths, so Bangkok is a perfect order. Pratunam is my latest food craze: it has the requisite stink from the canal and the idling cars at the massive intersection, the fluorescent lights and mating stray cats to make dining seem surreal. Plus half of Thailand's repertoire of wok wonders occupies one city block. No day is complete without a visit to the shopping centre Mahboonkrong (MBK); I love cruising the levels watching youthful conspicuous consumption. To really unpeel Bangkok, I like to jump from the old-fashioned part of town to the future city: from Banglamphu's reserved shophouses to Sukhumvit's scrapers, from the earnest river ferry to the zippy Skytrain. What a brilliantly confusing city.

Introducing Bangkok

A city of beguiling incongruities and overwhelming sensuality, Bangkok will scramble the expectations of even the most well-read traveller. A modern veneer of international brand names in blinking neon only partially disguises an encapsulation of all things Thai. As you emerge from the airport, the thick, jasmine-scented air envelops your body, the oceanic reverberation of distant traffic fills your ears, and you sense that Bangkok is a place you'll not easily forget.

Swept along by the vehicular current into the heart of the capital, you soon find yourself lodged in a labyrinth that draws together the essence of everything that is sacred and profane in Thailand. Gilded temple spires, gleaming shopping malls and ornate skyscrapers stand alongside tented noodle stands and blanket-on-the-pavement palm readers. Night falls and huge glittering discotheques fashioned to resemble UFOs and Roman palaces vie with massage parlours drenched in red neon for the attention of the orbiting inhabitants of a city that never sleeps. Time contracts as you realise just how overwhelming your choices are.

Yet in the midst of the melange of international influences and epoch-leaping technologies, Bangkok never loses sight of its essential *khwaam pen thai* or 'Thai-ness'. Outside the tallest skyscrapers, office employees stop to offer flowers, incense and prayers to roofed spirit shrines, diminutive echoes from the past. Wheeled carts at the curbside offer Thai herbal remedies and Buddhist amulets alongside espresso coffees and Nintendo game cartridges.

LOWDOWN

Population: 10 million

Time zone: UTC/GMT plus seven hours

Bowl of noodles: 35B

Skytrain ticket: 10B to 40B

Cup of brewed coffee: 25B

Three-star room: 1300B

Essential local drink: Sang Som with lime and soda

No-no: Don't touch the top of anyone's head, or point at anything with your feet

At times Bangkok seems like it's hurtling toward disaster. The city was laid out on the spongy Chao Phraya flood plains in the 18th century and is now reportedly sinking at a rate of nearly a metre a year as wells suck the water table dry. During the dry season, a thick traffic-induced haze fills busy intersections – in this city several hundred new vehicles are registered every day. Over half of Thailand's urban population lives in the capital and every bus from the provinces brings in yet more fortune seekers.

Maddening? Definitely. But the amazing thing is how well the city works. Public transport may be excruciatingly slow at times, but it is plentiful; try flagging a taxi in any other Asian capital at 3am. You can buy a bowl of mouth-watering *kŭaytĭaw* (rice noodles) from a street vendor while standing outside a US$200-a-night hotel; or have your muscles gently kneaded for an hour and a half at Wat Pho, the oldest temple in the city, for less than the price of a cinema ticket in most Western cities. Catch a ride aboard a canal taxi on the Thonburi side of Mae Nam Chao Phraya and you can disappear down shaded waterways where modern Bangkok is soon left behind.

Viewed from above, Bangkok resembles a quirky, skewed *mandala* (the quasi-circular diagrams created by Buddhist artists as objects for meditation). Much like Hindu-Buddhist mythology's Mt Meru, around which the cosmos unfolds in concentric continents alternating with slender cosmic oceans, Thailand's sweltering capital straddles a vast spider web of natural and artificial canals fanning out through the sultry river delta for over 1000 sq km. Crisscrossing the city in all directions, these murky green waterways conjure up a parallel universe in which 18th-century Siam collides with 21st-century Thailand.

Although today it's a city barely keeping up with the pace of its own hyper-development, Bangkok continues to lure rural Thais, Asian and Western investors, and curious visitors from around the world with its phantasmagoria of the carnal, spiritual and entrepreneurial. The capital remains easily the most exciting and dynamic city in Southeast Asia, with the region's largest foreign media correspondent base, largest fashion industry and most active contemporary cinema. As a primary gateway for investment in neighbouring Vietnam, Cambodia, Laos and Myanmar, the city also serves as a financial hub for mainland Southeast Asia.

As famed travel writer Pico Ayer, himself the cultural offspring of three continents, has noted about Bangkok – it is a city that is 'immutably and ineffably itself'.

ESSENTIAL BANGKOK *China Williams*

- Take a **motorcycle taxi** (p243) through town – this is the closest many people will come to an extreme sport.

- Wander through **Chinatown** (p91) – impossible to navigate, Chinatown's daily routine is thoroughly entertaining to watch.

- Hop on the **river ferry** (p241) at sunset – through the golden haze of pollution, Bangkok is heartbreakingly beautiful.

- Ride the **Skytrain** (p242) – from this vantage point, you can see into all those fortress garden estates.

- Hang out in **Mahboonkrong** (MBK; p181) – like pop music, MBK is mindless and fun.

City Life

City Life

BANGKOK TODAY

Bangkok comfortably rates as one of Asia's most intriguing and perpetually surprising cities. In terms of modernity it runs close behind Tokyo, Hong Kong and Singapore, with steady economic growth over the last 25 years bringing air-conditioned shopping malls, maple-and-chrome coffee shops, world-class architectural monuments and many other accoutrements of civilisation. Media, design, fine arts and other contemporary creative endeavours are all flourishing at levels that could almost compete with such world capitals as London and New York.

Yet in most ways, the city is as far from being tamed by international ideas and technology as when it was founded more than 200 years ago. Even the casual observer can see that Bangkok groans under the weight of an overburdened infrastructure. Road surfaces, whose area relative to the overall plan for a city this size is among the world's lowest percentages, remain insufficient for the number of Bangkok-registered cars, yet over a thousand new vehicles roll onto the streets every day. Meanwhile the City of Angels (the direct translation of Krung Thep, the city's Thai name) is sinking at a rate of nearly one metre per year as the city's hydraulic system continues to suck water out from the spongy Chao Phraya flood plains upon which the city sprawls. Bangkok's suburbs are now growing at a faster rate than the city centre, which has stabilised density in the older districts while spreading the demand for resources.

In spite of the environmental tightrope it walks, Bangkok continues to hold an intense allure for Thais and foreigners alike. An open investment climate and laissez-faire business attitude explain only part of the attraction. Socially speaking, Bangkok's legendary tolerance, which lends equal support to the monk and the playboy, to the beggar and the Benz dealer, complements the package. You can slurp down a chilli-laden plate of *kŭaytĭaw phàt khîi mao* ('shit-drunk' fried-rice noodles) from a street vendor before strolling into a world-class health spa. Bid your life savings on the Stock Exchange of Thailand or take an all-day canal tour for less than the price of a cinema ticket in most world capitals. For absolutely nothing, take a meditation cell at Wat Mahathat and contemplate your life's choices for days, weeks or the rest of your life. However sacred or profane, however slummy or highbrow your needs, Bangkok delivers.

And Bangkok does it all with a style and grace perhaps unrivalled anywhere else in the world, at least for a city of its size. In most neighbourhoods of the city the streets are remarkably free of litter, while even the most humble Bangkok residents tend to attire themselves in freshly laundered clothing. With jasmine blossoms hanging from every street shrine and incense smoke curling in the air, your nose may even forget to take note of omnipresent vehicular fumes.

The high value Thais traditionally place on *jai yen* (cool heart) – remaining unperturbed even in the most trying of situations – is alive and well in the Thai metropolis. Despite bumper-to-bumper traffic, the honking of auto horns is seldom heard, even during the city's legendary morning and evening rush-hour gridlocks. Service in local restaurants is conducted in calm, measured tones, rather than the frantic exchanges travellers may be more accustomed to in other huge cites.

Beyond the ever-present Thai spirit of place, even the most jaded traveller will be humbled by the city's sheer cultural diversity. Official estimates place Bangkok's population at nine million, though some sources claim this figure may be a million or two short. An astonishing 3600 residents compete for every square kilometre, constituting one of the highest density rates in Asia, and propelling a creative turbine that never ceases as the city's past and future coevolve, from farms to freeways, spirit shrines to art galleries.

As varied as it is vast, Bangkok offers residents and visitors alike the assurance they will never be bored. One can move across the city on water via 18th-century canals, in the air aboard the sleek BTS Skytrain or below ground in the high-tech Metropolitan Rapid Transit

Authority (MRTA) subway. When hunger beckons, residents are spoiled by a panoply of the finest Thai restaurants anywhere in the kingdom, along with a host of other Asian cuisines – Chinese, Japanese, Korean, Burmese, Malaysian, Sri Lankan and Indian, to name a few – and a broad range of European fare prepared by native chefs. When night falls, one can attend a classical Thai masked dance-drama performance followed by a jaunt to a club to hear a visiting DJ spin the latest world mixes.

Keeping the city vibrant at its core are the enviable freedoms that lie behind this phantasmagorical realm of choice. Metropolitan Bangkok boasts the only elected governorship in the nation – other provincial governors are ministry-appointed. The freedom to write just about anything one wants has made Bangkok Asia's largest base for foreign media correspondents. Thailand's openness to foreign investment has likewise developed Bangkok into the financial hub for mainland Southeast Asia, a role that has expanded quickly as Vietnam, Cambodia, Laos and Myanmar have opened up to travel and investment in the last 20 years or so.

While most of the time Bangkokians seem patently antipolitical, they are always the first in the country to stand up against their national leaders whenever their policies become unpopular. Throughout the city's modern history, Bangkok residents have taken to the streets in the hundreds of thousands to voice their opposition to administrative trends, most recently in the unseating of Prime Minister Thaksin Shinawatra in April 2006.

Meanwhile the city's burgeoning fine- and popular-arts scene provides a constantly changing social landscape of beauty, inspiration and challenge. More than 250 art galleries host rotating exhibitions of visual arts from both Thai and foreign artists. Public art has never been more popular, with daring neotraditional designs and colour schemes on restaurant walls, temple murals and anywhere else artists can find space. Socially engaged installations and exhibitions allow many city artists to participate in local and national politics at a level unrivalled in Thailand's history.

A growing fusion of Thai ideas with global media extends from painting and architecture to Thai cinema. Directorial efforts over the last 10 years have been so encouraging that Thai and foreign critics alike speak of a Thai 'new wave', almost entirely focused on Bangkok yet garnering awards and favourable mention at international film festivals abroad.

The city's ongoing self-consciousness as expressed in the arts has helped to boost urban pride, which in turn has led Bangkokians to put more thought into urban-planning issues. Realising that late-20th-century development changed the shape of Bangkok forever, residents are now looking towards the future with an eye for doing whatever possible to make their city a more pleasant and efficient place in which to work and live.

A bus in heavy traffic on Th Ratchaprarop, Pratunam (p94)

9

To relieve the lack of surface streets, the city boasts an extensive system of elevated freeways that now enable commuters to leapfrog the traffic congestion below. The BTS Skytrain, a sleek, elevated rail network that opened in 1999, has made a sizable dent in Bangkok traffic and allowed a large number of city residents to switch from the slow, often crowded city bus system. One unexpected benefit of the new system is that the Skytrain raises everyone riding it 12m above street level, affording glimpses of lush greenery and old Bangkok architecture not ordinarily visible below due to high walls. During the Skytrain's first years of operation, many Bangkokians expressed surprise that their city was actually more attractive than they'd previously believed.

Meanwhile the MRTA (Metro) subway links the 'old Bangkok' of Chinatown and Hualamphong with the 'new Bangkok' further east along Th Sukhumvit, the city's longest and broadest thoroughfare. Despite the once-popular sentiment that it couldn't be done, engineers dug the MRTA tunnels 23m below street level using the same techniques as for the 'Chunnel' between France and Great Britain.

Hence Bangkokians traversing the city today can choose among three levels, whether above the city via the Skytrain or elevated freeways, on the traditional roadways or beneath the city via the new subway. At one spot in Bangkok, Th Phra Ram IV is surmounted by a freeway flyover and, a bit higher, the Skytrain track, while below the street runs the subway line. Such layering is set to increase as both the Skytrain and Metro systems are scheduled to be extended over the next decade.

Concurrent with the ongoing growth of concrete, steel and asphalt is a countering, if not equal, movement in the development of green areas and public parks in Bangkok. Lumphini Park – Suan Lum in local parlance – is the city's oldest and until relatively recently the largest, with 58 hectares of grass, trees and an artificial lake, all very close to the city centre. A major recreational focus for people living in the older districts near Chao Phraya River, the park teems with people in the morning practicing t'ai chi, jogging or just taking a nap in the shade. On weekends during the cool season, the 80-piece Bangkok Symphony Orchestra performs, drawing classical music lovers from all over the city.

Meanwhile Rama IX Park, at 200 acres now the city's largest, is widely acclaimed for its well-tended collection of outdoor tropical flora as well as greenhouses filled with rare plants from around the world. Off Th Si Nakarin in the newer eastern side of the city, Rama IX Park is popular on weekends, yet nearly deserted during the week.

Although it doesn't boast the facilities of a full-scale public park, the large expanse of grass known as Sanam Luang in the former royal district of Ko Ratanakosin serves as an important locus for Thai picnickers, joggers and, during the hot season, kite-flyers. Just north of the Grand Palace and Wat Phra Kaew, Sanam Luang is also used for special events from time to time, and is the official cremation ground for infrequent royal funerals.

The latest Bangkok trend towards greenness is the creation of 'pocket parks' in unused and undeveloped areas of the city. Both of Bangkok's surviving 18th-century forts, Phra Sumen and Mahakan, have had adjacent lots planted with grass and trees to provide urbanites with relief from their mostly concrete, glass and steel existence.

All of these brave movements towards the city's future, whether in art, mass transport or urban planning, signal a new optimism for Bangkok. It's not unusual nowadays to hear a native Bangkokian comment, 'Ten years ago I was looking for another place to live in Thailand. Now I think I'll stay.'

HOT CONVERSATION TOPICS

- The fall of Thai Rak Thai – who will succeed Thaksin and company, and will they rid Bangkok of the early bar closing law enforced by Thaksin's 'new social order'?
- Siam Paragon – will the largest mall in Southeast Asia survive, and can the middle class afford to shop there?
- Press freedom – with magazine and newspaper editors unbridled by Thailand's richest man (Thaksin), Bangkokians have high expectations for the city's journalists.
- Coolest new cocktail bar-cum-disco – there's always a new one jockeying for position, with plenty of curbside critics ready to shoot it down.
- Thai models and superstars – where are they dining, what are they driving and are there any left who aren't *lûuk khrêung* (half-Thai, half-*faràng*)?

CITY CALENDAR

Although Bangkok shares a large number of festivals and fairs with the rest of Thailand, the truth is that most Bangkokians leave town on holidays if they can. Still, something is almost always going on, especially during the November to February cool season.

Dates for festivals typically vary from year to year, either because of the lunar calendar, which isn't quite in sync with the solar calendar, or because local authorities decide to change festival days. The Tourism Authority of Thailand (TAT) publishes an up-to-date *Major Events & Festivals* calendar each year.

On dates noted as public holidays, all government offices and banks close. For more on holidays, see p249.

Weather-wise, the best time of year to visit Bangkok is November to February, when temperatures drop to moderately warm and the skies are usually clear. March through May vivify the famous Noel Coward verse, 'In Bangkok at twelve o'clock they foam at the mouth and run, But mad dogs and Englishmen go out in the midday sun.' From June to October it rains almost daily, with occasional flash flooding in parts of the city.

JANUARY
BANGKOK INTERNATIONAL FILM FESTIVAL
www.bangkokfilm.org

Despite beginning only six years ago, the 10-day festival screens about 150 films from around the world, with an emphasis on Asian cinema. Screenings take place at the new Siam Paragon Cineplex (Map pp294–5), next to Siam Square. Events end with the awarding of the festival's Golden Kinnaree in a range of categories.

LATE JANUARY– EARLY FEBRUARY
RIVER OF KINGS
www.theriverofkingsbangkok.com

Initiated by Princess Ubol Ratana, and sponsored largely by TAT, this spectacular sound-and-light show is performed for 12 consecutive nights alongside Mae Nam Chao Phraya at Tha Ratchaworadit (between Tha Tien and Tha Chang). Enhanced by the illuminated Grand Palace and Wat Phra Kaew in the background, a combination of Thai dance, music and animation makes for an intensely visual experience. The storyline, which changes every year, typically involves royal heroism.

LATE FEBRUARY– EARLY MARCH
MAGHA PUJA
Magha Puja is held on the full moon of the third lunar month to commemorate the Buddha preaching to 1250 enlightened monks who came to hear him 'without prior summons'. The festival (called *Maakhá buuchaa* in Thai) culminates with a candle-lit walk around the main chapel at every wat. No alcohol can be legally sold on Magha Puja day, so virtually all of the city's bars close (although it's not a public holiday).

CHINESE NEW YEAR
Bangkok's large Thai-Chinese population celebrate their lunar new year, called *trùt jiin* in Thai, with a week full of house cleaning, lion dances and fireworks. The most impressive festivities, unsurprisingly, take place in Chinatown. Many businesses, particularly those that are Chinese owned, close down for a few days during the festival.

MARCH
BANGKOK GEMS & JEWELRY FAIR
http://gemsfair.thaigemjewelry.or.th

Held at Impact Exhibition & Convention Center, this has been Thailand's most important annual gem and jewellery trade show for over 35 years. Counting an attendance of over 30,000, the fair is a cooperative venture between the Department of Export Promotion, the Ministry of Commerce and the Thai Gem and Jewelry Traders Association.

KITE-FLYING SEASON
During the windy season, colourful kites battle it out over the skies of Sanam Luang and Lumphini Park.

Playing with water pistols during the Songkran Festival (below)

APRIL

SONGKRAN FESTIVAL

During Thailand's lunar new year celebration, Buddha images are 'bathed', monks and elders receive the respect of younger Thais through the sprinkling of water over their hands and a lot of water is tossed about for fun. Songkran gives everyone a chance to release their frustrations and literally cool off at the peak of the hot season.

Compared to most towns and cities in Thailand, Songkran in Bangkok is relatively tame as many Bangkokians leave town. The main venue for throwing water around with abandon is Th Khao San, where the foreigners outnumber the Thais. Still it's a lot of fun to spend at least one day in Khao San neighbourhood getting soaked.

MAY

VISAKHA PUJA

Falling on the 15th day of the waxing moon in the sixth lunar month, Visakha Puja (*Wísǎakhà buuchaa* in Thai) is considered the date of the Buddha's birth, enlightenment and *parinibbana* (passing away). Activities are centred on the local wat, with candle-lit processions, chanting and sermonising. No alcohol may be sold on this day.

ROYAL PLOUGHING CEREMONY

To kick off the official rice-planting season, either the king or the crown prince participates in this ancient Brahman ritual at Sanam Luang (Map p288). Thousands of Thais gather to watch, and traffic in this part of the city comes to a standstill.

MISS JUMBO QUEEN CONTEST

With fat-trends creeping across the globe, Thailand hosts a beauty pageant for extra-large (over 80kg) women who display the grace of an elephant at Nakhon Pathom's Samphran Elephant Park.

JULY

ASALHA PUJA

This Buddhist festival (*àsǎanhà buuchaa* in Thai) commemorates the day the Buddha preached his first sermon to his first five followers after attaining enlightenment. All Theravada Buddhist temples in the capital hold candle-lit processions at night. No alcohol may be sold on this day.

RAINS RETREAT (KHAO PHANSA)

A public holiday (p249) and the start of Buddhist *phansǎa* (rains retreat), traditionally this is when young men enter the monkhood for the rainy season and for all monks to station themselves in a monastery for the three months. It's a good time to observe a Buddhist ordination. No alcohol may be sold on this day.

SEPTEMBER

WORLD GOURMET FESTIVAL

The Four Seasons (formerly the Regent) hosts this 10-day feast, bringing in international chefs from all over the world. It's Bangkok's premier food event.

INTERNATIONAL FESTIVAL OF MUSIC & DANCE
www.thaiculturalcenter.com
This extravaganza of arts and culture is sponsored by the Thailand Cultural Centre.

VEGETARIAN FESTIVAL
A 10-day Chinese-Buddhist festival, *thêht-sàkaan kin jeh* wheels out streetside vendors serving meatless meals announced with yellow banners. The greatest concentration of vendors is found in Chinatown.

OCTOBER–NOVEMBER

KING CHULALONGKORN DAY
23 October

Rama V is honoured on the anniversary of his death at his revered Royal Plaza statue. Crowds of devotees come to make merit with incense and flower garlands.

KATHIN
A one-month period at the end of Buddhist *phansǎa,* during which new robes and other requisites of the monastic life are offered to the Sangha (Buddhist monkhood) at temples throughout Bangkok.

THAILAND INTERNATIONAL SWAN BOAT RACES
More than 20 international teams race traditional Thai-style long-boats along Mae Nam Chao Phraya and in Ayuthaya.

LOI KRATHONG
On the proper full-moon night (the full moon of the 12th lunar month), small lotus-shaped baskets or boats made of banana leaves containing flowers, incense, candles and a coin are floated on Thai rivers, lakes and canals. This intrinsically Thai festival (*lawy kràthong* in Thai) probably originated in Sukhothai. In Bangkok rather low-key

celebrations take place along the banks of Mae Nam Chao Phraya.

FAT FESTIVAL
Sponsored by FAT 104.5FM radio, Bangkok's indie-est indie bands gather for an annual mosh.

ASIATOPIA
Performance artists from across Southeast Asia converge on Bangkok's public spaces and theatres.

PRIDE WEEK
http://2006.pridefestival.org
A week-long festival of parades, parties and awards is organised by the city's gay businesses and organisations.

WAT SAKET FAIR
One of Bangkok's last great temple fairs is held in and around Wat Saket and the Golden Mount, welcoming pilgrims from all over Thailand and around the world to pay respect to the holy relics interred in the stupa here. During the festival, the temple grounds turn into a colourful fair selling flowers, incense, bells and saffron cloth as well as hundreds of other commercial trinkets and of course loads of Thai food.

DECEMBER

KING'S BIRTHDAY
5 December

On King Bhumibol's birthday, the city is festooned with lights and large portraits of the king are displayed in public. The highlight is a spectacular fireworks display near the Grand Palace.

BANGKOK JAZZ FESTIVAL
Started in 2003, the three-night jazz fest kicks off at Dusit Palace in commemoration of His Majesty the King's love of jazz. The line-up usually includes internationally known artists such as Larry Carlton, Earl Klugh and Bob James – focusing on the lighter side of jazz, per Thai public taste.

CULTURE

IDENTITY

Whether native or newcomer, virtually every Bangkokian you meet has a story. Although the majority no doubt find themselves in Bangkok owing to the simple fact that they were born in the city, a healthy percentage of the population hails from other parts of Thailand and from around the world. Some have followed the promise of work, while others have simply sought out one of the world's most vibrant social climates.

Climb into one of the capital's ubiquitous yellow-and-green taxis and the music issuing from your driver's radio or cassette player will often suggest where he's (virtually all Bangkok taxi drivers are male) from. If it's *măw lam,* with the churning sound of Thai-Lao bamboo panpipes *(khaen)* pounding out zydeco-like chord figures over a strong, simple rhythm, then chances are he moved to Bangkok from one of Thailand's distant northeastern provinces, such as Roi Et or Sakon Nakhon. Switch to *lûuk thûng,* a unique hybrid of Thai, Indian and Latin musical influences popular with rural audiences, and the driver almost certainly comes from a province closer to Bangkok, perhaps Suphanburi or Saraburi. And if it's syrupy Thai pop or an older, crooning Bangkok style called *lûuk krung,* then you've most likely hitched a ride with a city native.

Only a little more than half of the city's inhabitants are in fact true Bangkok Thais, ie those born of Thai parentage who speak Bangkok Thai as their first language. Although Thais are found in all walks of life, they are the backbone of the city's blue-collar work force, construction, automotive repair and river transport.

More than a quarter of the city's population is of Chinese or mixed Thai and Chinese descent. Many Chinese Thais in the capital can converse in at least one dialect from the old country, such as Cantonese, Hainanese, Hokkien or Chao Zhou, in addition to Thai. Although Chinese influence can be felt throughout Thailand's Chao Phraya delta, in Bangkok it is so strong that in certain areas of the city – such as Yaowarat, Bangkok's Chinatown, or Pathumwan, the city's wealthiest precinct – you can almost imagine you're in Hong Kong or Singapore rather than Thailand. Although Chinese Thais live in every quarter of the sprawling city, their presence is most noticeable in a densely populated core of multistorey shophouses along Th Charoen Krung and Th Yaowarat near Mae Nam Chao Phraya, a precinct known as Yaowarat, Sampeng or 'Chinatown'. Chinese in these areas tend to be engaged in all manner of commerce, from wholesale trade in auto parts to the manufacture of high-end kitchen utensils. In other parts of the city they dominate higher education, international trade, banking and white-collar employment in general.

Both immigrant and Thailand-born Chinese residents probably enjoy better relations with the majority population here than in any other country in Southeast Asia. Thai rulers in the 18th and 19th centuries made liberal use of Chinese businesspeople to infiltrate European trading houses, a move that helped defeat European colonial designs. The Thai monarchy also accepted the daughters of wealthy Chinese into the royal court as consorts, deepening political connections and adding a Chinese bloodline that extends to the current king.

Also prominent are people of South Asian descent, who make up Bangkok's second-largest Asian minority. Most trace their heritage to northern India, including many Sikhs who immigrated following the 1947 Partition of India. Other South Asian nationalities found in Bangkok include Sinhalese, Bangladeshis, Nepalis and Pakistanis. Most of the city's South Asians can be found in two areas. The heaviest concentration wedges itself in at the northern end of Th Yaowarat, between Th Chakraphet and Th Phahurat, in a neighbourhood known as Phahurat or, to English-speakers, Little India. South Asian residents are also more thinly spread along nearby Th Charoen Krung, near junctions with Th Silom and Th Surawong, an area collectively known as Bang Rak. In both areas they operate a multitude of successful retail businesses, particularly textile and tailor shops.

Centuries before the Thais migrated into the area, the Mae Nam Chao Phraya delta in and around Bangkok was home to the Mon. Bangkokians of Mon descent can still be found in some districts, particularly on Ko Kret, an island in the middle of the river in northern Bangkok and in neighbouring Pathum Thani Province. The Mon have their own language and culture, both of which have exercised a significant influence on modern Thai culture. The practice of Buddhism in Thailand in particular owes much to early Mon forms of Theravada Buddhism existent before and during the reign of King Rama IV, who by royal decree incorporated certain religious reforms key to Mon Buddhism. Thai cuisine has also been influenced by Mon cooking, producing such dishes as *khâo châe* (moist chilled rice served with sweetmeats, a hot-season speciality).

Malays, and Thais who are part-Malay and who adhere to Islam, make up the third-largest minority in Bangkok. Like residents of South Asian descent, many can be found living in Bang Rak, and like the majority of Thais, they tend to be found in blue-collar jobs. Other significant Asian minority groups found in Bangkok include Lao, Khmer, Vietnamese and Burmese.

People from the Middle East probably reached Thailand before most other ethnic groups, including the Thais themselves, having traded along the Thai coastlines in the early years of the first Christian millennium. The first global oil crisis in the 1970s saw a renewal of Arab business interests in Bangkok and today the area known as Nana, roughly extending from Soi 3 to Soi 11, along Th Sukhumvit, sees a high concentration of both residents and tourists from the Middle East.

Bangkok residents of European descent number around 25,000. The vast majority, unlike their Asian counterparts, find themselves in Thailand for only a few months or years for reasons of work or study. Perhaps reflecting their significant roles in the early development of Bangkok, residents of German and British descent appear to be most prominent.

All of Bangkok's diverse cultures pay respect to the Thai king. The monarchy is considered one of the most important stabilising influences in modern Thai political and cultural life, and on Coronation Day and the King's Birthday the city is festooned with strings of lights and portraits of the king.

Another cultural constant is Theravada Buddhism, the world's oldest and most traditional Buddhist sect. Around 90% of Bangkokians are Buddhists, who believe that individuals work out their own paths to *nibbana* (nirvana) through a combination of good works, meditation and study of the *dhamma* or Buddhist philosophy. The social and administrative centre for Thai Buddhism is the wat or monastery, a walled compound containing several buildings constructed in the traditional Thai style with steep, swooping roof lines and colourful interior murals; the most important structures contain solemn Buddha statues cast in bronze. The sheer number of wats scattered around the city – more than 300 – serves as a constant reminder that Buddhism retains a certain dominance even in increasingly secular Bangkok.

Bangkok manages to accommodate all comers in a wide variety of circumstances, whatever their nationality and creed, and no matter how little or how much money may line their pockets. Addicted to the city's throbbing, megalopolitan heartbeat, most would not choose to live elsewhere even if they could.

LIFESTYLE

Switch on the TV and tune in to a Bangkok channel around eight o'clock in the evening and let Thai soap-opera plots draw a rough outline of the Bangkok story. Most series are set in the capital, and although they are hardly realistic – the men are always handsome, the women beautiful, even their cars are spotless – the plot lines are propped up by Bangkok realities: a young Thai Isan girl from the northeastern countryside takes a cleaning job in a wealthy Bangkok household, and the resulting weekly culture clashes keep Thai viewers glued to the screen; a college student argues with his father, a *khâa râatchákaan* (civil servant), over whether he should spend a Saturday afternoon at Centrepoint, a fashionable-but-funky shopping area notorious for its tattoo parlours, punk hair salons and abundance of unaccompanied girls in revealing spaghetti-strap tops.

While there is a certain homogeneity to Bangkok Thais, individual lifestyles vary tremendously according to family background and income. If you could sneak a peek at what Bangkokians eat for breakfast, you'd have a fighting chance at guessing both. *Khâo tôm phúi*, an array of small dishes of dried fish, peanuts and pickled vegetables eaten with hot rice soup, indicates probable Chinese ancestry; add a plate of pricey sweet cured sausage and they're middle-class Chinese Thai. Spot a bowl of steaming *kaeng khĭaw-wăan* (sweet green

SÀNÙK

Although Bangkok is the most modern city in Thailand, the capital's cultural underpinnings are evident in virtually all facets of everyday life. First and foremost is the Thai sense of *sànùk*, loosely translated as 'fun'. In Thailand anything worth doing – even work – should have an element of *sànùk*, otherwise it automatically becomes drudgery. This doesn't mean Bangkokians don't work hard, just that they tend to approach tasks with a sense of playfulness. Nothing condemns an activity more than the description *mâi sànùk* (not fun). Whether in a bank or on a construction site, Bangkok Thais typically inject the activity with a little *sànùk* – flirtation between the sexes, jokes and mock insults.

curry) or *kaeng phèt* (red curry) over rice and it's likely your diner comes from mostly Thai genes, and prefers a basic, economic diet. The same Thai choosing ham, eggs and toast, chased with Starbucks coffee, has money and has probably travelled abroad. Meanwhile a *thai pàk tâi,* or someone from southern Thailand, might be digging into *khâo yam,* a spicy salad of rice, shaved lemon grass, toasted coconut, and tamarind sauce.

Walk the streets of Bangkok early in the morning and you'll catch the flash of shaved heads bobbing above bright ochre robes, as monks all over the city engage in *bindabàat,* the daily house-to-house alms food-gathering. Thai men are expected to shave their heads and don monastic robes temporarily at least once in their lives. Some enter the monkhood twice, first as 10-vow novices in their preteen years and again as fully ordained, 227-vow monks sometime after the age of 20. Monks depend on the faithful for their daily meals, permitted only before noon and collected from lay devotees in large, black-lacquered bowls.

Green-hued onion domes looming over rooftops belong to mosques and mark the immediate neighbourhood as Muslim, while brightly painted and ornately carved cement spires indicate a Hindu temple. Wander down congested Th Chakraphet in the Phahurat district to find Sri Gurusingh Sabha, a Sikh temple where visitors are very welcome. A handful of steepled Christian churches, including a few historic ones, have taken root over the centuries and can be found near the banks of Mae Nam Chao Phraya. In Chinatown large, round doorways topped with heavily inscribed Chinese characters and flanked by red paper lanterns mark the location of *sǎan jâo,* Chinese temples dedicated to the worship of Buddhist, Taoist and Confucian deities.

Thai royal ceremony remains almost exclusively the domain of one of the most ancient religious traditions still functioning in the kingdom, Brahmanism. White-robed, topknotted priests of Indian descent keep alive an arcane collection of rituals that, it is generally believed, must be performed at regular intervals to sustain the three pillars of Thai nationhood: sovereignty, religion and the monarchy. Such rituals are performed regularly at a complex of shrines near Wat Suthat in the centre of the city. Devasathan (Abode of Gods) contains shrines to Shiva and Ganesha and thus hosts priestly ceremonies in the Shaiva tradition, while the smaller Sathan Phra Narai (Abode of Vishnu) is reserved for Vaishnava ritual.

Animism predates the arrival of all other religions in Bangkok, and it still plays an important role in the everyday life of most city residents. Believing that *phrá phuum* or guardian spirits inhabit rivers, canals, trees and other natural features, and that these spirits must be placated whenever humans trespass upon or make use of these features, the Thais build spirit shrines to house the displaced spirits. These doll house–like structures perch on wood or cement pillars next to their homes and receive daily offerings of rice, fruit, flowers and water. Peek inside the smaller, more modest spirit homes and you'll typically see a collection of ceramic or plastic figurines representing the property's guardian spirits.

Larger and more elaborate spirit shrines stand alongside hotels and office buildings, and may contain elaborate bronze images of Brahma or Shiva. At virtually all times of the day and night, you'll see Thais kneeling before such shrines to offer stacks of flowers, incense and candles, and to pray for favours from these Indian 'spirit kings'.

The Thais may bestow Thai royal spirits with similar guardian qualities. The spirit of King Rama V, who ruled over Siam from 1868 to 1910 and who is particularly venerated for having successfully resisted colonialism, is thought to remain active and powerful in Bangkok today. Every Tuesday evening thousands of Bangkokians throng a bronze equestrian statue of Rama V standing opposite Abhisek Dusit Throne Hall, offering candles, pink roses, incense and liquor to the royal demigod.

One in 10 Thai citizens lives and works in Bangkok. Roughly 60% of the country's wealth is concentrated here, and per-capita income runs well above the average for the rest of the country – second only to Phuket, an island province in the south. The legal minimum daily wage in Bangkok and the adjacent provinces of Samut Prakan, Samut Sakhon, Pathum Thani, Nonthaburi and Nakhon Pathom amounted to 184B (US$4.85) in 2006, roughly 40B higher than in the rest of Thailand.

A typical civil servant in an entry-level government job earns around 7500B a month, but with promotions and extra job training may earn up to 15,000B. In the private sector

DOS & DON'TS

When Bangkokians greet each other, they place their palms together in the prayerlike *wâi* gesture, keeping the tips of the fingers somewhere between the chin and the nose, depending on the status of the person being greeted. If a Thai adult greets you with a *wâi*, you should *wâi* in response. Most Bangkokians are familiar with the Western-style handshake and will offer the same to a foreigner, although a *wâi* is always appreciated.

A smile and the all-purpose Thai greeting *'sà wàt dii khráp'* (if you're male) or *'sà wàt dii khâ'* (if you're female) go a long way towards smoothing any new interaction. When encounters take a turn for the worse, try to refrain from getting angry – it won't help matters, since losing one's temper means loss of face for everyone present. Talking loudly is perceived as rude behaviour by cultured Thais, whatever the situation.

The feet are the lowest part of the body (spiritually as well as physically), so don't point at people or things with your feet. Don't prop your feet on chairs or tables while seated. Never touch any part of someone's body with your foot.

In the same context, the head is regarded as the highest part of the body, so don't touch Thais on the head – or ruffle their hair. If you touch someone's head accidentally, offer an immediate apology or you'll be perceived as very rude.

an office worker starts at about the same level but will receive pay rises more quickly than those in government positions. Of course Bangkok thrives on private enterprise, from Talat Noi junk auto-parts shops eking out a profit of less than 500B a day to huge multinational corporations whose upper-level employees drive the latest BMW sedans.

Bangkok women typically control the family finances, and are more likely than men to inherit real estate. Women constitute close to half of the city's workforce, outranking many world capitals. In fields such as economics, academia and health services, women hold a majority of the professional positions – 80% of all Thai dentists, for example, are female.

Figures on Bangkok's infamous nightlife-based economy are difficult to come by, and civic leaders prefer to keep it that way. When Longman's *Dictionary of Contemporary English* defined Bangkok as 'a place where there are a lot of prostitutes', Thais filed diplomatic protests and staged demonstrations outside the British Embassy. The publishers immediately agreed to withdraw the edition from circulation, although Longman's blunder was echoed a few years later when Microsoft's *Encarta* extolled Bangkok as a 'commercial sex hub', resulting in a lawsuit and subsequent revision of the entry.

The infamous red-light districts that have perpetually captivated Western media attention are limited to a few areas of the city, and became further circumscribed in 2004 when the Thai government declared that henceforth no new 'entertainment services with female hostesses' would be permitted outside of three zones: Patpong, Ratchada and Royal City Ave (RCA).

Although often linked to tourism, Bangkok's commercial sex industry actually caters far more to the local market than to foreign visitors. Modern attitudes are changing rapidly, however, and as nonpaid extramarital sex becomes increasingly common, the percentage of Thai clients in Bangkok now runs considerably lower than in other parts of the country.

With the amount of time Bangkok drivers spend stuck in traffic, it's a wonder they have time to think about sex at all. The ocean of cars, trucks, buses, motorcycles and assorted other vehicles upon which Bangkokians have set themselves adrift dominates city life during the daytime and well into the evening. Practically every activity, whether social or work related, is planned around the ebb and flow of traffic. The construction of elevated freeways allowing vehicles to speed across at least some parts of the capital has helped improve the traffic situation to a noticeable degree over the last decade. Still, with roadways covering less than 10% of Bangkok's surface – compared to an international average of 25% – the steel-and-rubber currents remain sluggish.

Bangkok residents are also finally developing a new fondness for mass transit. Railcars on the BTS Skytrain are completely packed during commuter hours. While the MRTA subway, nicknamed 'the Metro', has been slower to take off, it has become a valuable complement to the Skytrain system, making more of the capital accessible without stepping into a car, bus or taxi. Officials continue to discuss plans to establish up to a light-rail circuit around Bangkok's perimeter fed by six 'spoke' lines linking the city centre with the suburbs.

Train pulling into the station at Siam Paragon shopping centre (p184)

FASHION

Unsurprisingly, Bangkok is Thailand's fashion hub, and in fact in all of Southeast Asia only Singapore is a serious rival. Bangkokians not only dabble in the latest American, European and Japanese designer trends, but they have an up-and-coming couture all their own. Shops run by modern Thai designers are particularly easy to find at the Emporium (p187), Gaysorn Plaza (p181), Siam Paragon (p184) and Siam Center (p183) shopping centres, and in the small lanes of Siam Square (p184). Siam Square focuses on inexpensive 'underground' Thai fashions favoured by university students and young office workers, while Emporium and Siam Center are much more upmarket. Local labels to look for include Dapper, Episode, Fly Now, Greyhound, Jaspal and Senada Theory. Chatuchak Weekend Market (p188) is another place to seek out Bangkok designs at bargain prices.

Take a stroll through Siam Square or Central World Plaza, especially on a weekend, and the explosion of styles and colours can't fail to impress. Even the self-tailoring applied to the black-and-white school uniforms shows a Thai sense of flair. On weekends the middle *soi* (lane) of Siam Square – an area known as Centrepoint – is filled with young Thais wearing the most outrageous clothing experiments they can create. It's not quite on a par with Tokyo's famous Harajuku district, but in a few years who knows what it may become?

Fashion shows grace the lobbies of various shopping centres around the city practically every weekend of the year. Since 1999 one of the biggest fashion events on the schedule has been the biannual Bangkok Fashion Week, a string of fashion shows in various venues around the city, including the Fashion Dome, a dome constructed over the middle of the lake at Benjakiti Park, adjacent to the Queen Sirikit National Convention Centre. The Bangkok International Fashion Fair, held in September, is mostly a trade event but it is usually open to the public at the weekend.

The Thai government's clumsily named Office of the Bangkok Fashion City promotes fashion events and aims to turn Bangkok into a world-class – rather than simply regional – fashion centre by 2012. The office, however, has clashed more than once with Thailand's culture minister, who regularly chastises the organisers of Bangkok Fashion Week for the skimpiness of some of the outfits displayed on the catwalks. Coupled with the conservative night-time entertainment venue closing times, such puritanism leads many in Bangkok's fashion community to question whether the city can attain world-class status with such government interference.

SPORT

Muay Thai (Thai Boxing)

The first spectator sport that comes to mind when one thinks of Bangkok is *muay thai,* also known as Thai boxing or kick boxing. Almost anything goes in this martial art, both in the ring and in the stands. If you don't mind the violence, a Thai boxing match is well worth attending for the pure spectacle – the wild musical accompaniment, the ceremonial beginning of each match and the frenzied betting throughout the stadium.

More formally known as Phahuyut (from the Pali-Sanskrit *bhahu* or 'arm' and *yodha* or 'combat'), Thailand's ancient martial art is arguably one of the kingdom's most striking national icons. Overflowing with colour and ceremony as well as exhilarating moments of clenched-teeth action, the best matches serve up a blend of such skill and tenacity that one is tempted to view the spectacle as emblematic of Thailand's centuries-old devotion to independence in a region where most other countries fell under the European colonial yoke.

Such a conclusion becomes all the more tempting when one takes into account the fact that many martial arts aficionados around the world agree that *muay thai* is the most efficient, effective and generally unbeatable form of ring-centred hand-to-hand combat practised today.

Unlike some martial disciplines, such as kung fu or qi gong, *muay thai* doesn't entertain the idea that esoteric martial-arts techniques can be passed only from master to disciple in secret. Thus the *muay thai* knowledge base hasn't fossilised and in fact remains ever open to innovation, refinement and revision. Undefeated Thai champion Dieselnoi, for example, created a new approach to knee strikes that was so difficult to defend that he retired at 23 because no-one dared to fight him anymore.

One of the most famous *muay thai* champions in recent years was Parinya Kiatbusaba, a male transvestite from Chiang Mai who arrived for weigh-ins wearing lipstick and rouge. After his 1998 triumph at Lumphini, Parinya used his earnings to pay for sex-change surgery and became a consultant for 2003's *Beautiful Boxer,* a cinematic version of his life. Another notable *muay thai* event occurred in 1999 when French fighter Mourad Sari became the first non-Thai fighter to take home a weight-class championship belt from a Bangkok stadium.

Several Thai *nák muay* (fighters) have gone on to triumph in world championships in international-style boxing. Khaosai Galaxy, the greatest Asian boxer of all time, chalked up 19 World Boxing Association bantamweight championships in a row before retiring undefeated in December 1991. At any given time Bangkok typically claims five concurrent international boxing champions, usually in the bantamweight and flyweight categories.

Bangkok's first permanent boxing stadium, Ratchadamnoen Stadium (known to Thais a Wethi Ratchadamnoen) was built on royal property along Th Ratchadamnoen Nok at the end of WWII, at about the same time Siam changed its name to Thailand. Originally an open-air affair that hosted fights only in the dry season, the structure gained a roof in 1951 so that *muay thai* could be enjoyed all year round. International boxing legend Rocky Marciano served as a guest referee for a Ratchadamnoen title fight in 1969. The Thai royal family has close ties with this stadium, which has a more formal atmosphere than its main Bangkok rival, Lumphini Stadium. Ratchadamnoen has maintained the same weekly fight schedule for many years: Monday at 5pm and 9pm, Wednesday and Thursday at 6pm and Sunday at 5pm.

In December 1956 the Royal Thai Army opened a second major boxing stadium, Lumphini, on Th Phra Ram IV near Lumphini Park. The atmosphere at Lumphini is looser and more populist than at Ratchadamnoen, and audience response tends to be livelier. Lumphini also has a policy of encouraging non-Thai boxers to compete and has been the site of several recent victories by fighters from Africa, Europe and America. Lumphini matches are scheduled every Tuesday and Friday at 6pm, and on Saturday at 5pm and 8.30pm.

Tàkrâw

Sometimes called 'Siamese football' in old English texts, *tàkrâw* refers to a game in which a woven rattan ball about 12cm in diameter is kicked around. The rattan (or sometimes plastic) ball is called a *lûuk tàkrâw. Tàkrâw* is also popular in several neighbouring countries.

It was originally introduced to the SEA Games by Thailand, and international championships tend to alternate between the Thais and Malays.

The traditional way to play *tàkrâw* in Thailand is for players to stand in a circle (the size of which depends on the number of players) and simply try to keep the ball airborne by kicking it soccer style. Points are scored for style, difficulty and variety of kicking manoeuvres. See p163 for more information about where you can see a game when visiting Thailand.

MEDIA

Thailand's 1997 constitution ensures freedom of the press, although the Royal Police Department reserves the power to suspend publishing licences for national security reasons. Editors generally exercise self-censorship in certain realms, especially with regard to the monarchy.

Thai press freedom reached its high-water mark in the mid-1990s, while Chuan Leekpai's Democrat Party was in power. Following the ascension of Thaksin Shinawatra's Thai Rak Thai Party in 2001, Thailand's media found themselves increasingly subject to interference by political and financial interests. Before the 2001 general election, Shin Corp, a telecommunications conglomerate owned by Prime Minister Thaksin's family, bought a controlling interest in iTV, Thailand's only independent TV station. Shortly thereafter, the new board sacked 23 iTV journalists who complained that the station was presenting biased coverage of the election to favour Thaksin and Thai Rak Thai. Almost overnight the station transformed from an independent, in-depth news channel to an entertainment channel with flimsy, pro-Thaksin news coverage.

Meanwhile relatives of cabinet minister and Thai Rak Thai Party secretary Suriya Jungrungreangkit purchased shares to become the third-largest shareholders of the Nation Group. Political coverage in the *Nation,* formerly known for its independent criticism of the Thai government, became much less aggressive.

The country's international reputation for press freedom took another serious dent in 2002 when two Western journalists were nearly expelled for reporting on a public

TOP FIVE MEDIA WEBSITES

- Asia Pacific Media Network (www.asiamedia.ucla.edu) Critical observer of the media in Thailand.
- Bangkok Post (www.bangkokpost.com) Contains the entire newspaper (except for ads and foreign-syndicated articles) daily, along with archives of stories dating back several years.
- Khao San Road (www.khaosanroad.com) Reports straight from the heart of mondo backpacker.
- The Nation (www.nationmultimedia.com) Another good source of local news, although the archive is less comprehensive than that of the Bangkok Post.
- ThaiDay (www.manager.co.th/IHT/ViewBrowse.aspx?BrowseNewsID=7300) A digest of Thai news published in English by Manager Media Group, run by Sondhi Limthongkul, the man who helped bring PM Thaksin down in 2006.

address presented by the Thai king on his birthday, a portion of which was highly critical of PM Thaksin. In 2004 Veera Prateepchaikul, editor in chief of the *Bangkok Post,* lost his job due to direct pressure from board members with ties to Thaksin and Thai Rak Thai. Allegedly the latter were upset with *Post* criticism of the way in which the PM had handled the 2003–04 bird-flu crisis (see p59).

Barely a week later, Rungruang Preechakul, editor of the Thai-language *Siam Rath Weekly News,* resigned, saying he could no longer endure the intense political pressure to avoid negative news about the Thaksin administration. Four of six full-time *Siam Rath* editors followed suit, as did well-known journalist Chatcharin Chaiwat, poet laureate Praiwarin Khaongarm and 18 other writers for the magazine.

Observers agree that by 2005 Thai press freedom had reached it lowest ebb since the 1970s era of Thai military dictatorship. However, as popular opinion turned against PM Thaksin in late 2005 and early 2006, virtually all media (save for military-run TV channel 11) shook off the cloak of self-censorship and joined the public clamour that resulted in the deposition of Thaksin.

LANGUAGE

Bangkokians conduct their daily lives using the Thai language almost exclusively. The dialect spoken in the capital is Central Thai, also known as Standard Thai, and this is the language taught in public schools throughout the country. Although as a written language Thai appears to be less than a thousand years old, the spoken language is much older. Thai has a very rich vocabulary that varies according to differences in social status, age, royal versus nonroyal and written versus spoken. See p262 for a brief explanation of the pronunciation, along with a list of useful words and phrases.

Street signs are often inconsistent in their transliteration of Thai names into Roman lettering. Most signage in Bangkok appears in Thai only, although you will also see plenty of signs that mix Thai with English and, in Chinatown, with Chinese. Many Chinese or Chinese-Thai residents can speak a dialect or two of Chinese, typically Chao Zhou, Hokkien or Cantonese.

Even though English is compulsory for the first six years of school, don't expect a lot of English to be spoken. Almost everyone knows a few words in English, but apart from university English majors or Thais who are heavily involved in international tourism, you won't find many Thais who speak it fluently.

See p245 for information on studying Thai in Bangkok.

ECONOMY & COSTS

Banking, finance, manufacturing wholesale and retail trade, transportation, tourism and energy dominate the immediate municipality, while the surrounding metropolitan area adds manufacturing, shipping, food processing and intensive farming to the list of top revenue producers.

Thailand is still recovering from the bursting of Southeast Asia's economic bubble in 1997, which largely stemmed from investor panic, with the rush to buy dollars to pay off debts creating a self-fulfilling collapse. During the initial financial crisis, the Thai currency (baht) depreciated roughly 40% against the US dollar, and dollar-backed external debt rose to over half of the country's GDP. This sudden, unforeseen drop in the national currency sounded the death knell for the long period of steady growth and economic stability during the '80s and most of the '90s.

Over the last five years negative growth has been replaced by 4% to 6% positive per-annum growth. In 2005 the after-effects of the December 2004 tsunami, combined with a nationwide drought, a few isolated incidences of avian influenza, continued unrest in southern Thailand and a precipitous increase in global oil prices battered the confidence of consumers and investors alike. Tourism was particularly affected, slowing to an income growth of only 0.5% compared to more than 25% the previous year. The slowdown can be blamed squarely on negative foreign perceptions of the aforementioned historical factors, even if their actual effect on travel is negligible to nonexistent.

Although world demand for principal Thai exports (particularly integrated circuits, computers and hard-disk drives) has been steady, the unexpected strengthening of the baht in the first half of 2006 is likely to apply the brakes to the export market. Interest-rate increases have also buffeted household consumption and domestic investment, and even the import market is slow despite the relatively strong baht.

HOW MUCH?

Khao San guesthouse room 200B to 400B

Midrange hotel room 1000B to 2000B

Skytrain ride 10B to 40B

Chao Phraya Express boat ride 9B to 32B

Cinema ticket 100B

Large Singha beer at a restaurant 80B

Bottle of drinking water 10B

Bowl of rice noodles from street vendor 25B

Air-con Thai restaurant meal, two dishes plus rice 200B

Two-hour traditional Thai massage 300B to 500B

Growth for 2006 and 2007 is projected at 4.5% to 5.6%, with inflation running between 3.5% and 4.5%. Thailand's account deficit is currently about 2.5% of GDP.

Currently one of the most talked-about economic issues among Bangkokians is the ongoing negotiations between Thailand and the USA in preparation for a free-trade agreement. If approved by both governments, the agreement will lead to the dropping of government tariffs on goods traded between the two countries, along with the removal of nontariff trade barriers. Lost in the debate is the fact that Thailand is negotiating similar treaties with India and Australia.

GOVERNMENT & POLITICS

The Bangkok Metropolitan Administration (BMA) administers the capital, which is segmented into 50 districts covering 1569 sq km. Since 1985 metropolitan Bangkok has boasted the country's only elected governorship (provincial governors are appointed). In 2004 Bangkok gubernatorial candidate Apirak Kosayodhin won a hotly contested race against a candidate backed by the ruling party, Thai Rak Thai. His victory was widely seen as a major loss of face for then–Prime Minister Thaksin Shinawatra, leader of Thai Rak Thai. Governor Apirak has named the reduction of corruption and traffic congestion as his main objectives.

The current climate for Bangkok governance has changed considerably following the establishment, in September 1997, of a new national constitution that guaranteed – at least on paper – more human and civil rights than had previously been codified in Thailand. As the first national charter to be prepared under civilian auspices, the 'people's constitution' has fostered great hope that Thailand will more quickly become a 'civic society' ruled by law, rather than social hierarchies.

At the national level, politics remain haunted and dominated by the economic crisis of the late 1990s. Prime minister of the day Chavalit Yongchaiyudh and his New Aspiration Party took the brunt of the blame for this crisis. Chavalit's successor, Chuan Leekpai, assigned a team of economists to right the economy, but they soon came under criticism for their top-down methods that neglected the rural and urban poor. Sensing a power vacuum, billionaire telecom tycoon Thaksin Shinawatra capitalised on widespread discontent and promised 'a million baht' to every village if elected – which later turned into a 'loan'.

Chuan lost the election (the first compulsory polls held in Thailand as per the 1997 constitution) and Thaksin took power in 2001. Amid accusations of widespread vote buying and violent protests in 16 provinces, Thailand's Election Commission launched an investigation into election conduct while the Counter-Corruption Commission (CCC) looked into allegations of graft and 'wealth concealment' in Thaksin's past. The new PM managed to escape the CCC investigation relatively unscathed, despite the discovery that only a week before the 2001 elections, Thaksin had transferred shares in his telecommunications empire to relatives, his chauffeur, his maid and others. Shortly thereafter, two of his domestic staff became among the top 10 shareholders in the Stock Exchange of Thailand (SET).

Through a shrewd combination of financial and political manoeuvres, Thaksin consolidated his power in a manner unprecedented for a democratically elected chief executive in Thailand. Placing political cronies and relatives in key positions in the media, government, armed forces and national police, the billionaire ruler all but silenced public debate about his governing abilities.

Although Thaksin and his nationalist party, Thai Rak Thai (Thai Love Thai), came to power on a raft of social programmes targeted at rural villagers, their political clout took a severe hit in early 2004 when it came to light that the administration had covered up the fact that Thai poultry had been infected with the avian flu since November 2003.

While many villagers outside Bangkok remained loyal, Bangkokians began rapidly losing faith in Thaksin and Thai Rak Thai. Thaksin made a irremediable error in January 2006 when his family sold its controlling interest in Shin Corporation, Thailand's largest telecom enterprise, to a Singapore buyer for a reported US$1.9 billion. Under a law Thaksin himself had pushed during his first term in office, allowing SET trades to be untaxed, his family owed not a single baht of tax on the sale.

Outraged Bangkokians hit the streets in a series of increasingly large demonstrations calling for the PM's ousting. In March 2006 Thaksin dissolved parliament and called for new elections the following month. Immediately the larger opposition parties, led by the Democrats, announced that they would boycott the election. As street demonstrations continued, activists urged citizens to vote 'no' on their ballots – a valid option in Thai elections. When the poll results failed to fill the minimum number of seats in the national assembly (representing areas where TRT candidates couldn't muster the 20% of the vote needed by law to win uncontested seats), Thaksin resigned. Journalists dubbed the people's win over an elected tyrant, 'Thailand's Silk Revolution'.

For the moment Deputy Prime Minister Chidchai Vanasatidya has taken the reins until a new government can be elected.

ENVIRONMENT
THE LAND
Occupying a space roughly midway along Thailand's 1860km north–south axis, Bangkok lies approximately 14° north of the equator, putting it on a latitudinal level with Madras, Manila, Guatemala and Khartoum. The rivers and tributaries of northern and central Thailand drain into Mae Nam Chao Phraya, which in turn disgorges into the Gulf of Thailand, a vast cul-de-sac of the South China Sea. Bangkok is partly surrounded by a huge, wet, flat and extremely fertile area known as 'the rice bowl of Asia' – more rice is grown here than in any other area of comparable size in all of Asia. Thailand has, in fact, been the world's top exporter of rice for at least the last 30 years.

Metropolitan Bangkok – which covers 1569 sq km and extends into the neighbouring provinces of Nonthaburi, Samut Prakan and Samut Sakhon – sits smack in the middle of this delta area, just a few kilometres inland from the gulf. A network of natural and artificial canals crisscrosses the city, although they are fewer in number in urban Bangkok than in surrounding provinces. All feed into Thailand's hydraulic lifeline, Mae Nam Chao Phraya, which snakes through the city centre and serves as an important transport link for cargo and passenger traffic, both within the city and upcountry.

Bangkok's main artery, Mae Nam Chao Phraya

GREEN BANGKOK

The Mae Nam Chao Phraya delta's natural environment has been forever altered by the founding and ongoing development of Bangkok. All of the city's canals, as well as Mae Nam Chao Phraya itself, would be considered polluted by most definitions, although plenty of Bangkok residents make daily use of these waterways for bathing, laundry, recreation and even drinking water (after treating it, of course). The worst water quality is found in the almost-black canals on the Bangkok side of the river. The city has undertaken efforts to clean up the canals over the last couple of decades, with some limited success. Foreigners who have been visiting Thailand for 20 years or more will have noticed some incremental improvements, particularly in the river. The post-1997 budget crisis in Thailand has visibly slowed the momentum gained in this direction.

Air quality varies from precinct to precinct but is generally worse at major traffic crossings. Along with carbon monoxide, lead and other poisons produced primarily by vehicle emissions, Bangkok's air has a fairly high concentration of particulate matter, including dust and debris brought in on the wheels of cars and trucks or created by ongoing construction projects. Relative to other cities in Asia, however, Bangkok doesn't even make the UN Environment Programme list of the region's 10 worst cities for air pollution – these honours are captured entirely by China and India. The worst precinct in Bangkok, Huay Khwang, has an average air quality index (AQI) of 58, which falls in the AQI scale's 'moderate quality' level.

In addition to several parks filled with trees and other vegetation, Bangkok relies on immense green areas to the west of the city as a means of detoxifying the air. One of the greatest threats to the environment is continued development, not only in the city centre, but also in outlying areas and neighbouring provinces. Realising the importance of maintaining green 'lungs' for the city, the Thai government maintains strict controls on development in these areas. They've had less success controlling development in the inner city, and almost no success controlling vehicle circulation, one of the most obvious problem areas. The 1999 introduction of the Skytrain, an elevated light-rail system that runs above some of the city's more sluggish avenues, came as a welcome relief to those who live or work in adjacent areas. Meanwhile the MRTA subway has provided yet another 'escape valve' for the traffic situation, and the city plans to construct seven commuter rail lines, in a spoke-and-wheel configuration around the city, to persuade more Bangkokians to leave their cars and motorcycles at home. See p242 for further Skytrain and subway information.

Ambient noise levels in Bangkok typically average 58 to 72dB, depending on the neighbourhood, with about 12% of the city slightly above the 70dBa at which researchers say hearing damage may result from long-term exposure. Lat Phrao, in the northern part of the city, rates the noisiest, most likely due to the above-average presence of expressways. The BMA is currently creating legal standards for ambient noise levels that will, ideally at least, monitor construction sites, entertainment venues and other sources of ambient noise.

The public rubbish collection system in Bangkok works fairly smoothly, with the city managing to dispose of around 90% of all solid waste produced, an average of 9000 tonnes per day. The piles of street rubbish commonly seen in some South and Southeast Asian capitals are noticeably fewer in Bangkok. Where the rubbish goes is another question altogether. Although some serious attempts to separate and recycle paper, glass and plastic are underway, an estimated 80% of all solid waste ends up at sanitary landfill sites outside Bangkok.

Bangkok has very strict standards for tap water and bottled drinking water. Bangkok tap water meets minimum international health standards and is technically potable.

URBAN PLANNING & DEVELOPMENT

When Bangkok became the new royal capital in 1782, the city was originally laid out in a traditional Buddhist mandala (monthon in Thai) plan, inspired by earlier capitals at Ayuthaya, Sukhothai and Chiang Mai. The Lak Meuang (City Pillar), palaces and royal monasteries stood at the centre, while Khlong Rop Krung was dug around the immediate perimeters to create an island called Ko Ratanakosin. Those nobles and merchants of value

Making an offering at Lak Meuang (p75), Ko Ratanakosin

to the royal court were encouraged to settle just outside Ko Ratanakosin, and other canals were dug to circumscribe this next layer out from the centre. This rough plan of inner and outer rings – land alternating with water – was a conscious attempt to pay homage to sacred Mt Meru (Phra Sumen in Thai) of Hindu-Buddhist mythology.

Early Bangkok was as much a citadel as a city. Today the massive whitewashed walls of Phra Sumen Fort still loom over one end of trendy Th Phra Athit, thrusting out towards Mae Nam Chao Phraya. This brick-and-stucco bunker was one of 14 city fortresses (*pom* in Thai) built along Khlong Banglamphu, which forms a bow-shaped arc carving an 'island' out of the Mae Nam Chao Phraya's left bank.

On the other side of the battlements, Khlong Banglamphu cuts away from the river at a sharp angle, creating the northern tip of Ko Ratanakosin, the royal island that once was the whole of Bangkok. Although often neglected by residents and visitors alike, here stands one of the capital's pivotal points in understanding the city's original plan.

In the other direction, the 7km-long canal curves gently inland towards another wall-and-bunker cluster, Mahakan Fort, marking the southern reach of Ko Ratanakosin. Of the 4m-high, 3m-thick ramparts that once lined the entire canal, only Phra Sumen and Mahakan have been preserved to remind us what 18th-century Bangkok really was about – keeping foreign armies at bay.

Beginning in the early-19th century, Thai kings relinquished the mandala concept and began refashioning the city following European and American models, a process that has continued to this day. Open trade with the Portuguese, Dutch, English, French and Chinese had made the fortifications obsolete by the mid-19th century, and most of the original wall was demolished to make way for sealed roadways. By 1900 these roadways were lined with two-storey, brick-and-stucco Sino-Gothic shophouses inspired by Rama V's visits to Singapore and Penang.

Following WWII, when the Japanese briefly occupied parts of the city, Thai engineers built bridges over Mae Nam Chao Phraya and began filling in canals to provide space for new roads and shophouses. Although many residents continued to occupy stilted houses along the *khlong* (canals) and to move about their neighbourhoods by boat, a future of cars and asphalt was inevitable. In the 1960s and '70s the capital's area doubled in size, yet scant attention was paid to managing growth. Well into the 1980s, as adjacent provinces began

25

filling with factories, housing estates, shopping malls, amusement parks and golf courses, urban planning was virtually nonexistent.

Bangkok's first official city plan was issued in 1992, and nowadays the BMA employs engineers and urban-planning experts full time to tackle growth and make plans for the future. So far most planning remains confined to paper – noble ideas without supporting actions. In theory city authorities have the power to regulate construction by zones, and to monitor land use, but in practice most new developments follow capital, with little thought given to such issues as parking, drainage, or social and environmental impact. For the most part city planners seem preoccupied with the immediate exigencies of maintaining basic city services.

Arts ■

Arts

It's no exaggeration to say that Bangkok has been Southeast Asia's contemporary-art capital since the city was founded in the late 18th century. Early Chakri kings weren't satisfied to merely invite artists and artisans from previous Thai royal capitals such as Ayuthaya, Sukhothai and Chiang Mai. Whether via political coercion of neighbouring countries or seductive promises of wealth and position, Bangkok's rulers had access to the artistic cream of Cambodia, Laos and Myanmar. Mon and Khmer peoples living in the Thai kingdom also contributed much to the visual-arts scene.

The great artistic traditions of India and China, the subtle renderings of Indo- and Sino-influenced art in neighbouring countries, and the colonial and postcolonial cultural influx from Europe also played huge roles in early Bangkok art. Likewise the decades surrounding the two world wars, Thailand's military dictatorships of the '50s, '60s and '70s, and the following protest-fuelled democracy movement brought a healthy dose of politics and social conscience to the Thai modern-art scene. In the more tightly connected modern world of aero- and cyberspace, influences from just about every corner of the globe now find free play in Bangkok.

TOP FIVE MUSEUMS & GALLERIES

- National Museum (p75) Stodgy presentation, deluxe collection.
- Jim Thompson's House (p97) The original model for expat-fantasy Thai homes.
- Thavibu Gallery (p96) The city's best collection of regional artists.
- H Gallery (p96) Cutting-edge artists with international ambitions.
- Chulalongkorn Art Centre (p97) Fast-rotating collection of Thai and international artists.

VISUAL ARTS

The wat served as a locus for the highest expressions of Thai arts for roughly 800 years, from the Lanna to Ratanakosin eras. Accordingly Bangkok's 400-plus Buddhist temples are brimming with the figuratively imaginative, if thematically formulaic, art of Thailand's foremost muralists. Always instructional in intent, such painted images range from the depiction of the *Jataka* (stories of the Buddha's past lives) and scenes from the Indian Hindu epic Ramayana, to elaborate scenes detailing daily life in Thailand. Artists traditionally applied natural pigments to plastered temple walls, a fragile medium of which very few examples remain.

The city's earliest surviving temple painting, dating from between 1657 and 1707, can be found at Wat Chong Nonsi (Map pp278–9). Nineteenth-century religious painting has fared better, with Ratanakosin-style (old Bangkok) temples being more highly esteemed for their painting than their sculpture or architecture. Typical temple murals feature rich colours and lively detail. Some of the finest are found in the National Museum's Wihan Phutthaisawan (Phutthaisawan (Buddhaisawan) Chapel; see p75).

The study and application of mural painting remains very much alive. Modern temple projects are undertaken somewhere within the capital virtually every day of the year, often using improved techniques and paints that promise to hold fast much longer than the temple murals of old. A privileged few in Bangkok's art community receive handsome sums for painting the interior walls of well-endowed ordination halls. Chakrabhand Posayakrit's postmodern murals at Wat Tritosathep Mahaworawihan in Banglamphu have been hailed as masterworks of Thai Buddhist art.

Thai artists have long been sculpting masters, using wood, stone, ivory, clay and metal, and employing a variety of techniques – including carving, modelling, construction and casting – to achieve their designs. Bangkok's most famous sculptural output has been bronze Buddha images, coveted the world over for their originality and grace. Nowadays, historic bronzes have all but disappeared from the art market in Thailand. Most are zealously protected by temples, museums or private collectors.

In 1913 the Thai government opened the School of Arts & Crafts in order to train teachers of art and design, as well as to codify the teaching of silversmithing, nielloing, lacquering and woodcarving in traditional Thai styles. It was an effort that was badly timed as interest in Thai classicism began to weaken in the aftermath of WWI, perhaps the first event in world history to inspire rank-and-file urban Thais to ponder global issues.

The beginnings of Thailand's modern visual-arts movement are usually attributed to Italian artist Corrado Feroci, who was invited to Thailand by Rama VI (King Mongkut) in 1924. In 1933 Feroci founded the country's first School of Fine Arts (SOFA).

Feet of the giant reclining Buddha at Wat Pho (p78), Ko Ratanakosin

Public monuments sponsored during the Phibul Songkhram government (1938–44) led the government to expand SOFA's status in 1943 so that it became part of the newly founded Silpakorn University (p77), Thailand's premier training ground for artists and art historians. Feroci continued as dean of the university and, in gratitude for his contributions, the government gave him the Thai name Silpa Bhirasri.

PHIBUL, FEROCI & THE DEMO

In 1939 Thai prime minister Phibul Songkhram decided that Bangkok needed a national monument commemorating the 1932 revolution that overthrew Thailand's system of absolute monarchy. Phibul chose Th Ratchadamnoen – originally built for royal motorcades – as the ideal spot for this 'Democracy Monument' (p85). Whether he chose it specifically to thumb his nose at royalty, or because it happened to be the city's broadest avenue, is a question that's better not asked in Thailand.

An ardent admirer of the steely nationalism of Adolf Hitler and Benito Mussolini, Phibul commissioned Corrado Feroci, an Italian artist who had previously designed monuments for Mussolini. Feroci, later known in Thailand by his government-conferred Thai name Silpa Bhirasri, in turn enlisted the help of his Thai students at Bangkok's School of Fine Arts (SOFA). Together they created a monument of structural simplicity and symbolic complexity.

To start with, Feroci and the students buried 75 cannonballs in the monument's base to signify the year of the coup, BE 2475 (AD 1932). Atop the base they raised four Art Deco 'wings' to represent the role of the Thai army, navy, air force and police in the 1932 coup. Each wing stands 24m high, in homage to the date – 24 June – of the coup. The wings surround a turret containing a bronze cast of the original (long-supplanted) constitution.

Four bas-relief human forms around the base of the wings represent the original coup conspirators, the Thai armed forces, the Thai people and the personification of 'Balance and Good Life'. Nowhere on the monument will you find any symbols of Buddhism or the monarchy.

Today few people know that 'the Demo', as it has been dubbed by foreign residents, was commissioned by a leader who himself had not been democratically elected. Phibul, appointed prime minister by Siam's military rulers in 1938, renamed the country 'Thailand', introduced the Western solar calendar and cooperated with the Japanese when they invaded Thailand in 1940. After the Japanese were expelled from Thailand at the end of WWII, Phibul was imprisoned and then exiled to Japan. In 1948 he returned and bullied his way back into the prime minister's seat during another military coup. Ousted in 1957 by a rival military man, Field Marshal Sarit Thanarat, Phibul returned to Japan, where he died in 1964.

In 1944 Bhirasri established the National Art Exhibition, which became an important catalyst for the evolution of Thai contemporary art. The first juried art event in Thai history, the annual exhibition created new standards and formed part of a heretofore nonexistent national art agenda. In the absence of galleries, the competition served as the only venue in Bangkok – in all of Thailand, for that matter – where young artists could display their work publicly. Among the most celebrated art of the period were works of realism painted by Chamras Khietkong, Piman Moolpramook, Sweang Songmangmee and Silpa Bhirasri himself.

Other artists involved in this blossoming of modern art, including Jitr (Prakit) Buabusaya, Fua Haripitak, Misiem Yipintsoi, Tawee Nandakhwang and Sawasdi Tantisuk, drew on European movements such as impressionism, postimpressionism, expressionism and cubism. For the first time in the Thai modern-art movement, we also saw a move towards the fusion of indigenous artistic sources with modern modes of expression, as seen in the paintings by Prasong Patamanuj and the sculptures of Khien Yimsiri and Chit Rienpracha.

Another watershed in Thai modern art arrived when King Bhumibol took up the brush and easel. Under the skilled tutelage of Fua Haripitak, the Thai monarch painted almost constantly between 1958 and 1967, turning out a respectable body of work ranging from realistic to abstract. The example of the king's success inspired many Thais in all stations of life to take up painting and other fine arts.

Meanwhile, while writing and lecturing against the iron rule of Field Marshal Sarit Thanarat (1957–59), Thai Marxist academic Jit Phumisak founded the Art for Life (*sila-pa phêa chee-wít*) movement, which had many parallels with the famous Mexican school in its belief that only art with social or political content was worth creating. This movement gained considerable ground during the 1973 democracy movement, when students, farmers and workers joined hands with Bangkok urbanites to resist Thanom Kittikachorn's right-wing military dictatorship. Much of the art (and music) produced at this time carried content commenting on poverty, urban and rural inequities, and political repression, and were typically executed boldly and quickly. Painters Sompote Upa-In and Chang Saetang became the most famous Art for Life exponents.

In 1974, during a brief three-year period of democracy, the Art for Life movement spawned the Artist Front of Thailand. Among the group's more famous and controversial works was a series of huge, politically themed billboards installed along the entire length of Th Ratchadamnoen.

Later in the same decade, a contrasting but equally important movement in Thai art eschewed politics and instead updated Buddhist themes and temple art. Initiated by painters Pichai Nirand, Thawan Duchanee and Prateung Emjaroen, the movement combined modern Western schemata with Thai motifs, moving from painting to sculpture and then to mixed media. Today the most important artists working in this neo-Thai, neo-Buddhist school include Surasit Saokong, Songdej Thipthong, Monchai Kaosamang, Tawatchai Somkong and Montien Boonma. All are frequently exhibited and collected outside Thailand.

Since the 1980s economic boom years, secular sculpture and painting in Bangkok have enjoyed more international recognition, with impressionism-inspired Jitr Buabusaya and Sriwan Janehuttakarnkit among the very few to have reached this vaunted status. On Thailand's art stage, famous names include artists of the 'Fireball' school such as Vasan Sitthiket and Manit Sriwanichpoom, who specialise in politically motivated mixed-media art installations. These artists delight in breaking Thai social codes and means of expression. Even when their purported message is Thai nationalism and self-sufficiency, they are sometimes considered 'anti-Thai'.

In Manit's infamous *Pink Man On Tour* series of art events, he dressed artist Sompong Thawee in pink from head to toe and had him parade with a shopping cart through popular tourist sites to protest the selling of Thai culture. Less well known are Manit's evocative black-and-white photographic pieces denouncing capitalism and consumerism, often identified as unwelcome Western imports. A typical Vasan work dangles cardboard silhouettes from thick steel ropes, accompanied by the title *Committing Suicide Culture: the Only Way for Thai Farmers to Escape Debt*.

Thaweesak Srithongdee, one of several newer Thai artists who manage to skirt both the neo-Buddhist and Fireball movements, paints flamboyantly iconic human figures with bulging body parts. Sculptor Manop Suwanpinta similarly moulds the human anatomy into fantastic shapes that often intersect with technological features, such as hinged faces that open to reveal inanimate content.

Modern sculpture can be split into two camps, one imitating Western or Japanese trends, and the other reviving Thai themes but interpreting them in new ways. An example of the latter is a piece by Sakarin Krue-On, who fashioned a huge, hollow Buddha head from a mixture of clay, mud, papier-mâché, glue and turmeric. Entitled *Phawang Si Leuang* (Yellow Trance), the work was displayed lying on its side, nearly filling a small room, during a recent successful world tour.

Modern painting and sculpture are exhibited at dozens of galleries around Bangkok, from the delicately lit darlings of Thai high society to industrially decorated spaces in empty warehouses (see the boxed text, p96). Other venues and sources of support for modern Thai art include the rotating displays at Bangkok's luxury hotels, particularly the Grand Hyatt Erawan (p200), the Sukhothai Hotel (p203) and the Metropolitan (p202).

ARCHITECTURE
TEMPLES, FORTS & SHOPHOUSES

When Bangkok became the capital of the kingdom of Siam in 1782, the first task set before designers of the new city was to create hallowed ground for royal palaces and Buddhist monasteries. Indian astrologers and high-ranking Buddhist monks conferred to select and consecrate the most auspicious riverside locations, marking them off with small carved-stone pillars. Siam's most talented architects and artisans then weighed in, creating majestic and ornate edifices to astound all who ventured into the new capital.

The temples and palaces along the riverbanks of Mae Nam Chao Phraya transformed humble Bang Makok (as the city was known before it was made Thailand's capital) into the glitter and glory of Ko Ratanakosin (Ratanakosin Island), and their scale and intricacy continue to make a lasting impression on new arrivals. Whether approaching by river or by road, your eye is instantly caught by the sunlight refracting off the multitude of gilded spires peeking over the huge walls of Wat Phra Kaew (p79), the Temple of the Emerald Buddha. Inside the brick-and-stucco walls, you can easily lose yourself amid the million-square-metre grounds, which bring together more than a hundred buildings and about two centuries of royal history and architectural experimentation.

Early Bangkok was both a citadel and a city of temples and palaces. Today the massive whitewashed walls of Phra Sumen Fort (p86), punctured by tiny windows and topped with neat crenulations, still loom over the northern end of Th Phra Athit, facing Mae Nam Chao Phraya.

Erected in 1783 and named for the mythical Mt Meru (Phra Sumen in Thai) of Hindu-Buddhist cosmology, the octagonal brick-and-stucco bunker was one of 14 city fortresses built along Khlong Banglamphu, which forms an arc carving an 'island' out of the left bank of Mae Nam Chao Phraya. Today Santichaiprakan Park, a grassy strip lying in the bunker's shadow, receives river breezes that cool refugees from the smoky cafés and bars of Th Phra Athit. The 7km canal curves inland towards another wall-and-bunker

> **TOP FIVE BUILDINGS**
>
> - Bangkok Bank (Map pp284–5; cnr Soi Wanit 1 & Th Mangkhon) Classic century-old Ratanakosin, blending European and Chinese architecture.
> - Chalermkrung Royal Theatre (Map pp284–5; 66 Th Charoen Krung) The city's best surviving example of Thai Deco.
> - Chao Sua Son's House (Map pp284–5; Talat Noi) With its round doorway opening onto a central U-shaped courtyard, this is one of Thailand's only examples of traditional Chinese residential architecture.
> - Thai Wah II (Map pp292–3; Th Sathon Tai) Although only the second-tallest, this is the most tasteful of Bangkok's superscrapers.
> - Sukhothai Hotel (Map pp292–3; Th Sathon Tai) Fuses American architect Ed Tuttle's minimalist vision of traditional Thai temple arts with innovative hotel design.

cluster, Pom Mahakan, thus marking the southern end of Ko Ratanakosin. Of the 4m-high, 3m-thick ramparts that once lined the entire canal, only Phra Sumen and Mahakan have been preserved to show what 18th-century Bangkok was really about – keeping foreign armies at bay. For more information on Bangkok's layout, see p24.

Open trade with the Portuguese, Dutch, English, French and Chinese made the fortifications obsolete by the mid-19th century, and most of the original city wall was demolished to make way for sealed roadways. By 1900 these roadways were lined with two-storey Sino-Gothic shophouses inspired by Rama V's visits to Singapore and Penang.

Bangkok's oldest residential and business district fans out along Mae Nam Chao Phraya, between Saphan Phra Pin Klao (Phra Pin Klao Bridge) and Hualamphong Station. Largely inhabited by the descendants of Chinese residents who moved out of Ko Ratanakosin to make way for royal temples and palaces in the early 19th century, the neighbourhood is referred to as Sampeng (for the longest market lane, Soi Sampeng), or as Yaowarat (for the major avenue bisecting the neighbourhood) or by the English term 'Chinatown'. During the reign of Rama IV Chinatown expanded outside Khlong Banglamphu, so the king ordered another canal dug to the east, Khlong Padung Krung Kasem, to facilitate commercial transport as well as defence. One of the liveliest quarters of the capital, Bangkok's Chinatown encompasses a congested array of hardware, wholesale food, textile, printing, automotive and gold shops, mixed in with apartment buildings, pawnshops, Chinese temples, noodle-and-dim-sum cafés and the best Chinese banquet houses in the city.

In the 19th century Chinese architecture began exerting a strong influence on the city. In Talat Noi (Little Market), a riverside neighbourhood just south of the older Chinese district Yaowarat, Chinese entrepreneur Chao Sua Son founded a market where larger riverboats could offload wholesale goods to city merchants. Chao Sua Son's house (Map pp284–5) still stands, a rare example of traditional Chinese architecture in Thailand.

Talat Noi serves as a cultural and geographic bridge between the almost-exclusively Chinese ambience of Yaowarat Chinatown to the immediate north and the almost exclusively Western – historically speaking, if not in present-day Bangkok – district of European trading houses and embassies to the immediate south. A portion of Talat Noi was given over to Portuguese residents of Bangkok, who in 1787 built the Holy Rosary Church (Map pp284–5), the capital's oldest place of Christian worship. Originally assembled from wood, it was replaced with brick and stucco in the neogothic style after an 1890 fire. Today the interior is graced by Romanesque stained-glass windows, gilded ceilings and a very old, life-sized Jesus effigy that is carried in the streets during Easter processions.

ARCHITECTURAL ETHICS

Thailand has done a fine job of preserving historic religious architecture, from venerable stupas to ancient temple compounds. In fact, the Department of Fine Arts enforces legislation that makes it a crime to destroy or modify such monuments; even structures found on private lands are protected.

On the other hand Thailand has less to be proud of in terms of preserving secular civil architecture such as old government offices and shophouses. A few of Bangkok's Ratanakosin and Asian Deco buildings have been preserved, along with a handful of private mansions and shophouses, but typically only because the owners of these buildings took the initiative to do so.

Thailand has no legislation in place to protect historic buildings or neighbourhoods. Distinctive early Bangkok architecture is disappearing fast, often to be replaced by plain cement, steel and glass structures of little historic or artistic value.

Many other countries around the world have regulations that allow the registration of historic homes and whole neighbourhoods can be designated as national monuments. In neighbouring Laos, Unesco has helped to preserve the charming Lao-French architecture of Lǔang Prabang by designating the city as a World Heritage site.

While Bangkok has gone so far in the direction of modern development that it will never recover much of the charm of its 18th- to early-20th-century architecture, if the city or nation doesn't take steps to preserve historic secular architecture, there will soon be nothing left but an internationally homogenous hodgepodge of styles. For more information on architectural restoration and preservation, try **Unesco Bangkok** (www.unescobkk.org) and **modern Asian Architecture Network** (mAAN; www.m-aan.org).

South of Talat Noi at least 2 miles of the Chao Phraya riverside was once given over to such international mercantile enterprises as the East Asiatic Co, Chartered Bank, British Dispensary, Bombay Burmah Trading Co, Banque de l'Indochine and Messrs Howarth Erskine, as well as the Portuguese, French, Russian, British, American, German and Italian embassies. For the era, the architecture of this area – still known as Bang Rak – was Bangkok's most flamboyant, a mixture of grand neoclassical fronts, shuttered Victorian windows and beaux-arts ornamentation. Many of these old buildings have survived to the present, but all have been obscured by more modern structures along Th Charoen Krung. Hence the best way to appreciate them as a group is from the river itself, by boat.

Under Rama IV, the palace treasury found it could no longer cope with the complexities of burgeoning international trade, so the king granted a licence to Prince Mahissara Ratchaharuthai to establish the Book (as in book-keeping) Club in Talat Noi. The name was later changed to Siam Commercial Bank, today one of Thailand's three leading banks. At the original office in Talat Noi, bank tellers count the money behind iron-grill windows, as customers glide in and out on old tile floors.

Thais began mixing traditional Thai architecture with European forms in the late 19th and early 20th centuries, as exemplified by Bangkok's Vimanmek Teak Mansion (p90), the Author's Wing of the Oriental Hotel (p204), the Chakri Mahaprasat next to Wat Phra Kaew (p79), and any number of older residences and shophouses in Bangkok. This style is usually referred to as 'old Bangkok' or 'Ratanakosin'. The Old Siam Plaza shopping centre (p131), adjacent to Bangkok's Chalermkrung Royal Theatre, is an attempt to revive the old Bangkok school.

Disembark at the Mae Nam Chao Phraya pier of Tha Tien (Map p288), weave your way through the vendor carts selling grilled squid and rice noodles, and you'll find yourself standing between two rows of shophouses of the sort once found along all the streets near the river. The deep, shaded porticoes of the ground floor, topped by upper storeys with tall, shuttered windows and delicate plaster foliage, preserve the elegance of old Bangkok's 'grand Victorian ladies'. Inside, the ground floors display multihued tiles of French, Italian or Dutch design, while upper floors are planked with polished teak.

In the early 20th century architects left the Victorian era behind, blended European Art Deco with functionalist restraint and created Thai Art Deco. Built just before WWI, an early and outstanding example of this style is Hualamphong Station (p92). The station's vaulted iron roof and neoclassical portico are a testament to state-of-the-art engineering, while the patterned, two-toned skylights exemplify Dutch modernism.

Fully realised examples of Thai Deco from the 1920s and '30s can be found along Chinatown's main streets, particularly Th Yaowarat (Map pp284–5). Whimsical Deco-style sculptures – the Eiffel Tower, a lion, an elephant, a Moorish dome – surmount vertical towers over doorways. Atop one commercial building on Th Songwat perches a rusting model of a WWII Japanese Zero warplane. Placed there by the Japanese during their brief occupation of Bangkok in 1941, it coordinates perfectly with the surrounding Thai Deco elements. Other examples are the Chalermkrung Royal Theatre (Map pp284–5), the Royal Hotel (p195), Ratchadamnoen Stadium (Map pp286–7) and Bangkok's main post office (Map pp290–1).

OFFICE TOWERS, HOTELS & SHOPPING CENTRES

During most of the post-WWII era, the trend in modern Thai architecture – inspired by the German Bauhaus movement – was towards a boring International Style functionalism, and the average building looked like a giant egg carton turned on its side. The Thai aesthetic, so vibrant in prewar eras, almost disappeared in this characterless architecture.

The city has been moving skywards almost as quickly as it has expanded outwards. When the Dusit Thani hotel (p202) opened in 1970 it was the capital's tallest building, and even by the end of that decade fewer than 25 buildings stood taller than six floors. By the year 2000, nearly 1000 buildings could claim that distinction, with at least 20 of them towering higher than 45 floors.

On Th Sathon Tai is the Bank of Asia headquarters (p108), known locally as the 'Robot Building'. Thai architect Sumet Jumsai combined nut-and-bolt motifs at various elevations,

Sukhothai Hotel (p203) makes use of classical Thai architectural motifs

with a pair of lightning rods on the roof (arranged to resemble sci-fi robotlike antennae) and two metal-lidded 'eyes' staring out from the upper façade. The Robot Building represents one of the last examples of architectural modernism in Bangkok, a trend which had all but concluded by the mid-1980s.

Almost every monumental project constructed in Bangkok now falls squarely in the postmodernist camp, combining rationalism with decorative elements from the past. Proclaiming its monumental verticality like a colossal exclamation point, the 60-storey Thai Wah II building, also on Th Sathon Tai, combines rectangles and squares to create a geometric Egyptian Deco mosaic. At 305m the cloud-stabbing Baiyoke Tower II (home to the Baiyoke Sky Hotel; Map pp280–1) is currently the second-tallest structure in Southeast Asia, after Kuala Lumpur's Petronas Twin Towers. Stylistically it shows the inspiration of American post-Deco.

Pure verticality is now giving way to tiered skyscrapers, in accordance with the city's regulations for allowing light into city streets. The tiered Bangkok City Tower (Map pp290–1) stacks marble, glass and granite around recessed entryways and window lines to create a stunning 'Mesopotamia meets Madison Ave' effect. Everything 'neo' is in, including neo-Thai. The Four Seasons (p199), Sukhothai (p203) and Grand Hyatt Erawan (p200) are all examples of hotels that make extensive use of Thai classical motifs in layout and ornamentation.

MUSIC
Throughout Bangkok you'll find a mind-bending diversity of musical genres and styles, from the serene court music that accompanies classical dance-drama to the thumping house music played at dance clubs. Virtually every musical movement heard in the West has been turned upside down, and Bangkokians have piled yet more variations on top of them all.

CLASSICAL THAI
Classical central-Thai music *(phleng thai doem)* features a dazzling array of subtle textures, hair-raising tempos and pastoral melodies. It may sound strange to Western visitors due to its use of the standard Thai scale, which divides the octave into seven full-tone intervals

with no semitones. Thai scales were first transcribed by the Thai-German composer Peter Feit (whose Thai name was Phra Chen Duriyanga), who also composed Thailand's national anthem in 1932.

The classical orchestra or *pìi-phâat* can include as few as five players or more than 20. It was originally developed to accompany classical dance-drama and shadow theatre but is also commonly heard in straightforward concert performances. Leading the band is *pìi,* a straight-lined woodwind instrument with a reed mouthpiece and an oboelike tone; you'll hear it most at *muay thai* (Thai-boxing) matches. Plucked like a guitar, the four-stringed *phin* lends subtle counterpoint, while *ránâat èhk,* a bamboo-keyed percussion instrument resembling the xylophone, carries the main melodies. The slender *saw,* a bowed instrument with a coconut-shell soundbox, provides soaring embellishments, as does *khlùi* or wooden Thai flute.

One of the more noticeable *pìi-phâat* instruments, *kháwng wong yài,* consists of tuned gongs arranged in a semicircle and played in simple rhythmic lines to provide the music's underlying fabric. Several types of drums, some played with the hands, some with sticks, carry the beat, often through several tempo changes in a single song. The most important type of drum is *tà-phon*

Arts

MUSIC

> **OLD & IN FASHION**
>
> Classical Thai music received a huge boost in Thailand when the film *Hom Rong* (The Overture) was released in 2004. Based on the life story of Thai maestro Lŭang Pradit Phairoh (1881–1954), the film chronicles an era when Thai political leaders were trying to suppress traditional Thai music in favour of Western classical music in order to prove to would-be colonisers that Thais were 'civilised'. Despite the illicit nature of his endeavours, the hero perseveres in his study of the *ránâat èhk* (Thai wooden xylophone), eventually winning the hearts of the Thai people and restoring social status to Thai classical music. In the first few months after the film's opening, new students were practically standing in line to learn *ránâat èhk* at Bangkok music schools. There has been a corresponding leap in demand for the instruments.

(or *thon*), a double-headed hand drum that sets the tempo for the entire ensemble. Prior to a performance, the players offer incense and flowers to *tà-phon,* considered to be the conductor of the music's spiritual content.

THAI POP

Popular Thai music has borrowed much from Western music, particularly in instrumentation, but retains a distinct flavour of its own. The bestselling of all modern musical genres in Thailand remains *lûuk thûng* (literally 'children of the fields'). *Lûuk thûng* dates back to the 1940s, is analogous to US country and western music, and tends to appeal most to working-class Thais. Subject matter almost always cleaves to tales of lost love, tragic early death and the dire circumstances of farmers who work day in and day out and still owe money to the bank at the end of the year.

Lûuk thûng song structures tend to be formulaic as well. There are two basic styles: the original Suphanburi style, with lyrics in standard Thai, and an Ubon style sung in Isan (northeastern) dialect. Thailand's most famous *lûuk thûng* singer, Pumpuang Duangjan (see the boxed text, p36), rated a royally sponsored cremation when she died in 1992, and has a major shrine at Suphanburi's Wat Thapkradan, which receives a steady stream of worshippers.

Several popular magazines and TV programmes are dedicated to the promotion of the *lûuk thûng* industry, as are a few Thai films. Movies about *lûuk thûng* singers from the countryside trying to achieve stardom in Bangkok are an entire genre unto themselves, with the 2002 Thai box office hit *Mon Rak Transistor* the best of the pack (see p44).

Chai Muang Sing and Siriporn Amphaipong have been the most beloved *lûuk thûng* superstars for several years, with lesser lights coming and going. Other stars include former soap-opera star Got Chakraband and Monsit Khamsoi, whose trademark silky vocal style has proved enormously popular. One of the more surprising newcomers is Jonas Anderson, a blonde-haired, blue-eyed Swede who spent part of his childhood in northeastern Thailand and is now one of the hottest-selling *lûuk thûng* acts in the country.

ELECTRONIC POP QUEEN

The popularity of *lûuk thûng* skyrocketed in the 1960s with the stardom of Suraphon Sombatjalern, a kind of Thai country Dean Martin. But the most popular *lûuk thûng* star of all was Pumpuang Duangjan, whose life mirrored the dreams and tragedies of the songs that she sang.

The illiterate daughter of a farming family, Pumpuang left her rural town of Suphanburi to seek her fortune in the city. She joined a band as a dancer at the age of 14 and soon after eloped with the saxophone player (who later ran off with her sister) before becoming the band's lead singer. She eventually became one of Thailand's most famous, if tragic, musical heroines. The extraordinary range of her voice ensured her nationwide success across all social levels; she once sang a song penned for her by Princess Sirindhorn for a royal performance. Her personal life was marked by heartbreak, and she suffered a string of much-publicised failed love affairs. One of the most colourful rumours that circulated was that she paid her married lover's wife so that she might keep him as her own, only to have him spend all her money, run her into debt and abandon her for his original wife.

Pumpuang peaked in the 1980s when she pioneered the pop-style electronic *lûuk thûng*. She died in 1992, at the age of 31, from an immune system–related illness.

Part of the genre's popularity is due to the spectacular *lûuk thûng* shows that tour temple fairs around Thailand, combining song, dance, comedy and large casts attired in an array of costumes – from royalty to rambutans (a popular Thai fruit). Would-be aficionados can track down modern and classical *lûuk thûng* in most Bangkok music stores.

Another genre more firmly rooted in northeastern Thailand and nearly as popular in Bangkok, is *mǎw lam*. Based on the songs played on the Lao-Isan *khaen*, a wind instrument comprised of a double row of bamboolike reeds fitted into a hardwood soundbox, *mǎw lam* features a simple but insistent bass beat and plaintive vocal melodies. If *lûuk thûng* is Thailand's country and western, then *mǎw lam* is its blues. Jintara Poonlap and Chalermphol Malaikham continue to reign as queen and king of *mǎw lam*.

These and other singers also perform *lûuk thûng prá-yúk*, a blend of *lûuk thûng* and *mǎw lam* that is emerging as *mǎw lam* loses its 'country bumpkin' image. Purists eschew *lûuk thûng prá-yúk* in favour of rootsier, funkier *mǎw lam* artists such as Rumpan Saosanon. Meanwhile, Sommainoi Duangcharoen goes in a completely different direction, mixing a bit of jazz and even rap into his *mǎw lam*. Tune into Bangkok radio station Luk Thung FM (95.0 FM) for large doses of *lûuk thûng* and *mǎw lam*.

The 1970s ushered in a new style inspired by the politically conscious folk rock of the US and Europe, which the Thais dubbed *phleng phêua chii-wít* (literally 'music for life') after Marxist Jit Phumisak's earlier Art for Life movement. Closely identified with the Thai band Caravan – which still performs regularly – the introduction of this style was the most significant musical shift in Thailand since *lûuk thûng* rose in the 1940s.

Phleng phêua chii-wít has political and environmental topics rather than the usual love themes. During the authoritarian dictatorships of the '70s many of Caravan's songs were banned. Following the massacre of student demonstrators in 1976, some members of the band fled to the hills to take up with armed communist groups. Another proponent of this style, Carabao, fused *phleng phêua chii-wít* with *lûuk thûng*, rock and heavy metal, and spawned a whole generation of imitators as well as a chain of barnlike performance venues seating 1000 or more.

Thailand also has a thriving teen-pop industry (sometimes referred to as 'T-Pop') centred on artists who have been chosen for their good looks, then matched with syrupy song arrangements. GMM Grammy, Thailand's music industry heavyweight, dominates sales and promotion, with Bakery Music a distant second. One of Bakery's more commercially successful artists, Surattanawee 'Bo' Suviporn, became known mainly for her provocative style of dress, which young Thai women have been quick to emulate. The Bo phenomenon helped spawn Bakery's subsidiary label, Dojo City, whose artists are as popular for their fashion sense as for their music.

Singers who are *lûuk khrêung* – half-Thai, half-*faràng* (Western) – and sport Western names are particularly popular; for example, Nat Myria, Tata Young, Nicole Theriault and the original *lûuk khrêung* heartthrob Thongchai 'Bird' McIntyre. Teen girl pop singers Palmy and Mint play much the same musical roles in Bangkok as Britney Spears and Christina Aguilera play in the West.

Karaoke CDs and VCDs comprise a huge share of the music-retail market. Many major Thai artists – even alternative-rock groups – release subtitled VCDs specially formatted for karaoke-style sing alongs. Thai music videos are telecast 24 hours a day on Channel [V] Thailand, a music TV channel available on UBC cable.

THAI ALT, INDIE & HIP-HOP

In the 1990s an alternative pop scene – known in Thailand as *klawng sĕhrii* (free drum) or *phleng tâi din* (underground music) – grew in Bangkok. Hip-hop/ska artist Joey Boy not only explored new musical frontiers but released lyrics that the Department of Culture banned. One song, for example, included the Thai euphemism for male masturbation, *chák wâo* (pull a kite). Despite a recent drug bust, Joey Boy maintains a regular presence on the Thai music charts.

Modern Dog, a Britpop-inspired band of four Chulalongkorn University graduates, is generally credited with bringing independent Thai music into the mainstream, and their success prompted an explosion of similar bands and indie recording labels. Like Joey Boy, they're on the Bakery Music label, Thailand's first alternative label. Bakery's band Pru, another Thai take on Britpop, has been equally popular.

Crowd pleaser Loso (from 'low society') reinvented Carabao's Thai folk melodies and rhythms with indie guitar rock. Grammy responded with a rash of similar Thai headbangers designed to fill stadiums and outsell the indies. Along with Modern Dog, Pru and Day Tripper, major alternative acts in Thailand include punk metal band Ebola and the electronica/underground group Futon, which is made up of British, Thai and Japanese band members. Futon's remake of Iggy Pop's proto-punk classic 'I Wanna Be Your Dog' hit big in Thailand, and its album *Never Mind the Botox* has been distributed internationally.

Currently Thailand's biggest alt rock band is Silly Fools, who have been on a roll since their 1998 album *IQ 180* hit the charts. Meanwhile, Big Ass and Bodyslam are two groups who inject their songs with a strong dose of anti-Thaksin politics.

HALF CHILD

Leaf through any Thai fashion magazine and you'll come across at least two or three *lûuk khrêung* (literally 'half child') faces. Turn on the TV to watch Thai soap operas, commercials or music videos and you're even more likely to see the offspring of *faràng* (Western)–Thai couplings.

The *lûuk khrêung* weren't always a mainstay of Thai media. In the 1970s and '80s most *lûuk khrêung* were the children of male American servicemen stationed at one of the seven US military bases scattered around Thailand during the Indochina Wars. Their mothers may have been Thai women associated only briefly with their fathers; some were *mia châo* (rent wives). The resulting Amerasian children of these alliances were typically looked down upon by other Thais.

This perception began to change following Thailand's economic boom in the '80s and '90s, when *lûuk khrêung* who were schooled abroad or educated at bilingual international schools in Thailand became adults. A new wave of *lûuk khrêung* who were the children of expats with more permanent ties to Thailand was also born during this time, in circumstances deemed more 'respectable' within Thai society.

Coupled with the fading public memory of the Indochina Wars–related births, the stigma formerly attached to *lûuk khrêung* almost overnight became positive rather than negative. Fluency in English and whiter skin tones – apparently a Thai preference long before Europeans arrived in Thailand – lend *lûuk khrêung* significant advantage as media figures. Today a high proportion of models, actors, VJs, beauty queens and pop music stars are *lûuk khrêung*.

Among the most well-known *lûuk khrêung* in Thailand are Tata Young (music), Paula Taylor (music/film/TV), Sirinya Burbridge (modelling/film/Miss Thailand World Pageant), Sonya Couling (modelling), Nat Myria (music), Peter Corp Dyrendal (music), Ananda Everingham (TV/film) and Bird McIntyre (music/film).

The *lûuk khrêung* phenomenon has become so topical in Thailand nowadays that a 2006 TV soap opera, *Lady Mahachon*, revolved around a *lûuk khrêung* pop star (played by real-life *lûuk khrêung* pop star Paula Taylor) looking for her American father (Erich Fleshman, a bilingual American actor) whom she hadn't seen since early childhood.

TOP 10 THAI CDS

Most of these CDs are available from Tower Records in the Emporium (Map pp296–7) and at Central World Plaza (Map pp294–5). You can also order most of them online at www.nongtaprachan.com (in Thai) or www.ethaicd.com.

- *Bakery Music: Lust For Live* – A collection of live alt rock performances by Modern Dog, Chou Chou, Yokee Playboy, P.O.P. and Rudklao Amraticha.
- *Banyen Raggan: Khaw Du Jai Kawn* – A good introduction to *mǎw lam*.
- *Big Ass & Bodyslam: Big Body Concert* – Modern political rock.
- *Carabao: Made in Thailand* – Carabao's classic and internationally popular album.
- *Caravan: Khon Kap Khwai* – The album that kicked off the *phleng phêua chii-wít* movement.
- *Fong Nam: The Nang Hong Suite* – Brilliant Thai funeral music, but think New Orleans second-line cheer rather than dirge.
- *Joey Boy: Joey Boy's Anthology* – Thirteen ska/hip-hop tracks from Joey Boy's seven years with Bakery Music.
- *Loso: The Best of Loso* – Thai anthems of teen angst.
- *Pumpuang Duangjan: Best* – Compilation of the late *lûuk thûng* diva's most famous tunes.
- *Thaitanium: Thailand's Most Wanted* – Three MCs rap in a mix of gangsta English and Thai.

As in the West, some indie labels have been compelled to undergo mergers to survive. Bakery Music is now owned by BMG Entertainment, a division of Bertelsmann AG, the world's largest media conglomerate. Meanwhile, Grammy has developed two of its own subsidiary alt rock labels, Genie Records and Sanamluang. Truly independent labels to look for include Rehab, Junk Food, Werk and Spicy Disc. For the latest indie Thai, tune into Fat Radio, 104.5 FM (www.thisisclick.com/1045).

Aside from Fat Radio, the indie stuff is almost always reserved for concert performances or one-off club appearances. One spot with regular weekend concerts is the outdoor stage at Centerpoint, Siam Square. Bangkok's biggest indie event of the year is the Fat Radio–organised, Heineken-sponsored Fat Festival, a three-day outdoor music festival held annually in November.

Hip-hop is huge in Thailand in terms of radio play and CD sales, but few Thai groups are proficient in performing this genre. One that has become hugely successful is Thaitanium, an all-Thai group that does all its recording in New York and distributes its music independently in Thailand.

JAZZ & WORLD-MUSIC INFLUENCES

Yet another inspiring movement in modern Thai music has been the fusion of international jazz with Thai classical and folk styles. Fong Nam, a Thai orchestra led by the US composer Bruce Gaston, performs an inspiring blend of Western and Thai classical motifs, which has become a favourite for movie soundtracks, TV commercials and tourism promotions. Fong Nam plays regularly at Tawan Daeng German Brewhouse (p154). Another leading exponent of this genre is the composer and instrumentalist Tewan Sapsanyakorn (also known by the name Tong Tewan), who plays soprano sax, alto sax, violin and *khlùi*, all with equal virtuosity. Tewan's compositions are frequently based on Thai melodies but the improvisations and rhythms are drawn from diverse jazz sources including artists such as Sonny Rollins and Jean-Luc Ponty. Other notable groups that are fusing international jazz and indigenous Thai music include Kangsadarn and Boy Thai; the latter adds Brazilian samba and reggae to the mix.

THEATRE & DANCE

Traditional Thai theatre consists of five dramatic forms. *Khǒn* is a formal, masked dance-drama that depicts scenes from the Ramakian (the Thai version of India's Ramayana); it was originally performed only for the royal court. *Lákhon* is a general term that encompasses several types of dance-drama (usually for nonroyal occasions), including *mánohraa*, the

Traditional dance at the Sala Rim Nam restaurant (p159)

southern Thai version based on a 2000-year-old Indian story, and Western theatre. *Lí-keh* is a partly improvised, often bawdy folk play featuring dancing, comedy, melodrama and music. *Lákhon lék* or *hùn lŭang* is puppet theatre, and *lákhon phûut* is modern spoken theatre.

KHŎN

In all *khŏn* performances, four types of characters are represented – male humans, female humans, monkeys and demons. Monkey and demon figures are always masked with the elaborate headpieces often seen in tourist promo material. Behind the masks and make-up, all actors are male. Traditional *khŏn* is very expensive to produce – Ravana's retinue alone (Ravana is the Ramakian's principal villain) consists of more than 100 demons, each with a distinctive mask.

Perhaps because it was once limited to royal venues and hence never gained a popular following, the *khŏn* or Ramakian dance-drama tradition nearly died out in Thailand. Bangkok's National Theatre (p158) was once the only place where *khŏn* was regularly performed for the public; the renovated Chalermkrung Royal Theatre now hosts occasional *khŏn* performances, enhanced by laser graphics and hi-tech audio.

Scenes in traditional *khŏn* and *lákhon* performances (see below) come from the 'epic journey' tale of the Ramakian, with parallels to Homer's *Odyssey* and the myth of Jason and the Argonauts. The central story revolves around Prince Rama's search for his beloved Princess Sita, who has been abducted by the evil 10-headed demon Ravana and taken to the island of Lanka. In his search and in the final battle against Ravana, Rama is assisted by a host of mythical half-animal, half-human characters including the monkey-god Hanuman (see p41 for details on the differences between the Indian Ramayana and the Thai Ramakian).

LÁKHON

The more formal *lákhon nai* (inner *lákhon*, which means that it is performed inside the palace) was originally performed for lower nobility by all-female ensembles. Today it's a dying art, even more so than the royal *khŏn*. In addition to scenes from the Ramakian, *lákhon nai* performances may include traditional Thai folk tales; whatever the story, text is always sung. *Lákhon nâwk* (outer *lákhon,* performed outside the palace) deals exclusively with folk tales and features a mix of sung and spoken text, sometimes with improvisation. Male and female performers are permitted. Like *khŏn* and *lákhon nai,* performances are increasingly rare.

Much more common these days is the less-refined *lákhon chaatrii,* a fast-paced, costumed dance-drama usually performed at upcountry temple festivals. *Chaatrii* stories are often influenced by the older *mánohraa* theatre of southern Thailand.

A variation on *chaatrii* that has evolved specifically for shrine worship, *lákhon kâe bon* involves an ensemble of about 20, including musicians. At an important shrine such as Bangkok's Lak Meuang (p75), four *kâe bon* troupes may alternate, each for a week at a time, as each performance lasts from 9am to 3pm and there is usually a long list of worshippers waiting to hire them.

LÍ-KEH

In the outlying working-class neighbourhoods of Bangkok you may be lucky enough to come across the gaudy, raucous *lí-keh.* This theatrical art form is thought to have descended from drama rituals brought to southern Thailand by Arab and Malay traders. The first native public performance in central Thailand came about when a group of Thai Muslims staged *lí-keh* for Rama V (King Chulalongkorn) in Bangkok during the funeral commemoration of Queen Sunantha. *Lí-keh* grew very popular under Rama VI (King Vajiravudh), peaked in the early 20th century and has been fading slowly since the 1960s.

Most often performed at Buddhist festivals by troupes of travelling performers, *lí-keh* is a colourful mixture of folk and classical music, outrageous costumes, melodrama, slapstick comedy, sexual innuendo and sociopolitical commentary. *Faràng* – even those who speak fluent Thai – are often left behind by the highly idiomatic language and gestures. Most *lí-keh* performances begin with the *àwk khàek,* a prelude in which an actor dressed in Malay costume takes the stage to pay homage to the troupe's teacher, and to narrate a brief summary of the play. For true *lí-keh* aficionados, the visit of a renowned troupe is a bigger occasion than the release of an international blockbuster at the local cinema.

LÁKHON LÉK

Lákhon lék (little theatre; also known as *hùn lŭang,* or royal puppets), like *khŏn,* was once reserved for court performances. Metre-high marionettes made of *khòi* paper and wire, and wearing elaborate costumes modelled on those of *khŏn,* were used to convey similar themes, music and dance movements.

Two to three puppet masters were required to manipulate each *hùn lŭang* – including arms, legs, hands, even fingers and eyes – by means of wires attached to long poles. Stories were drawn from Thai folk tales, particularly *Phra Aphaimani* (a classical Thai literary work), and occasionally from the Ramakian. *Hùn lŭang* is no longer performed, as the performance techniques and puppet-making skills have been lost. The *hùn lŭang* puppets themselves are highly collectable; the National Museum has only one example in its collection. Surviving examples of a smaller, 30cm court version called *hùn lék* (little puppets) are occasionally used in live performances; only one puppeteer is required for each marionette in *hùn lék.*

Another form of Thai puppet theatre, *hùn kràbàwk* (cylinder puppets), is based on popular Hainanese puppet shows. It uses 30cm hand puppets carved from wood and viewed only from the waist up. *Hùn kràbàwk* marionettes are still crafted and used in performances today, most notably at the Joe Louis Puppet Theatre in Bangkok (see p158).

LÁKHON PHÛUT

Lákhon phûut (speaking theatre, or live contemporary theatre, as it is known in the West) is enjoyed by a small elite audience in Bangkok. Virtually the entire scene, such as it is, centres on two venues: Patravadi Theatre (p158) and the Bangkok Playhouse.

LITERATURE
CLASSICAL

The written word has a long history in Thailand, dating back to the 11th or 12th century when the first Thai script was fashioned from an older Mon alphabet. Sukhothai's king Phaya Lithai is thought to have composed the first work of Thai literature in 1345. This was *Traiphum Phra Ruang*, a treatise that described the three realms of existence according to Hindu-Buddhist cosmology. According to contemporary scholars, this work and its symbolism continues to have considerable influence on Thailand's art and culture.

Of all classical Thai literature, however, the Ramakian is the most pervasive and influential. Its Indian precursor, the Ramayana, came to Thailand with the Khmers 900 years ago, first appearing as stone reliefs on Prasat Hin Phimai and other Angkor temples in the northeast. Eventually, during the reign of Rama I (King Buddha Yodfa), Thailand developed its own version of the epic. This contained 60,000 stanzas and was a quarter longer than the original.

The 30,000-line *Phra Aphaimani*, composed by poet Sunthorn Phu in the late 18th century, is Thailand's most famous classical literary work. Like many of its epic predecessors around the world, it tells the story of an exiled prince who must triumph in an odyssey of love and war before returning to his kingdom.

During the Ayuthaya period, Thailand developed a classical poetic tradition based on five types of verse – *chan, kàap, khlong, klawn* and *râi*. Each form uses a complex set of rules to regulate metre, rhyming patterns and number of syllables. During the political upheavals of the 1970s several Thai-newspaper editors, most notably Kukrit Pramoj, composed lightly disguised political commentary in *klawn* verse. Modern Thai poets seldom use the classical forms, preferring to compose in blank verse or with songlike rhyming.

CONTEMPORARY

The first Thai-language novel appeared only about 70 years ago, in direct imitation of Western models. Thus far, no more than 10 have been translated into English.

The first Thai novel of substance, *The Circus of Life* (1929) by Arkartdamkeung Rapheephat, follows a young, upper-class Thai as he travels to London, Paris, the USA and China in the 1920s. The novel's existentialist tone created quite a stir in Thailand when it was released, and it became an instant bestseller. The fact that the author, himself a Thai prince, took his own life at the age of 26 added to the mystique surrounding this work.

The late Kukrit Pramoj, former ambassador and Thai prime minister, novelised Bangkok court life from the late 19th century through to the 1940s in *Four Reigns* (1953), the longest novel ever published in Thai. *The Story of Jan Darra* (1966), by journalist and short-story writer Utsana Phleungtham, traces the sexual obsessions of a Thai aristocrat as they are passed to his son. Director-producer Nonzee Nimibutr turned the remarkable novel into a rather melodramatic film (see p43). Praphatsorn Seiwikun's rapid-paced *Time in a Bottle* (1984) turned the dilemmas of a fictional middle-class Bangkok family into a bestseller.

Many Thai authors, including the notable Khamphoon Boonthawi (*Luk Isan*; 1976) and Chart Kobjitt (*Time*; 1993), have

> ### TOP FIVE NOVELS SET IN BANGKOK
>
> - *Sightseeing* (2004), Rattawut Lapcharoensap
> - *Jasmine Nights* (1994), SP Somtow
> - *Bangkok 8* (2003), John Burdett
> - *Four Reigns* (1953), Kukrit Pramoj (*Si Phaendin;* translated 1981)
> - *A Woman of Bangkok* (1956), Jack Reynolds

been honoured with the SEA Write Award, an annual prize presented to fiction writers from countries in the Association of Southeast Asian Nations (ASEAN). A one-stop collection of fiction thus awarded can be found in *The SEA Write Anthology of Thai Short Stories and Poems* (1996).

When it comes to novels written in English, Thai wunderkind SP Somtow has written and published more titles than any other Thai writer. Born in Bangkok, educated at Eton and Cambridge, and now a commuter between two 'cities of angels' – Los Angeles and Bangkok – Somtow's prodigious output includes a string of well-reviewed science fiction/fantasy/horror stories. These include *Moon Dance* (1989), *Darker Angels* (1997) and *The Vampire's Beautiful Daughter* (1997). The Somtow novel most evocative of Thailand and Thai culture is *Jasmine Nights* (1994), which also happens to be one of his most accessible reads. Following a 12-year-old Thai boy's friendship with an African American boy in Bangkok in the 1960s, this semiautobiographical work seamlessly blends Thai, Greek and African myths, American Civil War lore and a dollop of magical realism.

Thai-American Rattawut Lapcharoensap's *Sightseeing* (2004), a collection of short stories set in present-day Thailand, has been widely lauded for its deft portrayal of the intersection between Thai and foreign cultures, both tourist and expat.

All Soul's Day (1997) by Bill Morris is a sharp, well-researched historical novel set in Bangkok c 1963. The story, which involves vintage Buicks and the American military build-up prior to the second Indochina War, would do Graham Greene proud.

Expat writer Christopher G Moore covers the Thai underworld in his 1990s novels *A Killing Smile* (1991), *Spirit House* (1992), *A Bewitching Smile* (1992) and a raft of others. His anchor is firmly hooked in the go-go bar scene, and his description of Bangkok's sleazy Thermae Coffee House (called 'Zeno' in *A Killing Smile*) is the closest literature comes to evoking the perpetual male adolescence to which such places cater.

Most other efforts in the 'expat-adventures-in-Bangkok' genre aren't worth looking up, though a few – particularly Jake Needham's *The Big Mango* (2002; the first expat novel to be translated into Thai) – are entertaining. The John Grisham–style legal thriller *Laundry Man* (2003), also by Jake Needham, is set mostly in Bangkok.

One recent surprise is John Burdett's *Bangkok 8* (2003), a page-turner in which a half-Thai, half-*faràng* police detective investigates the murder of a US Marine in Bangkok. Along the way we're treated to vivid portraits of the gritty capital and insights into Thai Buddhism.

CINEMA

Bangkok Film launched Thailand's film industry with the first Thai-directed silent movie, *Chok Sorng Chan* (Double Luck), in 1927. Silent films proved to be more popular than talkies right into the 1960s, and as late as 1969 Thai studios were still producing them from 16mm stock. Perhaps partially influenced by India's famed *masala* (curry mix) movies – which enjoyed a strong following in post-WWII Bangkok – film companies blended romance, comedy, melodrama and adventure to give Thai audiences a little bit of everything.

The arrival of 35mm movies in Thailand around the same time brought a proliferation of modern cinema halls and a surge in movie making. During this era Thai films attracted more cinema-goers than *nǎng faràng* (movies from Europe and America), and today many Thais consider the '60s to be a golden age of Thai cinema. More than half of the approximately 75 films produced annually during this period starred the much-admired on-screen duo Mit Chaibancha and Petchara Chaowaraj.

Despite the founding of a government committee in 1970 to promote Thai cinema, Thai film production in the '70s and early '80s was mostly limited to inexpensive action or romance stories. A notable exception, *Luk Isan* (Child of the Northeast; 1982), based on a Thai novel of the same name, follows the ups and downs of a farming family living in drought-ridden Isan. *Luk Isan* became one of the first popular films to offer urban Thais an understanding of the hardships endured by many northeasterners, and initiated a social-drama subgenre that continues to this day.

The Thai movie industry almost died during the '80s and '90s, swamped by Hollywood extravaganzas and the boom era's taste for anything imported. From a 1970s peak of about 200 releases per year, by 1997 the Thai output shrank to an average of only 10 films a year. The Southeast Asian economic crisis that year threatened to further bludgeon the ailing industry, but the lack of funding coupled with foreign competition brought about a new emphasis on quality rather than quantity. The current era boasts a new generation of seriously good Thai directors, several of whom studied film abroad during Thailand's '80s and early '90s boom period.

Recent efforts have been so encouraging that Thai and foreign critics alike speak of a current Thai 'new wave'. Avoiding the soap operas of the past, the current crop of directors favour gritty realism, artistic innovation and a strengthened Thai identity. Pen-Ek Ratanaruang's *Fun Bar Karaoke* is a 1997 satire of Bangkok life in which the main characters are an ageing Thai playboy and his daughter; the film received critical acclaim for its true-to-life depiction of

The EGV cinema (p160) in the Siam Discovery Center

modern urban living, blended with sage humour. It was the first feature-length outing by a young Thai who is fast becoming one of the kingdom's most internationally noted directors. The film played well to international audiences but achieved only limited box office success at home. Similarly Nonzee Nimibutr's *2499 Antaphan Krong Meuang* (Dang Bireley's Young Gangsters) was hailed abroad – winning first prize at the 1997 Brussels International Film Festival – but was only modestly successful in Thailand.

A harbinger for the Thai film industry was Nonzee Nimibutr's 1998 release of *Nang Nak,* an exquisite retelling of the Mae Nak Phrakhanong legend, in which the spirit of a woman who died during childbirth haunts the home of her husband. This story has had no fewer than 20 previous cinematic renderings. *Nang Nak* not only features excellent acting and period detailing, but manages to transform Nak into a sympathetic character rather than a horrific ghost. The film became the largest-grossing film in Thai history, out-earning even *Titanic,* and earned awards for best director, best art director and best sound at the 1999 Asia-Pacific Film Festival.

In 1999 director Pen-Ek Ratanaruang came out with his second feature, a finely crafted thriller set in Bangkok called *Ruang Talok 69* (6ixtynin9). Like his first film it was a critical success that saw relatively little screen time in Thailand.

The 2000 film *Satree Lex* (The Iron Ladies) humorously dramatises the real-life exploits of a Lampang volleyball team made up almost entirely of transvestites and transsexuals. At home, this Yongyoot Thongkongtoon–directed film became Thai cinema's second-largest-grossing film to date, and was the first Thai film ever to reach the art house cinemas of Europe and the US on general release.

The next Thai film to garner international attention was 2000's *Suriyothai,* a historic epic directed by Prince Chatri Chalerm Yukol. Forty months and US$20 million in the making, the three-hour film lavishly narrates a well-known episode in Thai history in which an Ayuthaya queen sacrifices herself at the 1548 Battle of Hanthawaddy to save her king's life. Although rich in costumes and locations, it flopped overseas and was widely criticised for being ponderous and overly long. Recently, legendary American producer-director Francis Ford Coppola re-edited the film to create a shorter, more internationally palatable version *(The Legend of Suriyothai),* albeit of limited appeal.

The year 2000 also introduced the Pang brothers, Danny and Oxide, to Thai and foreign film festival audiences with the release of *Krung Thep Antara* (Bangkok Dangerous). Influenced in equal parts by Hong Kong director John Woo and American writer-director Quentin Tarantino, this story of a deaf-mute hit man who finds love won a Discovery Award at the Toronto Film Festival and runner-up Best Director in Seattle. Although the Pangs hail from Hong Kong, Thailand has become their main cinematic inspiration.

Fah Talai Jone (2000), directed by Wisit Sasanatieng, presents a campy and colourful parody of quasi-cowboy Thai melodramas of the '50s and '60s. The film received an honourable mention at Cannes (where it was quickly dubbed a cult hit) and took an award at the Vancouver International Film Festival. When Miramax distributed the film in the USA, it was called *Tears of the Black Tiger.*

In 2001 Nonzee Nimibutr returned with *Jan Dara,* a cinematic rendition of Utsana Pleungtham's controversially erotic 1966 novel of the same name. Filmed almost entirely on

43

sound stages save for outdoor scenes shot in Lǔang Prabang, Laos, the film was critically compared with Vietnam's famous *The Scent of Green Papaya* (1993).

Encouraged by critical acclaim abroad and box office receipts at home, Thai producers nearly tripled their output from a total of 12 Thai-language movies in 2001 to around 30 new productions in 2002. Quality continues to improve as well, and Thai films have assumed a newly favoured identity on the international film scene. The Vancouver International Film Festival, for example, increased its screening of Thai films from three in 2001 to five in 2002.

For evidence that Thailand's role in world cinema will continue to expand, you don't need to look any further than Pen-Ek's *Mon Rak Transistor* (Transistor Love Story). This acclaimed film broke new ground by seizing a thoroughly Thai theme – the tragicomic odyssey of a young villager who tries to crack the big time *lûuk thûng* music scene in Bangkok – and upgrading production values to international standards. The 2001 release was honoured with a special Directors' Fortnight showing at Cannes 2002, and went on to earn Best Asian Film at the Seattle International Film Festival 2002 and the Audience Award at the Vienna International Film Festival 2002.

One of Thai cinema's finest moments arrived in 2002 when Cannes chose *Sut Sanaeha* (Blissfully Yours) for the coveted Un Certain Regard (Of Special Consideration) screening, an event that showcases notable work by new directors. Directed by 31-year-old Apichatpong Weerasethakul, the film dramatises a budding romance between a Thai woman and an illegal Burmese immigrant.

Another favourite on the 2002 festival circuit, and a blockbuster in Thailand as well, was Jira Malikul's film *15 Kham Deuan 11* (Mekhong Full Moon Party). The storyline juxtaposes folk beliefs about mysterious 'dragon lights' emanating from Mekong River with the scepticism of Bangkok scientists and news media, and also with Thai Buddhism. As with *Mon Rak Transistor*, the film affectionately evokes everyday Thai culture for the whole world to enjoy. It's also the first Thai feature film where most of the script is written in the Isan dialect, necessitating Thai subtitles.

The year 2003 saw *Faen Chan* (My Girl), a nostalgic but well-directed and acted drama/comedy about childhood friends who become re-acquainted as adults when one of them is about to marry. Directed by a team of six young Thais, the film was hugely successful in Thailand and garnered attention abroad as well.

TOP FIVE THAI FILMS

- *Mon Rak Transistor* (Transistor Love Story; 2002), director Pen-Ek Ratanaruang
- *Faen Chan* (My Girl; 2003), directors Vitcha +Gojiew *et al*
- *15 Kham Deuan 11* (Mekhong Full Moon Party; 2002), director Jira Malikul
- *Nang Nak* (1998), director Nonzee Nimibutr
- *Satree Lex* (The Iron Ladies; 2000), director Yongyoot Thongkongtoon

A further watershed occurred when the 2004 Cannes Film Festival awarded Apichatpong's dreamlike *Sut Pralat* (Tropical Malady) the Jury Prize. None of Apichatpong's films have generated much interest in Thailand, however, where they are seen as too Western in tone. Much better-received box office–wise, both in Thailand and abroad, was director's Prachya Pinkaew's *Ong Bak* (2004), widely hailed around the world as one of the finest 'old-school' martial arts films of all time.

Other signs that Thai cinema has reached a global platform include the shift of the prestigious CineAsia convention and trade show, which focuses on the Asia-Pacific film market, to Bangkok in 2003, after eight years' residence in Hong Kong. One of the reasons cited for the move was the availability of more than 300 screening venues in Bangkok.

The successful inauguration of the Bangkok International Film Festival (BKKIFF) in January 2002 further demonstrates that Thailand lies at the epicentre of a growing film industry. The 2006 BKKIFF screened over 150 films, and was attended by celebrities such as Catherine Deneuve, Oliver Stone, Willem Dafoe, Christopher Lee and Rita Moreno.

Food & Drink

Food & Drink

HISTORY & CULTURE

Bangkok's cooks concoct a seemingly endless variety of dishes, whether from 300-year-old court recipes, the latest in Euro-Thai fusion or simple dishes guided by seasonal and regional availability.

Standing at the crossroads of many ancient and culturally continuous traditions dominated by India, China and Asian Oceania, Thailand has adapted cooking techniques and ingredients from all three of these major spheres of influence, as well as the culinary kits carried by passing traders and empire builders from the Middle East and southern Europe. Over the centuries, indigenous rudiments have fused with imported elements to produce a distinctive native cuisine that is instantly recognisable.

Appreciation of Thai food is so central to Thai cultural identity that many Thais naively assume that non-Thais are physically or mentally unable to partake of the cuisine. Foreign visitors or residents won't be asked simply whether they like to eat Thai food. Rather they will be asked 'Kin aahǎan thai pen mǎi?' ('Do you know how to eat Thai food?'). It is almost assumed that to enjoy Thai cooking you must be either born Thai or trained in the difficult art of feeling exhilarated over a plate of well-prepared phàt thai (rice noodles stir-fried with egg, tofu and peanuts).

Of course the one aspect of Thai cuisines that does require getting used to for many people, even other Asians, is the food's relatively high chilli content. This is why the second-most-common question asked of a foreigner about to slip a spoon into a bowl of kaeng khǐaw-wǎan (green curry) is 'Kin phèt dâi mǎi?' ('Can you eat spicy food?').

Unlike their Indian counterparts, Thai cooks assemble curry pastes and other relatively elaborate seasoning concoctions quickly from fresh rather than powdered, dried or preserved ingredients. Exceptions include the fermentation and pickling processes favoured for certain condiments and seasonings. In classic Thai dishes, the use of butter or lard is extremely rare, and limited to East-West fusion experiments.

You will quickly discover that eating is one of life's great pleasures in Bangkok. The average Bangkokian takes time out to eat, not three times per day, but four or five. Sitting down at a roadside rót khěn (vendor cart) after an evening at the cinema or nightclubbing, a Thai may barely have finished one steaming bowl of noodles before ordering a second round, just to revel in the experience a little longer.

Of course regional Thai cuisines form only part of the vast menu of cooking styles available in Bangkok. With well over 25% of the population claiming Chinese ancestry, Chinese cuisines loom large. Although Chinese traders had lived along Chao Phraya riverbanks for hundreds of years, during the royal capital's late 18th-century shift from Ayuthaya to Bangkok the Chinese were moved to a single area of town known as Sampeng or Yaowarat – the city's Chinatown. Since most Chinese immigrants to Thailand hailed from southern China, you'll mainly find southern Chinese cooking styles, predominantly Cantonese, Chao Zhou and Hokkien. Between 8pm and midnight, when traffic subsides to a steady hum, is the best time to trawl Sampeng's restaurants and roadside stalls for the city's best Chinese food.

Nearby Phahurat district has a similar history with regard to immigration from the Indian subcontinent. A stroll down Th Chakkaphet will bring you nose-to-nose with a rich variety of Indian tea shops, Bombay sweets vendors, roti and samosa carts and tiny restaurants serving cuisines from nearly every region of north India, particularly Punjabi, Gujarati and Nawabi cuisines.

Another ethnic neighbourhood has more recently developed around Soi 3, Th Sukhumvit. Known as Nana, this area began attracting a heavy concentration of residents and visitors from Middle Eastern and North African countries in the 1970s, when the Grace Hotel – one of the largest hotels in Bangkok at the time – became a favourite of Arab tour groups. The number of restaurants and food vendors along Soi 3 and adjacent smaller *soi* continues to multiply, and today there are probably a hundred different Middle Eastern food venues in the neighbourhood.

ETIQUETTE

While Thai table manners would hardly ever be described as 'formal' in the Western sense, there are plenty of subtleties to be mastered. Using the correct utensils and eating gestures will garner much respect from Thais, who generally think Western table manners are coarse.

Originally Thai food was eaten with one's fingers, and it still is in certain regions of the kingdom. Some foods, such as *khâo nǐaw* (sticky rice), are eaten with the fingers everywhere. In the early 1900s restaurateurs began setting their tables with forks and spoons to affect a 'royal' setting, and it wasn't long before fork-and-spoon dining became the norm in Bangkok and later spread throughout the kingdom.

The *sâwm* (fork) and *cháwn tó* (tablespoon) are placed to the left of the plate, and usually wrapped in a paper or cloth napkin. In simpler restaurants, these utensils are laid bare on the table or may not arrive until the food is served. Some restaurants place a steel or glass container on each tabletop, in which a supply of clean forks and spoons is kept.

To most Thais, pushing a fork into one's mouth is almost as uncouth as putting a knife in the mouth for Westerners. Thais use forks to steer food onto the spoon, to eat chunks of roasted meat served as *kàp klâem* (snacks eaten with drinks) and to spear sliced fruit served at the end of the meal. Even so, the fork is never placed all the way into the mouth. Noodle soups are eaten with a spoon in the left hand (for spooning up the broth) and chopsticks in the right.

Whether at home or in a restaurant, Thai meals are always served 'family style', that is, from common serving platters. Traditionally, the party orders one of each kind of dish – perhaps a curry, a fish, a stir-fry, a *yam* (hot and tangy salad), a vegetable dish and a soup, taking care to balance cool and hot, sour and sweet, salty and plain. One dish is generally large enough for two people. One or two extras may be ordered for a large party.

Dishes are typically served more or less all at once, rather than in courses. If the host or restaurant staff can't bring them all to the table at the same time, then the diners typically wait until everything has arrived before digging in. One exception to this rule is if a *yam* or other *kàp klâem* is ordered, as these are sometimes served as an appetiser with drinks before the main meal. When these dishes come out with everything else, they will be eaten first.

Thais aren't fussy about dishes being served piping hot, so no-one minds if the dishes sit untouched for a while. In fact, it's considered impolite to take a spoonful of steaming-hot food, as it implies that you're so ravenous or uncivilised that you can't wait to gorge yourself. The one exception to the cooling rule is noodle dishes, which are typically served right from the pan.

Empty plates are placed in front of every person at the beginning of the meal, and diners take a little from each serving platter and put it onto these plates. When serving yourself from a common platter, put no more than one spoonful onto your plate at a time. It's customary at the start of a shared meal to eat a spoonful of plain rice first – a gesture that recognises rice as the most important part of the meal.

For the most part, *tôm yam* (chilli and lemon-grass soup) and other soups aren't served in individual bowls, except in more elegant restaurants or those aimed at tourists. You serve yourself from the common bowl, spooning broth and ingredients over your rice or into your own bowl. Sometimes serving spoons are provided. If not, you simply dig in with your own spoon.

Don't pick up a serving platter to serve yourself. Proper Thai etiquette requires leaving the platter on the tabletop and reaching over to it with your spoon, even if it means stretching your arm across the table. If you can't reach the serving platter, it's best to hand your plate to someone near the platter, who can then place some food on it. Most Thais will do this automatically if they notice you're out of platter range. Whatever you do, don't incline a serving platter over your individual plate – this is considered a very rude and greedy gesture.

Never ask someone to pass food your way, but rather wait for them to offer you more. Thais are constantly looking out for each other at meal times – making sure no-one's plate is empty – and will usually give you more food than you can eat. Don't be surprised if another diner in your party spoons food directly onto your plate, just like your mother did when you were a child. This is a completely normal gesture in Thai dining custom and carries no particular import other than showing hospitality towards a foreign guest.

Thais want you to enjoy the food, and at some point in the meal your host or one of your dining companions will pause for a second, smile and ask, '*Àràwy măí?*' ('Is it delicious?') The expected answer, of course, is '*Àràwy*' (delicious) or '*Àràwy mâak*' (very delicious).

Always leave some food on the serving platters as well as on your plate. To clean your plate and leave nothing on the serving platters says to your hosts 'you didn't feed me enough'. This is why Thais tend to over-order at social occasions – the more food left on the table, the more generous the host appears.

Cigarettes often appear both before and after a meal, but it is considered impolite to smoke during a meal. Thais will often step away from the table to smoke, mainly because ashtrays aren't usually placed on dining tables. It's not customary in Thailand to ask permission to smoke before lighting up, though this is beginning to change in Bangkok society. To be on the safe side, always ask, '*Sùup bùrìi dâi măi?*' ('Is it OK to smoke?'). Note that Thai law forbids smoking in any air-conditioned public area, including restaurants and bars.

HOW THAIS EAT

Aside from the occasional indulgence in deep-fried savouries, most Thais sustain themselves on a varied and healthy diet filled with many fruits, rice and vegetables mixed with smaller amounts of animal protein and fat. The Thais' main culinary satisfaction seems to come not from eating large amounts of food at any one meal but rather from nibbling at a variety of dishes with as many different flavours as possible throughout the day.

Thais extend a hand towards a bowl of noodles, a plate of rice or a banana-leaf-wrapped snack with amazing frequency. There are no 'typical' times for meals, though in Bangkok diners tend to cluster in local restaurants at the customary noon to 1pm lunch break. Even so, it's not at all unusual for a bank clerk or shop owner to order in a bowl of *kǔaytǐaw* (rice noodles) some time midmorning, and perhaps again around 3pm or 4pm.

Nor are certain kinds of food restricted to certain times of day. Practically anything can be eaten first thing in the morning, whether it's sweet, salty or chilli-ridden. *Khâo kaeng* (curry over rice) is a very popular morning meal, as are *khâo mǔu daeng* (red pork over rice) and *khâo man kài* (sliced steamed chicken cooked in chicken broth and garlic and served over rice).

Lighter morning choices, especially for Thais of Chinese descent, include deep-fried chunks of *paa-thâwng-kǒh* (fried wheat pastry) dipped in warm *náam tâo-hûu* (soya milk).

Kúay jáp, a thick broth of sliced Chinese mushrooms and bits of chicken or pork, is another early-morning Bangkok favourite. Thais also eat noodles, whether fried or in soup, with great gusto in the morning or as a substantial snack at any time of day or night.

As the staple with which almost all Thai dishes are eaten – noodles, after all, are still seen as a Chinese import – rice *(khâo)* is considered an absolutely indispensable part of the daily diet. Most Bangkok families will put on a pot of rice, or start the rice cooker, just after rising in the morning to prepare a base for the day's menu. All other dishes, aside from noodles, are considered *kàp khâo* (side dishes) that supplement this central *aahǎan làk* (staple).

Plaa (fish) finds its way into almost every meal, even if it's only in the form of *náam plaa* (fish sauce), a thin, clear, amber sauce made from fermented anchovies, which is used to salt Thai dishes, much as soy sauce is used in eastern Asia. Chicken is the next favourite source of protein, and is prepared in a variety of fashions, from curries and stir-fries to barbecues. Pork is particularly enjoyed by Chinese Thais while shunned by most Muslim Thais. Although beef isn't as popular as fish or chicken, there are some Bangkok favourites such as *néua phàt náam-man hǎwy* (beef stir-fried in oyster sauce) and northeastern Thailand's *néua náam tòk* (literally 'waterfall beef').

Thais are prodigious consumers of fruit. You'll find vendors pushing glass-and-wood carts filled with a rainbow of fresh sliced papaya, pineapple, watermelon and coconut, and a more muted palette of salt-pickled or candied seasonal fruits. These are usually served in a small plastic bag with a thin bamboo stick to use as an eating utensil.

Because many restaurants in Thailand are able to serve dishes at only a slightly higher price than they would cost to make at home, Thais dine out far more often than their Western counterparts. Any evening of the week you'll see small groups of Thais – usually males – clustered around roadside tables or in outdoor restaurants, drinking Thai-brewed beer or rice liquor while picking from an array of dishes, one morsel at a time. These are *kàp klâem,* dishes specifically meant to be eaten while drinking alcoholic beverages, often before an evening meal or while waiting for the larger courses to arrive. *Kàp klâem* can be as simple as a plate of *mét má-mûang thâwt* (fried cashews) or as elaborate as one of the many types of *yam,* containing a blast of lime, chilli, fresh herbs and a choice of seafood, roast vegetables, noodles or meats.

Thais tend to avoid eating alone. Dining with others is always preferred from the Thai perspective because it means everyone has a chance to sample several dishes. When forced to fly solo by circumstance – such as during lunch breaks at work – a single diner usually sticks to one-plate dishes such as fried rice or curry over rice.

Diners at an outdoor restaurant at Tha Chang, Ko Ratanakosin (p126)

STAPLES & SPECIALITIES

Just as Bangkok Thai has become 'Standard Thai' in schools and government offices throughout the country, so Bangkok Thai cooking is today considered 'classic Thai' cuisine. The region's central position and, more importantly, its wealth relative to the rest of the country mean that spices, seasonings and produce hailing from any corner of the kingdom are easily available. Coconuts from the south, bamboo shoots from the north, *maeng-daa* (water beetle) from the northeast – all find their way into Bangkok markets.

RICE

Bangkok sits right in the middle of Mae Nam Chao Phraya delta, the country's 'rice bowl'. Thailand has led the world in rice exports since the 1960s, and the quality of Thai rice, according to many discerning Asians, is considered the best in the world. Thailand's *khâo hǎwm málí* (jasmine rice) is so coveted that there is a steady underground business in smuggling bags of the fragrant grain to neighbouring countries.

Rice is so central to Thai food culture that the most common term for 'eat' is *kin khâo* (literally 'consume rice'), and one of the most common greetings is *'Kin khâo láew réu yang?'* ('Have you consumed rice yet?') All the dishes eaten with rice – whether curries, stir-fries, soups or other food preparations – are simply classified as *kàp khâo* (with rice). Only two dishes using rice as a principal ingredient are common in Thailand, *khâo phàt* (fried rice) and *khâo mòk kài* (chicken biryani), neither of which is native to Thailand.

Cooked rice is usually referred to as *khâo sǔay* – literally 'beautiful rice', yet another clue to how thoroughly Thais esteem this staple. When you order plain rice in a restaurant you may use this term or simply *khâo plào*, 'plain rice'. Restaurants may serve rice by the plate *(jaan)* or you can order a *thǒh* or large bowl of rice, lidded to keep the rice warm and moist, and notched along the rim to accommodate the handle of a rice scoop. *Thǒh* may be practical thick-sided plastic affairs or more elaborate engraved, footed aluminium bowls with fancy serving spoons to match.

NOODLES

Exactly when the noodle reached Thailand is difficult to say, but it probably arrived along trade routes from China, since the preparation styles in Thailand are similar to those of southern China.

You'll find four basic kinds of noodles in Bangkok. Hardly surprising, given the Thai fixation on rice, is the overwhelming popularity of *kǔaytǐaw,* made from pure rice flour mixed with water to form a paste, which is then steamed to form wide, flat sheets. The sheets are then folded and sliced into *sên yài* (flat 'wide line' noodles 2cm to 3cm wide), *sên lék* ('small line' noodles about 5mm wide) and *sên mìi* ('noodle line' noodles only 1mm to 2mm wide). *Sên mìi* dry out so quickly that they are sold only in their dried form.

At most restaurants or vendor stands specialising in *kǔaytǐaw,* you can choose between *sên yài* or *sên lék* noodles when ordering.

The king of Thai noodles *kǔaytǐaw* comes as part of many dishes. The simplest, *kǔaytǐaw náam,* is *kǔaytǐaw* served in a bowl of plain chicken or beef stock with bits of meat and pickled cabbage, and coriander leaf as garnish. Season your noodle soup by choosing from a rack of small glass or metal containers on the table (see the boxed text opposite).

Another dish, *kǔaytǐaw phàt,* involves the quick stir-frying of the noodles in a wok with sliced meat, *phàk kha-náa* (Chinese kale), soy sauce and various seasonings. Two other ways to order Thai rice noodles are *kǔaytǐaw hâeng* (dry *kǔaytǐaw*) and *kǔaytǐaw râat nâa* (*kǔaytǐaw* with gravy). For *kǔaytǐaw hâeng,* rice noodles are doused in very hot water to heat them up and soften them, then tossed in a soup bowl with garlic oil and topped with the usual ingredients that make up *kǔaytǐaw náam,* save the broth. *Kǔaytǐaw râat nâa* involves braising the noodles in a light gravy made with cornstarch-thickened stock, adding meats and seasonings to taste and serving the finished product on an oval plate. A seafood version of the latter, *kǔaytǐaw râat nâa tháleh,* is one of the most popular versions in Bangkok. *Râat nâa* (or *lâat nâa,* as it's more typically called in Bangkok), the shortened name for any *kǔaytǐaw râat nâa* dish, is frequently used when ordering.

Chilli-heads must give *kǔaytǐaw phàt khîi mao* (drunkard's fried noodles) a try. A favourite lunch or late-night snack, this spicy stir-fry consists of wide rice noodles, fresh basil leaves, chicken or pork, seasonings and a healthy dose of fresh sliced chillies.

Probably the most well-known *kǔaytǐaw* dish among foreigners is *kǔaytǐaw phàt thai,* usually called *phàt thai* for short, a plate of thin rice noodles stir-fried with dried or fresh shrimp, bean sprouts, fried tofu, egg and seasonings. The cook usually places little piles of ground peanuts and ground dried chilli along the edge of the plate, along with lime halves and a few stalks of spring onion, for self-seasoning.

Another kind of noodle, *khanǒm jiin,* is produced by pushing rice-flour paste through a sieve into boiling water, in much the same way as pasta is made. *Khanǒm jiin* is eaten doused with various curries. The most standard curry topping, *náam yaa* (herbal sauce), contains a strong dose of *krà-chai* (Chinese key), a root of the ginger family used as a traditional remedy for a number of gastrointestinal ailments, along with ground fish.

PERK UP YOUR NOODLE

Much as chicken soup is viewed as something of a home cold remedy in the West, rice-noodle soups in Thailand are often eaten to ward off colds, hangovers or general malaise. When you're presented with a bowl of noodles and the array of condiments available to season them, you must be prepared to become your own pharmacist, mixing up the ingredients to create the right flavour balance and, by implication, to set body and soul right.

If you see a steel rack containing four lidded glass bowls or jars on your table, it's proof that the restaurant you're in serves *kǔaytǐaw* (rice noodles). Typically these containers offer four choices: *náam sôm phrík* (sliced green chillies in white vinegar), *phrík náam plaa* (*phrík khǐi nǔu*, or mouse-dropping chilli, in fish sauce), *phrík pòn* (dried red chilli, flaked or ground to a near powder) and *náamtaan* (plain white sugar).

In typically Thai fashion, these condiments offer three ways to make the soup hotter – hot and sour, hot and salty, and just plain hot – and one to make it sweet. Some *kǔaytǐaw* vendors substitute *thùa pòn* (ground peanuts) for the *phrík náam plaa*, which is provided in a separate bowl or saucer instead.

The typical noodle eater will add a teaspoonful of each one of these condiments to the noodle soup, except for the sugar, which usually rates a full tablespoon. Until you're used to these strong seasonings, we recommend adding them a bit at a time, tasting the soup along the way to make sure you don't go overboard. Adding sugar to soup may appear strange to some foreign palates, but it does considerably enhance the flavour of *kǔaytǐaw náam* (rice-noodle soup).

In addition to the condiments rack, a conscientious *kǔaytǐaw* vendor will provide a bottle of *náam plaa* (fish sauce) for those who want to make the soup saltier without adding the spice.

The third kind of noodle, *bà-mìi*, is made from wheat flour and sometimes egg (depending on the noodle maker or the brand). It's yellowish in colour and always the same size, about 1.5mm in diameter. *Bà-mìi* is sold only in fresh bundles and, unlike both *kǔaytǐaw* and *khanǒm jiin*, it must be cooked just before serving. The cooking procedure is simple – plunge a bamboo-handled wire basket full of *bà-mìi* into boiling water or broth and leave it for two to three minutes. Add broth plus meat, seafood or vegetables and you have *bà-mìi náam*. Served in a bowl with a small amount of garlic oil and no liquid, it's *bà-mìi hâeng*.

Some restaurants serve both *bà-mìi* and *kǔaytǐaw*, but the best *bà-mìi* is found at shops or vendor carts that specialise in *bà-mìi* and *kíaw*. *Kíaw* is a triangle of *bà-mìi* dough wrapped around ground pork or ground fish (or a vegetable substitute at vegetarian restaurants). These dumplings may be boiled and added to soup, or fried to make *kíaw thâwt*. One of the most popular *bà-mìi* dishes is *bà-mìi kíaw puu*, a soup containing *kíaw* and *puu* (crab).

Finally there's *wún sên*, an almost-clear noodle made from mung-bean starch and water. Sold only in dried bunches, *wún sên* (literally 'jelly thread') is easily prepared by soaking in hot water for 10 to 15 minutes. It's used for only three dishes in Thailand. The first and typical, *yam wún sên*, is a hot and tangy salad made with lime juice, fresh sliced *phrík khǐi nǔu* (mouse-dropping chilli), mushrooms, dried or fresh shrimp, ground pork and various seasonings. A second appearance is in *wún-sên òp puu*, bean-thread noodles baked in a lidded clay pot with crab and seasonings. Lastly, *wún sên* is a common ingredient in *kaeng jèut*, a bland, Chinese-influenced soup containing ground pork, soft tofu and a few vegetables.

CURRIES

In Thai, *kaeng* (rhyme it with the English 'gang') is often translated as 'curry', but it actually describes any dish with a lot of liquid and can thus refer to soups (such as *kaeng jèut*) as well as the chilli-based curries such as *kaeng phèt* (red curry) for which Thai cuisine is famous. The preparation of all chilli-based *kaeng* begins with a *khrêuang kaeng*, created by grinding fresh ingredients with a mortar and pestle to form an aromatic, extremely pungent-tasting and rather thick paste. Typical ingredients in a *khrêuang kaeng* include dried chilli, galangal (also known as Thai ginger), lemon grass, kaffir lime (peel, leaves or both), shallots, garlic, shrimp paste and salt. Coriander seeds and cumin are added for green curries.

Most *kaeng* are blended in a heated pan with coconut cream, to which the chef adds the rest of the ingredients (meat, poultry, seafood and/or vegetables), along with coconut milk to further thin and flavour the *kaeng*. Some recipes will omit coconut milk entirely to

Pots of Thai curries at Talat Aw Taw Kaw (p146)

produce a particularly fiery *kaeng* known as *kaeng pàa* (forest curry). Another *kaeng* that does not use coconut milk is *kaeng sôm* (sour curry), made with dried chillies, shallots, garlic and Chinese key pestled with salt, shrimp paste *(kà-pì)* and fish sauce. Cooked with tamarind juice and green papaya to create an overall tanginess, the result is a soupy, salty, sweet-and-sour ragout that most Westerners would never identify with the word 'curry'.

Thai curry cuisine revolves around three primary *kaeng*. *Kaeng phèt* (hot curry), also known as *kaeng daeng* (red curry) and *kaeng phèt daeng* (red hot curry), is the most traditional and is often used as a base to create other curries. This curry paste should be quite spicy, with its deep red colour coming from a copious number of red chillies. *Kaeng phánaeng*, by contrast, is a relatively mild curry where the heat is reduced by the presence of crushed peanuts. *Kaeng khîaw-wǎan*, literally 'green sweet curry', substitutes green chillies for red, and adds a large dose of ground cumin seed along with Thai eggplants the size of ping-pong balls.

Although Thais are familiar with international curry powder or *phǒng kàrìi*, it's employed only in a few Hokkien Chinese–influenced dishes such as *puu phàt phǒng kàrìi* (cracked crab stir-fried with curry powder and eggs). The use of the Anglo-Indian term 'curry', *kàrìi* in Thai, is applied only to *kaeng kàrìi kài*, the one dish in the Thai repertoire that most approximates a true Indian curry. The word *kàrìi* also happens to be Thai slang for 'prostitute', and is thus the source of endless puns that intentionally confuse cooking with sex.

A few extra seasonings such as *phàk chii* (coriander leaf), *bai ma-krùt* (kaffir lime leaves), *bai hohráphaa* (sweet basil leaves) and *náam plaa* may be added to taste just before serving. Bangkok Thais like their curries a bit sweeter than those from other regions of Thailand. Note that the best place to find good curries is a *ráan khâo kaeng* (rice-curry shop), rather than a regular restaurant.

Most Bangkokians eat curries only for breakfast or lunch, hence the average *ráan khâo kaeng* is open 7am to 2pm only. Among the Thais it is considered a bit odd to eat curries in the evening, and hence most restaurants (tourist restaurants excepted) don't offer them on the evening menu.

HOT & TANGY SALADS

Standing right alongside *kaeng* in terms of Thai-ness is the ubiquitous *yam*, a hot and tangy salad containing a blast of lime, chilli, fresh herbs and a choice of seafood, roast vegetables, noodles or meats. Bangkokians prize *yam* dishes so much that they are often eaten on their own, without rice, before the meal has begun.

Lime juice provides the tang, while the abundant use of fresh chilli produces the heat. Other ingredients vary considerably, but plenty of leafy vegetables and herbs are usually present, including lettuce (often lining the dish) and mint leaves. Lemon grass, shallots, kaffir lime leaves and *khêun chàai* (Chinese celery) may also come into play. Most *yam* are served at room temperature or just slightly warmed by any cooked ingredients.

On Thai menus, the *yam* section will often be the longest. Yet when these same menus are translated into English, most or all of the *yam* are omitted because Thai restaurateurs harbour the idea that the delicate *faràng* (Western) palate cannot handle the heat or pungency. The usual English menu translation is either 'Thai-style salad' or 'hot and sour salad'.

Without a doubt, *yam* are the spiciest of all Thai dishes, and *yam phrík chíi fáa* (spur chilli *yam*) is perhaps the hottest. A good *yam* to begin with if you're not so chilli tolerant is *yam wún sên*: bean-thread noodles tossed with shrimp, ground pork, coriander leaf, lime juice and fresh sliced chilli. Another tame *yam* that tends to be a favourite among Thais and foreigners alike is *yam plaa dùk fuu,* made from fried shredded catfish, chilli and peanuts with a shredded-mango dressing on the side. Because of the city's proximity to the Gulf of Thailand, Bangkok eateries serve a wide variety of seafood *yam*. *Yam* may also be made with vegetables (*yam thùa phuu,* made with angle beans), fungi (*yam hèt hǎwm,* made with shiitake mushrooms) or fruit (*yam sôm oh,* made with pomelo).

STIR-FRIES & DEEP-FRIES

The simplest dishes in the Thai culinary repertoire are the stir-fries *(phàt),* brought to Thailand by the Chinese, who are of course world famous for being able to stir-fry a whole banquet in a single wok. Despite stir-fry's Chinese origins, *phàt* dishes are never served in Thailand with soy sauce as a condiment, except in Chinese restaurants. Instead they come with *phrík náam plaa* (mouse-dropping chilli in fish sauce) on the side.

The list of *phàt* dishes seems endless. Most are better classified as Chinese, such as *néua phàt náam-man hǎwy*. Some are clearly Thai-Chinese hybrids, such as *kài phàt phrík khǐng,* in which chicken is stir-fried with ginger, garlic and chilli – ingredients shared by both traditions – but seasoned with fish sauce. Also leaning towards Thai – because cashews are native to Thailand but not to China – is *kài phàt mét mámûang hìmáphaan* (sliced chicken stir-fried in dried chilli and cashews), a favourite with *faràng* tourists.

Perhaps the most Thai-like *phàt* dish is the famed lunch meal *phàt bai kà-phrao,* a chicken or pork stir-fry with garlic, fresh sliced chilli, soy and fish sauce, and lots of holy basil.

Another classic Thai stir-fry is *phàt phèt* (literally 'hot stir-fry'), in which the main ingredients are quickly stir-fried with red curry paste and tossed with sweet basil leaves before serving. This recipe usually includes seafood or freshwater fish, such as shrimp, squid, catfish or eel.

Stir-fry chicken, pork, beef or shrimp with black pepper and garlic and you have *phàt phrík thai kràthiam,* a relatively mild recipe often ordered as a 'fill-in' dish during a larger meal. For lovers of fresh vegetables, *phàt phàk kha-náa* (Chinese kale stir-fried in black bean sauce) is worth looking out for, as is *phàt phàk ruam* (mixed vegetables).

Thâwt (deep-frying in oil) is mainly reserved for snacks such as *klûay thâwt* (fried bananas) or *pàw-pía* (egg rolls). An exception is *plaa thâwt* (fried fish), which is the most common way any fish is prepared. Many Thai recipes featuring whole fish require that it be fried first, usually in a wok filled with cooking oil (until the outside flesh is crispy to a depth of at least 1cm). Although to Western tastes this may appear to dry the fish out, in Thailand most fish fried in this way will then be topped with some sort of sauce – lime gravy or a cooked chilli-onion mixture – which will remoisten the dish. Some fish, such as mackerel, will be steamed first, then lightly pan-fried in a smaller amount of oil to seal in the moisture.

Only a few dishes require ingredients to be dipped in batter and then deep-fried, such as *kài thâwt* (fried chicken) and *kûng chúp pâeng thâwt* (batter-fried shrimp).

SOUPS

Thai soups fall into two broad categories, *tôm yam* and *kaeng jèut,* that are worlds apart in terms of seasonings. *Tôm yam* is almost always made with seafood, though chicken may also be used. *Tôm yam kûng (tôm yam* with shrimp) can be found in nearly all Thai restaurants as well as in many serving non-Thai cuisine. It is often translated on English menus as 'hot-and-sour Thai soup', although this often misleads non-Thais to relate the dish to Chinese hot-and-sour soup, which is milder and thinner in texture, and includes vinegar.

Lemon grass, kaffir lime peel and lime juice give *tôm yam* its characteristic tang. Fuelling the fire beneath *tôm yam*'s velvety surface are fresh *phrík khîi nŭu* (mouse-dropping chilli) and sometimes half a teaspoonful of *náam phrík phǎo* (a paste of dried chilli roasted with *kà-pì*, or shrimp paste). Improvisation comes into play with this dish as cooks try to outdo one another in providing a savoury soup with at least one or two 'mystery' ingredients.

Many cooks add galangal to add fragrance to the soup. Aside from lemon grass and galangal resting on the bottom of the bowl, solids in this soup are confined to shrimp and straw mushrooms. Coriander leaf is an important garnish for both appearance and fragrance.

Tôm yam is meant to be eaten with rice, not sipped alone. The first swallow of this soup often leaves the uninitiated gasping for breath. It's not that the soup is so hot, but the chilli oils that provide the spice tend to float on top.

Of the several variations on *tôm yam* that exist, probably the most popular with Westerners is the milder *tôm khàa kài* (literally 'boiled galangal chicken', but often translated as 'chicken coconut soup'). The lime and chilli are considerably muted in this soup by the addition of coconut milk.

Kaeng jèut covers the other end of the spectrum; a soothing broth seasoned with little more than soy or fish sauce and black pepper. Although the number of variations on *kaeng jèut* are many, common ingredients include *wún sên* (mung-bean starch noodles), *tâohûu* (tofu), *hŭa chai tháo* (Chinese radish) and *mŭu sàp* (ground pork).

FRUIT

The omnipresent *phŏn-lá-mái* (literally 'fruit of the tree', a general term for all fruit) testifies to the Thais' great fondness for fruit, which they appear to consume at every opportunity. An evening meal is normally followed by a plate of sliced fresh fruit, not pastries or Western-style desserts – no doubt one reason Thais stay so slim, as a rule.

Other common year-rounders include *máphráo* (coconut), *faràng* (guava; also colloquial name for Westerner), *khanŭn* (jackfruit), *mákhǎam* (tamarind), *sôm khǐaw-wǎan* (mandarin orange), *málákaw* (papaya), *sôm oh* (pomelo), *taeng moh* (watermelon) and *sàppàrót* (pineapple). All are most commonly eaten fresh, and sometimes dipped in a mixture of salt, sugar and ground chilli. Fruit juices of every kind are popular as beverages (see p56).

No discussion of Thai fruit is complete without a mention of durian *(thúrian)*, dubbed 'the king of fruits' by most Southeast Asians yet despised by many foreigners. A member of the aptly named *Bombacaceae* family, this heavy, spiked orb resembles a piece of medieval weaponry. Inside the thick shell lie five sections of plump, buttery and pungent flesh. Legions of connoisseurs as well as detractors have laboured to describe the durian's com-

---

SEASONAL FRUITS

The watchful visitor could almost fix the calendar month in Thailand by observing the parade of fruits appearing – sweet mangoes in March, mangosteens in April, rambeh in May, custard apples in July, golden-peel oranges in November and so on.

Chom-phûu (Rose apple) Small, applelike texture, very fragrant; April to July.

Lam yai (Longan) 'Dragon's eyes'; small, brown, spherical, similar to rambutan; July to October.

Lámút (Sapodilla) Small, brown, oval, sweet but pungent smelling; July to September.

Mangkhút (Mangosteen) Round, purple fruit with juicy white flesh; April to September.

Máfai (Rambeh) Small, reddish-brown, sweet, apricotlike; April to May.

Mámûang (Mango) Several varieties and seasons.

Náwy nàa (Custard apple) July to October.

Ngáw (Rambutan) Red, hairy-skinned fruit with grapelike flesh; July to September.

plex flavour. Probably the best description is that of 19th-century British natural historian and obvious durian-devotee Alfred Russell Wallace, who wrote: '…custard flavoured with almonds, intermingled with wafts of flavour that call to mind cream cheese, onion sauce, brown sherry and other incongruities…neither acid, nor sweet, nor juicy, yet one feels the want of none of these qualities for it is perfect as it is.'

The durian's ammonialike aroma is so strong that many hotels in Thailand, as well as Thai Airways International, ban the fruit from their premises.

Durian seasons come and go throughout the year depending on the variety. One of the largest and most expensive durians, native to Thailand and widely exported, is the *mǎwn thawng* or 'golden pillow'.

SWEETS

English-language Thai menus often have a section called 'Desserts', even though the concept doesn't exist in Thai cuisine, nor is there a translation for the word. The closest equivalent, *khǎwng wǎan*, simply means 'sweet stuff' and refers to all foods whose primary flavour characteristic is sweetness. Sweets mostly work their way into the daily Thai diet in the form of between-meal snacks, so you won't find *khǎwng wǎan* in a traditional Thai restaurant. Instead, they're prepared and sold by market vendors or, more rarely, by shops specialising in *khǎwng wǎan*.

Khǎwng wǎan recipes and preparation techniques tend to require more skill than other dishes. The cook spends the morning making up *khǎwng wǎan*, which are bundled into banana leaves, poured into pandanus-leaf cups or cut into colourful squares. These are then arranged on large trays and taken to local markets or wheeled on carts through the streets to be sold by the *chín* (piece).

Prime ingredients for many Thai sweets include grated coconut, coconut milk, rice flour (from white rice or sticky rice), cooked sticky rice (whole grains), tapioca, mung-bean starch, boiled taro and various fruits. For added texture and crunch, some sweets may also contain fresh corn kernels, sugar-palm kernels, lotus seeds, cooked black beans and chopped water chestnuts. Egg yolks are a popular ingredient for *khǎwng wǎan* – including the ubiquitous *fǎwy thawng* (literally 'golden threads') – probably influenced by Portuguese desserts and pastries introduced during the early Ayuthaya era.

Thai sweets similar to the European concept of 'sweet pastry' are called *khànǒm*. Here again the kitchen-astute Portuguese were influential. Probably the most popular type of *khànǒm* in Thailand are the bite-sized items wrapped in banana or pandanus leaves, especially *khâo tôm kà-thí* and *khâo tôm mát*. Both consist of sticky rice grains steamed with *kà-thí* (coconut milk) inside a banana-leaf wrapper to form a solid, almost taffylike mass. *Khâo tôm kà-thí* also contains fresh grated coconut, while *khâo tôm mát* usually contains a few black beans or banana. *Tàkôh,* a very simple but popular steamed sweet made from tapioca flour and coconut milk over a layer of sweetened seaweed gelatine, comes in small cups made from pandanus leaves. A similar blend, minus the gelatine and steamed in tiny porcelain cups, is called *khanǒm thûay* (cup pastry).

Coconut milk also features prominently in several soupier sweets with colourful names. In the enormously popular *klûay*

Sweets for sale at a street stall

bùat chii (bananas ordaining as nuns), banana chunks float in a white syrup of sweetened and slightly salted coconut milk. *Bua láwy* (floating lotus) consists of boiled sticky-rice dumplings in a similar coconut sauce. Substitute red-dyed chunks of fresh water chestnut and you have *tháp thim kràwp* (crisp rubies). As at a modern ice-cream parlour, you can often order extra ingredients, such as black beans, sugar-palm kernels or corn kernels, to be added to the mix. Crushed ice is often added to cool the mixture.

DRINKS
FRUIT DRINKS
With the abundance of fruit growing in Thailand, the variety of juices and shakes available in markets, street stalls and restaurants is extensive. The all-purpose term for fruit juice is *náam phŏn-lá-mái*. When a blender or extractor is used, you've got *náam khán* (squeezed juice), hence *náam sàppàrót khán* is freshly squeezed pineapple juice. *Náam âwy* (sugar-cane juice) is a Thai favourite and a refreshing accompaniment to *kaeng* dishes. A similar juice from the sugar palm, *náam taan sòt,* is also very good, and both are full of vitamins and minerals. Mixed fruit blended with ice is *náam pon* (literally 'mixed juice').

BEER
Advertised with such slogans as *'pràthêht rao, bia rao'* ('our land, our beer'), the Singha label is considered the quintessential Thai beer by *faràng* and locals alike. Pronounced *sĭng*, it claims about half the domestic market. Singha's original recipe was formulated in 1934 by Thai nobleman Phya Bhirom Bhakdi, the first Thai to earn a brewmaster's diploma in Germany. Many beer drinkers believe the strong, hoppy brew to be one of the best produced in Asia. The barley for Singha is grown in Thailand, the hops are imported from Germany and the alcohol content is a heady 6%. It is sold in brown glass bottles (both 33cl and 66cl) with a shiny gold lion on the label as well as cans. It is available on tap as *bia sòt* (draught beer) – much tastier than either bottled or canned brew – in many Bangkok pubs and restaurants.

Singha's biggest rival, Beer Chang, matches the hoppy taste of Singha but pumps the alcohol content up to 7%. Beer Chang has managed to gain an impressive following mainly because it retails at a significantly lower price than Singha and thus offers more bang per baht.

Boon Rawd (the makers of Singha) responded with its own cheaper brand, Leo. Sporting a black-and-red leopard label, Leo costs only slightly more than Beer Chang but is similarly high in alcohol.

Kloster, similarly inspired by German brewing recipes, is a notch smoother and lighter than Singha, has an alcohol content of 4.7% and generally costs about 5B to 10B more per bottle. Look for a straight-sided green bottle with a label that looks like it was designed in 18th- or 19th-century Germany.

Dutch-licensed but Thailand-brewed Heineken comes third after Singha and Chang in sales rankings. Other Thai-brewed beers, all at the lower end of the price spectrum, include Cheers and Beer Thai. More variation in Thai beer brands is likely in the coming years as manufacturers scramble to command market share by offering a variety of flavours and prices.

RICE WHISKY
Rice whisky is a favourite of the working class in Bangkok, since it's more affordable than beer. It has a sharp, sweet taste not unlike rum, with an alcohol content of 35%. The most famous brand for many years was Mekong (pronounced *mâe khŏhng*), but currently the most popular brand is the slightly more expensive Sang Som. Both come in 750mL bottles called *klom* or in 375mL, flask-shaped bottles called *baen*.

More expensive Thai whiskies produced from barley and appealing to the can't-afford-Johnnie-Walker-yet set include Blue Eagle, 100 Pipers and Spey Royal, each with a 40% alcohol content. These come dressed up in shiny boxes, much like the expensive imported whiskies they're imitating.

CELEBRATING WITH FOOD
During *trùt jiin* (Chinese New Year), Bangkok's Chinese population celebrates with a week of house cleaning, lion dances, fireworks and restaurant feasting. Naturally the most impressive festivities take place in Chinatown. Favourite foods eaten during *trùt jiin* include 'mooncakes' – thick, circular pastries filled with sweetened bean paste or salted pork – and lots of noodles.

During the famous Vegetarian Festival, *thêhtsàkaan kin jeh,* also centred on Chinatown, virtually every Chinese eatery in the city puts on a lengthy Chinese vegetarian menu, advertised by yellow-and-red pennants in front of the restaurants.

History

History

THE RECENT PAST

Bangkok started the new millennium riding a tide of events that set new ways of governing and living in the capital. The most defining of these occurred in July 1997 when, after several months of warning signs that were ignored by almost everyone in Thailand and the international community, the Thai currency went into a deflationary tailspin and the national economy screeched to a virtual halt. Bangkok, which rode at the forefront of the 1980s double-digit economic boom, was more adversely affected than elsewhere in Thailand in job losses and massive income erosion.

Two months after the economic crash, the Thai parliament voted in a new constitution that guaranteed – at least on paper – more human and civil rights than had hitherto been codified in Thailand. The 'people's constitution' fostered great hope in a population emotionally battered by the 1997 economic crisis.

When then–prime minister Chavalit Yongchaiyudh failed to deal effectively with the economy, he was forced to resign. An election brought former prime minister Chuan Leekpai back into office and he handled the crisis reasonably well, acting as an international public-relations man for the crisis. By early 2000, following a financial restructuring coached by the International Monetary Fund (IMF), Bangkok's economy began to show signs of recovery.

Bangkok local-government elections in mid-2000 found Thai Citizen Party candidate Samak Sundaravej elected to office in a surprise landslide. Among Samak's first official acts was a crackdown on police who were extorting money from street vendors. Although the campaign had little demonstrable effect on corruption, it won the hearts of many residents. Samak also made the support and expansion of the Bangkok Mass Transit System (BTS) Skytrain and Metropolitan Rapid Transport Authority (MRTA) subway a major priority and promised to build affordable flats for low-income residents.

In January 2001 billionaire and former police colonel Thaksin Shinawatra became prime minister following a landslide victory in compulsory nationwide elections – the first in Thailand to be held under the strict guidelines established in the 1997 constitution. Thaksin came into power along with a new party called Thai Rak Thai (TRT; Thai Love Thai), espousing a populist platform at odds with the man's enormous wealth and influence.

The sixth-richest ruler in the world as of late 2003, when he first came to power Thaksin owned the country's only private TV station, while his family owned Shin Corporation, the country's largest telecommunications company and owner of the largest mobile phone service concession, Advance Info Service (AIS). Shin Corp also owns Asia's first privately owned satellite

Thaksin Shinawatra

1548–68	1767
Thonburi Si Mahasamut founded on the west bank of Mae Nam Chao Phraya as a trade centre for Siam	Ayuthaya, Siam's royal capital, is sacked by the Burmese

company, Shin Satellite, and holds significant shares in Thai Air Asia, a subsidiary of the Malaysia-based Air Asia.

Days before he took the prime ministerial office, Thaksin transferred his shares in Shin Corp to his siblings, chauffeur and even household servants. The country's TRT-dominated anticorruption commission cleared the PM of all fraud charges connected with the shares transfer.

Thaksin publicly stated his ambition to keep his party in office for four consecutive terms, a total of 16 years. Before he had even finished his first four-year term, however, many Thai citizens were annoyed with the government's slowness to right perceived wrongs in the countryside and had begun to plague the administration with regular large-scale demonstrations.

A coalition of northeastern Thai farmers calling themselves the Assembly of the Poor established a permanent tent-and-shanty encampment outside Bangkok's Government House to make their grievances known around the clock via colourful protest banners. Most demonstrations pled for government relief from hardships caused by the shrinking economy, while some demanded that the government dismantle World Bank or Asian Development projects, such as the Kheuan Pak Mun (Pak Mun Dam), that have been established without their consent. TRT promised land reform to help farmers, but the issues continue to smoulder, leaving observers to wonder if Thailand wasn't heading for a period of unrest similar to that seen in the 1970s. In early 2003 Governor Samak ordered 10,000 Bangkok Metropolitan Administration (BMA) workers to dismantle the encampment and bus many of the 1200 inhabitants to Ubon Ratchatani Province in northeastern Thailand.

Furthering Thaksin's eventual downfall was a stubborn tendency to reject all criticism from within and outside Thailand as 'un-Thai'. In 2002 two *Far Eastern Economic Review* correspondents were nearly ejected from Thailand for reporting on business connections between Thaksin and the Crown Prince. Although in the end they were allowed to remain in the kingdom, the censorious action shocked many observers for whom Thailand was Southeast Asia's greatest bastion of press freedom.

In 2003 Thaksin announced a 'war on drugs' that would free the country of illicit drug use within 90 days. Lists of drug dealers and users were compiled in every province and the police were given arrest quotas to fulfil or else lose their jobs. Within two months over 2000 Thais on the government blacklist had been killed. The Thaksin administration denied accusations by the UN, the US State Department, Amnesty International and Thailand's own human rights commission that the deaths were extrajudicial killings by Thai police. Independent observers claim that the 'war on drugs' did not reduce dope use, but simply raised drug prices, thus making the trade even more attractive to organised crime throughout the region.

Meanwhile in the south, a decades-old Muslim nationalist movement, responding to the Thaksin administration's strengthening culture of authoritarianism, began reheating. Sporadic attacks on police stations, schools, military installations and other government institutions resulted in a string of Thai deaths. Although targets were usually government officials or civil servants, Buddhist monks and a many Thai civilians also became victims.

Tensions in the south took a turn for the worse when Thai police gunned down 112 machete-wielding Muslim militants – most of them teenagers – inside a historic mosque in Pattani in April 2004. Five months later police broke up a large demonstration in southern Thailand, and while they were transporting around 1300 arrestees in overcrowded trucks, 78 died of suffocation or from being crushed under the weight of other arrestees.

Three other crises in public confidence shook Bangkok and the nation that same year. Firstly, avian influenza turned up in Thailand's bird population and, when it became known that the administration had been aware of the infections since November 2003, the EU and Japan banned all imports of Thai chicken. Avian flu claimed the lives of eight Thais – all of whom were infected while handling live poultry – before the crisis was under control.

1767	1782
Phaya Taksin takes the Siamese throne and moves the capital to Thonburi	Phaya Chakri crowned; founds new capital at Bang Makok

Large neighbourhoods in Bangkok were quarantined, particularly near Chatuchak Weekend Market in northern Bangkok, where live birds and fighting cocks are sold. Fearing that droppings could contaminate the capital, city workers captured and killed tens of thousands of pigeons in central Bangkok as well. Although there was no evidence to suggest that eating cooked chicken put people at risk, Bangkok restaurants suffered a huge loss of custom, and most were forced to quit serving chicken altogether. By mid-2004 the epidemic had cost the Thai economy 19 billion baht.

Just as the bird flu seemed under control, the Interior Ministry announced that, as of 1 March 2004, all entertainment establishments in Thailand would be required to close at midnight. In Bangkok the government exempted three districts – Patpong, Ratchada and Royal City Avenue (RCA) – in an all-too-apparent attempt to appease the city's most powerful mafia dons. Public reaction against this decision was so strong (mafia figures who control other areas of the city reportedly announced a billion-baht price on the prime minister's head) that the government back-pedalled, allowing nightspots to stay open till 1am, regardless of zoning. It is thought that approximately 100,000 Thai jobs were lost due to the enforcement of what the Thaksin administration termed the 'new social order' policy.

Immediately on the heels of the uproar over new closing hours came the government's announcement that the Electricity Generating Authority of Thailand (EGAT) and other state enterprises were being put on an accelerated schedule for privatisation. Tens of thousands of government employees demonstrated in Bangkok streets and, once again, the government backtracked, putting privatisation plans on hold for the time being.

Another issue for public debate has been the government's ongoing negotiations with the USA to create a US–Thailand free trade agreement (FTA). Proponents – among whom Thaksin was the most visible and outspoken – see the FTA as a way for Thailand to clear trade barriers and expand Thai exports deeper to the world's largest consumer market. Opponents say an imbalance between the two economies means that Thailand has more to lose in increased competition than it has to gain.

Of more immediate concern to Bangkok, the Tourism Authority of Thailand (TAT) announced it intended to clear 'unwanted buildings and communities' from Ko Ratanakosin (Ratanakosin Island) and the Mae Nam Chao Phraya riverside to create an area of landscaped parks and sweeping river views. Among the buildings targeted for demolition or relocation are the Office of the Council of State, the National Theatre, the Thai Dancing School, Thammasat University, the Navy Club, Pak Khlong Market, and illegal businesses and residences at Tha Phra Chan and Tha Chang. When plans materialise, these ideas will no doubt meet with fierce protest from local communities. Thus far the only changes to the Ko Ratanakosin cityscape has been the pleasant addition of walkways along the Banglamphu waterfront.

In the 2004 Bangkok gubernatorial race Democrat Apirak Kosayodhin scored an upset victory over Paveena Hongsakul, an independent candidate with the unofficial support of the ruling TRT, capturing 40% of the vote. Apirak won on promises to upgrade city services and mass transit, and to make city government more transparent – a direct challenge to Thaksin's self-dubbed CEO leadership style. Staying true to his word, shortly after taking office, Governor Apirak approved funds to allow planning of extensions to the BTS Skytrain, going against Thaksin's own desire to cap expansion of the system.

During the February 2005 general elections, the Thaksin administration scored a second four-year mandate in a landslide victory, surprising academic critics who expected the TRT would be called to account for its bungling of the bird flu, drug war deaths, early bar closing and privatisation crises. Armchair observers speculated the blame lay with the opposition's lack of a positive platform to deal with these same problems. Thaksin thus became the first Thai leader in history to be re-elected to a consecutive second term.

However time was running short for Thaksin and his party, who continued to blunder in public. The final straw came in January 2006, when Thaksin announced that his family

1809–24	1824–51
Rama II (King Buddha Loetla) ascends the throne, assumes the task of restoring art and culture damaged by Burmese invasions	Rama III (King Nang Klao) develops trade with China, and promotes domestic agriculture

had sold off its controlling interest in Shin Corp to a Singapore investment firm. Three days before the sale, Thaksin had successfully lobbied for new legislature exempting all transactions on the Stock Exchange of Thailand (SET) from capital-gains tax. Thaksin's family thus paid no tax at all on the US$1.9 billion the sale earned, a situation that enraged the millions of Thai villagers who made up TRT's rank-and-file support.

It also came to light that a year earlier Thaksin had managed to persuade the TRT-dominated National Assembly to make it possible for foreigners to own more than 49% of companies listed on the SET. As if that weren't enough, it had become common knowledge throughout the business community that Thaksin had used his influence as prime minister to land lucrative mobile phone coverage for Shin Corp not only in Thailand but also in India and Myanmar as well.

In light of these embarrassing revelations, many of the PM's most highly placed supporters turned against him, most pointedly media mogul Sondhi Limthongkul, once Thaksin's close friend. Sondhi organised a series of massive anti-Thaksin rallies in Bangkok, culminating in a rally at Bangkok's Royal Plaza on 4 and 5 February 2006 that drew over 100,000 protestors. Through former prime minister and current Privy Council chairman Prem Tinsulanonda, the group submitted a petition to the king pleading for Thaksin's censure and removal from office.

Retired major general Chamlong Sri Luang, a former Bangkok governor and one of Thaksin's earliest and strongest supporters, also turned against his ally, joining the leadership of the street demonstrations. During February and into March the weekly series of protests expanded their coverage into commercial districts such as Siam Square, taking an economic toll on retail sales, SET prices and the national currency. Two of Thaksin's ministers resigned from the cabinet and from the TRT, signalling that even members of his own party were beginning to share the growing distaste for the prime minister.

The prime minister responded by dissolving the National Assembly and scheduling snap elections for 2 April 2006. The opposition was aghast, since the scheduling didn't allow time for National Assembly members to change parties given the constitution's mandatory 90-day waiting period before a new party member can stand for office.

The Democrats and other major opposition parties thus announced that they would boycott the 2 April polls, while many leaders advised people to attend the polling but to check the 'No' box next to all TRT candidate's names. The results gave the TRT another victory with 66% of the popular vote. However, in the Democrat-controlled south, 38 TRT candidates failed to gain the 20% of the vote necessary to take National Assembly seats. In effect this meant that the government could not convene, and that elections would have to be scheduled yet again in order to establish a new government.

At first Thaksin refused to step down, but after a private audience with the king, he announced his official resignation on 4 April. The fact that the large, widespread demonstrations in Bangkok never erupted into violence led observers to dub Thaksin's unseating as a 'Thailand's Silk Revolution'.

DIVINE ANGER

Bangkok's Erawan Shrine (San Phra Phrom in Thai; p98), the capital's most revered non-Buddhist religious site, suffered tragedy just after midnight on 21 March 2006, when 27-year-old Thanakorn Pakdeepol entered the shrine and destroyed the gilded plaster image of Brahma with a hammer. Pakdeepol, who had a history of mental illness and depression, was almost immediately attacked and beaten to death by two Thai rubbish collectors in the vicinity.

Although the government ordered a swift restoration of the statue, its destruction became a galvanising omen for the anti-Thaksin movement, which was in full swing at the time. At a political rally the following day, protest leader Sondhi Limthongkul suggested that the prime minister had masterminded the Brahma image's destruction in order to replace the deity with a 'dark force' allied to Thaksin. Rumours spreading through the capital claimed that Thaksin had hired Cambodian shamans to put spells on Pakdeepol so that he would perform the unspeakable deed.

1851	1893–1910
Rama IV (King Mongkut) comes to power, courts relations with the West and encourages the study of science	Siam accedes border territories to the French and British empires

By-elections for the contested seats in parliament were to be held on 23 April. At this juncture it is unclear what the outcome may be, although the most likely scenario includes a repeated lack of decisiveness, which would lead to further inconclusive elections and a possible constitutional crisis.

FROM THE BEGINNING
AYUTHAYA & THONBURI

Before it became the capital of Thailand in 1782, the tiny settlement known as Bang Makok was merely a backwater village opposite Thonburi Si Mahasamut on the banks of Mae Nam Chao Phraya, not far from the Gulf of Siam.

Thonburi Si Mahasamut itself had been founded on the west bank by a group of wealthy Thais during the reign of King Chakkaphat (r 1548–68) as an important relay point for sea- and riverborne trade between the Gulf of Siam and Ayuthaya, 86km upriver. Ayuthaya served as the royal capital of Siam – as Thailand was then known – from 1350 to 1767. Encircled by rivers with access to the gulf, Ayuthaya flourished as a river port courted by Dutch, Portuguese, French, English, Chinese and Japanese merchants. By the end of the 17th century the city's population had reached a million and Ayuthaya was one of the wealthiest and most powerful cities in Asia. Virtually all foreign visitors claimed it to be the most illustrious city they had ever seen, beside which London and Paris paled in comparison.

Throughout four centuries of Ayuthaya reign, European powers tried without success to colonise the kingdom of Siam. An Asian power finally subdued the capital when the Burmese sacked Ayuthaya in 1767, destroying most of its Buddhist temples and royal edifices. Many Siamese were marched off to Pegu (Bago, Myanmar today), where they were forced to serve the Burmese court.

After this devastating defeat, the Siamese regrouped under Phaya Taksin, a half-Chinese, half-Thai general who decided to move the capital further south along Mae Nam Chao Phraya, closer to the Gulf of Siam. Thonburi Si Mahasamut was a logical choice.

Taksin eventually came to regard himself as the next Buddha, and his behaviour became increasingly violent and bizarre. Monks who wouldn't worship him as the Maitreya (the future Buddha) would be flogged. Disapproving of his religious fantasies and fearing the king had lost his mind, his ministers deposed Taksin and then executed him in the custom reserved for royalty – by sealing him inside a velvet sack (so that no royal blood touched the ground) and beating him to death with a scented sandalwood club in 1782.

THE CHAKRI DYNASTY & THE PORT OF BANGKOK

One of Taksin's key generals, Phaya Chakri, came to power and was crowned in 1782 as Phra Yot Fa. Fearing Thonburi to be vulnerable to Burmese attack from the west, Chakri moved the Siamese capital across the river to a smaller settlement known as Bang Makok (olive plum riverbank), named for the trees that grew there in abundance. As the first monarch of the new Chakri royal dynasty – which continues to this day – Phaya Chakri was later dubbed King Rama I.

The first task set before the planners of the new city was to create hallowed ground for royal palaces and Buddhist monasteries. Astrologers divined that construction on the new royal palace should begin on 6 May 1782, and ceremonies consecrated Rama I's transfer to a temporary new residence a month later. Construction of permanent throne halls, residence halls and palace temples followed. The plan of the original buildings, their position relative to the river and the royal chapel, and the royal parade and cremation grounds to the north of the palace (today's Sanam Luang) exactly copied the royal compound at Ayuthaya. Master

1911–25	1932
Rama VI (King Vajiravudh) makes education compulsory	People's Party launches bloodless revolution; Siam becomes a constitutional monarchy

craftsmen who had survived the sacking of Ayuthaya created the designs for several of the more magnificent temples and royal administrative buildings in the new capital.

Upon completion of the royal district in 1785, at a three-day consecration ceremony attended by tens of thousands of Siamese, the city was given a new name: 'Krungthep mahanakhon amonratanakosin mahintara ayuthaya mahadilok popnopparat ratchathani burirom udomratchaniwet mahasathan amonpiman avatansathit sakkathattiya witsanu-kamprasit'. This lexical gymnastic feat translates roughly as: 'Great City of Angels, the Repository of Divine Gems, the Great Land Unconquerable, the Grand and Prominent Realm, the Royal and Delightful Capital City full of Nine Noble Gems, the Highest Royal Dwelling and Grand Palace, the Divine Shelter and Living Place of Reincarnated Spirits'.

Foreign traders continued to call the capital Bang Makok, which eventually truncated itself to 'Bangkok', the name most commonly known to the outside world. The Thais, meanwhile, commonly use a shortened version of the name, Krung Thep (City of Angels) or, when referring to the city and burgeoning metropolitan area surrounding it, Krung Thep Mahanakhon (Metropolis of the City of Angels).

The break with Ayuthaya was ideological as well as temporal. As Chakri shared no bloodline with earlier royalty, he garnered loyalty by modelling himself as a Dhammaraja (*dhamma* king) supporting Buddhist law rather than a Devaraja (god king) linked to the divine.

Ayuthaya's control of tribute states in Laos and western Cambodia (including Angkor, ruled by the Siamese from 1432 to 1859) was transferred to Bangkok, and thousands of prisoners of war were brought to the capital to work as coolie labour. Bangkok also had ample access to free Thai labour via the *phrai luang* (commoner/noble) system, under which all commoners were required to provide labour to the state in lieu of taxes.

Using this immense pool of labour, Rama I augmented Bangkok's natural canal-and-river system with hundreds of artificial waterways feeding into Thailand's hydraulic lifeline, the broad Mae Nam Chao Phraya. Chakri also ordered the construction of 10km of city walls and *khlong rop krung* (canals round the city), to create a royal 'island' – Ko Ratanakosin – between Mae Nam Chao Phraya and the canal loop. Sections of the 4.5m-thick walls still stand in Wat Saket and the Golden Mount, and water still flows, albeit sluggishly, along the canals of the original royal district.

Under the second and third reigns of the Chakri dynasty, more temples were built and the system of rivers, streams and natural canals surrounding the capital was augmented by the excavation of additional waterways. Waterborne traffic dominated the city, supplemented by a meagre network of footpaths, well into the middle of the 19th century.

Temple construction remained the highlight of early development in Bangkok until the reign of Rama III (King Nang Klao; r 1824–51), when attention turned to upgrading the

WATERWORLD

Portuguese priest Fernão Mendez Pinto was the first to use the epithet 'Venice of the East', referring not to Bangkok but to Ayuthaya, in a letter to the Society of Jesus in Lisbon in 1554. Two hundred years later it was used to describe Bangkok as well. In 1855 British envoy Sir John Bowring noted in his reports: 'The highways of Bangkok are not streets or roads but the river and the canals. Boats are the universal means of conveyance and communication.'

On the eve of the coronation of Rama VI in 1911, a young and adventurous Italian nobleman named Salvatore Besso wrote:

'The Venice of the Far East – the capital still wrapped in mystery, in spite of the thousand efforts of modernism amid its maze of canals, and in spite of the popularity of the reigning monarch...From the crowded dock-roads of the River...which reminds one of the Giudecca, across the intricate mass of...the Chinese quarter...which, whilst resembling Canton, is still more Venetian. Were it not for the queues, almond eyes and odours, decidedly Oriental, the illusion would very often be complete...'

1938–39	1941
Phibul Songkhram becomes Siam's first prime minister and changes the country's name to Thailand	Japanese invade, first bombing and then occupying Bangkok; Phibul collaborates

port for international sea trade. The city soon became a regional centre for Chinese trading ships, slowly surpassing even the British port at Singapore.

By the mid-19th century Western naval shipping technology had eclipsed the Chinese junk fleets. Bangkok's rulers began to feel threatened as the British and French made colonial inroads into Cambodia, Laos and Burma. This prompted the suspension of a great iron chain across Mae Nam Chao Phraya to guard against the entry of unauthorised ships.

WATERWAYS & ROADWAYS

During the reign of the first five Chakri kings, canal building comprised the lion's share of public-works projects, changing the natural geography of the city. City planners added two lengthy canals to one of the river's largest natural curves. The canals Khlong Rop Krung (today's Khlong Banglamphu) and Khlong Ong Ang were built to create Ko Ratanakosin. The island quickly accumulated an impressive architectural portfolio centred on the Grand Palace, the political hub of the new Siamese capital, and the adjacent royal monastery, Wat Phra Kaew.

Throughout the early history of the Chakri dynasty, royal administrations added to the system. Khlong Mahawawat was excavated during the reign of Rama IV (King Mongkut; r 1851–68) to link Mae Nam Chao Phraya with Mae Nam Tha Chin, thus expanding the canal-and-river system by hundreds of kilometres. Lined with fruit orchards and stilted houses draped with fishing nets, Khlong Mahawawat remains one of the most traditional and least visited of the Bangkok canals.

Khlong Saen Saeb was built to shorten travel between Mae Nam Chao Phraya and Mae Nam Bang Pakong, and today is heavily used by boat-taxi commuters moving across the city. Likewise Khlong Sunak Hon and Khlong Damoen Saduak link up the Tha Chin and Mae Klong. Khlong Prem Prachakon was dug purely to facilitate travel for Rama V (King Chulalongkorn; r 1868–1910) between Bangkok and Ayuthaya, while Khlong Prawet Burirom shortened the distance between Samut Prakan and Chachoengsao Provinces.

When Rama IV loosened Thai trade restrictions, many Western powers signed trade agreements with the monarch. He also sponsored Siam's second printing press and instituted edu-

Long-tail boats

1957–63	1964–73
Strongman General Sarit Thanarat wrests power from Phibul, abolishes the constitution and eventually succumbs to cirrhosis	Military dictators allow the USA to establish several army bases; period of communist insurgency begins

cational reforms, developing a school system along European lines. Although the king courted the West, he did so with caution and warned his subjects: 'Whatever they have invented or done which we should know of and do, we can imitate and learn from them, but do not wholeheartedly believe in them'. Rama IV was the first monarch to show his face to Thai commoners in public.

In 1861 Bangkok's European diplomats and merchants delivered a petition to Rama IV requesting roadways so that they could enjoy horseback riding for physical fitness and pleasure. The royal government acquiesced and established a handful of roads suitable for horse-drawn carriages and rickshaws. The first – and the most ambitious

RIVER REALITY

One of the main physical transformations the city underwent during the 16th-century founding of Thonburi was the digging of a canal to short cut a large bend in Mae Nam Chao Phraya, thus hastening water transport to Siam's capital to the north, Ayuthaya.

Much of the volume of Mae Nam Chao Phraya's original rivercourse gradually diverted to the canal short cut. Today most visitors and residents are unaware that the section of river running along the western edge of Ko Ratanakosin is a canal. The original river loop, now assumed to be a *khlong* (canal), has taken on the name Khlong Bangkok Noi.

road project for nearly a century to come – was Th Charoen Krung (also known by its English name, New Rd), which extended 10km south from Wat Pho along the east bank of Mae Nam Chao Phraya. This swath of hand-laid cobblestone, which took nearly four years to finish, eventually accommodated a tramway as well as early automobiles.

Shortly thereafter Rama IV ordered the construction of the much shorter Bamrung Meuang and Feuang Nakhon roads to provide access to royal temples from Charoen Krung. His successor Rama V added the much wider Th Ratchadamnoen Klang to provide a suitably royal promenade – modelled after the Champs Elysées and lined with ornamental gardens – between the Grand Palace and the expanding commercial centre to the east of Ko Ratanakosin.

RESISTANCE TO COLONIALISM & THE 1932 REVOLUTION

Towards the end of the 19th century, Bangkok's city limits encompassed no more than a dozen square kilometres, with a population of about half a million. Despite its modest size, the capital successfully administered the much larger kingdom of Siam – which then extended into what today are Laos, western Cambodia and northern Malaysia. Even more impressively, Siamese rulers were able to stave off intense pressure from the Portuguese, the Dutch, the French and the English, all of whom at one time or another harboured desires to add Siam to their colonial portfolios. By the end of the century France and England had established a strong presence in every one of Siam's neighbouring countries – the French in Laos and Cambodia, and the British in Burma and Malaya.

Facing increasing pressure from British colonies in neighbouring Burma and Malaya, Rama IV signed the 1855 Bowring Treaty with Britain to reduce import/export duties and to allow access to former trade monopolies. Wishing to head off any potential invasion plans, Rama V acceded Laos and Cambodia to the French and northern Malaya to the British between 1893 and 1910. The two European powers, for their part, were happy to use Thailand as a buffer state between their respective colonial domains.

Was it a simple historical accident that Siam became the only South or Southeast Asian country never to be ruled by a foreign power? Or was the structure of Thai society itself is responsible for resisting European colonialisation? Whatever the reason, Bangkok's ability to maintain Siam's independence meant that the kingdom was free to draw upon the talents of any architect or transport developer in the world, a freedom that helps explain the enormous variety – both planned and unplanned – in the capital today.

Siam's future seemingly secured, Rama V gave Bangkok 120 new roads during his reign, inspired by street plans from Batavia (the Dutch colonial centre now known as Jakarta),

1973	1976
Kukrit Pramoj's civilian government takes charge	Paramilitary groups kill hundreds of demonstrators at Thammasat University; military regains government control

RAMA V CULT

A bronze figure of a military-garbed leader on horseback may seem like an unlikely shrine, but Bangkokians are flexible in their expression of religious devotion. Most importantly, the figure is no forgotten general – this is Rama V (King Chulalongkorn; r 1868–1910) who is widely credited for steering the country into the modern age and for preserving the country's independence from European colonialism. Rama V abolished prostration before the king as well as slavery and *corvée* (the requirement that every citizen be available for state labour when called). He courted relations with European nations and the USA: railways were built, a civil service was established and the legal code restructured.

The cult is particularly strong in Bangkok, since its members tend to be middle-class and nouveau-riche Thais with careers in commerce or the professions. However, all over Thailand, Rama V portraits are selling briskly. Some devotees place the portraits at home altars, while others wear tiny, coloured porcelain likenesses of the king on gold chains around their necks in place of the usual *phrá phim* (Buddhist amulet). In some social circles Rama V amulets are now more common than any other *phrá phim*.

Many Bangkokians also pay regular homage to his equestrian statue at Royal Plaza, leaving offerings of candles, flowers (predominantly pink roses), incense and bottles of brandy to the king's spirit. The most auspicious time to leave offerings at the statue-cum-shrine is Tuesday evening, when thousands of worshippers will turn up between dusk and dawn. The biggest day of the year at the shrine is 23 October, the anniversary of the king's death.

No single event occurred to ignite the Rama V movement. Its growth can, however, be traced to a series of events beginning with the 1991 military coup – which caused the intelligentsia to once again lose faith in the constitutional monarchy – and followed by the 1990–92 economic recession and 1997–98 baht crash. Along with worsening traffic and a host of other problems, these events brought about an unfocussed, general mistrust of modern politics, technology and affluence. Many Thais began looking for a new spiritual outlet with some historical relevancy. They seized on Rama V, a king who – without the help of a parliament or the military – brought Thai nationalism.

Ironically Rama V conceded substantial Thai territory to French Indochina and British Malaya during his reign – a total loss of land greater than any Thai king had allowed since before the Sukhothai era. Rama V also deserves more of the blame for 'Westernisation' than any other single monarch. He was the first king to travel to Europe, which he did in 1897 and again in 1907. After seeing Europeans eating with forks, knives and spoons, he discouraged the Thai tradition of taking food with the hands; he also introduced chairs to the kingdom (before his reign, Thais sat on the floor or on floor cushions). Following one European visit he asked his number-one concubine to grow her hair long after the European fashion; by custom Thai women had kept their hair cropped short since the Ayuthaya period.

Calcutta, Penang and Singapore. Germans were hired to design and build railways emanating from the capital, while the Dutch contributed the design of Bangkok's Hualamphong Railway Station, today considered a minor masterpiece of civic Art Deco.

In 1893 Bangkok opened its first railway line, extending 22km from Bangkok to Pak Nam, where Mae Nam Chao Phraya enters the Gulf of Thailand; at that time it cost just 1B to travel in first class. A 20km electric tramway opened the following year, running parallel to the left bank of Mae Nam Chao Phraya. By 1904 three more rail lines out of Bangkok had been added: northeast to Khorat (306km), with a branch line to Lopburi (42km); southsouthwest to Phetchaburi (151km); and south to Tha Chin (34km).

Italian sculptor Corrado Feroci contributed several national monuments to the city and helped found the country's first fine-arts university. Americans established Siam's first printing press along with the kingdom's first newspaper, the *Bangkok Recorder*, in 1864. The first Thai-language newspaper, *Darunovadha,* came along in 1874 and by 1900 Bangkok boasted three daily English-language newspapers, the *Bangkok Times, Siam Observer* and *Siam Free Press.*

As Bangkok prospered, many wealthy merchant families sent their children to study in Europe. Students of humbler socioeconomic status who excelled at school had access to government scholarships for overseas study as well. In 1924 a handful of Thai students in Paris formed the Promoters of Political Change, a group that met to discuss ideas for a future Siamese government modelled on Western democracy.

1981	1992
General Prem Tinsulanonda becomes prime minister after a military coup but is able to stabilise Thai politics	General Suchinda Kraprayoon ousted; civilians regain government

After finishing their studies and returning to Bangkok, three of the 'Promoters', lawyer Pridi Banomyong and military officers Phibul Songkhram and Prayoon Phamonmontri, organised an underground 'People's Party' dedicated to the overthrow of the Siamese system of government. The People's Party found a willing accomplice in Rama VII (King Prajadhipok; r 1925-35), and a bloodless revolution in 1932 transformed Thailand from an absolute monarchy into a constitutional one. Bangkok thus found itself the centre of a vast new civil service, which, along with its growing success as a world port, transformed the city into a mecca for Thais seeking economic opportunities.

Rama V statue at Royal Plaza (p89)

WWII & THE STRUGGLE FOR DEMOCRACY

Phibul Songkhram, appointed prime minister by the People's Party in December 1938, changed the country's name from Siam to Thailand and introduced the Western solar calendar. When the Japanese invaded Southeast Asia in 1941, outflanking Allied troops in Malaya and Burma, Phibul allowed Japanese regiments access to the Gulf of Thailand. Japanese troops bombed and briefly occupied parts of Bangkok on their way to the Thai–Burmese border to fight the British in Burma and, as a result of public insecurity, the Thai economy stagnated.

Phibul resigned in 1944 under pressure from the Thai underground resistance, and after V-J Day in 1945 was exiled to Japan. Bangkok resumed its pace towards modernisation, even after Phibul returned to Thailand in 1948 and took over the leadership again via a

THE KING

If you see a yellow Rolls Royce flashing by along city avenues, accompanied by a police, you've just caught a glimpse of Thailand's longest-reigning monarch – and the longest-reigning living monarch in the world – King Bhumibol Adulyadej. Also known as Rama IX (the ninth king of the Chakri dynasty), Bhumibol was born in the USA in 1927, while his father Prince Mahidol was studying medicine at Harvard University.

Fluent in English, French, German and Thai, His Majesty ascended the throne in 1946 following the death of his brother Rama VIII (King Ananda Mahidol), who died in a handgun accident.

An ardent jazz composer and saxophonist when he was younger, King Bhumibol has hosted jam sessions with the likes of jazz greats Woody Herman and Benny Goodman. His compositions are often played on Thai radio.

His Majesty administers royal duties from Chitralada Palace in the city's Dusit precinct, north of Ko Ratanakosin. As protector of both nation and religion, King Bhumibol presides over several important Buddhist and Brahmanist ceremonies during the year. Among the more colourful are the seasonal robe-changing of the Emerald Buddha (p80) in Wat Phra Kaew and the annual Royal Ploughing Ceremony (p12), in which rice is ceremonially sown at Sanam Luang to ensure a robust economy for the coming year.

The king and Queen Sirikit have four children: Princess Ubol Ratana (born 1951), Crown Prince Maha Vajiralongkorn (1952), Princess Mahachakri Sirindhorn (1955) and Princess Chulabhorn (1957).

Now in his 60th regnal year, and about to celebrate his 80th birthday, the king is preparing for his succession. For the last few years the crown prince has performed most of the royal ceremonies the king would normally perform, including those mentioned above and handing out academic degrees at university commencements.

Along with nation and religion, the monarchy is very highly regarded in Thai society – negative comment about the king or any member of the royal family is a social as well as legal taboo.

1997	2001
Baht crashes; new democratic constitution unveiled	Tycoon Thaksin Shinawatra elected prime minister, attempts to run Thailand 'CEO'-style

FIVE BOOKS ABOUT BANGKOK

- *Bangkok: Place, Practice and Representation,* Marc Askew (2002) – A detailed look at how geography, culture and politics shaped the capital from its founding to the present day.
- *Bangkok: The Story of a City,* Alec Waugh (1971) – Fascinating account of the city and its residents in the 1960s. Paul Bowles originally came to Bangkok to write this book but, when his wife's illness forced him to return to Tangiers, he suggested that novelist and travel writer Alec Waugh (brother of Evelyn Waugh) finish the job.
- *Bangkok, Vol. 1,* William Warren (2002) – Warren, an American resident of Bangkok for nearly half a century, has written several titles with Bangkok as a theme. His latest blends personal impressions with accounts of some of the city's most celebrated personalities, from Anna Leonowens (of *The King & I* fame) to silk magnate Jim Thompson.
- *Old Bangkok,* Michael Smithies (1986) – Smithies, an independent academic and long-time resident of Thailand, delves deep into the stories behind the capital's historical districts.
- *The Intimate Economies of Bangkok: Tomboys, Tycoons, and Avon Ladies in the Global City,* Ara Wilson (2004) – A historically based ethnography that combines feminist theory with mainstream anthropology.

military coup. Over the next 15 years, bridges were built over Mae Nam Chao Phraya, canals were filled in to provide space for new roads and multistorey buildings began crowding out traditional teak structures.

Another coup installed Field Marshal Sarit Thanarat in 1957, and Phibul Songkhram once again found himself exiled to Japan, where he died in 1964. From 1964 to 1973 – the peak years of the 1962–75 Indochina War – Thai army officers Thanom Kittikachorn and Praphat Charusathien ruled Thailand and allowed the US to establish several army bases within Thai borders to support the US campaign in Indochina. During this time Bangkok gained notoriety as a R&R spot for foreign troops stationed in Southeast Asia.

In October 1973 the Thai military brutally suppressed a large prodemocracy student demonstration at Thammasat University in Bangkok, but Rama IX (King Bhumibol; r 1946–) and General Krit Sivara, who sympathised with the students, refused to support further bloodshed, forcing Thanom and Praphat to leave Thailand. Oxford-educated Kukrit Pramoj took charge of a 14-party coalition government and steered a leftist agenda past the conservative parliament. Among Kukrit's lasting achievements were a national minimum wage, the repeal of anticommunist laws and the ejection of US military forces from Thailand.

The military regained control in 1976 after right-wing, paramilitary civilian groups assaulted a group of 2000 students holding a sit-in at Thammasat, killing hundreds. Many students fled Bangkok and joined the People's Liberation Army of Thailand (PLAT), an armed communist insurgency based in the hills, which had been active in Thailand since the 1930s.

Bangkok continued to seesaw between civilian and military rule for the next 15 years. Although a general amnesty in 1982 brought an end to the PLAT, and students, workers and farmers returned to their homes, a new era of political tolerance exposed the military once again to civilian fire.

In May 1992 several huge demonstrations demanding the resignation of the latest dictator, General Suchinda Kraprayoon, rocked Bangkok and the large provincial capitals. Charismatic Bangkok governor Chamlong Srimuang, winner of the 1992 Magsaysay Award (a humanitarian service award issued in the Philippines) for his role in galvanising the public to reject Suchinda, led the protests. After confrontations between the protesters and the military near the Democracy Monument resulted in nearly 50 deaths and hundreds of injuries, King Bhumibol summoned both Suchinda and Chamlong for a rare public scolding. Suchinda resigned, having been in power for less than six weeks, and Chamlong's career was all but finished.

Bangkok grew from a mere 13 sq km in 1900 to an astounding metropolitan area of more than 330 sq km by the turn of the century. Today the city encompasses not only Bangkok proper, but also the former capital of Thonburi across Mae Nam Chao Phraya to the west, along with the densely populated 'suburb' provinces, Samut Prakan to the east and Nonthaburi to the north. More than half of Thailand's urban population lives in Bangkok.

2004	2006
The 26 December Indian Ocean tsunami claims over 5000 lives and 3000 missing along Thailand's Andaman coast	Thaksin resigns after mass demonstrations force a snap election in which his party loses seats in the National Assembly

Sights

Sights

Flashy and fickle, devout and loyal, Bangkok is every mutation of the Thai personality fused together in one sprawling landmass. At first glance only the concentration of concrete towers differentiates the new city from the old, but closer inspection reveals the formula for a spellbinding city: enough diversity to make a trip across town feel like a journey through the past, present and future. A simple sketch of Bangkok's layout fails to convey the chaos that the city has acquired, first along its original streets, the *khlong* (canals), and then along their modern replacements, asphalt roads. In between the major arteries, *soi* (small lanes) run in serpentine patterns like streams through rocky outcrops. Almost every new outing is a wild-goose chase, rarely delivering you where your map hypothesised. Frustrated and sweaty, recent arrivals begin to appreciate the Buddhist precept of 'being in the present'.

While officially Bangkok is divided into administrative districts, occasionally marked by bilingual road signs, the character of a neighbourhood is more loosely defined by historical roles, modern commerce, and immigrant communities who have held fast to the traditions of their homelands. Along the banks of Mae Nam Chao Phraya (the city's only tangible boundary), the ancient monuments of king, country and religion were planted in the flood plains, providing physical proximity to divinity for the mortals trapped by reincarnation. In the ancient district of Ko Ratanakosin (Ratanakosin Island), the rituals and visuals of Thai Buddhism clog the sidewalks as monks file in and out of temple lecture halls and vulnerable mortals scour the amulet market for a trustworthy bodyguard.

Following the grand boulevard of Th Ratchadamnoen leads to Banglamphu, whose small villages of yellow-and-green shophouses once supplied the royal palace with its many ornate necessities. Some of the old mercantile and artisanal families still remain alongside a newer crop of artists, thoughtful inheritors of a celebrated past. The regal enclave of Dusit, fashioned after the capitals of Europe, sits like a crown on the northern apex of Banglamphu. Moving inland towards the main railway station, Hualamphong, is the cramped and chaotic district of Chinatown, bearing all the hallmarks of the mother country.

To the north and east, the city pours forward like an endless concrete spill. Skyscrapers, shopping centres and toll flyovers dominate the skyline in place of temples. Th Phra Ram I feeds into Siam Square, a popular shopping district, and eventually turns into Th Sukhumvit, a busy commercial centre where the internationals and cosmopolitans congregate. Between Siam Square and Th Sukhumvit, Th Withayu shelters many of the city's foreign embassies. South of these districts, Th Silom and Th Sathon form the backbone of Bangkok's financial district, yet another concentration of high-rise ranges.

Inspecting amulets at a stall in the amulet market (p169)

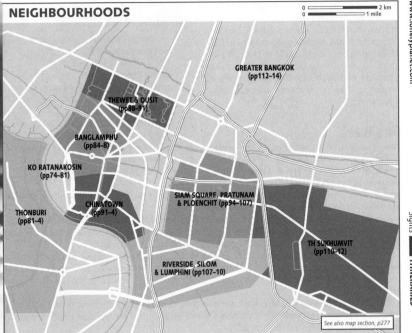

NEIGHBOURHOODS

GREATER BANGKOK (pp112–14)

THEWET & DUSIT (pp88–91)

BANGLAMPHU (pp84–8)

KO RATANAKOSIN (pp74–81)

THONBURI (pp81–4)

CHINATOWN (pp91–4)

SIAM SQUARE, PRATUNAM & PLOENCHIT (pp94–107)

TH SUKHUMVIT (pp110–12)

RIVERSIDE, SILOM & LUMPHINI (pp107–10)

See also map section, p277

ITINERARIES

One Day

Early in the morning, before the day gets steamy, go to **Wat Phra Kaew** (p79) and the **Grand Palace** (p79). These buildings represent the pinnacle of Thai religious architecture and are a must for first-time visitors. Afterwards, stroll down to **Wat Pho** (p78), which has enough quirky corners to escape the crowds, or to the **amulet market** (p169), which is so cramped with commerce that pavements become makeshift stores.

Charter a long-tail boat for a tour of Thonburi's **river canals** (p72), bordered by elegant and dilapidated houses balancing over watery yards. Most boat drivers will make a stop at **Wat Arun** (p82), which would nicely complete a morning's temple consumption. Have the driver drop you off at Tha Phra Athit for a stroll through the charming neighbourhood of **Banglamphu** (p84). Graze your way through lunch by sampling all the streetside snacks: tropical fruit, iced Thai coffee, satay. If you aren't already planted on Th Khao San, stop by for some cheap souvenirs or return for the night display of beer guzzlers and exhibitionists.

For dinner, go all-out touristy at one of the riverside or sky-high restaurants or dinner cruises for a main dish of scenery.

Three Days

With the cultural obligations out of the way, you can devote more time to self-improvement: shopping and pampering. The area around **Siam Square** (p180) has the largest concentration of shopping malls, ranging from mall-rat traps to label-whore temples. You can temporarily interrupt your shopping homage with a trip to **Jim Thompson's House** (p97), a serene example of old-style Bangkok living. It will make you dream of becoming a Bangkok transplant.

Be sure to ride the **Skytrain** (p242), a sleek, elevated tram that gives a bird's-eye view into the city's fortressed compounds and high-rise balconies. If those bargaining muscles have worn out, treat yourself to a rejuvenating, if strenuous, **Thai massage** (p163).

For dinner head to Th Sukhumvit, where you'll find **Vientiane Kitchen** (p144), the non-touristy version of a dinner show. Then do the night flight to the **go-go district** (p157) of Patpong or the chic **clubs** (p154) in Sukhumvit. Before you call it quits, do as the Thais do and grab one final meal from a vendor stall as an insurance policy against a hangover.

One Week

Now that you're accustomed to the noise, pollution and traffic, **Chinatown** (p91) should be added to your itinerary. A whole day can be spent here wandering the narrow streets, where commerce is an ancient art. Work your way over to **Phahurat** (p92), the Indian district, for lunch – one can't live on Thai food alone.

On the weekend, take the Skytrain to **Chatuchak Weekend Market** (p188) for intensive souvenir and necessity hunting. Past the kitchen supplies is an area where fighting cocks and fighting fish are as proudly displayed as antique Buddhas and used blue jeans.

For a little R&R, take a river ferry to **Ko Kret** (p113), a car-free island north of central Bangkok that defines relaxation. In open-air studios, Ko Kret artisans continue the age-old tradition of hand-thrown terracotta pottery. Their meditative process is the most intensive activity on the island.

With one week, you will also have time to peruse the goings-on about town, such as a traditional arts performance or a visiting DJ at a local club. You can also find a favourite street vendor, the best souvenir of all.

ORGANISED TOURS

Mastering Bangkok is the urban aficionado's version of conquering Everest. But not everyone enjoys slogging through the sprawl and for those sensible folks there are many tours exploring Bangkok's historic and cultural sights, as well as outlying areas.

River & Canal Tours

The car has long since become Bangkok's conveyance of choice, but there was a time, and there are still places today, where roads are made of water, not asphalt.

ASIA VOYAGES Map pp278–9
☎ 0 2651 9768-9; fax 0 2651 9770; www.asia-voyages.com; Menam Riverside Hotel, 2074 Th Charoen Krung; from 8000B

This company operates the stout but elegant *Mekhala*, which delivers passengers to Ayuthaya and Bang Pa-In as part of a two-day trip that includes an overnight stay on the boat with a candlelight dinner at the foot of a picturesque temple. A minibus returns guests to Bangkok's Menam

BANGKOK STREET SMARTS

- Good jewellery, gems and tailor shops aren't found through a túk-túk driver.
- Skip the 10B túk-túk ride; you'll pay more with time and money in the end.
- Ignore 'helpful' locals who tell you that tourist attractions and public transport are closed for a holiday or cleaning.
- Don't expect to have any pedestrian rights; yield to anything with more metal than you.
- Walk outside the tourist strip to hail a taxi who will use the meter.

Riverside Hotel. The trip can also be done in reverse with a minivan to Ayuthaya and return by boat.

CHAO PHRAYA EXPRESS BOAT
☎ 0 2623 6001, 0 2623 6143; www.chaophraya boat.co.th

You can observe urban river life by boarding a Chao Phraya Express boat at any *tha* (pier) and taking it in either direction to its final stop. The trip is the cheapest introduction to one of Bangkok's most photogenic places. Boats pass children swimming in the muddy waters, huge cargo ships groaning under the weight of sand being shipped to construction sites, and wake-skipping long-tailed boats. At sunset the famed missile-shaped Wat Arun (p82) and the riverside towers of the luxury hotels are bathed in red and orange hues.

The terminus for most northbound boats is Tha Nonthaburi; for most southbound boats it's Tha Sathon (also called Central Pier), close to the Saphan Taksin Skytrain station. Some boats terminate further south at Wat Ratchasingkhon. See p241 for information on fares and timetables.

The company also offers a one-day river pass (100B) for unlimited trips aboard the Chao Phraya Tourist Boat, which stops at 10 major piers from 9.30am to 3pm and has a distracting loudspeaker guide. Even guidebook writers who sightsee at warp speed don't find this pass offers much better value than the average 10B fare.

The company that manages the river express boats also provides various weekend boat cruises. One of the most popular is the **Sunday tour** (adult/child 430/350B; 8am-6pm from Tha Maharat) to Bang Pa-In Palace near Ayuthaya, Bang Sai Handicrafts Centre and the bird sanctuary at Wat Phailom in Pathum Thani Province. The tour price does not include lunch or admission fees. You can also use this service (one way adult/child 350/300B) for an independent trip to Ayuthaya (p214).

MANOHRA CRUISES:
AYUTHAYA Map pp278-9
☎ 0 2477 0811; www.manohracruises.com; Bangkok Marriott Resort & Spa, 257 Th Charoen Nakhon; cruises US$850-1150

The nautical equivalent of the *Eastern & Oriental Express* train, the *Manohra 2* has been transformed into a luxury cabin cruiser that travels to and from Ayuthaya, the ancient capital. Decorated with antiques and Persian carpets, the craft represents the ultimate in Mae Nam Chao Phraya luxury. A three-day trip to Bang Pa-In and Ayuthaya aboard *Manohra 2* stops en route at Ko Kret and docks overnight in front of a temple along the river. In the morning guests 'make merit' and continue on to visit Bang Pa-In and Ayuthaya. On the third day the tour visits Bang Sai.

MANOHRA CRUISES:
BANGKOK Map pp278-9
☎ 0 2476 0021; www.manohracruises.com; Bangkok Marriott Resort & Spa, 257 Th Charoen Nakhon; sunset/dinner cruise 750/1500B

The best-looking vessels on the river are Manohra Cruises' restored teak rice barges that evoke the splendour of old Siam. *Manohra* and *Manohra Moon* are employed for sunset and dinner cruises that sail past the river's famous landmarks: Wat Phra Kaew, Wat Arun and Silom's skyscrapers. Manohra Cruises also offers overnight river trips to Ayuthaya (see above).

MITCHAOPAYA COMPANY Map p288
☎ 0 2225 6179; fax 0 26236168; Tha Chang; fares 800-1200B

The main company that nets canal-bound tourists has a desk at Tha Chang. Fares are based on duration aboard a long-tail boat. The cheapest trip lasts an hour and visits Wat Arun (p82) and the Royal Barges National Museum (p82), both places that can be visited more cheaply independently. Add more time and you can take in a floating market, canalside temples and orchid farms. It is customary to buy your boat driver a drink from one of the floating vendors you meet along the route.

Those on restricted budgets might find that these tours are only value if you're with a large group.

Bicycle Tours

Make arrangements by phone or Internet for the following tours.

ABC AMAZING BANGKOK CYCLIST TOUR
☎ 0 2665 6364; www.realasia.net; weekday/weekend all inclusive 1500/2000B

Several dedicated cyclists organise daily bike tours through a scenic riverside neighbourhood in Thonburi. You travel by long-tail boat to the *khlong*-crossed villages of stilt houses, green gardens and old ladies wrapped up in market sarongs. Instead of asphalt and traffic, you'll negotiate narrow concrete pathways bridging the canal below and occasionally yielding to a few motorbikes driven by kids half your age. Weekend tours also take in a floating market and what is touted as a 'super special' lunch.

GRASSHOPPER ADVENTURES
☎ 0 2628 7067; www.grasshopperadventures.com; all inclusive US$20

For the two-wheeled warriors, this touring company hits the streets of Bangkok for a sightseeing tour of Ko Ratanakosin before the traffic hits. In addition to the famous temples, you will cruise through little streets and alleys that you might otherwise miss with your nose in a map. The company also organises multiday trips throughout Southeast Asia should you evolve into a cycling convert.

KO RATANAKOSIN

Eating p126; Shopping p169; Sleeping p193

Bordering the eastern bank of Mae Nam Chao Phraya, this area is a veritable Vatican City of Thai Buddhism filled with some of the country's most honoured and holy sites: Wat Phra Kaew, the Grand Palace and Wat Pho. These are also the most spectacular tourist attractions the city has to offer and an obligation for even the most unmotivated students of culture and history.

This collection of religious and architectural treasures wasn't accidental. Rama I (King Buddha Yodfa; r 1782–1809) intended to recreate the glory of the sacked Siamese capital of Ayuthaya by constructing a new island city – one that would be fortified against future attacks – and to elevate the newly established dynasty in the imagination and adoration of the populace. Both intentions succeeded. The Burmese and other noncommercial invaders never staged an assault on the new capital and the Chakri dynasty survives to the present day.

The ancient city has matured in modern times to a lively district of contradictions that only Thailand can juggle. The temples, with their heavenly status, are tethered to earth by nearby food markets shaded by dull green umbrellas like clusters of mushrooms. In the shadows of the whitewashed temple walls are Buddhism's ancient companions – the animistic spirits who govern fortune and fate, neatly packaged into amulets.

Come here to survey the street life as much as the famed attractions. The area is best visited early in the morning, before the sun reaches its maximum strength. The wide pavements that circumnavigate the major sights and the inside courtyards of the temples are unfortunately devoid of shade, a necessary refuge from the tropical sun. Some of the more elegant visitors carry a sun umbrella to preserve their skin.

Rip-off artists prowl the tourist strip, using the country's legendary hospitality

KO RATANAKOSIN & THONBURI TOP FIVE

- Amulet Market (p169) Monks and collectors inspect these sacred objects for authenticity and protective powers.
- Lak Meuang (opposite) Don't bother with some hokey tourist show; if traditional dance is on your itinerary, wander over to the city shrine to see if a commissioned dance is in progress.
- Wat Arun (p82) A militaristic-looking temple decorated with delicate flower mosaics.
- Wat Phra Kaew and Grand Palace (p79) The Hollywood blockbusters of Thai architecture.
- Wat Pho (p78) A rambling complex full of hidden sights and corners.

to earn a dishonest day's wages. Disregard any strangers who approach you inquiring about where you are going or that attractions are closed. Save the one-on-one cultural exchange for genuine folks outside the tourist zone.

Orientation

Forming almost a tear-drop shape, Ko Ratanakosin's boundaries are defined by Mae Nam Chao Phraya on the western side, Th Phra Pin Klao on the northern side and Th Atsadang, which follows Khlong Lawt, on the eastern side. The district's attractions are concentrated in the area south of Sanam Luang, making for a walkable outing. Two main river piers – Tha Maharat and Tha Chang – service this district, making transport a scenic and relaxed experience. This is also a popular area from which to hire boats for tours into Thonburi's canals.

South of Th Na Phra Lan is primarily a tourist zone with a few warehouses abutting the river as reminders that daily life still exists. North of the Grand Palace is Sanam Luang, an oval park where joggers shuffle along in the early morning hours. Alongside Sanam Luang the National Museum and the National Theatre stand with stoic resolve.

On the far eastern side of Wat Phra Kaew are government ministry buildings reflecting a pronounced Western architectural influence – an interesting contrast to the flamboyant Thai architecture across the street.

TRANSPORT KO RATANAKOSIN

Bus Air-con 503, 508, 511 and 512, ordinary 3, 25, 39, 47, 53 and 70

Ferry Tha Maharat, Tha Chang and Tha Tien

LAK MEUANG Map p288
ศาลหลักเมือง

Cnr Th Ratchadamnoen Nai & Th Lak Meuang; admission free; ☺ **8.30am-5.30pm; ferry Tha Chang, air-con bus 508, 511 & 512, ordinary bus 15, 47, 53 & 59**

What would otherwise be an uninteresting mileage marker has both religious and historical significance in Thailand. Lak Meuang is the city shrine, a wooden pillar erected by Rama I in 1782 to represent the founding of the new Bangkok capital. From this point, distances are measured to all other city shrines in the country. But its importance doesn't stop there. The pillar is endowed with a spirit, Phra Sayam Thewathirat (Venerable Siam Deity of the State), and is considered the city's guardian. To the east of the main shrine are five other idols added during the reign of Rama V (King Chulalongkorn; r 1868–1910).

Like the sacred banyan trees and the holy temples, Lak Meuang receives daily supplications from Thai worshippers, some of whom commission classical Thai dancers to perform *lákhon kâe bon* (shrine dancing) as thanks for granted wishes. Some of the offerings also include those morbidly cute pigs' heads with sticks of incense sprouting from their foreheads.

Lak Meuang is across the street from the eastern wall of Wat Phra Kaew, at the southern end of Sanam Luang.

NATIONAL GALLERY Map p288
หอศิลปแห่งชาติ

☎ **0 2282 2639; Th Chao Fa; admission 30B;** ☺ **9am-4pm Wed-Sun; ferry Tha Phra Athit, air-con bus 508, 511 & 512, ordinary bus 47 & 53**

Housed in a weather-worn colonial building, the National Gallery displays traditional and contemporary art, mostly by artists receiving government support. Secular art is a fairly new concept in Thailand and some of the country's best examples of fine art reside in temples rather than galleries. Most of the permanent collection documents Thailand's homage to modern styles. One noteworthy exception is the *Musical Rhythm* sculpture, by Khien Yimsiri, which is considered one of the most remarkable fusions of Western and Thai styles during the mid-20th century. More uniquely Thai expressions can be seen in the rotating exhibits by young artists. The general opinion is that this gallery is not Thailand's best, but now that air-conditioning has arrived, it is a quiet place to escape the crowds and the sun. A weekend art market, set up in the museum courtyard, is accessible without admission.

The National Gallery is sandwiched between Thammasat University and the National Theatre in an early Ratanakosin-era building.

NATIONAL MUSEUM Map p288
พิพิธภัณฑสถานแห่งชาติ

☎ **0 2224 1333; Th Na Phra That; admission 40B;** ☺ **9am-4pm Wed-Sun; air-con bus 508, 511 & 512, ordinary bus 12, 47 & 53**

Thailand's National Museum is the largest museum in Southeast Asia and covers a broad range of subjects, from historical surveys to religious sculpture displays.

The history wing presents a succinct chronology of prehistoric, Sukhothai-, Ayuthaya- and Bangkok-era events and figures. Despite the hokey dioramas, there are some real treasures here: look for King Ramakamhaeng's inscribed stone pillar, the oldest record of Thai writing; King Taksin's throne; and the Rama V section.

The other parts of the museum aren't as well presented, but this might be part of the charm. Dimly lit rooms, ranging in temperature from lukewarm to boiling, offer an atticlike collection of Thai art and handicrafts.

In the central exhibits hall, there are collections of traditional musical instruments from Thailand, Laos, Cambodia and Indonesia, as well as ceramics, clothing and textiles, woodcarving, royal regalia, and Chinese art and weaponry. Perhaps most interesting is to watch the Thai school children's imaginations swell as they drink in their cultural legacy.

The art and artefact buildings cover every Southeast Asian art period and style, from Dvaravati to Ratanakosin. The collection is impressive but hard to digest due to poor signage and sheer volume.

The museum grounds also contain the restored **Phutthaisawan (Buddhaisawan) Chapel.** Inside the chapel (built in 1795) are some well-preserved original murals and one of the country's most revered Buddha images, Phra Phuttha Sihing. Legend claims the image came from Ceylon, but art historians attribute it to the 13th-century Sukhothai period.

Sights

KO RATANAKOSIN

Stone carving outside Phutthaisawan Chapel, National Museum (p75)

The museum buildings were originally built in 1782 as the palace of Rama I's viceroy, Prince Wang Na. Rama V turned it into a museum in 1884.

Taking a foreign-language tour will contribute greatly to your appreciation of the museum. Free tours are given in English on Wednesday (focusing on Buddhism) and Thursday (Thai art, religion and culture). Tours in German (Thursday), French (Wednesday) and Japanese (Wednesday) are also available. All tours start from the ticket pavilion at 9.30am.

SANAM LUANG Map p288
สนามหลวง

Bounded by Th Na Phra That, Ratchadamnoen Nai & Na Phra Lan; ferry Tha Chang, air-con bus 503, 508, 511 & 512, ordinary bus 15, 47, 53 & 59

On a hot day, Sanam Luang (Royal Field) is far from charming – a shadeless expanse of dying grass, ringed by flocks of pigeons and homeless people. Despite its shabby appearance, though, it fulfils many royal appointments.

This is the site of the annual Royal Ploughing Ceremony, in which the king officially initiates the rice-growing season (p12). After the rains, kite-flying season (mid-February to April) fills the open space with butterfly-shaped Thai kites. Matches are held between many teams, who fly either a 'male' or 'female' kite and are assigned a particular

territory, winning points if they can force a competitor into their zone.

Large funeral pyres are constructed here during elaborate, but infrequent, royal cremations. The most recent ceremonial cremation took place here in March 1996, when the king presided over funeral rites for his mother. Before that the most recent Sanam Luang cremations were held in 1976 for Thai students killed in prodemocracy demonstrations.

In a way the park is suffering a career crisis, having lost most of its full-time employment to other locales or the whims of fashion. Until 1982 Bangkok's famous Weekend Market was regularly held here (it's now at Chatuchak Park; see p188). Previously the wealthy came here for imported leisure sports. Today the cool mornings and evenings still attract a health-conscious crowd of joggers and walkers.

At the northern end of the park is the **statue of Mae Thorani**, the earth goddess (borrowed from Hindu mythology's Dharani), which stands in a white pavilion. Erected in the late 19th century by Rama V, the statue was originally attached to a well that provided drinking water to the public.

SARANROM ROYAL GARDEN Map p288
สวนสราญรมย์

Btwn Th Ratchini & Charoen Krung; ☺ 8.30am-4.30pm; ferry Tha Tien, air-con bus 503, 508 & 512, ordinary bus 12, 25 & 53

Easily mistaken for a European public garden, this Victorian-era green space was originally designed as a royal residence in the time of Rama IV (King Mongkut; r 1851–68). After the abdication of the king in 1932, the palace served as the headquarters of the People's Party, the political organisation that orchestrated the handover of the government. In 1960 the preserved open space became public. It provides a lovely stroll as evening approaches or after a day of sightseeing. There's a Victorian gazebo, paths lined with frangipani and a moat around a marble monument built in honour of Rama V's wife, Queen Sunantha, who died in a boating accident. The queen was on her way to Bang Pa-In Summer Palace in Ayuthaya when her boat began to sink. The custom at the time was that commoners were forbidden to touch royalty, which prevented her attendants from saving her from drowning.

The satellite corners of the park are filled with weightlifting equipment where a túk-túk driver might do some leg crunches in between hassling tourists. As the day cools various aerobics and dance classes practice their synchronization.

SILPAKORN UNIVERSITY Map p288
มหาวิทยาลัยศิลปากร
☎ 0 2623 6115; www.su.ac.th; 31 Th Na Phra Lan; ferry Tha Chang, air-con bus 508 & 512, ordinary bus 47 & 53

Thailand's universities aren't usually repositories for interesting architecture, but the country's premier art school breaks the mould. Housed in a former palace, the classical buildings form the charming nucleus of an early Thai aristocratic enclave and the traditional artistic temperament still pervades. The building immediately facing the Th Na Phra Lan gate houses the **Silpakorn University Art Centre** (Map p288; ☎ 0 2225 4350; www.art-centre.su.ac.th; Silpakorn University, Th Na Phra Lan; ⏰ 9am-7pm Mon-Fri, 9am-4pm Sat; river express Tha Chang, bus 25 & 53), which showcases faculty and student exhibitions. To the right of the building is a shady sculpture garden displaying the work of Corrado Feroci (also known as Silpa Bhirasri), the Italian art professor who helped establish Silpakorn's fine arts department.

The campus is cramped but well inhabited with outdoor sketchers. Stop by the Art Shop beside the gallery for unique postcards and books.

TH MAHARAT Map p288
ถนนมหาราช
Btwn Th Phra Chan, Th Na Phra Lan & Mae Nam Chao Phraya; ferry Tha Chang, air-con bus 503, 508 & 512, ordinary bus 47 & 53

The northern stretch of this street is one of Bangkok's most interesting. On the opposite side of Wat Mahathat's whitewashed walls, the street is monopolised by ancient Thai industries: herbal apothecaries and amulet dealers. In the cool season, medicinal bowls of ginger-infused broth are sold from steaming cauldrons to stave off winter colds. And outdoor displays of pill bottles are lined up and dusted daily like prized antiques. Each remedy bears a picture of a stoic healer, a marketing pitch that puts a human face on medicine. Further along, the

amulet market (*talàat phrá khrêuang;* see p169) spills out of its medieval warren into the street, forcing pedestrians to run zigzag patterns through the obstacles.

Just before Thammasat University are several narrow alleys lined with graduation gowns and leading to a riverside canteen. The makeshift restaurants of uneven wooden floors and narrow passages make a grown-up feel as overgrown as a kid does in a tree house. Each humble kitchen garners a view of the river and students congregate here for cheap eats before heading off to class. The fixings reflect Bangkok's peculiar student menu: a motley mix of Thai comforts and Western adaptations.

Grand plans by the municipal government have proposed that this area be demolished and redeveloped as a cultural theme park with more river vistas and shops catering to tourists. The plan has met with fierce resistance from residents, and many hope that this is one of many pipe dreams that ultimately gets smoked. But with Bangkok's love of reinvention, it is better to savour its few remaining medieval corners while they last.

THAMMASAT UNIVERSITY Map p288
มหาวิทยาลัยธรรมศาสตร์
☎ 0 2221 6111; www.tu.ac.th; 2 Th Phra Chan; ferry Tha Chang, air-con bus 508, 511 & 512, ordinary bus 47 & 53

Much of the drama that followed Thailand's transition from monarchy to democracy has unfolded on this quiet riverside campus. Thammasat University was established in 1934, two years after the bloodless coup that deposed the monarchy, to instruct students in law and political economy, considered the intellectual necessities for an educated democracy.

Overlooking the river is **Pridi Court**, anchored by a statue of Dr Pridi Phanomyong, the university founder and leader of the People's Party, the civilian organisation that advocated for a constitutional monarchy. Pridi had studied in Paris, served in various ministries, organised the Seri Thai movement (Thai resistance campaign against the Japanese during WWII) and was ultimately forced into exile when the postwar government was seized by a military dictatorship in 1947.

Although Pridi was unable to counter the dismantling of democrat reforms, the university he established continued his crusade. Thammasat was the hotbed of prodemocracy activism during the student uprising era of the 1970s. On 14 October 1973 (sìp-sìi tù-laa in Thai) 10,000 protesters convened on the parade grounds beside the university's Memorial Building demanding that the government reinstate the constitution. The military and police opened fire on the crowd, killing 77 and wounding 857. The massacre prompted the king to revoke his support of the military rulers and for a brief period a civilian government was reinstated. Thammasat was the site of more bloody protests on 6 October 1976 (hòk tù-laa), when students rallied against the former dictator Field Marshal Thanom Kittikachorn being allowed to return to Thailand after his exile. A plaque on the parade grounds commemorates these events.

WAT MAHATHAT Map p288
วัดมหาธาตุ

☎ 0 2221 5999; Th Mahathat; donation accepted;
🕑 9am-5pm; ferry Tha Chang, air-con bus 503, 508 & 512, ordinary bus 47 & 53

While other temples in the area claim all the fame, Wat Mahathat goes about the everyday business of a temple. Saffron-robed monks file in and out of the whitewashed gates, grandmas in their best silks come to make merit, and a tired soi dog trots from shade to food.

Founded in the 1700s, Wat Mahathat is a national centre for the Mahanikai monastic sect and houses one of Bangkok's two Buddhist universities, Mahathat Rajavidyalaya. The university is the most important place of Buddhist learning in mainland Southeast Asia – the Lao, Vietnamese and Cambodian governments send selected monks to further their studies here.

Mahathat and the surrounding area have developed into an informal Thai cultural centre of sorts, though this may not be obvious at first glance. The monastery offers meditation instruction in English (see p245).

WAT PHO Map p288
วัดโพธิ์(วัดพระเชตุพน)

☎ 0 2221 5910; Th Sanam Chai; admission 20B;
🕑 8am-6pm; ferry Tha Tien, air-con bus 503, 508 & 512, ordinary bus 12 & 53

This temple has a long list of credits: the oldest and largest wat in Bangkok, the longest reclining Buddha and the largest

STONE COLD STARE: WAT PHO'S ROCK GIANTS

Talk about a stiff crowd: Wat Pho is filled with giants and figurines carved out of granite. The rock giants first arrived in Thailand aboard Chinese junks as ballast and were put to work in Wat Pho, guarding the entrances of temple gates and courtyards. These comical figures were carved to resemble prominent and ordinary folks in ancient China. The giants with bulging eyes and Chinese opera costumes were inspired by warrior noblemen and are called Lan Than; notice their swords tucked behind their ornate robes. Wearing a fedoralike hat with a trimmed beard and moustache is a giant said to resemble Marco Polo, who introduced such European styles to the Chinese courts. The political nobleman wears his hair and moustache below his shoulders and carries a scroll in one hand; his long cloak indicates that he is a member of the aristocracy. The figure in a straw hat is a farmer, forever interrupted from his day's work cultivating the fields.

collection of Buddha images in Thailand, and the earliest centre for public education. But its best attraction is that it isn't as big an attraction as Wat Phra Kaew, meaning you've got this rambling complex nearly to yourself.

Narrow Th Chetuphon divides the grounds in two, with each section surrounded by huge whitewashed walls. The part open to the public is the northern compound. Once inside you'll find the interior layout confusing, so come to wander rather than to complete a checklist.

Enter from Th Chetuphon, off Th Maharat, into the eastern courtyard and the main bòt (chapel), which is constructed in Ayuthaya style and is strikingly more subdued than Wat Phra Kaew. Rama I's remains are interred in the base of the presiding Buddha figure in the bòt.

The images on display in the four wíhǎan (sanctuaries) surrounding the main bòt are worth investigation. Particularly beautiful are the Phra Jinnarat and Phra Jinachi Buddhas, in the western and southern chapels, both from Sukhothai. The galleries extending between the four chapels feature no fewer than 394 gilded Buddha images.

Encircling the main bòt is a low marble wall with 152 bas-reliefs depicting scenes from the Ramakian. You'll recognise some of these figures when you exit the temple past the hawkers with the mass-produced rubbings for sale; these are made from cement casts based on Wat Pho's reliefs.

As a temple site, Wat Pho (Temple of the Reclining Buddha) dates from the 16th century, but its current history really begins in 1781 with the complete rebuilding of the original monastery. During the reign of Rama III (King Nang Klao; r 1824–51), Wat Pho was an open university, and it maintains that tradition today as the national headquarters for the teaching and preservation of traditional Thai medicine, including Thai massage. On the temple grounds, there are un-air-conditioned massage pavilions that have recently reopened after a brief hiatus and there are air-con rooms available in the massage school, across the street from the temple (see p165). The two pavilions located nearby contain visual depictions of the body meridians and pressure points that were used to record the oral knowledge of the practice and are used as a teaching tool.

A collection of towering tiled stupas commemorates the first four Chakri kings and there are 91 smaller stupas. Rama IV ordered that the four stupas be surrounded by a wall to prevent future kings from joining the memorial. Note the square bell shape with distinct corners, a signature of Ratanakosin style. Other smaller *chedi* (stupa) clusters keep the ashes of royal descendants.

Small rock gardens and hill islands interrupt the tiled courtyards providing shade, greenery and quirky decorations. Inherited from China, these rockeries are cluttered with topiary, miniature waterfalls and small statues depicting daily life. **Khao Mor** is the most distinctive of the rock gardens. It is festooned with figures of the hermit credited with inventing yoga, in various healing positions. According to the tradition, a few good arm stretches should cure idleness.

If you enter the temple via Th Chetuphon, the less-used gate, you'll find you've left the best part for last. Near the Th Thai Wang gate is the tremendous **redining Buddha**, the temple's primary celebrity. At 46m long and 15m high, the supine figure illustrates the passing of the Buddha into nirvana. It is modelled out of plaster around a brick core and finished in gold

leaf. Mother-of-pearl inlay adorns the eyes and feet of this colossal figure, with the feet displaying 108 different auspicious *láksànà* (characteristics of a Buddha).

WAT PHRA KAEW & GRAND PALACE Map p288

วัดพระแก้ว/พระบรมมหาราชวัง

☎ 0 2623 5500; admission to both 250B; ⏱ 8.30am-3.30pm; ferry Tha Chang, air-con bus 503, 508 & 512, ordinary bus 2 & 25

The Temple of the Emerald Buddha (Wat Phra Kaew) gleams and glitters with so much colour and glory that its earthly foundations seem barely able to resist the celestial pull. Architecturally fantastic, the temple complex is also the spiritual core of Thai Buddhism and the monarchy, symbolically united in the temple's most holy image, the Emerald Buddha. Attached to the temple complex is the former royal residence, once a sealed city of intricate ritual and social stratification.

You enter Wat Phra Kaew and the Grand Palace complex through the third gate from the river pier. Tickets are purchased inside the complex. If anyone outside the complex tells you that it is closed, proceed to the official ticket window to confirm.

Past the ticket counters as you enter the compound are the brawny guardian giants known as *yaksha* from the Ramakian (the Thai version of the Indian Ramayana epic).

Beyond the gate is a courtyard with a **central bòt** (chapel) housing the Emerald Buddha. The spectacular ornamentation inside and out does an excellent job of distracting first-time visitors from paying their respects to the image. Here's why: the Emerald Buddha is only 66cm high and sits so high above worshippers in the main temple

TEMPLE ETIQUETTE

Wats are sacred places and should be treated with respect and formality. Wat Phra Kaew, especially, is very strict in its dress code. You may not enter the temple grounds if wearing shorts or a sleeveless shirt. The temple does have sarongs and baggy pants that are sometimes available on loan at the entrance. For walking in the courtyard areas you must wear shoes with closed heels and toes – sandals and flip-flops aren't permitted for foreigners. But you should remove your shoes before entering any building.

building that the gilded shrine is more striking than the small figure it cradles. There are always postcards if you miss it.

Outside of the main *bòt* is a stone statue of the Chinese goddess of mercy, Kuan Im, and nearby are two cow figures, representing the year of Rama I's birth.

In the cloisters that define the perimeter of the complex are extensive murals depicting scenes from the Ramakian. Divided into 178 sections, the murals illustrate the epic in its entirety, beginning at the north gate and moving clockwise around the compound. If the temple grounds seem overrun by tourists, the mural area is usually pleasantly abandoned and shady.

Adjoining Wat Phra Kaew is the **Grand Palace** (Phra Borom Maharatchawang), a former royal residence which today is used by the king only for certain ceremonial occasions. The current monarch lives in Chitralada Palace, which is closed to the public. Visitors are allowed to survey the Grand Palace grounds and exteriors of the four remaining palace buildings, which are interesting for their royal bombast.

At the eastern end, **Borombhiman Hall** is a French-inspired structure that served as a residence for Rama VI (King Vajiravudh; r 1910–25). In April 1981 General San Chitpatima used it as headquarters for an attempted coup. **Amarindra Hall**, to the west,

was originally a hall of justice but is used today for coronation ceremonies.

The largest of the palace buildings is the triple-winged **Chakri Mahaprasat** (Grand Palace Hall). Designed in 1882 by British architects, the exterior shows a peculiar blend of Italian Renaissance and traditional Thai architecture, a style often referred to as *faràng sài chá-daa* (Westerner wearing a Thai classical dancer's headdress), because each wing is topped by a *mondòp* (a layered, heavily ornamented spire). The tallest of the *mondòp*, in the centre, contains the ashes of Chakri kings; the flanking *mondòp* enshrine the ashes of Chakri princes who failed to inherit the throne.

The last building to the west is the Ratanakosin-style **Dusit Hall**, which initially served as a venue for royal audiences and later as a royal funerary hall.

Thai kings traditionally housed their huge harems in the inner palace area (not open to the public), which was guarded by combat-trained female sentries. The intrigue and rituals that occurred within the walls of this cloistered community live on in the fictionalised epic *Four Reigns*, by Kukrit Pramoj, which follows a young girl named Ploi growing up within the Royal City.

The admission fee to Wat Phra Kaew also includes entry to Dusit Park (p89).

THE EMERALD BUDDHA

The Emerald Buddha's lofty perch in Wat Phra Kaew signifies its high status as the 'talisman' of the Thai kingdom.

Neither the origin nor the sculptor of the Buddha is certain, but it first appeared on record in 15th-century Chiang Rai in northern Thailand. Legend says it was sculpted in India and brought to Siam by way of Ceylon, but stylistically it seems to belong to Thai artistic periods of the 13th to 14th centuries.

Sometime in the 15th century, this Buddha is said to have been covered with plaster and gold leaf and placed in Chiang Rai's own Wat Phra Kaew. Many valuable Buddha images were masked in this way to deter potential thieves and marauders during unstable times. Oftentimes, the true identity of the images were forgotten over the years until what is viewed as a divine accident allowed the image to show its precious core.

The Emerald Buddha experienced such a divine revelation when it was being transported to a new location. In a fall, the plaster covering broke off revealing a brilliant green figure (the Emerald Buddha is actually carved from nephrite, a type of jade). But this coming out was not the beginning of the figure's peaceful reign.

During territorial clashes with Laos, the Emerald Buddha was seized and taken to Vientiane in the mid-16th century. Some 200 years later, after the fall of Ayuthaya and the ascendancy of the Bangkok-based kingdom, the Thai army marched up to Laos and seized the Emerald Buddha. The return of this revered figure was a great omen for future fortunes of this new leadership. The Buddha was enshrined in then-capital Thonburi, but was later moved to Bangkok when the general who led the charge on Vientiane had assumed the throne and established the present Chakri dynasty as Rama I.

A tradition that dates back to this time is the changing of the Buddha's seasonal robes. There are now three royal robes: for the hot, rainy and cool seasons. The three robes are still solemnly changed at the beginning of each season by the king himself.

WHAT'S A WAT?

Planning to conquer Bangkok's temples? With this handy guide, you'll be able to keep your wits and your wats about you.

Bòt: a consecrated chapel where monastic ordinations are held.

Chedi (stupa): a large bell-shaped tower usually containing five structural elements symbolising (from bottom to top) earth, water, fire, wind and void; relics of the Buddha or a Thai king are housed inside.

Prang: a towering phallic spire of Khmer origin serving the same religious purpose as a *chedi.*

Wat: temple monastery.

Wíhăan: the main sanctuary for the temple's Buddha sculpture and where laypeople come to make their offerings; classic architecture typically has a three-tiered roof representing the triple gems, Buddha (the teacher), Dharma (the teaching) and Brotherhood (the followers).

Buddha Images

Elongated earlobes, no evidence of bone or muscle, arms that reach to the knees, a third eye: these are some of the 32 rules, originating from 3rd-century India, that govern the depiction of Buddha in sculpture and denote his divine nature. Other symbols to be aware of are the 'postures', which depict periods in the life of Buddha.

Sitting: Buddha teaching or meditating. If the right hand is pointed towards the earth, Buddha is shown subduing the demons of desire. If the hands are folded in the lap, Buddha is meditating.

Reclining: the exact moment of Buddha's passing into *parinibbana* (postdeath nirvana).

Standing: Buddha bestowing blessings or taming evil forces.

Walking: Buddha after his return to earth from heaven.

THONBURI

Eating p126

In the procession of Thai capitals, Thonburi enjoyed a brief 15-year promotion from sleepy port town to royal seat of power. If it weren't for timing, it might otherwise be a footnote in Thai history. Instead it is still revered as a patriotic and divinely inspired step in reuniting the country after the fall of Ayuthaya. The stories of the postwar reunification are filled with poetic symbolism: General Taksin, who expelled the Burmese and subdued rival factions, came across this spot in the river at dawn and pronounced it Ayuthaya's successor. But Taksin and his new capital were later deposed by a more strategic leader and position across the river.

Today Thonburi is basically a suburb of Bangkok but the surviving canals help preserve a riverine character that has been lost in the faddish capital. A vast network of canals and river tributaries still carry a motley fleet of watercraft, from paddled canoes to rice barges. In these areas many homes, trading houses and temples are built up on stilts with their front doors opening out to river, not road, traffic. It provides a fascinating glimpse into the past, when Thais still considered themselves *jâo náam* (water lords), and according to many residents, protects them from the seasonal flooding that plagues the capital.

Khlong Bangkok Noi is lined with lots of greenery and historic temples, reaching deep into the Bang Yai district, where a brief five-minute ride sheds the concrete entanglements of central Bangkok. Khlong Bangkok Yai was in fact the original course of the river until a canal was built to expedite transits. Today the tributary sees a steady stream of tourists on long-tail boat tours en route to touristy floating markets or Wat Intharam, where a *chedi* contains the ashes of Thonburi's King Taksin, who was assassinated in 1782. Fine gold-and-black lacquerwork adorning the main *bòt* doors depicts the mythical *naariiphŏn* tree, which bears fruit shaped like beautiful maidens.

Most tourists only meet the river-facing part of Thonburi between Khlong Bangkok Noi to Khlong Bangkok Yai, leaving the interior of the community predominately Thai with hardly an English sign or pestering túk-túk driver in sight. As the river ferries ricochet from stop to stop, a steady stream of commuters are shuttled to and from jobs in downtown Bangkok, as they wait impatiently for the Skytrain to be extended to their bedroom community.

Orientation

Thonburi occupies the western bank of the river and most of the attractions are directly across from Ko Ratanakosin. Two major bridges fuse the two banks together – Saphan Phra Pin Klao and Saphan Phra Phuttha Yot Fa (Memorial Bridge) – and husky cross-river ferries plod from one side to another. The river ferry stops at a few key Thonburi piers.

There are major roads that cut shipping and transport arteries through Thonburi, delivering passengers to the Southern bus station, along bland megahighway projects and characterless suburban stretches. Two minor rail lines depart from Thonburi: one line departs from Bangkok Noi (near Siriraj Hospital) and trundles west to Kanchanaburi, the other is a commuter line that departs from Wong Wian Yai to the gulf coast suburbs.

FORENSIC MEDICINE MUSEUM Map p288

พิพิธภัณฑ์นิติเวชศาสตร์สงกรานต์นิยมเสน

☎ 0 2419 7000; Forensic Medicine Bldg, Siriraj Hospital; admission 40B; ⏰ 9am-4pm Mon-Fri; ferry Tha Rot Fai

Pickled body parts, ingenious murder weapons and other crime-scene evidence are on display at this medical museum, intended to educate rather than nauseate. Among the grisly displays is the preserved cadaver of Si Ouey, one of Thailand's most prolific serial murderers and a frequent curse for misbehaving children. If you've finally found a museum that suits you here, try out the other nine dusty museums on the hospital premises.

The best way to get here is to take a river ferry to Tha Rot Fai (Railway Station Pier) in

Thonburi and follow the road to the second entrance into the Siriraj Hospital campus. The museum building will be on your left.

ROYAL BARGES NATIONAL MUSEUM Map p288

เรือพระที่นั่ง

☎ 0 2424 0004; Khlong Bangkok Noi; admission 30B, photography fee 100B; ⏰ 9am-5pm; tourist shuttle boat from Tha Phra Athit

Every foreign country has its famous religious monuments and museums, but how many have their own fleet of boats on display? As a former riverine culture, Thailand still maintains the royal barges, once used daily by the royal family for outings and events and now used only for grand ceremonies.

The royal barges are slender like their mainstream cousins, the long-tail boats, and are fantastically ornamented with religious symbolism. The largest is 50m long and requires a rowing crew of 50 men, plus seven umbrella bearers, two helmsmen and two navigators, as well as a flag bearer, rhythm keeper and chanter. *Suphannahong,* the king's personal barge, is the most important of the boats; made from a single piece of timber, it's the largest dugout in the world. The name means 'golden swan', and a huge swan's head has been carved into the bow. Lesser barges feature bows carved into other Hindu-Buddhist mythological shapes such as the *naga* (sea dragon) and the *garuda* (Vishnu's bird mount).

To mark auspicious Buddhist calendar years, the royal barges in all their finery set sail during the royal *kàthǐn,* the ceremony that marks the end of the Buddhist retreat (or *phansǎa*) in October or November. During this ceremony, a barge procession travels to the temples to offer new robes to the monastic contingent.

The barges are kept in sheds on the Thonburi side of the river, next to Khlong Bangkok Noi.

WAT ARUN Map pp280-1

วัดอรุณฯ

☎ 0 2891 1149; Th Arun Amarin; admission 20B; ⏰ 8.30am-5.30pm; cross-river ferry from Tha Tien to Tha Thai Wang

The missile-shaped temple that rises from the banks of the Mae Nam Chao Phraya is known as the Temple of Dawn, named after the Indian god of dawn, Aruna. It was here that King Taksin stumbled upon a small shrine used by the local people and interpreted the discovery as an auspicious sign for building a new Thai capital. King Taksin used the site for a palace, royal temple and home of the Emerald Buddha before relocating (along with the capital) to Bangkok.

The central feature of the temple, the 82m Khmer-style *prang* (spire), was constructed during the first half of the 19th century by Rama II (King Buddha Loetla; r 1809–24) and Rama III. From the river it is not apparent that this corn-cob shaped steeple is adorned with colourful floral murals made of glazed porcelain, a common temple ornamentation in the early Ratanakosin period, when Chinese ships calling at Bangkok used broken porcelain as ballast.

Also worth a look is the interior of the *bòt*. The main Buddha image is said to have been designed by Rama II himself. The murals date to the reign of Rama V; particularly impressive is one that depicts Prince Siddhartha (the Buddha) encountering examples of birth, old age, sickness and death outside his palace walls, an experience that

Detail of Wat Arun's 82m prang (spire)

led him to abandon the worldly life. The ashes of Rama II are interred in the base of the *bòt*'s presiding Buddha image.

GENUFLECTING IN THE CITY OF ANGELS

The trade winds blew many strange cultures into the tidal plain of Chao Phraya long before 747s unloaded holiday-makers. Portuguese seafarers were among the first Europeans to establish diplomatic ties with Siam and their influence in the kingdom was rewarded with prime riverside real estate, now occupied by their surviving Catholic churches. The French continued the Catholic traditions in Bangkok as the European balance of power shifted, and today refugees from Indochina fill the pews.

Centuries before Sukhumvit became the international district, the Portuguese claimed *faràng* (Western) supremacy and built **Church of Santa Cruz** (Map pp280–1; ☎ 0 2466 0347; Soi Kuti Jiin, Thonburi; ☾ Sat & Sun; cross-river ferry from Tha Pak Talat/Atsadang) in the 1700s. The land was a gift from King Taksin in appreciation of loyalty after the fall of Ayuthaya. The surviving church dates to 1913. Very little activity occurs on the grounds itself, but small village streets break off of the main courtyard into the area known as Kuti Jiin. On Soi Kuti Jiin 3, several houses sell the Portuguese-inspired cake named for the area.

In 1787 a Portuguese contingent moved across the river to the present-day Talat Noi district of Chinatown to found **Holy Rosary Church** (Map pp284–5; ☎ 0 2266 4849; 1318 Th Yotha, near River City; ☾ mass Mon-Sat 6am, Sun 6.15am, 8am & 10am; ferry Tha Si Phraya), known in Thai as Wat Kalawan, from the Portuguese 'Calvario'. As the Portuguese community dissipated and the church fell into disrepair, Vietnamese and Cambodian Catholics displaced by the Indochina wars adopted the parish. This old church has a splendid set of Romanesque stained-glass windows, gilded ceilings and a Christ statue that is carried through the streets during Easter celebrations.

Assumption Cathedral (Map pp290–1; ☎ 0 2234 8556; Soi Oriental, Th Charoen Krung; ☾ daily; ferry Tha Oriental) marks the ascendancy of the French missionary influence in Bangkok in the 1800s, during the reign of Rama II. The Romanesque church with its rich golden interior dates to 1910 and hosted a mass by Pope John Paul II in 1984. The schools associated with the cathedral are considered some of the best in Thailand.

Church of the Immaculate Conception (Map pp282–3; ☎ 0 2243 2617, ext 167; Soi 11, Th Samsen; ☾ variable; ferry Tha Thewet) dates back to 1674, but the present building claims an 1837 reconstruction and a Cambodian parish. One of the original church buildings survives and is now used as a museum housing holy relics.

On the periphery of the temple grounds are simple wooden cut-outs of Thai dancers luring visitors to take photographs of their mugs imposed onto the figures; be aware that a charge of 40B is required.

Wat Arun is located directly across from Wat Pho on the Thonburi side of the river; a cross-river ferry from Tha Tien is the jumping off point for a temple visit. You can also follow the interior road to Th Wang Doem, a quiet tiled street of wooden shophouses for an unstructured stroll.

BANGLAMPHU

Eating p126; Shopping p169; Sleeping p193

This is old Bangkok, once an aristocratic and artistic enclave of teak houses and tended gardens. Here trees still outnumber high-rises, fashion comes from the market not the malls and monks outnumber chauffeurs. Classic and charming, Banglamphu is pleasantly stuck in the 19th century.

Most of the district is a circuit-board of two-storey shophouses, each decorated with terracotta water gardens or potted plants and low-hanging shades that block out the mean sun. It is easy to lose your way in this neighbourhood where streets more closely mimic a maze than a thoroughfare.

During the Chinese New Year, it is customary for the merchants to do a little 'spring cleaning'. Swarms of workers scour the pavements, mop the floors and polish the neon signs. Once all the soap is rinsed away, the scene looks inexplicably just like it did before. These shops sell ordinary items that fill wardrobes, utility closets and kitchen pantries in a typical Thai home. Usually the businesses are dimly lit and packed to the ceiling with merchandise and run by the 'shirtless masters', older Thai-Chinese men who show off their merchant bellies on hot days.

But the most famous draw is Th Khao San, the backpacker enclave of guesthouses

BANGLAMPHU TOP FIVE

- Santichaiprakan Park (p86) The perfect spot for evening sunsets, cool river breezes and snacking with Thai families.
- Street stalls (p126) Graze the informal buffet of Banglamphu's street food.
- Th Khao San (p149) Backpacker mecca, beer hall and daily freak show.
- Wat Saket and Golden Mount (p87) Gain a little altitude in this flat city.
- October 14 Memorial (p86) Pay your respects to Thailand's political struggle.

and amenities. Th Khao San's travellers' scene has expanded beyond its namesake street into nearby *soi*. Although permanent expats deride the backpacker clones in Banglamphu, the services and affordability here are unrivalled in the city. The whole strip anticipates every traveller need: meals to soothe homesickness, cafés and bars for friendly chats with a fellow traveller on how to get to the Cambodian border, tailors, teeth whitening, you name it. Since this is a staging ground for trips elsewhere, Banglamphu creates an instant camaraderie that emerges to pacify the anxiety of plunging into the unknown.

Long before Banglamphu landed on travellers' itineraries, this was the original residential district for farmers and produce merchants from Ayuthaya who followed the transfer of the royal court to Bangkok in the late 18th century. The name means 'Place of Lamphu', a reference to the *lamphuu* tree (*Duabanga grandiflora*) that was once prevalent in the area. By the time of King Rama IV, Banglamphu had developed into a thriving commercial district by day and an entertainment spot by night, a role it still fulfils today.

Orientation

Banglamphu spreads from the river north of Th Phra Pin Klao and eventually melts into Dusit and Thewet around Th Krung Kasem. The royal boulevard of Th Ratchadamnoen Klang, lined with billboard-sized pictures of the king and queen, links the Grand Palace in Ko Ratanakosin with the new palace in Dusit. Lots of changes are in store for Th Ratchadamnoen Klang and plans for new museums hope to transform

TRANSPORT BANGLAMPHU

Bus Air-con 511 and 512, ordinary 3, 15, 32 and 53

Ferry Tha Phra Athit (aka Tha Banglamphu)

Khlong taxi Pier at Th Lan Luang and Th Ratchadamnoen Klang

the traffic corridor into a cultural promenade documenting Thailand's transition to democracy.

Book-ended by the major roads of Th Phra Athit and Th Ratchadamnoen Klang, the backpacker universe starts on Th Khao San and spreads down Soi Rambutri, Th Rambutri and even over the *khlong* to the residential *soi* off Th Samsen.

The avenue of mansions, Th Phra Athit arcs from the Sanam Luang area in the south and bends with the river and follows the *khlong* inland to Th Phra Sumen and intersects with Th Ratchadamnoen. This section also includes the area of Phra Nakhon south of Th Ratchadamnoen Klang on either side of Khlong Ong Ang.

DEMOCRACY MONUMENT Map pp286-7
อนุสาวรีย์ประชาธิปไตย
Traffic circle of Th Ratchadamnoen Klang & Th Din So; air-con bus 511 & 512, ordinary bus 2 & 82
The focal point of a grand European boulevard, the Democracy Monument is a stunning Deco creation erected in 1932 to commemorate Thailand's momentous transformation from absolute to constitutional monarchy. The monument was designed by Italian artist Corrado Feroci (Silpa Bhirasri) and evokes patriotic symbolism. There are 75 cannonballs buried in its base to signify the year BE (Buddhist Era) 2475 (AD 1932). The four wings of the monument stand 24m tall, representing 24 June, the day the constitution was signed, and each wing has bas-reliefs depicting soldiers, police and civilians who have helped build the modern Thai state.

During the era of military dictatorships, demonstrators often assembled in this historic spot to lobby for fulfilment of the 1932 revolution. And there were three bloody clashes between civilian demonstrators and the government: 14 October 1973, 6 October 1976 and 17 May 1972.

KING PRAJADHIPOK MUSEUM Map pp286-7
พิพิธภัณฑ์พระบาทสมเด็จพระปกเกล้าเจ้าอยู่หัว
☎ 0 2280 3413; 2 Th Lan Luang; ☯ 9am-4pm Tue-Sun; admission 40B; air-con bus 511 & 512, ordinary bus 2, khlong taxi to Tha Phan Fah
A visit to a royal museum might sound like a royal bore, but displays here deal with more than royal adoration. King Prajadhipok (Rama VII; r 1925–35) was a

diplomatic participant in history's march toward the future. He did not expect to become king nor did he rule for long before the bloodless coup unseated 150 years of dynastic rule. The intersection of history makes for great drama: the king's abdication occurred only two months after the sesquicentenary of the Chakri dynasty and was orchestrated by the new intellectual class of Thais who had returned home from European educations with dreams of democracy. The museum is housed in a neoclassical shophouse that was once a tailor shop for imported haute couture.

MAHAKAN FORT Map pp286-7
ป้อมมหากาฬ
Th Ratchadamnoen Klang; ☯ 8.30am-6pm; air-con bus 511 & 512, ordinary bus 2, khlong taxi to Tha Phan Fah
One of two surviving citadels that defended the old walled city, Mahakan Fort has been recently refurbished into a small green park overlooking Khlong Ong Ang. The octagonal fort is a picturesque stop en route to Golden Mount, but the back story on its conversion makes the site more compelling for political junkies. A small community of 55 simple wooden houses formerly surrounded the fort, but the Bangkok municipal government demolished the community in order to create a 'tourist' park, the modern term for urban renewal. The community blocked progress for 13 years and even proposed the development of another tourist attraction: a *lí-keh* museum honouring the dance tradition that traces its creation to a school located here in 1897. But the plans were rejected and now a green fence abruptly separates the green space from the houses that escaped removal.

MONK'S BOWL VILLAGE Map pp286-7
บ้านบาตร
Soi Ban Baat, Th Boriphat; ordinary bus 12 & 42, khlong taxi to Tha Phan Fah
This is the only remaining village of three established in Bangkok by Rama I for the purpose of handcrafting *bàat* (monk's bowls), the ceremonial bowls used to collect alms from the faithful every morning. As cheaper factory-made bowls are now the norm, the artisanal tradition has shrunk to a single alley of about half a

WORKING FROM HOME: ARTISAN VILLAGES

Long before multinational factories, Bangkok was a town of craftspeople who lived and worked in artisan villages, inheriting their skills and profession from their parents. Many villages made stylised arts and crafts for the palace and minor royalty living along the fashionable avenues of the time. Today most of the villages still remain, but the descendants of the craftspeople have become office workers commuting to jobs no longer based in their homes.

Soi Ma Toom (Map pp280–1; off Th Arun Amarin, across from the Naval Department) is a surviving example of the old home-and-factory paradigm. This quiet lane, just off of a traffic-clogged artery in Thonburi, is where the *ma toom* (bael fruit) is peeled, cut into horizontal slices and soaked in palm sugar to make a popular candy.

Surviving primarily on tourist patronage, the **Monk's Bowl Village** (see p85) dates back to the first Bangkok king and continues to create ceremonial pieces used by monks to collect morning alms.

Near the old timber yards and saw mills, **Woodworking Street** (Map pp278–9; Soi Pracha Narumit, Th Pracharat, Bang Sue) is still going strong with small Thai-Chinese owned factories fashioning wooden eaves, furniture and shrines. Shops are open daily and an annual street fair is celebrated in January.

dozen families. You can usually observe the process of hammering the bowls together from eight separate pieces of steel said to represent Buddhism's Eight-fold Path. The joints are fused in a wood fire with bits of copper, and the bowl is polished and coated with several layers of black lacquer. A typical *bàat*-smith's output is one bowl per day.

To find the village, walk south on Th Boriphat, south of Th Bamrung Meuang, then turn left onto Soi Ban Baat. At any of the houses that make them, you can purchase a fine-quality alms bowl for around 600B to 800B.

OCTOBER 14 MEMORIAL Map pp286-7
อนุสาวรีย์ 14 ตุลาคม
Khok Wua intersection, Th Ratchadamnoen Klang; air-con bus 511 & 512, ordinary bus 2 & 82
A peaceful amphitheatre commemorates the civilian demonstrators who were killed on 14 October 1973 by the military during a prodemocracy rally. Over 200,000 people assembled at the Democracy Monument and along Th Ratchadamnoen to protest the arrest of political campaigners and to express their discontent over the continued military dictatorship; over 70 demonstrators were killed when the tanks met the crowd. The complex is an interesting adaptation of Thai temple architecture for a secular and political purpose. A central *chedi* is dedicated to the fallen and a gallery of historic photographs lines the interior wall. Included in the redevelopment plans of Th Ratchadamnoen Klang is a museum that will occupy the underground portion of the amphitheatre.

PHRA SUMEN FORT & SANTICHAIPRAKAN PARK Map pp286-7
ป้อมพระสุเมร/สวนสาธารณะสันติชัยปราการ
Th Phra Athit; 5am-10pm; ferry Tha Phra Athit, ordinary bus 15, 30 & 53
Next to Mae Nam Chao Phraya in Banglam-phu stands one of Bangkok's original 18th-century forts. Built in 1783 to defend against potential naval invasions and named for the mythical Mt Meru (Phra Sumen in Thai) of Hindu-Buddhist cosmol-ogy, the octagonal brick-and-stucco bunker was one of 14 city fortresses constructed alongside Khlong Rop Krung (now Khlong Banglamphu).

Alongside the fort and fronting the river is a small, grassy park with an open-air pavilion, river views, cool breezes and picnickers. Daily aerobics classes are held here in the evenings and attract as many amused spectators as participants, forming an intoxicating spirit of community.

A walkway zigzags along the river – and in some cases is suspended right over it – from the fort to all the way to Saphan Phra Pin Klao. Follow this walk and along the way you can catch glimpses of old Ratanakosin-style buildings not visible from the street, such as those housing parts of the Buddhist Society of Thailand and the Food & Agriculture Organization.

QUEEN'S GALLERY Map pp286-7
หอศิลปสมเด็จพระนางเจ้าสิริกิติ์
0 2281 5360; www.queengallery.org; 101 Th Ratchadamnoen Klang; 10am-7pm Tue-Mon; admission 20B; air-con bus 511 & 512, ordinary bus 2, khlong taxi to Tha Phan Fah
This royally funded museum presents five floors of modern art. The building is sleek

and contemporary and the artists hail from the upper echelons of the conservative Thai art world. The attached shop is filled with fine arts books and gifts.

SAO CHING-CHA Map pp286-7
เสาชิงช้า

☎ 0 2281 2831; Th Botphram, btwn Th Tri Thong & Th Burapha; ordinary bus 12, 42, khlong taxi to Tha Phan Fah

It is easy to forget the powers of the Brahmans in Thai Buddhism, unless you happen upon the giant red poles of Sao Ching-Cha (the Giant Swing). During the second lunar month (usually in January), Brahman beliefs dictate that Shiva comes down to earth for a 10-day residence and should be welcomed by great ceremonies including the acrobatics of the Great Swing. Participants would swing in ever-heightening arcs in an effort to reach a bag of gold suspended from a 15m bamboo pole – many died trying.

The Brahmans had enjoyed a mystical position within the royal court, primarily in the coronation rituals. But after the 1932 revolution, the Brahmans' waning power was effectively terminated and the festival was discontinued during the reign of Rama VII.

Sao Ching-Cha is two long blocks south of the Democracy Monument and directly across from Wat Suthat. The framework of the giant swing still remains, and it's worth visiting to take a few pictures of this unusual site.

WAT BOWONNIWET Map pp286-7
วัดบวรนิเวศ

☎ 0 2281 2831; www.watbowon.org; Th Phra Sumen; admission free; ☼ 8am-5pm; ferry Tha Phra Athit, air-con bus 511

Wat Bowonniwet (commonly known as Wat Bowon) is the national headquarters for the Thammayut monastic sect, a reformed version of Thai Buddhism. The Thammayuts focused on reinstating purer ritual practices (based on Mon traditions) and orthodox theology expunged of folk beliefs. Rama IV, who set out to be a scholar not king, founded the Thammayuts and began the royal tradition of ordination at this temple. In fact, Mongkut was the abbot of Wat Bowon for several years. Rama IX (King Bhumibol; r 1946–) and Crown Prince Vajiralongkorn, as well as several other males in the royal family, have been temporarily ordained as monks here.

The temple was founded in 1826, when it was known as Wat Mai.

Bangkok's second Buddhist university, Mahamakut University, is housed at Wat Bowon. Selected monks are sent from India, Nepal and Sri Lanka to study here.

Because of its royal status, visitors should be particularly careful to dress properly for admittance to this wat – no shorts or sleeveless clothing are allowed.

WAT RATCHANATDA Map pp286-7
วัดราชนัดดา

☎ 0 2224 8807; Th Mahachai; admission free; ☼ 8am-5pm; air-con bus 511 & 512, ordinary bus 2, khlong taxi to Tha Phan Fah

Across Th Mahachai from Wat Saket, this temple is most stunning at night when the 37 spires of the metal palace are lit up like a medieval birthday cake. Displaying Burmese influences, it dates from the mid-19th century and was built under Rama III in honour of his granddaughter.

Behind the formal gardens is a well-known market selling Buddhist *phrá khrêuang* (amulets) in all sizes, shapes and styles. The amulets feature not only images of the Buddha, but also famous Thai monks and Indian deities. Full Buddha images are also for sale.

WAT SAKET & GOLDEN MOUNT Map pp286-7
วัดสระเกศ

☎ 0 2223 4561; soi off Th Boriphat; admission to summit of Golden Mount 10B; ☼ 8am-5pm; air-con bus 511 & 512, ordinary bus 2, khlong taxi to Tha Phan Fah

Bangkok is a sinking bowl, except for the manmade heights. Before glass and steel towers defied gravity, the only structure so bold did so with royal permission. Golden Mount (Phu Khao Thong) sits at the eastern entrance to Banglamphu and benevolently beams at Th Ratchadamnoen Klang below. Serpentine steps wind through the artificial hill shaded by gnarled trees and past small tombstones accompanied by photos of the deceased.

This hill was created when a large *chedi* under construction by Rama III collapsed because the soft soil would not support it. The resulting mud-and-brick hill was left to sprout weeds until Rama IV built a small *chedi* on its crest. Rama V later added to the structure and housed a Buddha relic from India (given to him by the British government) in the *chedi*. The concrete walls were added during WWII to prevent the hill from eroding.

Every November there is a big festival in the grounds of Wat Saket, which includes an enchanting candle-lit procession up the Golden Mount.

WAT SUTHAT Map pp286-7
วัดสุทัศน์

☎ 0 2224 9845; Th Botphram; admission 20B;
🕙 8.30am-5.30pm; ordinary bus 12 & 42, khlong taxi to Tha Phan Fah

Unlike Bangkok's postcard temples, Wat Suthat is peacefully abandoned, except for a few napping dogs and temple staff. The temple maintains a special place in the national religion because of its association with Brahman priests, who perform important ceremonies such as the Royal Ploughing Ceremony in May (p12). These priests also perform religious rites at two Hindu shrines near the wat – the **Thewa Sathaan** (Devi Mandir) on Th Siri Phong, and the smaller **Saan Jao Phitsanu** (Vishnu Shrine) on Th Din So. The former shrine contains images of Shiva and Ganesha while the latter is dedicated to Vishnu.

Wat Suthat holds the rank of Rachavoramahavihan, the highest royal temple grade. One of the oldest Ratanakosin-era religious structures in Bangkok, the *wíhǎan* has wooden doors carved by several artisans, including Rama II himself. Within the *wíhǎan*, the ashes of Rama VIII (King Ananda Mahidol, the current king's deceased older brother; r 1935–46) are contained in the base of the main Buddha image. There is also a gilded bronze

Wat Suthat

Buddha image, called Phra Si Sakayamuni, Thailand's largest surviving Sukhothai-period bronze, and colourful *Jataka* (murals depicting scenes from the Buddha's life).

THEWET & DUSIT
Eating p129; Shopping p169; Sleeping p197

Formerly a fruit orchard, Dusit was transformed into a mini-European city by Rama V (King Chulalongkorn). Like London and Paris, the planned district is bisected by wide avenues and lined with shady walkways. The effect is familiar and elegant, but hollow in spirit. You can walk for blocks and blocks and not spot any of the things that make Bangkok wonderful: street vendors, motorcycle taxis, random stores with blaring music. Somerset Maugham said it better in 1923 when driving through Dusit's main streets: 'They seem to await ceremonies and procession. They are like the deserted avenues in the park of a fallen monarch.'

Devotion to the venerated monarch is the primary purpose of an average Bangkokian's visit to Dusit. Many people come to make merit at the bronze statue of Rama V, which stands in military garb at the Royal Plaza. Although originally intended as mere historical commemoration, the statue has quite literally become a religious shrine, where every Tuesday evening thousands of Bangkok residents come to offer candles, flowers (predominantly pink roses), incense and bottles of whisky. Even in the hot noon sun, an imported luxury car might park along the avenue to pray in front of the proud statue.

Rama V is also honoured with an annual festival celebrating his accomplishments in modernising the country, abolishing slavery and maintaining the country's independence as other Southeast Asian countries were being colonised. During this festival (October 23) huge numbers of visitors converge on the plaza, accompanied by cacophonous loudspeakers and attendant food vendors, briefly disrupting Dusit's aloofness with Bangkok's engaging chaos.

For a visitors accustomed to more subdued spaces, Dusit and its well-maintained green spaces will provide a necessary break from Bangkok's incessant noise.

The riverside section of the district is referred to as Thewet and shelters a quiet backpacker scene as well as a popular flower market. Although guesthouses claim almost an entire *soi*, the neighbourhood seems oblivious to the money-making opportunities that come from catering to foreigners. Instead vendors prefer to follow the traditional course of business with Thais, allowing the foreigners to adjust to local customs. Largely a residential neighbourhood, Thewet is packed at rush hour with uniform-clad residents climbing aboard rickety buses for a sweaty commute to the office districts of Silom or Th Sukhumvit. At rush hour, Th Samsen is a near continuous stream of rattletrap buses and screaming túk-túk.

THEWET & DUSIT TOP FIVE

- Dusit Park (below) Victorian sense and Thai sensibilities merge in this royal enclave.
- Dusit Zoo (p90) A place where kids can stretch their legs and imaginations.
- Thewet Flower Market (p179) Orchids and air plants all wait patiently for an adoptive family at this quiet market.
- Thewet riverside restaurants (p129) Soak up the view of the Saphan Rama VIII.
- Wat Benchamabophit (p91) An Italian-marble temple reminiscent of an ice palace.

Orientation

Cradled between Th Samsen and the river, Thewet consists of a series of small *soi* and its name comes from the nearby temple, Wat Ratchathewet. Thewet's pavements are packed with vendors, making for an interesting stroll but an aggravating delay if you're in a rush.

Dusit begins east of Th Samsen and follows Th Phitsanulok and Th Si Ayuthaya to the district's most famous sites of Dusit Park, Dusit Zoo and Wat Benchamabophit. Further east is the present monarch's residence of Chitralada Palace, which is not open to the public. Although the sites are clustered together on the map, the distances between are long dull stretches that make walking seem like crossing a desert. Taxis and buses zoom down the main avenues at regular intervals to take you to your next destination.

Street stalls and food markets are most prolific near Thewet, but eating opportunities dry up quickly as you plunge into the hallowed promenades of Dusit. Be sure to be well watered and fed before embarking into Dusit on foot.

DUSIT PARK Map pp282-3

สวนดุสิต

☎ 0 2628 6300; bounded by Th Ratchawithi, Th U Thong Nai & Th Ratchasima; adult 250B, admission free with Grand Palace ticket; ⏰ 9.30am-4pm; bus 510 & 70

A modern country, King Chulalongkorn pronounced, needed a modern seat of government. And so the king moved the royal court to Dusit where he had built Beaux Arts institutions and Victorian manor houses. The royal residence was removed

Sights   THEWET & DUSIT

TRANSPORT THEWET & DUSIT

Bus Air-con 505 and 510, ordinary 3, 16, 18, 32, 53, 70 and 72

Ferry Tha Thewet

from the cloistered city of Ko Ratanakosin to the open and manicured lawns of Dusit Park. Confectionary buildings of European and Thai fusions housed the members of the royal family in a style that must have seemed as futuristic as today's skyscrapers. Today the maturing art of architecture has been kind to the romantic Victorian period and Dusit Park is a worthwhile escape from Bangkok's chaos and egg-carton Bauhaus buildings.

Because this is royal property, visitors should wear long pants (no capri pants) or long skirts and shirts with sleeves.

The highlight of the park is **Vimanmek Teak Mansion**, said to be the world's largest golden teak mansion. For all of its finery, huge staircases, octagonal rooms and lattice walls that are nothing short of magnificent, it is surprisingly serene and intimate.

Originally constructed on Ko Si Chang in 1868, the mansion was moved to the present site in 1910 and served as Rama V's residence. The interior of the mansion contains various personal effects of the king, and a treasure-trove of early Ratanakosin art objects and antiques. Compulsory English-language tours of the building last an hour. Don't expect to learn a lot en route as the guide's English is quite laboured and tours tend to overlap with one another.

Most rewarding to pretty-house admirers are the performances of Thai classical and folk dances staged beside the mansion at 10.30am and 2pm.

Immediately behind Vimanmek mansion is **Abhisek Dusit Throne Hall**. Visions of Moorish palaces and Victorian mansions must have still been spinning around in the king's head when he commissioned this intricate building of porticoes and fretwork fused with a distinctive Thai character. Built as the throne hall for the palace in 1904, it opens onto a big stretch of lawn and flowerbeds, just like any important European building.

Inside, the heavy ornamentation of the white main room is quite extraordinary, especially if you've been visiting a lot of overwhelmingly gold temples or traditional wooden buildings. Look up to just below the ceiling to see the line of brightly coloured, stained-glass panels in Moorish patterns.

The hall displays regional handiwork crafted by members of the Promotion of Supplementary Occupations & Related Techniques (Support) charity founda-

tion sponsored by Queen Sirikit. Among the exhibits are *mát-mìi* (cotton) and silk textiles, *málaeng tháp* collages (made from metallic, multicoloured beetle wings), damascene and nielloware, and *yaan líphao* basketry (a style of basketry using a type of vine).

Built in the early 1900s by Italian architects, the great neoclassical dome of the **Ananta Samakh** anchors Royal Plaza. The building is still used for its intended purpose: hosting foreign dignitaries. Frescoes in the dome ceiling depict the monarchs and the important works of the Chakri dynasty. The first meeting of the Thai parliament was held in this building before being moved to a facility nearby.

Beside the Th U Thong Nai gate, the **Royal Elephant Museum** showcases two large stables that once housed three white elephants, whose auspicious albinism automatically made them crown property. One of the structures contains photos and artefacts outlining the importance of elephants in Thai history, and explains their various rankings according to physical characteristics. The second stable holds a sculptural representation of a living royal white elephant kept at Chitralada Palace, home to the current Thai king. Draped in royal vestments, the statue is more or less treated as a shrine by the visiting Thai public.

Near the Th Ratchawithi entrance, two residence halls display the **HM King Bhumibol Photography Exhibitions**, a collection of photographs and paintings by the present monarch. Among the many loving photos of his wife and children are pictures of the king playing clarinet with Benny Goodman and Louis Armstrong in 1960.

Near the photography exhibits, the **Ancient Cloth Museum** presents a beautiful collection of traditional silks and cottons that make up the royal cloth collection.

DUSIT ZOO Map pp282-3
สวนสัตว์ดุสิต(เขาดิน)

☎ 0 2281 2000; Th Ratchawithi; adult/child 50/30B; ⏱ 8.30am-6pm; air-con bus 510, ordinary bus 18 & 28

The collection of animals at Bangkok's 19-hectare zoo comprises more than 300 mammals, 200 reptiles and 800 birds, including relatively rare indigenous species. Originally a private botanic garden for

Rama V, Dusit Zoo (Suan Sat Dusit or *khǎo din*) was opened in 1938 and is now one of the premier zoological facilities in Southeast Asia. The shady grounds feature trees labelled in English plus a lake in the centre with paddle boats for rent. There's also a small children's playground.

If nothing else, the zoo is a nice place to get away from the noise of the city and observe how the Thais amuse themselves – mainly by eating. A couple of lakeside restaurants serve good, inexpensive Thai food. Sunday can be a bit crowded – if you want the zoo mostly to yourself, go on a weekday.

WAT BENCHAMABOPHIT Map pp282-3
วัดเบญจมบพิตร (วัดเบญฯ)

☎ 0 2282 7413; cnr Th Si Ayuthaya & Th Phra Ram V; admission 20B; ⏰ 8am-5.30pm; ordinary bus 72
The closest Thailand will come to an ice palace, this temple of white Carrara marble (hence its alternate name, 'Marble Temple') was built at the turn of the century under Rama V. The large cruciform *bòt* is a prime example of modern Thai temple architecture. The base of the central Buddha image, a copy of Phra Phuttha Chinnarat in Phitsanulok, holds the ashes of Rama V. The courtyard behind the *bòt* has 53 Buddha images (33 originals and 20 copies) representing famous figures and styles from Thailand and other Buddhist countries – it's a great way to compare Buddhist iconography. If religious details aren't for you, this temple offers a pleasant stroll beside landscaped canals filled with blooming lotus and Chinese-style footbridges.

CHINATOWN
Eating p130; Shopping p179; Sleeping p198
Although many generations removed from the mainland, Bangkok's Chinatown could be a bosom brother of any Chinese city. The streets are crammed with shark-fin restaurants, gaudy yellow gold and jade shops, flashing neon signs in Chinese characters, and warbling Chinese crooners. But these characteristics are just window dressing for the soul of the neighbourhood: the tenacious entrepreneurial spirit.

Immigrants from the Teochew region of China came en masse to Bangkok as labourers in the late 1700s, during the creation of the new capital. Most came as impoverished peasants, started menial jobs and eventually established business empires. A pepper grinder who had a stall on Th Charoen Krung eventually tugged at his bootstraps hard enough to corner the country's herbal export trade. This was a breeding ground for such rags-to-riches stories, and many immigrant family names are now affixed to some of the country's largest businesses and economic engines. Thais have been ambivalent in their long-running relationship with this immigrant group. The peasant newcomers were despised until their fortunes turned; today attitudes are complimentary, now that affluence, rather than poverty, is the norm. The umbilical cord to the cultural motherland is still strong, but many descendants of immigrants consider themselves 100% Thai. The influence of the Chinese and their integration within the Bangkok community means that almost every Bangkokian claims some Chinese

Sights

CHINATOWN

GET LOST

Getting lost is the best gift Bangkok gives to visitors. Maps are never 100% accurate, neither are direction-givers, and every venture to the unknown is usually a wild-goose chase.

Chinatown (Map pp284–5) is a great neighbourhood to get lost in. Streets get whittled down into alleys, alleys into hallways, hallways into dead ends. On certain corners itinerant vendors give 'threading' facials, where taut strings are used to remove excess facial hair for the bearded ladies among us. There are also strange and greasy machine-shop districts that would make your mum clutch her purse.

Communities that run alongside the remaining canals are so modest that they nearly resemble slums. **Khlong Lawt** (Map pp286–7), **Khlong Saen Saeb** (Map pp286–7) and **Khlong Ong Ang** (Map pp284–5) are worth a look but you'd better go now, before a Bangkok official decides that tourists don't like anything from earlier than 1983.

Streets that are filled with the old yellow-and-green shophouses are reminders of Bangkok's connection to other port cities, like Singapore and Penang. **Th Atsadang** (Map pp284–5) and **Th Phra Sumen** (Map pp286–7) have some of the best examples built by middle-class merchants. The columns and ornate façades of the warehouses and shops near **Tha Tien** (Map p288) show off the success of wealthier businesses.

ancestry, a characteristic not prevalent in the rest of the country.

As the years go by, Bangkok's Chinatown will become less of a commercial core and more of a symbolic centre. That trend is already happening as the middle class flees the cramped district to the new suburbs (*mùu bâan* in Thai). For now, though, Chinese is the district's primary language, sometimes mixed with Thai to form a motley language soup spoken in the depths of the winding neighbourhood *soi*. Goods, people and services are on a continuous conveyor belt into and out of the area. The neighbourhood is self-segregated by profession with whole streets or blocks dedicated to sign making, gold and jewellery stores, and machine and tyre shops.

During Chinese New Year the neighbourhood swings into a joyous mood, with an increased number of vendors and shoppers haggling over auspicious gifts and tokens. Chinese calligraphers also join the pavement commerce.

At the western edge of Chinatown, near the intersection of Th Phahurat and Th Chakraphet, is a small but thriving Indian and Islamic district, generally called Phahurat or Little India. The dim alleys and affinity for commerce tie these two heritages together, although their particular expressions provide a fascinating diversity.

Orientation

Chinatown fans out along Mae Nam Chao Phraya between Saphan Phra Phuttha Yot Fa to the west and Hualamphong Railway Station to the east. Th Yaowarat and Th Charoen Krung are Chinatown's main arteries and provide the greatest diversity of services, from shopping and eating to promenading in the styles popular on the Chinese mainland, such as oversized designer sunglasses and chest-high pants. At night the district feels like a carnival, with the merriment of banquet dining and the dazzling spectacle of neon lights.

TRANSPORT CHINATOWN

Bus Air-con 507 and 508, ordinary 53, 73 and 75

Ferry Tha Ratchawong

Subway Hualamphong

CHINATOWN TOP FIVE

- **Talat Noi** (opposite) Stroll through this cramped neighbourhood of oil-stained machine shops.
- **Phahurat** (below) Bollywood-style markets of flashy colours and sequins galore.
- **Sampeng Lane** (p179) Regimented chaos and commerce are staged deep in the bowels of this outdoor market.
- **Seafood stalls** (p131) Devour such delicacies as king prawns and oysters while teetering on the edge of the gutter.
- **Wat Traimit** (p94) Meet the temple's handsome golden Buddha.

Getting into and out of the area by bus or cab is nearly impossible due to an impenetrable stream of traffic. The best transport is the river ferry, which will deliver you within a short walk of the heart of Chinatown. Walking is the most efficient and entertaining way to get around the neighbourhood. Follow the little *soi* into the claustrophobic pathways past warehouses and trinket shops, or walk west to see the subtle transition from Chinatown to Little India.

HUALAMPHONG RAILWAY
STATION Map pp284-5
สถานีรถไฟหัวลำโพง
Th Phra Ram IV; air-con bus 501, ordinary bus 25 & 75; subway Hualamphong

At the southeastern edge of Chinatown, Bangkok's main train station was built by Dutch architects and engineers just before WWI. It is one of the city's earliest and most outstanding examples of the movement towards Thai Art Deco, and the vaulted iron roof and neoclassical portico demonstrate an engineering feat that was state of the art in its time, while the patterned, two-toned skylights exemplify pure de Stijl Dutch modernism.

PHAHURAT Map pp284-5
พาหุรัด
West of Th Chakrawat; ferry Tha Saphan Phut, ordinary bus 53 & 73

Fabric and gem traders set up shop in this small but bustling Little India. Behind the more obvious storefronts are winding alleys that criss-cross Khlong Ong Ang where

Shopping for fabrics in Phahurat (opposite)

considered the last of the religion's 10 great gurus or teachers. *Prasada* (blessed food offered to Hindu or Sikh temple attendees) is distributed among devotees every morning around 9am, and if you arrive on a Sikh festival day you can partake in the *langar* (communal Sikh meal) served in the temple. Stores surrounding the temple sell religious paraphernalia.

TALAT NOI Map pp284-5
ตลาดน้อย

Bounded by the river, Th Songwat, Th Charoen Krung & Th Yotha; ferry Tha Si Phraya
This microcosm of *soi* life is named after a little market that once set up between Soi 22 and Soi 20, off Th Charoen Krung, selling goods from China. Streamlike *soi* turn in on themselves, weaving through people's living rooms, noodle shops and grease-stained machine shops. Opposite the River View Guesthouse, **San Jao Sien Khong** (unnamed *soi;* admission by donation; 6am-6pm) is one of the city's oldest Chinese shrines and is guarded by a playful rooftop terracotta dragon. A former owner of the shrine made his fortune collecting taxes on bird-nest delicacies.

merchants grab a bite to eat or make travel arrangements for trips home.

Just off Th Chakraphet is **Sri Gurusingh Sabha** (Th Phahurat; 9am-5pm), a gold-domed Sikh temple best viewed from Soi ATM. Basically it's a large hall, somewhat reminiscent of a mosque interior, devoted to the worship of the Guru Granth Sahib, the 16th-century Sikh holy book which is itself

SUPER SALE ON AISLE 9: CHINATOWN'S SHOPPING STREETS

Chinatown is the neighbourhood version of a big-box store divided up into categories of consumables.

Th Charoen Krung (Map pp284–5) Chinatown's primary thoroughfare is a prestigious address. Starting on the western end of the street, near the intersection of Th Mahachai, is a collection of old record stores. Talat Khlong Ong Ang consumes the next block, selling all sorts of used and new electronic gadgets. Nakhon Kasem is the reformed thieves' market where vendors now stock up on nifty gadgets for portable food prep. Further east, near Th Mahachak is Talat Khlong Thom, a hardware centre. West of Th Ratchawong, everything is geared towards the afterlife and the passing of life.

Th Yaowarat (Map pp284–5) A hundred years ago, this was a poultry farm; now it is gold street, the biggest trading centre of the precious metal in the country. Shops are always painted like the interior of a Chinese shrine: blood red and decorated with well-groomed toy dogs. Near the intersection of Th Ratchawong, stores shift to Chinese and Singaporean tourists' tastes: dried fruits and nuts, chintzy talismans and accoutrements for Chinese festivals. The multistorey buildings around Th Ratchawong were some of Bangkok's first skyscrapers and a source of wonder for the local people. There are a few Chinese apothecaries still around that smell like wood bark and ancient secrets.

Th Mittraphan (Map pp284–5) Sign makers branch off Wong Wian 22 July; Thai and Roman letters are typically cut out by a hand-guided lathe placed prominently beside the pavement.

Th Santiphap (Map pp284–5) Car parts and other automotive gear make this the place for kicking tyres.

Sampeng Lane (Soi Wanit 1; Map pp284–5) Plastic cuteness in bulk, from pencil cases to pens, stuffed animals and hair flotsam, all hang out near the eastern end of the alley. As it approaches Phahurat, every store switches stock to bolts of synthetic fabric.

Trok Itsaranuphap (Map pp284–5) An ancient fresh market splays along the southern portion of this cramped alley. After crossing Th Charoen Krung, funerary items for ritual burnings dominate the open-air stalls.

WAT MANGKON KAMALAWATT Map pp284-5
วัดมังกรกมลาวาส

☎ 0 2222 3975; Th Charoen Krung; ⏱ 9am-6pm; air-con bus 508, ordinary bus 73, ferry Tha Ratchawong

Explore the cryptlike sermon halls of this busy Chinese temple (also known as Leng Noi Yee) to find Buddhist, Taoist and Confucian shrines. During the annual Vegetarian Festival (p13), religious and culinary activities are centred here. But almost any time of day or night, this temple is packed with worshippers lighting incense, filling the ever-burning altar lamps with oil and making offerings to their ancestors. Offering oil is believed to provide a smooth journey into the afterlife and to fuel the fire of life. Mangkon Kamalawatt means 'Dragon Lotus Temple'. Surrounding the temple are vendors selling food for the gods – steamed lotus-shaped dumplings and oranges – that are used for merit making.

WAT TRAIMIT Map pp284-5
วัดไตรมิตร

☎ 0 2225 9775; cnr Th Yaowarat & Th Charoen Krung; admission 20B; ⏱ 9am-5pm; ferry Tha Ratchawong, ordinary bus 25 & 53, subway Hualamphong

Forgive us for being crabby, but there are some tourist attractions that don't seem to live up to the hype. Wat Traimit (Temple of the Golden Buddha) is one. Sure the gleaming, 3m-tall, 5.5-tonne, solid-gold Buddha image is handsome. But the precious figure is housed in a room so small it could double as a broom closet. And because the temple is firmly cemented in every tour guide's itinerary, tourists always outnumber worshippers. You don't need to travel across an ocean to watch people taking pictures or forgetting to take their shoes off.

The one redeeming thing about this temple is the mechanical horoscope machines that look like an import from a boardwalk amusement centre. Put a 5B coin in the machine that corresponds to the day of the week you were born, lights flash mystically and then a number appears that corresponds to a printed fortune.

If you'd like to know more about the main attraction, the Golden Buddha is sculpted in the graceful Sukhothai style

(notice the hair curls and elongated earlobes). The image was 'rediscovered' some 40 years ago beneath a plaster exterior when it fell from a crane while being moved to a new building within the temple compound. It has been theorised that the covering was added to protect it from marauding hordes, either during the late Sukhothai period or later in the Ayuthaya period when the city was under siege by the Burmese. The temple itself is said to date from the early 13th century.

SIAM SQUARE, PRATUNAM & PLOENCHIT

Eating p131; Shopping p180; Sleeping p199

Bangkok normally abhors organisation but this central shopping district is uncharacteristically convenient for unleashing cash. Bangkok's baht-flexing teenagers rule the closet-sized boutiques of Siam Square, an ageing open-air mall that dictates what's hot and what's not. Sealing out the elements are the modern shopping malls, like Mahboonkrong (MBK), Siam Discovery Center and Central World Plaza, that suck in passengers directly from the elevated footpaths of the Skytrain.

This is modern Bangkok, where flimsy fashion is no longer a saffron monk's robe but a flouncy skirt and clicky heels. Packs of teenagers shuffle across the concrete pathways, breaking every social more their ancestors ever created. Female students wear barely-there miniskirts, cutesy couples stroll hand-in-hand, hipsters (dèk naew) assume gangster styles from ghettos they've only heard rapped about. Give Bangkok another 10 years of disposable income and the city will join Tokyo and New York for pop power.

Behind the modern façade is a simple village of modest means centred on one of Bangkok's most famous canals, the soot-coloured Khlong Saen Saeb. Lined with rickety wooden shacks, drying laundry and the exposed interior of daily life, the khlong is the primary plumbing for many of its residents. Kids bathe in the water as morning commuter boats buzz by, housewives rinse out the family's dishes, and unwanted items are discarded into the murky depths.

Baan Krua, originally founded by immigrants from Cambodia and one of the city's most famous slums, has successfully fought off highway-construction plans to remain an intact village. The silk-weaving skills of early occupants caught the attention of Jim Thompson, a long-time Bangkok resident who developed the village's woven work into an international commodity.

The ever-present noise and suffocating exhaust fumes that clog this district fuel Bangkok's image as an unpleasant and difficult place to visit. In an attempt to spare their lungs, many residents wear surgical-style face masks with about as much ease as Easter bonnets. Oblivious to the pollution, pavement food vendors and shoe repairers return to their open-air shops every day, taking few or no health precautions.

Despite the intense sprawl, this area is a perfect concert between old and new Bangkok. The crowds file in and out of air-conditioned comfort, virtually ignoring the quiet cultural attractions of traditional wooden houses and Thai antiques. Conveniently located on the Skytrain line, this is also a central post for quick trips to other city points.

Orientation

Bangkok's miracle mile of shopping centres lines Th Phra Ram I from the corner of Th Phayathai to Th Chitlom. Pathumwan district is defined by the Th Phra Ram I and Th Phayathai intersection, including the area around the National Stadium (Map pp280–1). South of Th Phra Ram I, along Th Phayathai, is the campus of Chulalongkorn University, one of Thailand's most prestigious schools. At the Th Phra Ram I intersection of Th Ratchadamri, the area known as Ratchaprasong supports

SIAM SQUARE, PRATUNAM & PLOENCHIT TOP FIVE

- Erawan Shrine (p98) A modern expression of religion in the landscape.
- Jim Thompson's House (p97) A teak mansion with a junglelike garden and informative tours.
- Khlong Saen Saeb Canal Taxis (p241) Commute with the locals aboard the scrappy boats that trundle past canal ghettos.
- Mahboonkrong (MBK; p181) Indulge in air-con, junk food and plastic stuff.
- Wang Suan Phakkat (p107) Pretend you're a minor Thai royal in the quiet museum grounds.

the city's second outpost of luxury hotels, primarily serving businesspeople and holidaying shoppers. Heading north on Th Ratchadamri leads to Pratunam district, on the northern side of Khlong Saen Saeb. The huge shopping centres dissipate here into smaller markets and cottage industries, and wandering the *soi* offers an exploration of a human-sized environment. Pratunam is also home to Thailand's tallest skyscraper, the Baiyoke Skytower.

Also included in this section is the area extending east along Th Ploenchit and Th Withayu (Wireless Rd), where many embassies and expatriates reside. Lined with trees and expensive condo towers, Soi Lang Suan is the closest Bangkok comes to Fifth Avenue.

BANGKOK DOLL FACTORY & MUSEUM Map pp280-1
พิพิธภัณฑ์ตุ๊กตาบางกอกดอล
☎ 0 2235 3008; 85 Soi Ratchataphan (Soi Mo Leng), Th Ratchaprarop; admission free; ☼ 8.30am-5pm Mon-Sat; ordinary bus 62 & 77
Khungying Tongkorn Chandevimol became interested in dolls while living in Japan. Upon her return to Thailand, she began researching and making dolls, drawing from Thai mythology and historical periods. Today her personal collection of dolls from all over the world and important dolls from her own workshop are on display. You can also view the small factory where family members continue to craft the figures that are now replicated and sold throughout Thailand's tourist markets. A large selection of her dolls are also for sale.

It is difficult to find this well-hidden spot, but perseverance will reward any doll lover, especially the pint-sized connoisseurs. The museum is in Ratchathewi and is best approached via Th Si Ayuthaya heading east. Cross under the expressway past the intersection with Th Ratchaprarop and take the *soi* to the right of the post office. Follow this windy street until you start seeing signs.

CONTEMPORARY ART

A few decades ago, modern art in Thailand meant two things: imitation of Western styles or modern renditions of Buddha figures. But the 1990s changed all that. Increasing globalisation, foreign educations, and the economic crisis and subsequent recovery fuelled a visually stunning debate on canvas, in sculpture and through installations.

Artists not only changed the subjects they were 'allowed' to talk about, they also changed the venues where modern art and the public could meet, enabling greater freedom and creativity. Previously, the government-sponsored galleries narrowly defined what was and wasn't art. Now, young creatives have begun to put art into a social context, in bars and restaurants. This is more than just a business gimmick; it is revolutionary for a culture bound by social hierarchy. Commercial galleries provide yet another stage for young artists to interact with the public's questions about technique and intention. Despite the air of sophistication, exhibition openings pour liberal doses of Thailand's famed hospitality as well as free drinks.

In typical Bangkok style, the art scene lacks a centre. Socially, many artists and their work gather at the bohemian cafés along Th Phra Athit, while the commercial galleries prefer the business districts of Th Silom and Th Sukhumvit. **Eat Me Restaurant** (p136) shows rotating exhibits organised by H Gallery, and photography gets its just desserts at **Gallery F-Stop**, which shares space with **Tamarind Café** (p144). Art museums focusing on Thai artists, past and present, include the **National Gallery** (p75) and the **Queen's Gallery** (p86).

For profiles of Thai modern artists, pick up a copy of *Flavours: Thai Contemporary Art*, by Steven Pettifor, a leading Bangkok art critic. **Rama IX Museum** (www.rama9art.org) is an online resource for artists' portfolios and gallery profiles. Pick up a copy of the free *Art Connection* brochure for a map of contemporary galleries, or check the lifestyle magazines for exhibition opening nights.

The following is a list of noteworthy commercial and university galleries:

100 Tonson Gallery (Map pp294–5; ☎ 0 2684 1527; www.100tonsongallery.com; 100 Soi Tonson, Th Ploenchit; ☯ 11am-7pm Thu-Sat; Skytrain Chitlom) Pop aesthetics from big international and local names.

About Café\About Studio (Map pp284–5; ☎ 0 2639 8057; 418 Th Maitrichit; ☯ hours vary; subway Hualamphong) Considered the cool cat in town for cutting-edge Thai artists working in alternative and experimental media.

Bangkok University Art Gallery (Map pp278–9; ☎ 0 2350 3500; 3rd fl, Bldg 9, City Campus, Th Rama IV; ☯ 9.30am-7pm Tues-Sat) Bangkok's most experimental art school showcases emerging and established artists.

H Gallery (Map pp290–1; ☎ 0 1310 4428; www.hgallerybkk.com; 201 Soi 12, Th Sathon; ☯ noon-6pm Thu-Sat; Skytrain Chong Nongsi) Leading commercial gallery with ties to New York City galleries for emerging Thai abstract painters.

Jamjuree Gallery (Map pp280–1; ☎ 0 2218 3708/9; Jamjuree Bldg 8, Chulalongkorn University, Th Phayathai; ☯ 10am-7pm Mon-Fri, noon-6pm Sat & Sun; Skytrain Siam, subway Samyan) Chula university gallery for students' shows and affordable prices.

Numthong Gallery (☎ 0 2243 4326; Room 109, Bangkok Co-op Bldg, Th Toeddamri, Dusit; ☯ 11am-6pm Mon-Sat; Skytrain Ari) Shares space with artist collective Project 304 and focuses primarily on Thai artists.

Play Gallery (Map pp296–7; ☎ 0 2714 7888; www.playgroundstore.co.th; Playground!, 2nd fl, 818 Th Sukhumvit, Soi 55; ☯ 10am-11pm; Skytrain Thong Lor) Mainly urban and street art showcased in a design concept mall.

Surapon Gallery (Map pp292–3; ☎ 0 2638 0033-4; ☯ 11am-6pm Mon-Sat; 1st fl, Tisco Tower, Th Sathon; Skytrain Sala Daeng, subway Lumphini) Contemporary interpretations of Thai handicrafts with social messages.

Tadu Contemporary Art (Map pp278–9; ☎ 0 2645 2473; www.tadu.net; 7th fl, Barcelona Motors Bldg, 99/2 Th Thiam Ruammit; ☯ Mon-Sat 9:30am-6pm; subway Thailand Cultural Centre) Leading exhibition space for cutting-edge artists working in performance and installation art.

Tang Gallery (Map pp290–1; ☎ 0 2630 1114; basement, Silom Galleria, 91 9/1 Th Silom; ☯ 11am-7pm Mon-Sat) Bangkok's primary venue for modern artists from China.

Thavibu Gallery (Map pp290–1; ☎ 0 2266 5454; www.thavibu.com; 3rd fl, Silom Galleria, 91 9/1 Th Silom; ☯ 11am-7pm Tue-Sat, noon-6pm Sun) Artists from Cambodia, Thailand and Myanmar.

CHULALONGKORN
UNIVERSITY Map pp280-1
จุฬาลงกรณ์มหาวิทยาลัย

☎ 0 2215 0871; www.chula.ac.th; 254 Th Phayathai; air-con bus 502, ordinary bus 21, Skytrain
Siam, subway Samyan

Thailand's oldest and most prestigious university nestles into a leafy enclave south of
busy Th Phra Ram I. The centrepiece of the
campus is the promenade ground on the
east side of Th Phayathai where a seated
statue of Rama V (King Chulalongkorn) is
surrounded by purple bougainvillea and
offerings of pink carnations. The showcase
buildings display the architectural fusion
the monarch favoured, a mix of Italian
revival and Thai traditional. The campus has
a parklike quality, with noble tropical trees
considerately labelled for plant geeks. Of
the many species that shade the campus,
the rain trees with their delicate leaves are
considered symbolic of the school, even
commemorated in a school song, and the
deciduous cycle matches the beginning
and ending of each school year.

The university has two art galleries,
Jamjuree and the **Chulalongkorn Art Centre**
(Map pp280–1; ☎ 0 2218 2965; www.car
.chula.ac.th; Centre of Academic Resources
Bldg, 7th fl, Chulalongkorn University, Th
Phayathai; ⏰ 10am-7pm Mon-Fri; Skytrain
Siam, subway Samyan). The latter shows
Chula professors as well as major names
in the Thai and international modern art
scene; permanent exhibits include Thai art
retrospectives.

On the west side of Th Phayathai is the
teak **Thai Pavilion**, in which the Center of Arts
and Culture performs cultural displays on
the first Friday of each month.

JIM THOMPSON'S HOUSE Map pp294-5
บ้านจิมทอมป์สัน

☎ 0 2216 7368, 0 2215 0122; www.jimthompson
house.org; 6 Soi Kasem San 2, Th Phra Ram I;
adult/child 100/50B; ⏰ 9am-5pm; khlong taxi to
Tha Ratchathewi, Skytrain National Stadium

An A-plus museum for pretty things, Jim
Thompson's house is every faràng's (Westerner's) dream residence. American Jim
Thompson was an eagle-eyed collector of
Thai things, from residential architecture
to Southeast Asian art. He lived amid his
treasures at the end of an undistinguished
soi next to Khlong Saen Saeb in a house
that is now open to the public.

Jim Thompson's House

Born in Delaware in 1906, Thompson was
a New York architect who briefly served in
the Office of Strategic Services (a forerun-
ner of the CIA) in Thailand during WWII.
After the war he found New York too tame
compared to his beloved Bangkok. The
Thai silk that his neighbours made in the
adjacent village caught his eye and he sent
samples to fashion houses in Milan, London
and Paris, gradually building a worldwide
clientele for a craft that was in danger of
dying out.

A tireless promoter of traditional Thai
arts and culture, Thompson collected parts
of various derelict Thai homes in central
Thailand and had them reassembled in the
current location in 1959. Although for the
most part they're assembled in typical Thai
style, one striking departure from tradition
is the way each wall has its exterior side
facing the house's interior, thus exposing
the wall's bracing system.

While out for an afternoon walk in the
Cameron Highlands of western Malaysia in
1967, Thompson disappeared under mysterious circumstances and has never been
heard from since. That same year his sister
was murdered in the USA, fuelling various
conspiracy theories to explain the disappearance. Was it communist spies? Business
rivals? A man-eating tiger? The most recent

97

BANGKOK FOR FREE

The value of the Thai baht in international currencies might turn misers into spendthrifts, but there are still plenty of cheap and even free outings in the city.

Jet lag can be a blessing in Bangkok; it gets you up early enough to see the parade of uniforms: schoolchildren, all elbows and knees, hustle off to school wearing naval-inspired outfits; barefoot novice monks wrapped up in saffron robes make their morning alms route between the devout grandmothers freshly powdered in their tailored polyester shirts; government office workers swagger through the sidewalks in their khaki civil-servant garb; and shopkeepers in market knock-offs sweep out the stores and set out breakfast for the business' guardian spirits.

In the evenings, Bangkok really comes alive. The *soi* dogs wake up from their siesta and trot about town after a meal and a little tail, not much different than their human counterparts. Break dancers practise their moves on the elevated walkway in front of the National Stadium and Victory Monument Skytrain station. These two walkways are like urban parks with cuddling couples, illegal markets and lots of fashion exhibitionism.

More spectacular and synchronised are the evening aerobics classes in **Lumphini Park** (p109) and **Santichaiprakan Park** (p86). The techno beat, setting sun and crowd of bouncing bodies attracts many onlookers unabashed about laughing at the spectacle as well as participants.

---

theory (for which there is apparently some hard evidence) is that the silk magnate was accidentally run over by a Malaysian truck driver who hid his remains.

The Legendary American: The Remarkable Career & Strange Disappearance of Jim Thompson by William Warren, is an excellent book on Thompson, his career, house and intriguing disappearance.

Beware of well-dressed touts in the *soi* who will tell you Thompson's house is closed – it's just a ruse to take you on a buying spree. Admission proceeds go to Bangkok's School for the Blind.

LINGAM SHRINE Map pp294-5
ศาลเจ้าแม่ทับทิม
Nai Lert Park Hotel, Th Withayu; khlong taxi to Tha Withayu, Skytrain Ploenchit

Every village-neighbourhood has a local shrine, either a sacred banyan tree tied up with coloured scarves or a spirit house. But it isn't everyday you see a phallus garden, like the lingam shrine (Saan Jao Mae Thap Thim), tucked back behind the staff quarters of Nai Lert Park. Clusters of carved stone and wooden phalluses surround a spirit house and shrine built by millionaire businessman Nai Loet to honour Jao Mae Thap Thim, a female deity thought to reside in the old banyan tree on the site. Someone who made an offering shortly after the shrine was built had a baby, and the shrine has received a steady stream of worshippers – mostly young women seeking fertility – ever since.

If facing the entrance of the hotel, follow the small concrete pathway to the right, which winds down into the guts of the

building beside the car park. The shrine is at the end of the building next to the *khlong*.

RATCHAPRASONG INTERSECTION SHRINES Map pp294-5
Cnr Th Ratchadamri & Th Ploenchit; Skytrain Chitlom

A crowd in this part of town usually means a bargain market is nearby. But in this case the continuous activity revolves around the Hindu shrines credited for making this commercial corridor a success.

Beside the Erawan Hotel, **Erawan Shrine** (San Phra Phrom) is one of Bangkok's most famous contemporary shrines. The centrepiece is Brahma, the four-headed Hindu god of creation, who commands great respect in Thai Buddhism but not enough to warrant such popularity. The human traffic jam can be directly attributed to the perceived powers of the shrine during its 50-year history. Originally, a simple Thai spirit house occupied this spot during the construction of the original Erawan Hotel (named after Erawan, Indra's three-headed elephant mount). After several serious mishaps delayed the hotel's construction, the developers erected this Brahman shrine to ward off future injuries. Eventually the shrine took on an independent cult of its own and is perceived as a harbinger of material success.

Worshippers continuously cycle through, laying down marigold garlands or raising a cluster of joss sticks to their foreheads in prayer. They come to ask for good luck, health, wealth and love. When wishes are

(Continued on page 107)

1 *Diners at a riverside restaurant, Ko Ratanakosin (p126)* 2 *Sweets for sale (p55)* 3 *Pots of Thai curries at Talat Aw Taw Kaw (p146)* 4 *Street vendor selling fruit (p54)*

1 *The delights of Bangkok street food (p126)* 2 *One of Bangkok's myriad stir-fries (p53)* 3 *Vegetables and spices* 4 *Selection of meals*

1 *BTS Skytrain (p242)* 2 Chedi *(stupas) at Wat Pho (p78)*
3 *Interior of the River City Complex (p185)* 4 *Neon signs and traffic on Soi Thaniya in Patpong (p157)*

1 *Musician playing the drum at Erawan Shrine (p98)* **2** *Demon statue at the entrance to the ordination hall at Wat Arun (p82)* **3** *Murals depicting scenes from the Ramakian around the perimeter of the Wat Phra Kaew complex (p79)* **4** *Democracy Monument (p85)*

1 *Wat Phra Kaew (p79)* 2 *Display at the amulet market (p169)*
3 *Visitors enjoying the landscaped courtyard of the National Museum (p75)* 4 *Fortune teller in front of Wat Mahathat (p78)*

1 *Wat Arun (p82) at dusk*
2 *Royal barge (p82)* **3** *Making alms bowls the traditional way at Monk's Bowl Village (p85)*
4 *Golden Mount chedi (stupa; p87)*

1 *Riverside tables at Kaloang Home Kitchen (p129)* **2** *Paintings by local children decorate the walls at Dusit Zoo (p90)* **3** *Wat Benchamabophit (p91)* **4** *Thewet Flower Market (p179)*

1 *Dim sum on sale in Chinatown (p130)* **2** *Shopping for fabrics at Talat Phahurat (p179)* **3** *People and túk-túks outside Hualamphong Railway Station (p92)* **4** *Decorated pillar at the entrance to Wat Mangkon Kamalawatt (p94) in Chinatown*

(Continued from page 98)

granted, the worshippers show their gratitude by commissioning shrine musicians and dancers for a performance. The tinkling tempo, throaty bass and colourful dancers elevate the crowd into a celestial other world far from the ordinary street corner surrounded by idling cars and self-absorbed shoppers.

The businesses posted on the other cardinal points of the intersection have erected their own Hindu shrines in order to counter and copy the power of the Erawan Shrine, which is perceived to have made the Erawan Hotel a long-running success with upper-crust society. On the opposite side of the street is the **Trimurthi Shrine** (San Trimurthi), in front of the Central World Plaza. This shrine depicts the three supreme Hindu gods (Shiva, Vishnu and Brahma) and symbolises creation, destruction and preservation. On Tuesdays, many Thai teenagers come to this shrine to ask for success in love.

WANG SUAN PHAKKAT Map pp280–1
วังสวนผักกาด

☎ 0 2245 4934; Th Si Ayuthaya, btwn Th Phayathai & Th Ratchaprarop; admission 100B; ⊗ 9am-4pm; ordinary bus 72, Skytrain Phayathai

Everyone loves Jim Thompson's house, but no one has even heard of Wang Suan Phakkat (Lettuce Farm Palace), another noteworthy traditional Thai house museum. Once the residence of Princess Chumbon of Nakhon Sawan, the museum is a collection of five traditional wooden Thai houses linked by elevated walkways containing varied displays of art, antiques and furnishings. The landscaped grounds are a peaceful oasis complete with ducks, swans and a semienclosed, Japanese-style garden.

The diminutive **Lacquer Pavilion** at the back of the complex dates from the Ayuthaya period (the building originally sat in a monastery compound on the banks of Mae Nam Chao Phraya, just south of Ayuthaya) and features gold-leaf *Jataka* and Ramayana murals as well as scenes from daily Ayuthaya life. Larger residential structures at the front of the complex contain displays of Khmer, Hindu and Buddhist art, Ban Chiang ceramics and a collection of historic Buddhas, including a beautiful late–U Thong–style image. In the noise and confusion of Bangkok, the gardens offer a tranquil retreat.

RIVERSIDE, SILOM & LUMPHINI

Eating p135; Shopping p185; Sleeping p204, p201

During Bangkok's shipping heyday, the city faced outward toward the river to welcome foreign trading ships and European envoys. All along the Mae Nam Chao Phraya are the remnants of this mercantile era: the ornate French embassy, the crumbling Customs House and the elegant Oriental Hotel. On land, little lanes wind through abandoned warehouses, gated headquarters of ancient shipping companies, and the Muslim and Indian communities that replaced the European presence.

Th Charoen Krung, which runs parallel to the river and links Th Silom with Chinatown, was Bangkok's first paved road and was brought about by European residents who wanted a place for their horses and buggies. The water-based society complied so readily with the landlubbers' wishes that nearly all the canal routes are now asphalt. Today Charoen Krung is lined with silk and jewellery businesses targeted at the wealthy tourists staying at the riverside luxury hotels. Back behind the commercial façade is the residential section where curry shops are more likely to serve Indian-style roti than rice, and culturally mandated silken headdresses distinguish Muslim Thais from their Buddhist sisters.

As industries changed from commodities to intellectual property, the financial district migrated inland along Th Silom, which was once the outskirts of the riverside city. Windmills ('*silom*' in Thai) once dotted the landscape, conveying water to the area's rice fields. Silom's unpopulated past is illustrated in the European and Chinese cemeteries around Soi 11; many of the graves there had to be moved as the city grew around what was then the end of the earth.

Today Silom experiences a daily tide of people. Workers flood into the office towers in the morning, are released into the streets for lunch and return home aboard public transport in the evening. Foreigners sweat in their imported suits, maintaining the corporate appearance of New York and London in styles that are ill suited for the tropics. Thai secretaries prefer polyester suits that are sold off the rack at small markets, alongside bulk toiletries and thick-heeled sandals. Workers returning to the office after lunch are usually loaded down with plastic bags of food for midafternoon snacks: in Thailand the snack table is the equivalent of the Western water cooler.

In the heart of the business zone is Bangkok's most infamous attraction, the strip clubs of Patpong. Mainly the stuff of pulp fiction, Patpong has mellowed greatly since its naughty nightlife heyday, but it is no accident that this skin party occurs so close to the buttoned-up world of international business. Accommodating Bangkok knows how to entertain the traditionally male-dominated world of business.

Just when Bangkok seemed hopelessly congested, foresighted city planners built Lumphini Park, the city's central green space, where kids learn to ride bikes, grandmas stretch out stiff joints and Thais maintain their slim physique. Fresh air never tasted so good.

Work and play, not sightseeing, usually bring people to this area of town, but there are a few noteworthy attractions to inject some culture into daily business. Boasting the greatest concentration of skyscrapers, Th Silom is also the hot spot for dinner and drinkers atop a vertigo-inducing roof.

Orientation

Th Silom runs roughly west to east from Th Charoen Krung to Lumphini Park and Th Phra Ram IV. A more residential and small-scale commercial strip is Th Surawong, which runs parallel to Th Silom on the north side.

The modern-day diplomatic enclave is along the highway stretch of Th Sathon, friendly to modern Bangkok's favourite toy, the automobile. Th Sathon runs parallel to Th Silom to the south and is divided into northbound (Th Sathon Neua) and south-

bound (Th Sathon Tai). On a small street off Th Sathon is the Immigration Office, a frequent pilgrimage site for every foreigner living in Bangkok.

Following the course of the river, Th Charoen Krung runs north to south intersecting with these cross-town routes.

Lumphini Park is bounded by Th Sarasin, Th Phra Ram IV, Th Withayu and Th Ratchadamri. East of the park is the new night bazaar and the boxing stadium. Just off the southeastern corner of the park is the area known as Soi Ngam Duphli, the backpacker predecessor of Th Khao San's guesthouse scene.

Th Silom is hopelessly backed up with traffic and is best avoided at almost every hour but daybreak. The Skytrain is a better alternative for reaching destinations on this street, especially during rush hour. Traffic moves more regularly on Th Sathon, if you need to take a cab in or out of the area quickly, or relatively quickly.

BANK OF ASIA Map pp290-1
ธนาคารเอเชีย
Cnr Th Sathon Tai & Soi Pikun; ☒ **not open to the public**
During the crazy 1980s, when no building project was too outlandish or expensive, architect Sumet Jumsai created his now-famous 'Robot Building' for the Bank of Asia. Few were keen on it at the time, but now it seems quaint and retro. The building's whimsical façade is best viewed on the Skytrain between Surasak and Chong Nonsi stations.

RIVERSIDE, SILOM & LUMPHINI TOP FIVE

- Oriental Hotel (p204) Relive the steamship era of globetrotting aristocrats with tea and crumpets at this legendary establishment.
- Lumphini Park (opposite) Stroll among exercisers and exercise-observers in this peaceful park.
- Patpong (p157) Find out how ping-pong has diversified since summer camp.
- Queen Saovabha Memorial Institute (opposite) Confront your fear of snakes at this humanitarian snake farm.
- Sri Mariamman Temple (p110) Thai temples will look austere after you've visited this riotously coloured Hindu building.

TRANSPORT RIVERSIDE, SILOM & LUMPHINI

Bus Air-con 502 and 505, ordinary 15, 22 and 62
Ferry Tha Si Phraya, Tha Oriental and Tha Sathon
Skytrain Sala Daeng, Chong Nonsi and Surasak
Subway Silom and Lumphini

KUKRIT PRAMOJ HOUSE Map pp290-1
บ้านหม่อมราชวงศ์คึกฤทธิ์ปราโมช
☎ 0 2286 8185; Soi 7 (Phra Phinij), Th Narathiwat Ratchankharin; admission 50B; ⏰ 10am-5pm Sat & Sun; Skytrain Chong Nonsi

Author and statesman Mom Ratchawong Kukrit Pramoj once resided in this charming complex now open to the public for tours. Surrounded by a manicured garden, five teak buildings introduce visitors to traditional Thai architecture and to the former resident, who authored more than 150 books (including *Four Reigns*) and served as prime minister of Thailand.

LUMPHINI PARK Map pp292-3
สวนลุมพินี
⏰ 5am-8pm; air-con bus 505, ordinary bus 13, subway Lumphini & Silom, Skytrain Sala Daeng & Ratchadamri

Named after Buddha's birthplace in Nepal, this is Bangkok's largest and most popular park. A big artificial lake in the centre is surrounded by broad, well-tended lawns, wooded areas and walking paths – it's the best outdoor escape from Bangkok without leaving town.

One of the best times to visit the park is in the early morning before 7am, when the air is fresh (well, relatively so for Bangkok) and legions of Chinese are practising t'ai chi. Meanwhile, vendors set up tables to dispense fresh snake's blood and bile, considered health tonics by many Thais and Chinese. A weight-lifting area in one section becomes a miniature 'muscle beach' on weekends. Facilities include a snack bar, an asphalt jogging track, a picnic area, toilets and a couple of tables where women serve Chinese tea.

During the kite-flying season (mid-February to April), Lumphini becomes a favoured flight zone, with kites *(wâo)* for sale in the park.

OLD CUSTOMS HOUSE Map pp290-1
กรมศุลกากร
Soi 36, Th Charoen Krung; ⏰ closed to the public; ferry Tha Oriental

Like other shipping attendants, the Old Customs House front-door faces the river ceremoniously decorated in columns and transom windows. Built in the 1880s, this crumbling edifice now houses the fire brigade and is hauntingly beautiful as its shutters sag from neglect and laundry flaps on the unpainted balconies. There are plans to resurrect this building as the Aman Resort in 2007.

QUEEN SAOVABHA MEMORIAL INSTITUTE (SNAKE FARM) Map pp290-1
สถานเสาวภา
☎ 0 2252 0161; 1871 Th Phra Ram IV; admission 70B; ⏰ 8.30am-4.30pm Mon-Fri, 8.30am-noon Sat & Sun; air-con bus 507, ordinary bus 4, 47 & 50, Skytrain Sala Daeng, subway Samyan

Venomous snakes such as the formidable cobra and pit viper live a peaceful and altruistic existence at this farm affiliated with the Thai Red Cross. The snakes are milked daily to make snake-bite antivenins, which are distributed throughout the country. When the institute was founded in 1923, it was only the second of its kind in the world (the first was in Brazil).

Tourists are welcome to view the milkings (11am and 2.30pm Monday to Friday, 11am Saturday and Sunday) and feedings (2.30pm Monday to Friday) or to stroll the small garden complex where the snakes are kept in escape-proof cages. The snakes tend to be camera shy during nonperformance times, although it is exhilarating to spot a camouflaged king cobra poised to strike.

The open-air auditorium at the Queen Saovabha Memorial Institute (Snake Farm)

The booklet titled *Guide to Healthy Living in Thailand*, published by the Thai Red Cross in conjunction with the US embassy, is available here.

This institution received its historical name in honour of Queen Saovabha, wife of Rama V, who championed a wide variety of medical causes and education, including a school for midwives and other modern birthing practices.

SRI MARIAMMAN TEMPLE Map pp290-1
วัดพระศรีมหาอุมาเทวี(วัดแขก)

☎ 0 2238 4007; cnr Th Silom & Th Pan; admission free; ⏱ 6am-8pm; ferry Tha Oriental, Skytrain Chong Nonsi

Arrestingly flamboyant, this Hindu temple is a wild collision of colours, shapes and deities. Built in the 1860s by Tamil immigrants, the principal temple features a 6m façade of intertwined, full-colour Hindu deities, topped by a gold-plated copper dome. The temple's main shrine contains three supremes: Jao Mae Maha Umathewi (Uma Devi; also known as Shakti, Shiva's consort) at the centre; her son Phra Khanthakuman (Khanthakumara or Subramaniam) on the right; and her elephant-headed son Phra Phikkhanesawora (Ganesha) on the

left. Along the left interior wall sit rows of Shivas, Vishnus and other Hindu deities, as well as a few Buddhas. Thai and Chinese devotees come to pray along with Indians as the Hindu gods figure just as prominently in their individualistic approach to religion.

The official name of the temple is Wat Phra Si Maha Umathewi in Thai, but sometimes it is shortened to its colloquial name Wat Khaek – *khàek* is a common expression for people of Indian descent. The literal translation is 'guest', an obvious euphemism for any group of people not particularly wanted as permanent residents; hence most Indian Thais don't appreciate the term.

TH SUKHUMVIT
Eating p140; Shopping p186; Sleeping p205

Like Bangkok as a whole, Th Sukhumvit lacks a centre and spreads out along kilometres worth of asphalt from what could be called the centre of Bangkok all the way to the Gulf of Thailand. From an aerial view, the street must look like a felled tree with neighbourhood streets branching off at right angles.

Sukhumvit was the city's first car suburb, pushing modernity ever deeper into the rice paddies. But it has since surpassed modernity to become truly a global village: a very wealthy global village. Aristocratic Thai families who have recently returned from years abroad resume their elevated status at home but preserve customs acquired in New York, London or Paris. Mama might make curry but breakfast is toast with English marmalade. Mixed Thai-*faràng* households are so common along Sukhumvit that one could forget that most Thai children don't have pointy Western noses. This is also the primary address for the city's most recent expat arrivals, from Japanese engineers to Lebanese importers. Whole neighbourhoods are populated by company families temporarily transplanted to the tropics. Middle-class lives in the West are transformed into upper-class status in Thailand, and families are expected to contribute to the local economy by hiring maids, gardeners and other household staff. Yuppie couples decked out in the latest fashions and fully bilingual, perhaps more so in English, entertain stylishly in sky-piercing condos and cart the kids off to international school.

Some traditionalists fear that Thai will soon become a service language within the capital city. If new Bangkok gave a hoot about introspection, surely an identity crisis would follow. But Sukhumvit's only bother is the traffic. Despite the fears and the lack of temples, Sukhumvit still exemplifies some of the best parts of Thailand's urban character: the mouths of *soi* are always filled with food vendors, motorcycle taxis will cart you home for hardly a sneeze and the neighbours still play their country music way too loud.

Orientation

Th Sukhumvit starts on the eastern side of Soi Ruam Rudi and extends all the way to the Gulf of Thailand. The *soi* that branch off Th Sukhumvit are conveniently numbered, with the even-numbered *soi* on the southern side of the street, and the odd-numbered *soi* occupying the northern side. The drawback to such an uncharacteristically simple design is that the even- and odd-numbered *soi* don't line up sequentially (Soi 11 lies directly opposite Soi 8). In some cases, the *soi* are better known by an alternative name, such as Soi Nana (Soi 3), Soi Asoke (Soi 21), Soi Phrom Phong (Soi 39) and Soi Thong Lor (Soi 55).

Sukhumvit has two distinct personalities. Lower Sukhumvit, below Soi Asoke, is dominated by the sex tourist scene around Nana Entertainment Plaza and Soi Cowboy. Above Soi Asoke, the street is more generic and filled with the bulk of international residents. Soi Thong Lor and beyond is primarily Thai. The Eastern bus station is at Soi Ekamai (Soi 63).

As with other parts of the city, Th Sukhumvit is almost always congested with traffic, especially at rush hour and at bar-closing time. A short cut through the back *soi*, known as the 'Green Route', is used

www.lonelyplanet.com

TH SUKHUMVIT TOP FIVE

- Ban Kamthieng (below) Cultural studies in this pretty teak building make learning not so taxing.
- Q Bar (p157) and Bed Supperclub (p155) Go clubbing among a happening crowd of expats and Bangkok hi-sos (socialites).
- Emporium Shopping Centre (p187) High-powered shopaholics can get their fix at this glamorous mall.
- International restaurants (p140) Craving nachos, kidney pie or pasta? All can be rustled up along Th Sukhumvit.
- Skytrain (p242) Peek into the neighbourhood's many fortressed mansions.

by savvy cabs and locals to circumvent the creeping pace of Th Sukhumvit.

BENJAKITI PARK Map pp296-7
สวนเบญจกิติ

Th Ratchadaphisek; ☯ 5am-8pm; subway Sirikit Centre

The latest addition to Bangkok's emaciated green scene, this 130-rai (20.8-hectare) park encircles a large lake on the former grounds of the Tobacco Monopoly, just behind the Queen Sirikit Convention Centre, marking the queen's sixth cycle (72nd birthday). Another 300 rai (48 hectares) of former factory buildings is earmarked for transformation into a manmade rainforest in 2008.

SIAM SOCIETY & BAN KAMTHIENG Map pp296-7
สยามสมาคม/บ้านคำเที่ยง

☎ 02661 6470; 131 Soi Asoke (Soi 21), Th Sukhumvit; Ban Kamthieng admission 100B; ☯ 9am-5pm; Skytrain Asoke, subway Sukhumvit

Past the elevated Skytrain tracks and the roar of traffic, the Siam Society transports visitors to a northern Thai village with its excellent Ban Kamthieng house museum. Ban Kamthieng is a traditional 19th-century home that was located on the banks of Mae Ping in Chiang Mai. Now relocated to Bangkok, the house presents the daily customs and spiritual beliefs of the Lanna tradition. Communicating all the hard facts as well as any sterile museum (with detailed English signage and engaging video installations), Ban Kamthieng instils in the

TRANSPORT TH SUKHUMVIT

Bus Air-con 501, 508, 511 and 513, ordinary 2 and 25

Skytrain from Nana to On Nut stations

Subway Sukhumvit and Phetchaburi

visitor a sense of place, from the attached rice granary and handmade tools to the wooden loom and woven silks. Best of all you can wander and wonder without having to share space with shutterbugs.

Next door to Ban Kamthieng are the headquarters of the prestigious Siam Society, publisher of the renowned *Journal of the Siam Society* and a valiant preserver of traditional Thai culture. This is a good place to visit for those with a serious interest in Thailand. A reference library is open to visitors and Siam Society monographs are for sale. Almost anything you'd want to know about Thailand (outside the political sphere, since the society is sponsored by the royal family) can be researched here.

THAILAND CREATIVE & DESIGN CENTER Map pp296-7
ศูนย์สร้างสรรค์งานออกแบบ
☎ 0 2664 8448; www.tcdc.or.th; 6th fl, Emporium, Th Sukhumvit; ⏲ 10.30am-10pm Tue-Sun; Skytrain Phrom Phong

Move over Scandinavian minimalism, this is the dawning of Thai style. This new museum is a government-backed initiative intended to incubate design innovation, which is seen as Thailand's next step in the global marketplace now that labour is no longer competitive. Rotating exhibits feature profiles of international products and retrospectives of regional handicrafts and creativity. Material ConneXion is a permanent library of design-related materials, the first of its kind in Asia.

GREATER BANGKOK

Surrounding the previously defined neighbourhoods are residential suburbs and a few scattered attractions. Once rice fields, voracious Bangkok has expanded in every possible direction with little alluring charm. Chatuchak, in the northern section of the city, is one noteworthy area with a popular weekend market (p188). Other attractions listed here are located in otherwise uneventful areas.

Orientation

Many of these sites lie beyond the inner-city expressway. Some are conveniently located along the Skytrain route, which has made it possible to travel to the northern regions of town in less than a day. Chatuchak and Victory Monument are both in the northern section of town en route to the airport and easily accessible by public transport. The other attractions listed here will require several forms of public transport (and lots of time and patience) or personal transport. The prisons are located west of Chatuchak and the river and north of central Bangkok. In the far-eastern part of town is Rama IX Royal Park.

BANG KWANG & KHLONG PREM PRISONS Map pp278-9
เรือนจำบางขวางและคลองเปรม
Bang Kwang ☎ 0 2967 3311; fax 0 2967 3313; Th Nonthaburi Nonthaburi; ⏲ visiting hours vary; ferry Nonthaburi; Khlong Prem ☎ 0 2580 0975; 33/3 Th Ngam Wang Wan, Chatuchak; ⏲ visiting hours vary; ferry Nonthaburi, Skytrain Mo Chit

Thailand's permissive reputation is juxtaposed by strict antidrug laws that often land foreign nationals in a prison system with feudal conditions. A sobering and charitable expedition is to visit an inmate, bringing them news of the outside, basic supplies and reading materials. The regulations for visitations are quite involved and require pre-arrival research (see p250). You must dress respectfully (long sleeves and long pants), bring your passport for registration purposes and have the name and

---

CONDO-FIED ENGLISH

Peppering documents, ad campaigns and pop songs with English is a sure-fire status symbol in Thailand. This isn't unconscious fluency, but premeditated posturing. The thinking goes like this: the language associated with the richest nations of the world will surely divert just a little of that wealth to the business venture that masters a few key phrases. The most creative and excessive use of English as a good omen are the billboard ads for new condominiums. 'Beyond expectation' is a commonplace sales pitch. 'The ultimate in luxury living in prestige village' is another superlative that might make Muhammad Ali blush. The residents in the ads are always beautiful *lûuk khrêung* (half-Thai, half-*faràng*) impeccably dressed and enjoying a sweat-free existence in the tropics. They stare out at a misty future enjoying 'the best of tomorrow today, in the most extravagant, exciting, trendy place in the universe'.

GREATER BANGKOK TOP FIVE

- Chatuchak Weekend Market (p188) So much stuff to buy, so little time.
- Children's Discovery Museum (below) A place where kids are encouraged to touch everything.
- Ko Kret (below) Relax on this laid-back island, light years behind bustling Bangkok.
- Safari World (p114) When the jungles of Bangkok become too ordinary, take the kids to this park, on the outskirts of town.
- Victory Point (p146) A night market around Victory Monument that typifies the provinces.

building number of the inmate you plan to visit. Inmate information can be obtained from most embassies. Visiting hours and days vary depending on the building the inmate is housed in.

Male inmates who have received sentences of 40 years to life (often for drug offences) are detained in Bang Kwang Prison, north of central Bangkok. To reach the prison, take the Mae Nam Chao Phraya ferry north to Nonthaburi (the last stop); the prison is 500m from the pier.

Women are detained in the Bang Khen section of Khlong Prem Prison. From Nonthaburi, take a minibus (15B) to the prison, or take the Skytrain to Mo Chit and then a taxi to the prison gates.

CHILDREN'S DISCOVERY MUSEUM Map pp278-9
พิพิธภัณฑ์เด็กกรุงเทพมหานคร

☎ 0 2615 7333; Queen Sirikit Park, Th Kamphaeng Phet 4; adult/child 150/120B; ☻ 9am-5pm Tue-Fri, 10am-6pm Sat & Sun; Skytrain Mo Chit
Through hands-on activities, learning is well disguised as fun at this museum opposite Chatuchak Weekend Market (p188). Kids can stand inside a bubble, see how an engine works, or role-play as a firefighter. Most activities are geared to primary-school-aged children. There is also a toddlers' playground at the back of the main building.

KO KRET
เกาะเกร็ด

Remember what quiet sounds like? How about the chatter of cicadas? If the answer is no and no, then you must escape the thunderdome to this car-free island in the middle of Mae Nam Chao Phraya. It is a sleepy little village encircled by one half-hearted attempt at a road. The primary profession appears to be napping and even the life of a stray dog on Ko Kret seems enviable.

The island's claim to fame is the hand-thrown terracotta pots that are sold at markets throughout Bangkok. This island and the pottery tradition date back to one of Thailand's oldest settlements of Mon people, who were a dominant tribe of central Thailand between the 6th and 10th centuries AD. There are two **pottery centres** on the island where you can buy the earthenware and watch the potters work; one is on the east coast and the other is on the north coast. From **Wat Paramai Yikawat** (Wat Mon), which has an interesting Mon-style marble Buddha, go in either direction to find the pottery shops.

Baan Dvara Prateep (☎ 0 2538 4212; www.baandvaraprateep.com; 53/3 Moo 5, Ko Kret) offers multiday yoga and meditation retreats in a traditional wooden house on the west coast of the island.

The easiest way to reach Ko Kret is to take a northbound Chao Phraya Express boat to Nonthaburi and then hire a long-tail boat (per person for two hours 350B) from there. Another option is the equivalent of sneaking in the back door. From Tha Nonthaburi, dodge the pesky tour operators and hop on a public Laem Thong boat (10B) continuing north. Disembark at Tha Pak Kret and wait for a cross-river ferry to Ko Kret (1B), which is just across the way. *Voilà*, you're on the island and you did it all by yourself. Ko Kret has several piers, so remember to return to Tha Pa Fai for your indirect trip home.

RAMA IX ROYAL PARK Map pp278-9
สวนหลวง ร.๙

Soi 103 (Soi Udom Suk), Th Sukhumvit; admission 10B; ☻ 5am-6pm; ordinary bus 2, 23 & 25, transfer to green minibus at Soi 103
Opened in 1987 to commemorate King Bhumibol's 60th birthday, this green area covers 81 hectares and has a water park and botanic garden. Since its opening, the garden has become a significant horticultural research centre. A museum with an exhibition on the king's life sits at the park's centre. There are resident lizards, tortoises and birds. A flower and plant sale is held here in December.

SAFARI WORLD Map pp278-9
ซาฟารีเวิลด์

☎ 0 2518 1000; www.safariworld.com; 99 Th Ramindra 1, Miniburi; adult/child 780/570B; ⏰ 9am-5pm

Claiming to be world's largest 'open zoo', Safari World is divided into two parts, the drive-through Safari Park and the Marine Park. In the Safari Park, visitors drive through eight habitats with giraffes, lions, zebras, elephants, orang-utans, and other African and Asian animals. A panda house displays rare white pandas. The Marine Park focuses on stunts by dolphins and other trained animals. Safari World is 45km northeast of Bangkok, and best reached by car.

VICTORY MONUMENT Map pp280-1
อนุสาวรีย์ชัยสมรภูมิ

Th Ratchawithi & Phayathai; Skytrain Victory Monument; ordinary bus 12, 62

A busy traffic circle revolves around this obelisk monument that commemorates a 1939 Thai victory against the French in Laos. But the monument is only a landmark for observing the social universe of the local university students. An elevated walkway circumnavigates the roundabout, funnelling the pedestrian traffic in and out of the Skytrain station as well as providing a gathering spot for break dancers, flirting gangs of guys and gals, and lots of fashion experiments. Because Victory Monument is outside of the core of Bangkok, the neighbourhood is less cosmopolitan and more reminiscent of provincial towns elsewhere in the country.

West of the roundabout is **Phayathai Palace** (King Mongkut Hospital, 315 Th Ratchawithi; admission free; ⏰ 8.30am-4.30pm

GOING WILD WITH THE KIDS IN BANGKOK

Most people might assume that Bangkok is no place for children, but its untamed parts aren't limited to the naughty zones. This notorious city has lots of family-friendly corners, where kids can commune with nature and each other.

Join the novice monks and other Thai children as they sprinkle tiny pellets of fish food (sold on the pier) into the river at **Tha Thewet** (Map pp282–3; Th Samsen; ⏰ 7am-7pm), transforming the muddy river into a brisk boil of flapping bodies.

Near the old Portuguese quarter in Thonburi, **Wat Prayoon** (Map pp280–1; 24 Th Prachathipok, cnr Thetsaban Soi 1, beside Memorial Bridge; ⏰ 8am-6pm; cross-river ferry from Tha Pak Talat/Atsadang) is an artificial hill cluttered with miniature shrines and a winding path encircling a turtle pond. Vendors sell cut fruit for feeding to the resident turtles.

In Chinatown, **Wat Chakrawat** (Map pp284–5; Th Chakrawat; ⏰ 8am-6pm; ferry Tha Ratchawong) has a small pond where two lazy crocodiles float the day away.

Other critter parks in town include the **Queen Saovabha Memorial Institute** (Snake Farm; p109), **Dusit Zoo** (p90) and **Safari World** (left).

Mon-Fri), a country cottage built by King Chulalongkorn (Rama V) in 1909 for retreats into what was then the country. The surviving throne hall encased in French glass doors and a fanciful tiered roof is now part of a hospital complex, but is open to the public. There isn't much in the way of tourist displays but it's worth it to survey the architecture of the buildings and escape the sightseeing masses.

Walking Tours

Walking Tours

Walk through the world's worst traffic jam? Sounds absurd, but Bangkok by foot really is charming. Without a doubt, every block will be filled with something you've never seen before – blind troubadours with portable karaoke machines, stray dogs wearing T-shirts, vendors selling everything plus the kitchen sink. The added challenge is that Bangkok's pavements are as traffic clogged as its roads, turning a leisurely stroll into an adventure sport of dodging broken asphalt and inexplicable puddles, ducking under huge umbrellas or canvas awnings pitched right at the level of your forehead, or squeezing through a bottleneck at a stall selling desserts that look like tacos.

GOING WITH THE FLOW

For a day of sightseeing, you'll need a good map, comfortable shoes and lots of water. Don't bring your Western concept of pavement etiquette. You're in Asia now, and the rules of personal space – not to mention the laws of physics – are completely different. Human traffic in Bangkok acts like flowing water: if there is an empty space, it will quickly be filled with a warm body, regardless of who was where in some unspoken queue. With an increase of mass (a motorcycle or pushcart), a solid state is achieved and the sea of pedestrians can be pushed out of the way in a textbook example of might-makes-right. Once you master these simple concepts, you can enjoy shuffling along with the flow.

KO RATANAKOSIN STROLL

Bangkok's most famous sites are cradled in Ko Ratanakosin (Ratanakosin Island). In the days when Bangkok was known as the 'Venice of the East', Khlong Banglamphu and Khlong Ong Ang – two lengthy adjoining canals to the east – were probably large enough for the area to seem more like an island than it does today. The canals were enlarged in the early period of the city in an effort to re-create the island-city of Ayuthaya (Thailand's former capital, which was sacked by the Burmese).

This circular walk starts at Tha Chang, accessible by Chao Phraya river ferries. From the pier, file east past the market toward Th Na Phra Lan. On your left-hand side is **Silpakorn University** (1; p77), Thailand's first fine-arts university. The university campus includes part of an old Rama I palace and an art gallery showing works by students and professors.

Just past the intersection with Th Na Phra That is the third gate and the official tourist entrance to Thailand's holiest temple, **Wat Phra Kaew** (2; p79), and the formal royal residence, the **Grand Palace** (3; p79). All visitors to the palace and temple grounds must be appropriately attired – no shorts, tank tops or other dress considered unacceptable for temple visits. Temple staff can provide wraparound sarongs for bare legs.

Exiting via the same gate, take a right and cross Th Ratchadamnoen Nai to reach **Lak Meuang** (4; City Pillar; p75), a shrine to Bangkok's city spirit. Traditionally, every city in Thailand must have a foundation stone that embodies the city's guardian deity and from which intercity distances are measured. This shrine is one of Bangkok's most important sites of animistic worship; believers throng the area day and night, bringing offerings of flowers, incense, whisky, fruit and even cooked food.

From Lak Meuang, follow Th Sanam Chai south until you come to Th Chetuphon (the second street on your right after

Passengers travelling on the Chao Phraya Express (p72) on Mae Nam Chao Phraya

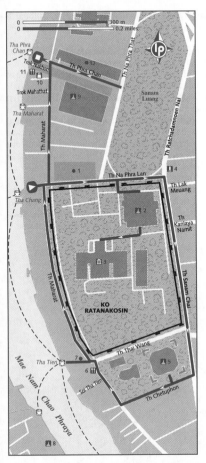

WALK FACTS

Start Tha Chang (river ferry)
End Tha Phra Chan (river ferry)
Distance 2.5km
Duration One to two hours
Fuel Stops Rub Aroon (p126), Trok Nakhon food vendors (p133)

the palace walls end, approximately 600m from the pillar). Turn right onto Th Chetuphon and enter **Wat Pho** (5; p78) through the second portico. Meander through the grounds on your way to the massive reclining Buddha. Wat Pho is the national repository for traditional massage and operates an affiliated training school with pavilions located on the temple grounds for weary foot soldiers.

Turn right at Th Maharat, and savour all this cultural intensity at **Rub Aroon** (6; p126), a friendly café serving Thai standards and fresh fruit drinks. Stroll north to Th Thai Wang and turn left to see a row of rare, early Ratanakosin-era **shophouses** 7. If you continue along Th Thai Wang to the river you'll arrive at Tha Tien (a Chao Phraya Express pier), where you can catch one of the regular cross-river ferries to **Wat Arun** (8; p82), to see its striking Hindu-Khmer stupa.

Back on the east side of the river, retrace your steps to Th Maharat and turn left to continue the walking tour north. After crossing Th Na Phra Lan, Th Maharat becomes a healing centre of herbal apothecaries and footpath amulet sellers. On your right is **Wat Mahathat** (9; p78), Thailand's most respected Buddhist university. Take a left into the narrow alley immediately after Trok Mahathat to the **amulet market** (10; p169), a warren of vendors selling *phrá khrêuang* (religious amulets) representing various Hindu and Buddhist deities.

If you're hungry, snake your way back to Th Maharat and continue to the next alley, Trok Nakhon, which leads past more amulet stalls and stores selling graduation gowns to a dim alternative world of **food vendors** (11; p133), some with a river view. The food here is very good and inexpensive – to order, all you'll need to do is point.

Renewed and refuelled, follow the last stretch of Th Maharat to the gates of **Thammasat University** (12; p77), which is known for its law and political science faculties. To return home follow the crowds to Tha Phra Chan and take a cross-river ferry to Tha Bangkok Noi, where you can pick up the Chao Phraya Express in either direction.

OLD BANGLAMPHU WALK

Beyond the manic scene of Th Khao San, Banglamphu is a unique collection of bohemian and traditionalist Thais, the cultural inheritors of the neighbourhood's artistic legacy.

Start at the *khlong* (canal) taxi pier near Saphan Phan Fah. Walk out to Th Ratchadamnoen Klang, the main boulevard, and turn left. This thoroughfare was built during Thailand's military dictatorship era for the purposes of cultivating nationalistic sentiments. Billboard-sized pictures of the king and queen line the avenue and preserve the royal family in their prime rather than the present.

Continue across the street at the first stop light to reach **Wat Ratchanatda** (1; p87) and its Burmese-style iron castle. Cross the multilane street to the **Queen's Gallery** (2; p86).

Stop in at **Old Bangkok Inn** (3; p194) for a cup of coffee or tea and to soak up the ambience of this old shophouse. Continue west on Th Phra Sumen to the intersection of Th Din So.

To your right is **Saphan Chalerm Wan Chat 4**, a bridge named in honour of Thailand's first constitution and the birth of the modern Thai nation in 1932. Just across the bridge is **Thai Nakorn** (5; p179), a 75-year-old shop that sells nielloware, a traditional craft that was formerly made in this village. Retrace your steps and follow Th Din So south towards the **Democracy Monument** (6; p85), Bangkok's most striking memorial to the constitutional revolution. From 'the Demo', back-track along the left-hand side of Th Din So. Many of the shophouses that line the road on Th Din So date to the reigns of Rama V

WALK FACTS

Start Tha Phan Fah (*khlong* taxi)
End Tha Phra Athit (river ferry)
Distance 1.8km
Duration One to 1½ hours
Fuel Stops Old Bangkok Inn (p194), Ton Pho (p129)

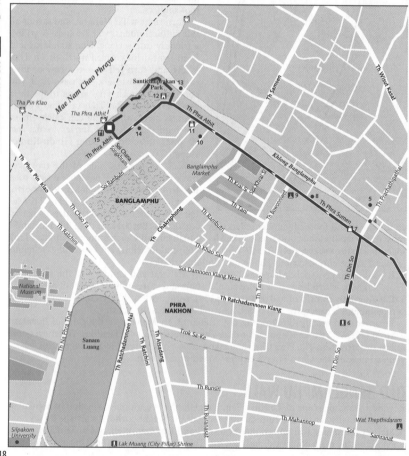

(King Chulalongkorn; r 1868–1910) and Rama VII (King Prajadhipok; 1925–35). Since the entire block to the northwest of the Democracy Monument belongs to Wat Bowonniwet, the shop owners pay rent directly to the temple.

Turn left on Th Phra Sumen, which is lined with **national regalia shops 7**: red-white-and-blue national flags and orange Buddhist flags, cardboard cutouts of the king, and house-shrine photos of the monarchy. These are the only stores like them in the city.

Further down the street is a remnant of the **old city gate 8**, one of Bangkok's original 16 when the city was walled. Once built of timber, it was replaced by this larger brick-and-stucco version during the reign of Rama V and restored in 1981.

On the opposite side of the street is **Wat Bowonniwet (9; p87)**, one of the most highly venerated Buddhist monasteries in Bangkok and headquarters for the strict Thammayut monastic sect.

Further along, Th Phra Sumen changes its name to Th Phra Athit after crossing Th Chakraphong. Before the bend in the road, you'll pass a ruined brick **palace gate 10** on your left. Although the 18th-century palace, once the residence of Rama I's youngest brother, is long gone, local residents maintain a small spirit house in front of the gate out of respect for the Chakri dynasty.

A few doors down is **Passport (11; p170)**, a bookstore that acts as the intellectual hub of Banglamphu's young creatives. An upstairs café usually has a few intense conversations or quiet book-thumbers.

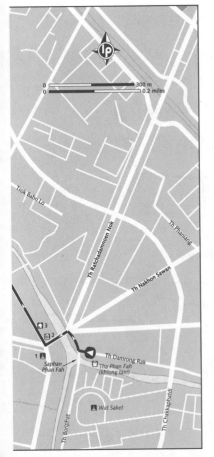

As the street approaches Mae Nam Chao Phraya and turns southward, the corner is guarded by the 18th-century **Phra Sumen Fort (12; p86)**, the centrepiece of the Santichaiprakan Park. Directly behind the fort is **Khlong Banglamphu 13**, one of the original canals built to defend the city from land attacks. Standing in the park are Banglamphu's last two remaining *lamphuu* trees, from which the area derives its name. A riverfront promenade follows Mae Nam Chao Phraya southwest from the park to Tha Phra Athit.

For this walk, return to Th Phra Athit and continue south. You'll pass a mixture of modern shophouses and old mansions on either side of the road, the latter built to house Thai nobility during the late-19th and early-20th centuries. **Ban Phra Athit 14**, at No 201/1, once belonged to Chao Phraya Vorapongpipat, finance minister during the reigns of Ramas V, VI and VII. One of the most splendidly restored Ratanakosin-era buildings in the neighbourhood, it now belongs to a private company, but a coffee shop within the grounds is open to the public.

End the walking tour at the Tha Phra Athit pier with a lunch at the river-facing **Ton Pho (15; p129)** restaurant.

PHRA NAKHON MEANDER

Subdued and refined, the area south of Wat Saket combines antique shops, old wooden houses and mystical religious shrines. It rarely appears on sightseeing itineraries but is a Thai gem.

From the *khlong* taxi pier, turn left over Saphan Phan Fah to **Golden Mount (1; p87)** for a panoramic view of the city.

Return to Th Boriphat, which is lined with **teak shops** 2 selling carved lintels and other decorations for turning your apartment into a Thai restaurant. Cross Th Bamrung Meuang and turn left at Soi Ban Baat into **Monk's Bowl Village** (3; p85) to see a surviving artisan village. Backtrack to Th Bamrung Meuang and turn left to the spindly red **Sao Ching-Cha** (4; p87), a gatelike structure that hosted a death-defying Brahmin spectacle. To the right of the Giant Swing is the Bangkok City Hall (BMA building), forgettable except for the **marble sign** 5 in front of the square spelling out Bangkok's official Thai name; we spy a photo-op. On the other side of the Giant Swing is **Wat Suthat** (6; p88), one of the holiest temples in Thailand and a repository of Brahmin rituals that continue to this day to be interwoven with royal ceremonies.

Continue to the crescent-shaped shop-house on the corner of Th Din So and Bam-rung Meuang where **religious shops** 7 sell huge Buddhas and other temple needs. Wealthy families make merit by donating these items to their local temples. Technically Buddhas are rented, not sold, and the hubbub surrounding a shop filled with vaguely human forms is sacrilegiously humorous. The huge

WALK FACTS

Start Tha Phan Fah (*khlong* taxi)
End Tha Saphan Phut (river ferry)
Distance 4km
Duration Two hours
Fuel Stop Arawy (p126)

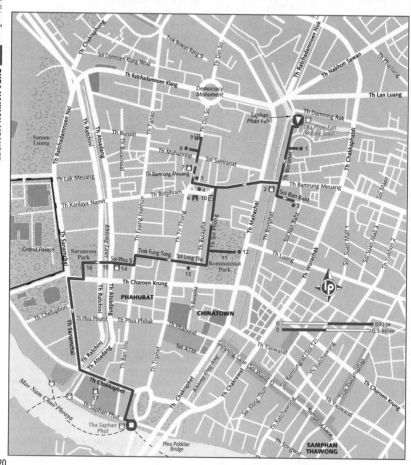

figures arrive wrapped up like abductees in monk's robes aboard pick-up trucks. Then begins the touch-up process on their golden paint jobs. Afterwards the images are arranged by size in hopes of an adoption.

Turn right on Th Din So to **Thewa Sathaan 8**, a Brahmin shrine containing the images of Shiva, Ganesha and Vishnu, who are regarded as bringing fertility and security to the country and the monarchy. Stop in at **Arawy** (9; p126) for a spot-on green curry.

Backtrack to Th Bamrung Meuang and turn right on Th Siri Phong to the **San Jao Phitsanu 10**, a small shrine dedicated to Vishnu amid a leafy traffic median. Continue south for a peek over the temple wall at the parts of the grounds you might have missed: the sacred banyan tree and various rock statues.

Turn left into **Rommaninat Park 11**, a pretty green space of fountains and walking paths. In the northeast corner of the park is the **Corrections Museum** (12; donations accepted; 🕑 8.30am-4pm Mon-Fri), a rehabilitated

People exercising in front of Sao Ching-Cha (Giant Swing; p87), with Wat Suthat in background

colonial building covering the park's former career as a prison in the early 1900s. Most displays are in Thai but the maintenance staff and other hangers-on turn the tour into a social event, giggling at the gruesome displays of torture used in the good old days.

Exit from the same gate and cross the street to follow the **khlong 13** through the neighbourhood on Soi Long Tha, past fruit vendors, noodle shops, laundry and the neighbourhood shrine. This is what Bangkok looked like when the city's footpaths were riverbanks.

At Fuang Nakhon turn left and then right on Soi Phra Si past the heavily ornamented **shopfronts 14** decorated in a style often referred to as Sino-Portuguese. In the early 20th century, these buildings where the height of fashion and sold new luxury goods, like motor cars, to the modernising country. Today the fashions have shifted to downtown malls and the old buildings are mainly warehouses. Cross Th Atsadang to **Saphan Hok 15**, a simple lever bridge across Khlong Lawt, the inner-city moat that transformed Ko Ratanakosin into an island. Small trading ships from Mon settlements would dock near here on trading missions.

Enter the **Saranrom Royal Garden** (16; p76), a park favouring English Victorian gardens with tropical perfumes and earnest exercisers. Exit near the fountain to the old ministry buildings and turn left on Th Sanam Chai all the way to Th Triphet and **Pak Khlong Market** (17; p179), Bangkok's wholesale flower and vegetable market. End the tour at Tha Saphan Phut.

CHINATOWN SHOPPING SPREE

Chinatown is packed – every inch of it is used to make a living. From the fresh-food market festooned with carcasses to the plastic beeping toy stores, commerce never rests. This walking tour plunges into crowded claustrophobic alleys lined with vendors selling a greater variety of goods than the modern shopping centres. At points you'll be shocked, disgusted and thoroughly amazed – just come prepared for crowds and smells.

Start at Tha Ratchawong, along the banks of Mae Nam Chao Phraya and reached via river taxi. Walk along Th Ratchawong, the main street leading away from the pier. Ratchawong was a fashionable corridor in the early 1900s: Chinese opera houses and pretheatre banquet restaurants lined the street for the recently introduced fad of going out on the town. Today the street is filled with glorified warehouses selling wholesale products that get divided up and sold in smaller quantities at other markets.

Turn right at **Sampeng Lane** (1; Soi Wanit 1; p179); you won't see a street sign here because the corner is packed with vendors' stalls, but you'll know it by the queue of people slowly shuffling into the alley. You have now entered the shopping fun house, where the sky is completely obscured and bargains lie in ambush – that is if you really want 500 Hello Kitty pens, a tonne of stuffed animals and books of stickers. Sampeng was originally a trading centre built in 1782 near the river for goods bound for the international markets.

After about 100m, Sampeng Lane crosses Th Mangkon. On either side of the intersection are two of Bangkok's oldest commercial buildings, a **Bangkok Bank 2** and the venerable **Tang To Kang 3** gold shop, which are both more than 100 years old. The exteriors of the buildings are classic early Ratanakosin, showing lots of European influence; the interiors are heavy with hardwood panelling. Good luck spotting these as you squeeze against your neighbour to allow a delivery of overstuffed boxes to pass.

Continue another 60m or so to Trok Itsaranuphap, where you'll take a left onto a wider lane past rows of vendors selling fried pork skins and other delicacies. Down the lane on your right is **Talat Kao (4**; Old Market). This market has been operating continuously for more than 200 years. All manner of freshwater and saltwater fish and shellfish are displayed here, alive or filleted – or, sometimes, half alive and half filleted. The action runs from 4am to 11am – any later and you'll only find slick sidewalks and piles of rubbish.

From Trok Itsaranuphap, continue to Th Yaowarat, a main Chinatown thoroughfare. This section of Th Yaowarat is lined with large and small gold shops; for price and selection, this is probably the best place in Thailand to purchase a gold chain (sold by the *bàat,* a unit of weight equal to 15g). To cross the road, shadow a few Thai shoppers possessing that innate Bangkok ability to dodge traffic.

On the other side of Yaowarat, on Trok Itsaranuphap, is **Talat Leng-Buai-la 5**. A spry 80 years old, it was once the city's central vegetable market before Pak Khlong usurped the position. Today the market sells mainly Chinese ingredients for the local community. Popular purchases are fresh cashews, lotus seeds, and shiitake mushrooms. The first section is lined with vendors purveying cleaned chickens, plucked ducks, scaled fish, unnaturally coloured vats of pickled food and prepackaged snacks – hungry yet? **Hong Kong Noodles (6**; p130), on the left side of the alley, does a rollicking business catering to appetites aroused by the such sights.

Cross the next major intersection, Th Charoen Krung, and turn left. Continue for 20m to **Wat Mangkon Kamalawatt (7**; p94), one of Chinatown's largest and liveliest temples. Along this stretch of the street, neighbouring shops sell fruit, cakes, incense and ritual burning paper, all for offering at the temple. Head back to Trok Itsaranuphap and continue past funerary stalls selling paper versions of 21st-century comforts to be ritually burned, enabling the departed to travel to the next life in style. Slide past the beef-jerky vendor to the termination of the *soi* at Th Yommarat Sukhum. Turn right on to Th Phla Phla Chai and follow the bend in the road into the blazing sun, past more religious shops, back to Th Charoen Krung. About midblock, this tour poetically ends beside a coffin shop.

If the commingling of death and commerce has you energised, take your wallet on an outing to other outdoor markets (p179) in Chinatown.

WALK FACTS

Start Tha Ratchawong (river ferry)
End Th Charoen Krung
Distance 1.5km
Duration One hour
Fuel Stop Hong Kong Noodles (p130)

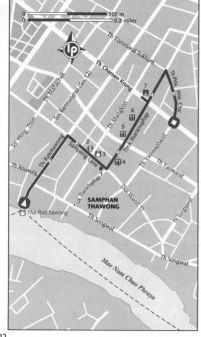

Eating

Eating

Wherever you go in Bangkok, there is food. *Rót khĕn* (vendor carts) deploy across the city outfitted with portable woks, charcoal stoves or deep-fryers ready to whip up a quick snack or a sit-down meal. There is so much variety on the streets that you can go weeks without stepping inside a restaurant.

When you make the leap inside, your best options for great Thai food are Spartan closets run by mum, dad and the kids. Some of the most famous food shops regularly covered in the Thai-language press are a few tables shy of being a home kitchen and look more like a carport than a palace. For folks more interested in food than finery, Bangkok is the great liberator from tablecloth suffocation and penguin-suit waiters. Even

THAI RESTAURANTS WORTH WOOING

- Le Lys (p137) Run by a Thai-French couple for cosy and relaxed hybrid dishes.
- Ruen Mallika (p144) Classic Thai for cultural lovebirds.
- Hemlock (p127) Artful dishes for the bookish and bohemian.
- Blue Elephant (p135) Conservative dining for history-buff executives.
- In Love (p129) River views for courting Thai seafood.

when karma has delivered fame and fortune, the elite still love their street eats. Your fellow diners at a famous outdoor stall might include a wealthy student just returned from a semester abroad or a low-level civil servant who has never left her home province. When it comes to good eats, Asia's famous obsession with status takes a back seat. Best of all, these proven grub shops won't siphon away a car payment.

That doesn't mean you can't dine in decadence. As a cosmopolitan centre, Bangkok loves to spend money and has many stylish spots that cater to a mood, from sky-high perches to riverside pavilions and modern minimalist dens. Italian is king in the fine-dining sphere, with Mediterranean-Californian styles not far behind. Those refreshing flavours of citrus and seafood translate better into this tropical climate than the heavy sauces of traditional French cuisine, the usual haute contender. The city's playboy side is indulged in the ever-changing fashionable restaurants, intended more for high-priced 'kissing and telling' than culinary adventures. With that said, there are a minority of true matchmakers bringing together harmonious food unions between East and West.

Bangkok also offers a host of homesickness cures for its many immigrant communities. Chinatown is naturally a good area for Chinese food. In a corner of Chinatown known as Phahurat and around Th Silom, Indian residents keep themselves and the culinary traveller

ALL THAT GLITTERS ISN'T GOOD

The Thai word for 'restaurant' literally means 'food shop', which communicates the simplicity of eating Thai food. This is comfort food, communal and relaxed, without formality or fussiness. In the sphere of food, Thailand is surprisingly egalitarian, much more so than the West, where feudal-style class distinctions are inherent in its culinary traditions. While the French invented what was adopted as regal cuisine in the West, the Thai royalty enjoyed recognisable family recipes, only with more bounty and ceremony than the commoners. Dishes for the royal family became another kind of Thai handicraft: fruit was carved to look like flowers and elaborate sweets were hand moulded to look like strands of gold. Though modern-day restaurants in Bangkok boast royal Thai menus, they are really merging the Western concept of ambience and Western ingredients into standard Thai dishes.

'Dressing up' Thai food is a popular experiment in Bangkok restaurants based on a simple premise: old standards get a nouveau makeover with exotic ingredients and artful arrangement. Add a beautiful setting and a serious price tag, and *voilà*, you've got a tourist trap. Invariably the spices have been tamed, the foreign ingredients clash, and only visitors and expats seem impressed. Without the chillies, Thais swear it has no taste. And why would a Thai pay a lot for a meal that would be better at home or on the street? Until proven wrong, we're sticking to the maxim that fluorescent lighting is the best indicator of a good Thai restaurant.

well fed. In the crowded bazaarlike area of Little Arabia, just off Th Sukhumvit, there is such fabulous Arabic cuisine that no-one would fault you for doing one too many hummus nights. Meat pies, nachos, corn bread, runny eggs – whatever mama used to make has been recreated by an expat entrepreneur for those far-from-home cravings.

Opening Hours

Restaurants serving Thai food are generally open from 10am to 8pm or 9pm, although some places are open later. Foreign-cuisine restaurants tend to keep only dinner hours, although this varies. Thais are consummate eaters and are always within reach of a snack or light meal, so meal times are quite flexible, although restaurants tend to get crowded around 8pm.

Muslim-run restaurants sometimes close in observance of religious or cultural holidays, some close on Friday, while others close on Monday. Most Thai and Chinese restaurants view holidays as a chance to feed more customers and therefore rarely lock up the metal gates for the day.

Bangkok has recently passed a city-wide ordinance banning street vendors from setting up shop on Monday. The footpaths are so uncluttered on these days that a roadside eater might feel both hunger and abandonment by their favourite rice mama.

How Much?

A bowl of noodles or a stir-fry dish bought from a street vendor should cost 25B to 30B, depending on the portion size and ingredients. Climbing up the scale are the canteen shops that have a selection of premade dishes, sturdier chairs and a roof. For these luxuries, you'll probably pay 30B to 40B.

Thai restaurants with an army of servers and laminated menus usually offer main dishes for around 80B to 150B. Add ambience, air-con and fancy uniforms, and a main jumps to about 120B to 200B. Anything above 300B will deliver you into the arms of some of the city's fanciest restaurants. An exception is the restaurants in top-end hotels, which feature prices close to what you'd expect to pay at any flash hotel in the world.

PRICE GUIDE	
$$$	over 300B a meal
$$	150–299B a meal
$	under 150B a meal

In most parts of the city, Western food occupies the high end of the scale, costing from 200B to 350B. One obvious exception is Banglamphu, where *faràng* (Western) food comes in under 200B a plate.

Booking Tables

If you have a lot of friends in tow or will be attending a formal restaurant (including hotel restaurants), reservations are recommended. Bookings are also recommended for Sunday brunch and dinner cruises.

Otherwise, you shouldn't have a problem scoring a table at most restaurants in the city, especially if you arrive during off-peak hours. Following the European tradition (or because of the wretched evening commute), peak dinner time starts around 8pm. The lunchtime crush typically starts around noon and lasts close to an hour.

Tipping

You shouldn't be surprised to learn that tipping in Thailand isn't as exact as it is in Europe (tip no-one) or the USA (tip everyone). Thailand falls somewhere in between, and some areas are left open to interpretation. Everyone agrees that you don't tip streetside vendors, although some vendors add a little surcharge when tallying up a bill for a foreigner. To avoid getting annoyed about this double-pricing scheme, consider it an implicit tip.

When eating at a restaurant, tipping becomes more a game of finesse. Some people leave roughly 10% at any sit-down restaurant where someone fills their glass every time they take a sip. Others don't. Most upscale restaurants will apply a 10% service charge to the bill. Some patrons leave extra on top of the service charge; others don't. The decision is up to you.

KO RATANAKOSIN & THONBURI

After a day of sightseeing in these historic neighbourhoods, there are surprisingly few restaurants geared toward hunger and heat relief. Once the sun sets, several riverside restaurants soak up the night-time view of the dual temples (Wat Phra Kaew and Wat Arun), but vistas rarely coincide with good victuals.

RUB AROON Map p288   Thai $
Th Maharat, Ko Ratanakosin; mains 60-150B; ⏱ 10am-7pm; ferry Tha Tien, ordinary bus 512
There aren't a lot of options for a sit-down meal in Ko Ratanakosin, but this traveller-friendly café is a pleasant exception. The restored shopfront opens directly onto the street with cosy seating and gentle service. The dishes are basic and delicious and served alongside fruit drinks and coffees for sipping away tropical fatigue.

TALAT WANG LANG Map p288   Thai $
Th Phrannok & Trok Wang Lang, Thonburi; snacks/mains from 5/60B, ⏱ 10am-8pm; ferry Tha Wang Lang
Beside Siriraj Hospital is a busy market that sprawls west from Tha Wang Lang. Many of the vendors prepare specialties from southern-style curries and *phàt phèt sataw* (spicy red curry stir-fry with nitta seeds). The theory is that southern Thai food took root here because of the nearby train sta-tion that served southern destinations. Organic produce is available at **Bo Pak**, a small store directly in front of the ferry pier.

BANGLAMPHU

With more villagelike qualities than other parts of Bangkok, this area's strength is its abundant street food. Every alley wide enough to hold a wok is claimed as a make-shift dining room. Because of the back-packer presence, Western and vegetarian food is plentiful and cheap.

ARAWY Map pp286-7   Vegetarian Thai $
152 Th Din So; mains 35-40B; ⏱ 7am-7pm; air-con bus 508, 511 & 512, khlong taxi Tha Phan Fah
This king of vegie spots is marked by a Roman-script sign that reads 'Alloy' ('deli-cious'). There's hardly any room for custom-ers among the vats of curries and stockpiles of ingredients, but squeezing in beside the TV and a box of palm oil is worth it. This is one of the city's best Thai vegetarian res-taurants. The restaurant is just opposite the City Hall and a few doors from a 7-Eleven store.

CHOCHANA Map pp286-7   Israeli $
Soi off Th Chakraphong; mains 100-150B; ⏱ 11am-11pm; air-con bus 511 & 512, ordinary bus 2 & 82, ferry Tha Phra Athit
One of Khao San's longest-running Israeli restaurants, Chochana is tucked away in a tiny alley beside the petrol station and serves gut-filling falafel-and-hummus plates

---

BANGLAMPHU STREET BUFFET

In Banglamphu, every crack between buildings is a kitchen. It is dank and anti-atmospheric, but the food is fab and the strange setting makes chowhounds feel like Indiana Jones.

To spare the shopping housewives from feeling peckish, a **khànǒm jiin stand** (Map pp286–7; beside the Tan Hua Seng supermarket, Th Chakraphong) sets up directly behind the vendor selling puffed rice treats.

The bar **Spyglass** (Map pp286–7; Th Phra Athit) opens up during the day to feed lunchtime workers premade curries and stir-fries. The whopping bill comes to 20B for one choice or 30B for two choices over rice. And those beautiful slivers of colour are tear-inducing chilli peppers.

Trok Surat is lined with several Muslim street vendors. A **khâo mòk kài** (chicken biryani) seller sets up on Fridays. In the forecourt of an old wooden house, **SM Lokanda** (Map pp286–7; Trok Surat; mains 40B) sells a choice of two or three premade Muslim curries piquantly spiced with turmeric and generous pieces of chicken, a hearty break from the Thai curry crawl.

Th Khao San is an obvious choice for late-night snacks: *shwarma* sandwiches, stand-and-gulp *phàt thai*, fruit and satay.

Near the 7-Eleven on Th Rambutri, post-imbibing Thais fend off a hangover with a bowl of *jóhk* (rice porridge). Soi Rambutri has more streetside eating, with grilled fish, chicken and cold beer.

with a side order of blaring Israeli comedy sketches on the communal TV. Don't overlook the tasty baba ghanoush and *jachnoon* (a Sabbath cake).

CHOTE CHITR
Thai $

☎ 0 2221 4082; 146 Th Phraeng Phuton; ☾ 10am-10pm; mains 60-150B; air-con bus 508, khlong taxi Tha Phan Fah

Antique family-owned restaurants adorn this old section of town where middle-class Thais, unconcerned with the latest restaurant import, eat the way their parents and grandparents did before them. When it comes to retrograde eating, perhaps no other world cuisine can command such respect. Of the long list of specialities, Chote Chitr is famous for *mee krob* (sweet-and-spicy crispy fried noodles), a dish that is beginning to lose favour among modern Thais. The *yam hua plee* (banana flower salad) is another shy celebrity. To get here walk south on Th Tanao, past Th Bunsiri, and turn right into the Phraeng Phuton area across from the bank.

HEMLOCK
Map pp286-7
Thai $

☎ 0 2282 7507; 56 Th Phra Athit; mains 80-200B; ☾ 5.30-11.30pm; ferry Tha Phra Athit

Living-room-sized restaurants line Th Phra Athit and form a social gathering point for Banglamphu's Thai bohemians (writers, artists and intellectuals) and nongovernment organisation (NGO) type *faràng*. This cosy gem has enough style to feel like a special night out but doesn't skimp on flavour or preparation. The eclectic menu reads like an ancient literary work, reviving old dishes from the aristocratic kitchens across the country. Try the flavourful *mîang kham* (tea leaves wrapped around ginger, shallots, peanuts, lime and coconut flakes) or *yam khà-moi* (thieves' salad).

ILLY CAFÉ
Map pp286-7
Thai $

Th Chakraphong; mains 50-150B; ☾ 10am-10pm; ordinary bus 53, ferry Tha Phra Athit

Parts of Banglamphu are cool in a Greenwich Village sort of way – eclectic, funky and nostalgic – and Illy Café continues the emerging aesthetic. Big picture windows look out on the busy street where housewives climb in and out of asthmatic buses and backpackers stumble past with small apartments strapped to their backs. You can enjoy that hard-won holiday ritual of nursing a cup of coffee here. Or stop by around midday for honest Thai food. At night, grab some beers in the upstairs lounge filled with vintage décor and the neighbourhood's lo-sos (bohemian Thais who don't have as much money as the high-society types hanging out across town).

JAY FAI
Map pp286-7
Thai $

☎ 0 2223-9384; 327 Th Maha Chai; mains 250B; ☾ 5pm-midnight; ordinary bus 508 & 5, khlong taxi Tha Phan Fah

Another venerable spot, Jay Fai is known for its 'millionaire' noodles. The lowly street dish, *kǔaytǐaw phàt khîi mao* (drunken noodles), gets a *Pygmalion* makeover, loaded up with such fresh seafood and premium ingredients that BMWs outnumber motorcycles. Honestly, we're content with the 30B variety, but it's curious to know that fame can command such prices.

JEY HOY
Map pp286-7
Thai-Chinese $

Soi 2, Th Samsen; mains 50-100B; ☾ 6pm-midnight; air-con bus 505, ordinary bus 53, ferry Tha Phra Athit

Just over the *khlong* bridge, this popular open-air restaurant commandeers the corner with a big tray of fresh seafood displayed on a bed of ice. The iron chef beats mercilessly at the prominently displayed

Cook at work with a wok, Jey Hoy

wok, creating lickety-split Hokkien specials, such as *puu phàt phong kàrìi* (crab stir-fried with curry powder and egg). Tables radiate out of the restaurant and along the footpaths – an indication that the food must be good enough to hold diners' attention.

KHRUA NOPPARAT Map pp286-7   Thai $
Th Phra Athit; mains 60-100B; ⏰ 10.30am-9.30pm Mon-Sat; ordinary bus 53, ferry Tha Phra Athit
This plain Jane is filled with fluorescent lighting and cheap furniture, which leaves more resources for the food. The small plates should encourage the Thai tradition of over-ordering. Everything is good, so just focus on chewing your way through the multipage menu. Once you find a few favourites, you are ready to pull up a chair alongside a motorcycle taxi driver at one of the working-class canteens set up under a shade tree.

MAY KAIDEE Map pp286-7   Vegetarian Thai $
Sub-soi off Soi Damnoen Klang Neua & Th Tanao; mains 50B; ⏰ 11am-9.30pm; air-con bus 511, ordinary bus 59, ferry Tha Phra Athit
May Kaidee started doing vegetarian around the same time that fisherman pants became the backpacker uniform. She knows her audience: easy on the chillies, heavy on the coconut milk and light on the fishiness. And she doesn't even wince when new arrivals ask for chopsticks for their curries. Even though the dishes are tweaked, the scene is 100% Bangkok: *lûuk thûng* (Thai country music) blares over the restaurant speakers and the wok clangs in time with the music. To find this restaurant from Th Khao San, cross Th Tanao and follow the little soi near Sirinthip Guesthouse; take the first left for 50m. There is a second branch on **Th Samsen** (Map pp286–7), just over the bridge. May Kaidee also offers cooking lessons.

PRASIT SOMONTA   Thai $
☎ 0 2622 2349; 474-476 Th Tanao; mains 100B; ⏰ 10am-10pm; air-con bus 508, khlong taxi Tha Phan Fah
Past the new-fangled chicken rotisserie is a friendly log-cabin restaurant with big picnic table seating and walls adorned with famous Thai actors. This is a new venture in a neighbourhood known for longevity and royal pedigree. And the Isan

---

DINING WITH A VIEW

- Crepes & Co (p141) Peek into a tropical garden from this breezy cottage.
- Rang Mahal (p144) A sea of concrete towers meets the horizon from this rooftop perch.
- Ton Pho (opposite) Watch the muddy Chao Phraya river, hulking barge boats and zippy long-tail boats.
- Sirocco (p138) So high in the sky that you can tickle the moon.
- River Bar Café (p146) Sassy and classy glass box overlooking the Chao Phraya River.

---

menu is even more incongruous, considering that the owner is Thai-Chinese and had never eaten the fiery dishes of the northeast until he met his wife from Chaiyapoom. But the comfortable setting and curious contradictions make this a welcoming spot for neat freaks made nervous by streetside dining.

RANEE'S GUESTHOUSE
Map pp286-7   Vegetarian Thai $
77 Trok Mayom off Th Chakraphong; mains 70-120B; ⏰ 7am-midnight; ordinary bus 59, air-con bus 508, ferry Tha Phra Athit
Quantity-loving vegetarians will appreciate this guesthouse kitchen. Vegetable stir-fries are cooked to perfection and can be enjoyed in a quiet garden courtyard where the owner's children have their own imaginary dinner party. Specify if you want brown rice.

ROTI-MATABA Map pp286-7   Muslim Thai $
Cnr Th Phra Athit & Th Phra Sumen; mains 50-80B; ⏰ 7am-8pm Tue-Sun; ordinary bus 53, ferry Tha Phra Athit
Opposite Phra Sumen Fort, this claustrophobic spot does delicious southern-Thai-style meals, such as roti, *kaeng mátsàmàn* (Muslim curry), chicken korma and chicken or vegetable *mátàbà* (a sort of stuffed Indian pancake). It has a bilingual menu and a gruff army of aproned young servers. An upstairs air-con dining area and outdoor tables barely provide enough seating for its loyal fans. The procedure for eating and paying requires telepathic Thai abilities: you seat yourself and flag down one of the waiters (who will pretend that you don't

Staff working at Roti-Mataba (opposite)

exist), but you pay downstairs where miraculously they have a bill waiting. Wonders never cease.

SIAM HOUSE Map pp286-7   Thai $$
☎ 0 2281 6237; 591 Th Phra Sumen; mains 150-300B; ⏰ 6pm-midnight; air-con bus 511, khlong taxi Tha Phan Fah

This classic Sino-Portuguese house has fallen off the map of 'in' spots, especially after a parade of name changes. But civil servants still bestow their discriminating taste buds on the authentic Thai dishes at lunchtime.

THIP SAMAI Map pp286-7   Thai $
☎ 0 2221 6280; 313 Th Mahachai; mains 60-100B; ⏰ 7pm-3am; air-con bus 508, ordinary bus 5, khlong taxi Tha Phan Fah

For new arrivals, every plate of *phàt thai* is better than the last. But for those teethed on these fried noodles, Thip Samai surpasses expectations. The venerable restaurant still serves up the wok special amid austere footpath seating but the plump shrimp and delicate egg-wrapped crepes fetch more than pocket change.

TON PHO Map pp286-7   Thai $
☎ 0 2280 0452; Th Phra Athit; mains 60-100B; ⏰ 10am-10pm; ferry Tha Phra Athit

This dockside restaurant, overlooking the muddy Mae Nam Chao Phraya, is an excellent stop for authentic Thai. The restaurant's décor has as much charm as a school cafeteria, adding anecdotal evidence to the city-wide conviction that good food doesn't deserve to be sullied with the Western concept of ambience.

THEWET

The primary draw to this sleepy neighbourhood are the riverside restaurants that drink in the cool river breezes and grill whole fish for communal picking.

IN LOVE Map pp282-3   Thai $$
☎ 0 2281 2900; Th Krung Kasem; mains 150-200B; ⏰ 11am-10pm; air-con bus 506 & 53; ferry Tha Thewet

The old Silver Spoon (Chon-Ngern) has changed its name but not its view of the elegant Saphan Phra Ram VIII (King Rama XIII Bridge). Nothing says Thailand like sitting out en plein on a glorified pier picking tender meat off a whole fish, such as the restaurant speciality of *plaa kràphong nêung mánao* (steamed sea bass with lemon).

KALOANG HOME KITCHEN
Map pp282-3   Thai $
☎ 02 281 9228; 2 Th Si Ayuthaya; mains 90-150B; ⏰ 11am-11pm; air-con bus 506, ordinary bus 53, ferry Tha Thewet

Little more than a converted pier, Kaloang Home Kitchen could teach the high-end restaurants a thing or two about five-star

GRUBHOUND FAVOURITES

- Soi Polo Fried Chicken (p139) Fried chicken to put the colonel to shame.
- Khrua Aroy Aroy (p136) Meet the real curry McCoy, not the guesthouse impostors.
- Talat Wang Lang (p126) A market of finger-lickin' good Southern Thai.
- Chote Chitr (p127) A stand-in Thai grandma for old-fashioned family recipes.
- MBK Food Court (p132) A mall food court for street eats without the diesel fumes.

service. The crowd is solely Thai with more beer guzzlers than rice gobblers. But food is never forgotten and the deep-fried snakehead fish often adorns the table along with sweating bottles of beer. Finding this place is half the fun: follow Th Si Ayuthaya towards the river and turn right at the temple past the kids playing badminton, and keep going till the end of the street.

CHINATOWN & PHAHURAT

When you say Chinatown, Bangkokians begin dreaming of noodles, usually prepared by street vendors that line Th Yaowarat after dark. During the annual Vegetarian Festival, the neighbourhood embraces meatless meals with yellow-flagged street stalls. Phahurat has several Indian restaurants and an afternoon samosa vendor near Soi ATM.

BA-MII HONG KONG
Map pp284-5   Thai- Chinese $
Cnr Th Yaowarat & Soi Yaowaphanit; mains 50B;
6pm-midnight; air-con bus 73, ferry Tha Ratchawong
At night Th Yaowarat turns into a fluorescent-lit carnival of outdoor eating. Set up next to the gold shop, Bà-Mii Hong Kong serves *bà-mìi* (egg noodles) and *kíaw* (shrimp-stuffed wontons) with capitalistic variety. Customers tick off their choices on an order sheet after hunting down a table.

CHIANG KII Map pp284-5   Chinese $
54 Soi Bamrungrat; mains 100B; 5-10pm;
air-con bus 73, ferry Tha Ratchawong
It might take a few years of slurping down rice everyday to develop a true apprecia-

tion of Chiang Kii's *khâo tôm plaa* (rice soup with fish). Fresh butterfish and sea bass are used in the otherwise humble dish, along with a well-seasoned broth and little cubes of pork slightly sweetened in palm sugar.

HONG KONG NOODLES
Map pp284-5   Chinese $
136 Trok Itsaranuphap, Th Charoen Krung; mains 30B;
10am-8pm; air-con bus 73, ferry Tha Ratchawong
Deep in the heart of a vendor-lined *soi*, Hong Kong Noodles does a busy trade in steaming bowls of roast-duck noodles. If you can find a seat, there's a nice vista of the surrounding commerce.

HUA SENG HONG
Map pp284-5   Thai-Chinese $
0 2222 0635; 371-373 Th Yaowarat; mains 100-200B; 10am-midnight; air-con bus 73, ferry Tha Ratchawong
Shark fin might draw in some tourists but it's the homemade noodle dishes *(hâwy thâwt)*, dim sum and other Thai-Chinese favourites at Hua Seng that really satisfy the empty belly and clear the conscience.

LAEM THONG Map pp284-5   Thai-Chinese $
0 2224 3591; 38 Soi Bamrungrat, Th Charoen Krung; mains 20-25B; 9am-7pm; air-con bus 73, ferry Tha Ratchawong
A small canteen shop, Laem Thong specialises in southern Chinese cuisine with a

WAVING THE YELLOW FLAG

During the annual Vegetarian Festival (in September/October), Bangkok's Chinatown becomes a virtual orgy of nonmeat cuisine. The festivities centre on Wat Mangkon Kamalawatt, on Th Charoen Krung, but food shops and stalls all over the city post yellow flags to announce their meat-free status.

Celebrating alongside the ethnic Chinese are Thais who look forward to the special dishes that appear during the festival period. Most restaurants will put their normal menus on hold and instead prepare soybased substitutes to standard Thai dishes like *tôm yam* (hot and sour soup), *kaeng mátsàmàn* (Muslim curry), and *kaeng khǐaw-wǎan* (green curry). Of the special festival dishes, yellow Japanese-style noodles *(soba)* appear in stir-fried dishes along with meaty mushrooms and big hunks of vegetables.

Along with abstinence from meat, the 10-day festival is celebrated with special visits to the temple, often requiring worshippers to dress in white.

wide assortment of seafood, rice noodles and dumplings. You just point and order. It isn't fancy but neither is Chinatown.

OLD SIAM PLAZA

Map pp284-5   Thai $

Cnr Th Phahurat & Th Triphet; mains 30-40B;
🕙 **10am-5pm; air-con bus 73, ferry Tha Saphan Phut**
Wedged between the western edge of Chinatown and the northern edge of Phahurat, this three-storey shopping plaza has a 3rd-floor food centre serving Thai and Chinese food. The 1st floor provides a quick lesson in Thai desserts, with vendors selling all the streetside sweets within a quieter space.

ROYAL INDIA Map pp284-5   Indian $$

☎ **0 2221 6565; 392/1 Th Chakraphet; mains 100-250B;** 🕙 **10am-10pm; air-con bus 73, ferry Tha Saphan Phut**
A legend in expat circles, Royal India prepares honest dishes from northern India. Barely visible from the main road, the restaurant huddles in the shadows of a small *soi* giving it an in-the-know speakeasy quality. But the crowds find it at lunch when tables are shared between parties and travellers from different continents and generations share their globetrotting resumes.

SHANGARILA RESTAURANT

Map pp284-5   Chinese $$$

☎ **0 2235 7493; 206 Th Yaowarat; mains 220-500B;** 🕙 **11am-10pm; air-con bus 73, ferry Tha Ratchawong**
This massive, banquet-style restaurant prepares a variety of Cantonese cuisine for ravenous families. The dim sum lunches are worth muscling your way past the outdoor steam tables.

SOI TEXAS SEAFOOD STALLS

Map pp284-5   Thai-Chinese $$

Cnr Th Phadungdao & Th Yaowarat; mains 150-250B;
🕙 **6-10pm; air-con bus 73, ferry Tha Ratchawong**
On a yet another food corner, this street sprouts outdoor barbecues, iced seafood trays and sidewalk seating. Servers dash every which way, cars plough through narrow openings, and before you know it you're tearing into a plate of grilled prawns like a starved alley cat.

BEYOND RICE: OUTSTANDING IMPORTS

- Chochana (p126) Scratch the ketchup itch with fries and Israeli sandos.
- Mizu's Kitchen (p137) Japanese versions of mac 'n' cheese and other cafeteria commandos.
- Sallim Restaurant (p138) Scoff down fiery Southern Thai and Muslim curries.
- Café Le Notre (below) Desserts so rich they should pay for themselves.
- Great American Rib Company (p142) A manly meal of big slabs of slow-roasted Southern barbecue.

SIAM SQUARE, PRATUNAM & PLOENCHIT

When you just can't stomach another meal of rice, take yourself immediately to Siam Square for the guilty pleasure of international fast food. These spiffy air-con joints overflow with Thai students more adept at handling a hamburger than most *faràng* are with chopsticks. Fear not mediocrity: there is a veritable restaurant row around Soi Lang Suan, off Th Ploenchit.

BAN KHUN MAE Map pp294-5   Thai $

☎ **0 2658 4112; Soi 8, Siam Square; mains 50-90B;** 🕙 **11am-10pm; Skytrain Siam**
Welcome to Mama's House, a homey little spot for respectable Thai food at hospitable prices. Once you master this menu, you are ready to strike out on your own into the vendor stalls where the same quality is delivered for half the price.

CAFÉ LE NOTRE Map pp294-5   French $$$

☎ **0 2250 7050; Natural Ville Executive Residences, 61 Soi Lang Suan; mains 300B;** 🕙 **6am-10pm; Skytrain Ploenchit**
Ooh la, la, la, grab your Fendi and your prettiest gal pals for an afternoon dessert fest at this Parisian chain café that puts its confections and its patrons on display. Rich and decadent chocolate pastries, brioche and macaroons go quickly for the nibblers, and light fare fills out the menu's skeletal figure.

DELHI DARBAR RESTAURANT

Map pp280-1   Indian $$

☎ 0 2254 3704; 122/61 Soi Somprasongruam, Th
Ratchadamri; 150-200B; ⏰ 10am-10pm; ordinary
bus 77, khlong taxi Tha Pratunam

Need a jolt out of your food pattern? Go
hunting through chaotic Pratunam market
for this family-run Indian restaurant. The
menu covers Muslim fare from the north
and south of the subcontinent. But the best
success is finding it: from Baiyoke Skytower
follow the traffic away from Th Ratcha-
prarop and turn right on the first *soi* and
right again directly across from 7-Eleven.

FOOD LOFT Map pp294-5   International $$

☎ 0 2655 7777; 7th fl, Central Chitlom Shopping
Center, Th Ploenchit; meals 100-400B; ⏰ 10am-
10pm; Skytrain Chitlom

Taking the mall food court one step further,
Food Loft has added ambience, a view of
the city and international options. Some of
the city's most beloved restaurants have
stations here so that lunch can be a globetrotting experience.

FUJI JAPANESE RESTAURANT

Map pp294-5   Japanese $$

☎ 0 2611 7166; Mahboonkrong (MBK) Center, Th
Rama I; mains 50-250B; ⏰ 11am-10pm; Skytrain
National Stadium

It is a source of great consternation for
Bangkok, but quality Japanese food is

---

sorely lacking. Everyone then settles for
this Japanese chain, which will scratch the
wasabi itch without depleting the baht
reserves. There are other branches through-
out the city, including the **Emporium** (Map
pp296-7; Th Sukhumvit).

GIANNI'S RISTORANTE

Map pp294-5   Italian $$$

☎ 0 2252 1619; 34/1 Soi Tonson; Th Ploenchit;
mains 260-600B; ⏰ 6-11pm; Skytrain Chitlom

The Italians dominate the top end of Bangkok's cuisine scene. Pasta and pizza lure
noodle-loving Thais and tomato-deprived
expats. Gianni's distinguishes itself from the
pack like a family patriarch. It has helped
push the city beyond rudimentary to nearly
fluent appreciation of Italian cuisine. Homemade sausages, lobster-stuffed ravioli and
braised lamb shanks transport taste buds
to the Adriatic. Wine lovers rave about the
huge and unique selection. Reservations
recommended.

KHAO MAN KAI SIAM Map pp294-5   Thai $

Siam Chicken (on front door); 280 Th Phra Ram I;
mains 35-50B; ⏰ 10am-9pm; Skytrain Siam

On the Siam Square side of Th Phra Ram I
and in the shadow of the Siam Skytrain
station, this slick and sterile spot still
maintains the calling card of a traditional
khâo man kài (chicken rice) shop: dangling
chicken carcasses in front of the kitchen.
The fresh lemon grass broth and spicy
dipping sauce keep the traditions of this
time-honoured comfort food and the air-
con means you can enjoy it free from car
exhaust fumes.

MBK FOOD COURT Map pp294-5   Thai $

4th fl, Mahboonkrong (MBK) Centre, cnr Th Phayathai & Th Phra Ram I; mains 30-60B; ⏰ 10am-
10pm; Skytrain Siam

It sounds ridiculous to recommend eating
at a shopping mall in such a culinary capital, but the malls have ushered Bangkok's
street food options into soothing air con-
ditioning with bilingual menus. And some
have even distinguished themselves in Thai
chowhound circles. MBK, for example, ex-
cels at duck and beef noodles in herb broth
and for *khâo khǎa mǔu* (stewed pork leg).
See, the modern world isn't so bad. All the
mall food courts play the coupon game:
buy the pretend money from the desk and
be refunded the remainder.

THE HUNT FOR A PLATE OF RICE

If you're staying on or near Soi Kasem San 1, you don't
have to suck motorcycle fumes crossing Th Phra Ram
I and Th Phayathai to find something to eat. A row of
vendors with tables along the east side of the *soi* cater
mainly to lunching Thais and a few *faràng* patrons.

A small village of food vendors (Map pp294–5;
⏰ closed Sunday) set up within one of the alleys of
Siam Square, just to the right of Siam Square's Scala
cinema. If approaching this alley from Th Phayathai,
look for the sign that reads 'food centre'.

Lots of lunch stalls spring up along Soi Tonson
(Map pp294–5) and connecting *soi* behind the Sind-
horn building. Keep an eye out for *kaeng tai plaa,* a
Southern curry.

Deep in the *soi* near Chulalongkorn University is
the **Suan Luang Night Market** (Map pp280–1; Soi 5
btwn Soi 22 & 16, Th Ban That Thong), it closes off a
multiblock radius for dinnertime.

MIDNIGHT KAI TON Map pp294-5   Thai $

Th Phetburi; mains 30-40B; 7pm-4am; ordinary bus 77, khlong taxi Tha Pratunam

Drive around Bangkok at night and you'll pass large pockets of sleeping businesses suddenly interrupted by a shock of fluorescent lights and crowds of outdoor tables. Of the night-dining pockets, Pratunam's intersection of Th Ratchadamri and Th Phetburi draws Thais from near and far for *khâo man kài*. This dish is the ultimate in comfort food, simple and wholesome, but this food shop makes just enough adjustments to make it worth a special trip. Their famous dipping

HOTEL BUFFET BONANZA

Perhaps we're food curmudgeons, but we've been under-whelmed by many of the highly touted hotel restaurants, which have more in common with graduation dinners at the country club than culinary orgasms. Where the hotels really excel is the mind-blowingly decadent buffets. Fountains of chocolate, oysters on the half shell, pretty pink salmon, dishes from every major cuisine. Roman vomitoriums eat your heart out; we've got to do another buffet round.

At the high-end hotels, lunch buffets are typically 1000B, and dinner and brunch buffets 1500B to 2000B. Smaller hotels are significantly cheaper. Reservations are required. Hours are typically lunch noon to 2pm, dinner 6pm to 10pm, and brunch buffets on weekends 11am to 3pm.

Colonnade Restaurant (Map pp292–3; ☎ 0 2344 8888; 1st fl, Sukhothai Hotel, 13/3 Th Sathon) Dah-ling, you've got to brag to the neighbours about this cherry-on-top Sunday brunch. Free-flowing champagne, made-to-order lobster bisque, caviar, imported cheeses, foie gras and a jazz trio for background music. Reservations essential, months in advance.

Four Seasons (Map pp294–5; ☎ 0 2250 1000; Four Seasons Hotel, 155 Th Ratchadamri) The Four Seasons' highly regarded restaurants, Shintaro, Biscotti and Madison, set up steam tables for their decadent weekend brunch buffet. Next stop fistfuls of foie gras.

Marriott Cafe (Map pp296–7; ☎ 0 2656 7700; JW Marriott, 4 Soi 2, Th Sukhumvit) American-style abundance fills the buffet tables with fresh oysters, seafood, pasta and international nibbles at its daily buffet. There are also activities for children.

Oriental Hotel (Map pp290–1; ☎ 0 2655 9900; Oriental Hotel, Soi Oriental, Th Charoen Krung) The Oriental has two options: Lord Jim's is a chic glass-enclosed restaurant that overlooks the river and serves a weekend brunch buffet of seafood. The Riverside Terrace serves evening barbecue buffets within fishing distance of the river.

Shanghai 38 (Map pp290–1; ☎ 0 2238 1991; Sofitel Silom, 188 Th Silom) Perched on the 38th floor, this Chinese restaurant dishes up a daily dim-sum buffet and a panoramic view.

Afternoon tea lives on at the Author's Lounge in the Oriental Hotel

EDIBLE GLOBALISATION

Pasta with curry, steak slathered in chillies, ketchup on pizza? Dishes you recognise from home have been Thai-ed up to suit local tastes. Known as 'inter' (for 'international'), these Western-Thai fusions are not as self-conscious as their haute cousins or as well dressed, and appear more in markets and canteens than fine-dining restaurants. The flavour-forward university students are great champions of inter food. Interested in sampling edible versions of globalisation? Check out Pasta Lover: Thai Style, a vendor in the **lunchtime market** (Map pp292–3) on the corner of Th Sala Daeng & Soi Yommarat. A steak vendor (pronounced Thai style as 'sa-teak') sets up on Soi Convent (Map pp290–1) at night. More inter options can be found at the food stalls (Map p288) between the river and the amulet market near Thammasat University.

sauce has zesty bits of bite-sized ginger and the broth tastes nutritious enough to cure what ails you. There are several overflow restaurants nearby but Midnight Kai Ton is the second shop from the corner.

REUR TA SIAM GUAY TIEW
Map pp294-5   Thai $
☎ 0 2252 8353; Soi 3, Siam Square, Th Phra Ram 1; mains 40-100B; ⏰ 9am-9pm; Skytrain Siam
Back in the days when canals were the city's thoroughfares, the vendor cart floated from house to house. Now that life has moved to solid ground, this restaurant and others like it pay tribute to those days by serving noodles out of stylised boats. Teenagers love this place and often stand in line to get *kŭaytĭaw reua* (boat noodles) with red pork and other rice dishes.

SANGUAN SRI Map pp294-5   Thai $
59/1 Th Withayu; mains 60-150B; ⏰ 11am-2.30pm; Skytrain Ploenchit
Bangkok is such a sensory overload that many places melt into the landscape unless they scream at you in neon lights or Roman lettering. Sanguan Sri certainly disappears within its concrete bunker, which looks like a forgotten office filled with old-fashioned ink stamps and tropically wilted paper. But it is really a culinary landmark for generations of Thai managers and upper-level office workers. The food is straight from the bosom of a Thai grandmother: *kaeng khĭaw-wăan* (green curry), *kaeng jèut* (soup

with glass noodles and minced pork), *yam plaa kràwp* (crispy dried fish salad) and *mìi kràwp râat nâa kài* (crisp-fried noodles with chicken in a gravy sauce). There is no English sign and no English menu, so you may need to enlist a Thai friend for this venture.

TALAT SAM YAN Map pp280-1   Thai $
Chulalongkorn Soi 6, near cnr of Th Phayathai & Th Phra Ram IV; mains 50B; ⏰ noon-midnight; subway Samyan
This two-storey pavilion has a busy fresh-food market on the 1st floor along with a lunch and dinner emporium on the 2nd floor. During lunch, the meals are a curious Thai adaptation of the Western heart-attack special: slabs of meat that are slathered in sweet and spicy sauces and then wrapped in processed cheese. At dinner the meals are more health-friendly Thai dishes.

THANG LONG Map pp294-5   Vietnamese $
☎ 0 2251 3504; 82/5 Soi Lang Suan, Th Ploenchit; mains 80-185B; ⏰ 11am-2pm & 5-9pm; Skytrain Chitlom
Although Thailand and Vietnam are nearly kissing cousins, Vietnamese food in Bangkok is a date occasion, rather than the immigrant outpost you might expect. Poised at genteel Lang Suan, Thang Long is Bangkok's latest mistress, a classy place zipped up in sophisticated minimalist décor and serving inspired modern Vietnamese cuisine.

WHOLE EARTH RESTAURANT
Map pp294-5   Vegetarian Thai $$
☎ 0 2252 5574; 93/3 Soi Lang Suan; mains 120-200B; ⏰ 11.30am-2pm & 5.30-11pm; Skytrain Chitlom
Mainly a lunchtime draw, this popular expat restaurant does very down-to-earth and wholesome, if not hugely exciting, international veg food.

RIVERSIDE, SILOM & LUMPHINI

In the heart of the financial district, Silom has a lot more variety than you might assume. At lunchtime the area goes into a feeding frenzy, with whole lunchtime villages of street vendors and lip-smacking

SWIMMING IN STREET FOOD

So many office workers, so many mouths to feed. Lunchtime eats clog every pedestrian corridor in the financial district. **Talat ITF** (Map pp290–1; Soi 10, Th Silom) has a string of food stalls running the length of the *soi*, purveying pots of curry and miles of noodles. More central eats can be found at lunch stalls (Map pp290–1) along quieter Soi Sala Daeng 2. A midday vendor ekes out a small business selling chicken biryani at a **khâo mòk kài stall** (Map pp290–1; Th Convent) in front of the Irish X-Change.

buffets at the nearby English-Irish pubs. Dinner offerings are a little more gourmet, with a handful of elegant restaurants preparing fusion and royal Thai cuisine intended to make a good impression for visiting VIPs.

Towards the western end of Th Silom, Indian and Muslim eateries begin making an appearance. Unlike in Indian restaurants elsewhere in Bangkok, the menus don't necessarily exhibit the usual, boring predilection towards North Indian Moghul-style cuisine.

Bordering the river, the luxury hotels sponsor elaborate restaurants with elegant views and predictable hotel food.

Strangled by several surface highways, Lumphini has very little neighbourhood personality but still boasts many dinner restaurants because land is under less demand than the coveted properties north of Lumphini Park. Off the main roads are smaller streets sprouting food villages. The area known as Soi Ngam Duphli boasts some neighbourhood standards worth chewing on if you're in the neighbourhood and need air-con.

BAAN KHANITHA Map pp292-3   Thai $$

☎ 0 2253 4638-9; 69 Th Sathon Tai; mains 150-350B; ☽ 11am-2pm & 6-11pm; ordinary bus 22, subway Lumphini

Baan Khanitha has moved from its charming old house on Soi Ruam Rudi to this corner command post, but it still earns respect from expats for considerate and accommodating Westernised Thai food. Tender palates are given access to the subtle complexity of Thai flavours in such dishes as the wing bean salad and deep-fried squid curry.

BAN CHIANG Map pp290-1   Thai $

☎ 0 2236 7045, 14 Soi Si Wiang, Th Surasak; mains 90-150B; ☽ 11.30am-9.30pm; Skytrain Surasak

Named after the archaeological site in northeastern Thailand, Ban Chiang is a tourist spot that deserves referrals. Traditional Thai and Isan cuisine fills the menu in a cosy wooden house with eclectic décor. Not everything is mind-blowing, but solid standards include *yam plaa dùk fuu* (shredded fish salad), *phàt phàk khánáa* (stir-fried greens) and *kài phàt khǐng hèt hǎwm* (chicken stir-fried with mushroom and ginger). To get here go east on Soi Si Wiang and look for the junglelike garden barely tamed by an overwhelmed wooden fence.

BLUE ELEPHANT Map pp290-1   Thai $$

☎ 0 2673 9353; 233 Th Sathon Tai; mains 200-500B; ☽ 11am-2pm & 5-11pm; Skytrain Surasak

The Blue Elephant got its start in Brussels more than two decades ago as an exotic outpost of royal Thai cuisine. After spreading to other foreign cities, the Blue Elephant boldly chose Bangkok, the cuisine's birth mother, as its ninth location. Set in a stunning Sino-Portuguese colonial building with service fit for royalty, it is a noble contender for fine dining within striking distance of the city's luxury hotels.

CIRCLE OF FRIENDS Map pp290-1   Thai $

☎ 0 2237 0080; Soi 10, Th Sathon; mains 60-100B; ☽ 11.30am-3pm; Skytrain Surasak

This unpretentious café shares space with Saeng-Arom Ashram and exudes a gentle tranquillity. There are lots of vegie options and all the Thai standards along with an eclectic group of bookish Thais. The walk through the neighbourhood is part of the draw.

C'YAN & GLOW

Map pp292-3   International $$$

☎ 0 2625 3333; Metropolitan Hotel, 27 Th Sathon Tai; 7-course meal 2500B; ordinary bus 22, subway Lumphini

The young, fabulous and conspicuously rich just adore C'yan, a sleek minimalist fashion plate that injects Bangkok's stodgy hotel food-scape with youthful flavours. The Mediterranean-inspired dishes focus on fresh and intense combinations created by Amanda Gale, a protégée of Australian

Eating   **RIVERSIDE, SILOM & LUMPHINI**

DINNER CRUISES

The river is lovely in the evenings, with the skyscrapers' lights twinkling in the distance and a cool breeze chasing the heat away. A dozen or more companies run regular dinner cruises along Mae Nam Chao Phraya. Some are mammoth boats so brightly lit inside that you'd never know you were on the water; others are more sedate and intimate, allowing patrons to see the surroundings. Several of the dinner boats cruise under the well-lit Saphan Phra Ram IX, the longest single-span cable-suspension bridge in the world.

Loy Nava (Map pp290–1; ☎ 0 2437 4932; www.loynava.com; set menu 1200B; ☼ cruises 6-8pm & 8-10pm) Travels from Tha Si Phraya aboard a converted rice barge.

Manohra Cruises (Map pp278–9; ☎ 0 2477 0770; www.manohracruises.com; Bangkok Marriott Resort & Spa, 257/1-3 Th Charoen Nakhon; 1550B; ☼ 7.30-10pm) A restored rice barge, Manohra is the grandest of them all.

Yok Yor Restaurant (Map pp290-1; ☎ 0 2863 0565; yokyor.co.th; Thonburi; dinner 300-320B plus surcharge 120B; ☼ 8-10pm) The long-running floating restaurant on the Thonburi side of the river also runs a dinner cruise for the average folks, mainly Thais celebrating birthdays.

celebrity chef Neil Perry. Although the dining crowd is fickle, we predict C'yan's formula will soon be duplicated throughout the city. Another Gale venture, Glow has a sanatorium effect, with health-conscious spa food to offset the ill-effects of guzzling Bangkok's toxic sludge. The spirulina noodles topped with a crown of greens is a nutty and peppery dish that proves there is life beyond chillies.

EAT ME RESTAURANT

Map pp290-1   International $$
☎ 0 2238 0931; Soi Phiphat 2, off Th Convent; mains 200-400B; ☼ 6pm-1am; Skytrain Sala Daeng
A little bit of Sydney has blossomed here off Th Silom, helping give Bangkok more cosmo cred. Chic, minimalist décor is accessorised by rotating art exhibits supplied by H Gallery, the city's leading contemporary gallery. And, lest we forget, the creative and modern food – from pumpkin risotto to tuna tartare – spans the globe.

GALLERY CAFÉ Map pp290-1   Thai $$
☎ 0 2234 0053; 1293-5 Th Charoen Krung; mains 120-220B; ferry Tha Si Phraya
The closer you get to the luxury hotels near the river, the less likely you are to get a good or affordable Thai meal. Most couldn't pass muster outside of Kansas and generally the more Thai antiques on display, the more suspicious potential diners should be. This upmarket gallery-cum-café breaks the mould, not in the food department, but in value. For the price you get decent foreign adaptations of Thai food, plus a dining

room full of antiques and other works of art, and no nagging phobias about cleanliness.

HARMONIQUE Map pp290-1   Thai $
☎ 0 2237 8175; Soi 34, Th Charoen Krung; mains 60-150B; ☼ 11am-10pm Mon-Sat; ferry Tha Oriental
A tiny but refreshing oasis set in a former Chinese residence, Harmonique is an expat favourite for thrifty romantic dinners. The food is that peculiar adaptation of guesthouse Thai that has been pioneered for folks scared of chillies and fish sauce, but it is the ambience of fairy lights, a central banyan tree and marble-topped tables that has spared Harmonique from our chopping block.

INDIA HUT Map pp290-1   Indian $$
☎ 0 2635 7876; Th Surawong; mains 90-250B; ☼ 11am-10pm; ferry Tha Oriental
Bearing a self-styled logo that blatantly rips off Pizza Hut, this Indian restaurant, across from the Manorha Hotel, specialises in Nawabi (Lucknow) cuisine. Try the vegetarian samosas, fresh prawns cooked with ginger or the homemade paneer (unfermented cheese) in tomato and onion curry. The stiff white tablecloths, upholstered chairs and shopping-mall sterility is oppressive when the restaurant isn't crowded, but once the tables fill up, the place feels like a palace.

KHRUA AROY AROY Map pp290-1   Thai $
Th Pan, Th Silom; mains 40-80B; ☼ 8am-9pm; Skytrain Chong Nonsi
Across Th Pan from Wat Khaek, this simple kitchen lures in post-worshippers with big vats of curries spicy enough to put hair on

smooth chests. The surrounding colours create a visual scream fest while the calm broad-hipped rice mama ladles a little more radioactive liquid on to your plate.

LE LYS Map pp290-1 French-Thai $$
☎ 0 2287 1898; 104 Soi 7, Th Narathiwat Ratchanakharin; mains 150-300B; ⊗ noon-10pm; Skytrain Chong Nonsi

More of a dinner party at a friend's house than a restaurant, Le Lys has uprooted its living/dining room to a new location in Sathorn and all their friends have followed. You'll still find all the pleasant Thai dishes, *pétanque* (French lawn bowling) in back yard and the same gentle hospitality.

LE NORMANDIE Map pp290-1 French $$$
☎ 0 2236 0400; Oriental Hotel, Soi 38, Th Charoen Krung; 3-/7-course meals 1000/4000B; ferry Tha Oriental; ⊗ dinner 6-11pm

Bangkok, like the rest of the world, knows about fine, fine dining from the French. This high perch overlooking the river is the pinnacle of Bangkok's upper crust. Michelin-starred chefs and other noteworthy know-it-alls are imported along with the finest ingredients for this culinary court. Reservations are necessary and formal attire (including jackets) is required.

MALI RESTAURANT
Map pp292-3 Thai & Western $
☎ 0 2679 8693; Soi 1, Th Sathon; mains 50-150B; ⊗ 11am-10pm; ordinary bus 13, subway Lumphini

The regular neighbourhood characters stop into this homey restaurant serving Thai and Western food. Inside the restaurant each surface is covered with Thai handicrafts and knick-knacks celebrating a 1950s revival.

MIZU'S KITCHEN Map pp290-1 Japanese $
☎ 0 2233 6447; Soi Patpong 1, Th Silom; mains 80-150B; ⊗ noon-1am; Skytrain Sala Daeng, subway Silom

Not a lot has changed in Mizu's since the city's R&R days when the trattoria-style chequered tablecloths and calendar girl pin-ups first appeared to lure in American GIs. Even the menu is an old-fashioned fusion of Japan and the West before cooks became chefs – back when fresh vegetables meant opening a can. It's hard to differentiate between the dishes – they're all warm

and salty and a perfect option for a slurred-speech night out in Patpong.

MUSLIM RESTAURANT
Map pp290-1 Muslim $
1356 Th Charoen Krung; mains under 40B; ⊗ 10am-8pm; ferry Tha Oriental

Near the intersection of Th Charoen Krung and Th Silom, this aptly named restaurant has been feeding various Lonely Planet authors for more than 20 years. The faded walls and stainless-steel tables are the opposite of smart décor, but an assortment of curries and roti are displayed in a clean glass case for easy pointing and eye-catching allure.

NAAZ Map pp290-1 Muslim-Thai $
Soi 43, Th Charoen Krung; mains 50-70B; ⊗ 7.30am-10.30pm Mon-Sat; ferry Tha Oriental

Around the corner from the central post office is Naaz (pronounced 'Naat' in Thai), a little living-room kitchen serving some of the city's richest *khâo mòk kài* (chicken biryani). The milk tea is also very good, and daily specials include chicken *masala* and mutton korma. For dessert, the house speciality is *firni*, a Middle Eastern pudding spiced with coconut, almonds, cardamom and saffron.

NGWAN LEE LANG SUAN
Map pp292-3 Thai $$
☎ 0 2250 0936; cnr Soi Lang Suan & Th Sarasin; mains 150-300B; ⊗ 6pm-3am; Skytrain Chitlom

Roll up your sleeves for a night of extreme eating in this seafood mess hall. Like the

WILL EMIGRATE FOR FOOD
Ever been stuck in some office park back home with no food options and had to forage for a meal from a petrol station? That will never happen in Bangkok. Wherever people live, work or are thinking of going to, there is food. Hike into the deepest wilderness and there'll be a wok that has beaten you there. Even the drudgery of filing immigration papers can be timed with a delicious lunch. Along with the immigration office, Soi Suan Phlu (Map pp292–3) also boasts a number of good eats. Directly across from the day market is a famous duck-noodle shop as well as several unsung lunch-in-a-hurry spots just steps from the immigration office.

crab shacks found in coastal towns, Ngwan Lee has zero pretension so that you and your food can make a mess together. Grilled king prawns the size of lobsters, fiery *tôm yam kûng* (hot and sour soup with shrimp), crab curry and other Thai-Chinese hits spill off the table while the various beer-girl promoters make their rounds. Post-partying Thais stop in for a quick bite after the bars on Th Sarasin close.

RAMENTEI Map pp290-1 Japanese $

☎ 0 2234 8082; Soi 6, Th Silom; mains 100-150B; 🕑 6-11pm; Skytrain Sala Daeng, subway Silom
So much Zen calm surrounds an otherwise fire-alarm kitchen at this factory of Japanese lunches. Grab a seat in front of the open kitchen to watch the cooks beat the ingredients into compliance. Meanwhile shy businessmen bury themselves in books and newspapers while waiting for the arrival of steaming bowls of soup big enough to drown any hunger.

RAN NAM TAO HU YONG HER

Map pp290-1 Chinese $

☎ 0 2236 7237; 2/5 Soi 19, Th Silom; mains 30-100B; 🕑 10am-10pm; Skytrain Surasak
One of many nondescript shopfront restaurants, Ran Nam Tao Hu (Soy Milk Restaurant) stands out for its northern Chinese cuisine. When the owner first opened shop, Mandarin was her only language, but Thai has been added now and comically fractured English appears on the menu too. Peking cuisine is known for its dumplings, whether fried, steamed or baked, as well as everyone's favourite scallion pancakes.

RATSSTUBE Map pp292-3 German $$

☎ 0 2287 2822; Soi Goethe; mains 200-350B; 🕑 11am-2.30pm & 5.30-10pm Mon-Fri, 11am-10pm Sat & Sun; ordinary bus 13, subway Lumphini
The leafy grounds of the Goethe Institut, off Soi Atakanprasit, are so pleasant that a date with this rococo restaurant is well worth the trip. Come for homemade sausages, hearty set lunches and a sturdy clientele.

SALLIM RESTAURANT

Map pp290-1 Muslim $

☎ 0 2237 1060; Soi 32, Th Charoen Krung; mains 50-80B; 🕑 11am-9pm; ferry Tha Si Phraya
This place could pose a challenge for the hygiene conscious, but the food is

fabulous. Don't even bother looking at the English menu, which in no way corresponds to the daily offerings. Instead leap into one of the southern Thai curries (*kaeng kài, néua* or *plaa*) served with your choice of rice or roti.

SARA-JANE'S Map pp290-1 Italian & Thai $

☎ 0 2676 3338; 55/21 Th Narathiwat Ratchanakharin; mains 50-200B; 🕑 11am-10.30pm; Skytrain Chong Nonsi
You can be as big of a *faràng* as you want to be at Sara-Jane's, a long-running favourite with the expat crowd. Don't like fish sauce? No reason to grin and bear it here; just ask for it be omittwed. Hate tofu in your *phàt thai*? Can't eat chillies in your *sôm-tam*? They can oblige too. What arrives might not be Thai food anymore, but you're among friends. There is another branch in Th Withayu (Map pp294–5; Sindhorn Bldg, Th Withayu), but this location tends to have better food.

SIROCCO & SKY BAR

Map pp290-1 International $$$

☎ 02 624 9554; 63rd fl State Tower, cnr Th Silom & Th Charoen Krung; mains 500-800B; air-con bus 502 & 504; ferry Tha Oriental
Need a restaurant to impress? Thanks to its altitude on top of the State Tower, amid the Silom skyscrapers, Sirocco quite literally takes people's breath away and leaves them with wide-eyed boasts after returning to ground level. But the heavenly location has bestowed little perfection on the menu, which is expensive and amateurish. As one overheard Australian patron put it, 'They're selling ambience here'.

OH SO BANGKOK: THE BEST IN OPEN-AIR DINING

- Soi Texas Seafood Stalls (p131) Footpath dining featuring grilled prawns the size of speed humps.
- Ngwan Lee Lang Suan (p137) Pig out at this seafood mess hall.
- Oriental Hotel Buffet (p133) Stunning river setting and enormous portions for the well dressed.
- Soi 38 Night Market (p144) An after-party of late-night grubbing.
- Suan Luang Night Market (p132) Don your PJs and grab a bowl of noodles for a good night's sleep.

High-altitude dining at Sirocco (opposite)

SOI POLO FRIED CHICKEN

Map pp292-3   Thai $

☎ 0 1252 2252; 137/1-3 Soi Polo, Th Withayu; mains 100-150B; Skytrain Ploenchit

Fried chicken tastes good in any language, but Soi Polo's chicken could tar and feather the colonel and his kin. Crispy on the outside, moist and meaty inside and sprinkled with fried garlic bits – even people afraid of food love this place. Don't forget to order *khâo nǐaw* (sticky rice) for soaking up the spicy dipping sauces.

SOI PRADIT MARKET Map pp290-1   Thai $

Soi 20, Th Silom ☺ 10am-10pm; mains 25-35B; ferry Tha Oriental

Bangkok's magic is working if you start craving street-stall meals instead of air-con luxury. During the day, fruit vendors and closet-sized noodle shops line this narrow *soi* leading to Mirasuddeen Mosque. Look for the duck-noodle shop (identified by a, um, duck sign) or rickety tables selling zesty *khànǒm jiin* (stark white rice noodles served with curries). The woks are still sizzling at night when more sit-down stalls appear.

SOMBOON SEAFOOD

Map pp290-1   Thai $$

☎ 0 2233 3104; cnr Th Surawong & Th Narathiwat Ratchanakharin; mains 150-250B; ☺ 4pm-midnight; Skytrain Chong Nonsi

Towards the eastern end of Th Surawong, about a 10-minute walk west of Montien Hotel, Somboon's is known for having the best crab curry in town. Soy-steamed sea bass *(plaa kràphong nêung sii-íu)* is also a speciality. The dining room is a human-sized version of the fish tanks where the daily specials bide their time.

SUAN LUM NIGHT BAZAAR

Map pp292-3   Thai $

Th Rama IV; mains 80-150B; ☺ 5pm-midnight; subway Lumphini

Sure it is loud, gaudy and touristy, but so is Thailand. And nowhere else can deliver as boisterous a good time than the football-field-sized beer gardens at Suan Lum Night Bazaar. It's also the antidote to the misconception that a Thai meal should be surrounded by antiques and silk costumes. Heaps more authentic, Suan Lum has the girls dressed up in promotional uniforms, tacky pop-song stage shows, cold German beer and spicy Thai food. There is talk that Suan Lum is headed for the wrecking ball, but until the bulldozers arrive, we're sceptical.

TAMIL NADU Map pp290-1   Indian $

5/1 Soi 11, Th Silom; mains 50-120B; ☺ 10am-10pm; Skytrain Chong Nonsi

No décor? No bother. This family-run spot doesn't want to distract its international customers from the comforts of its home-style southern Indian dishes chased afterwards by a cup of sweet milk tea. Obliging

MISS CONGENIALITY: NOODLE SOUP

If food competed in beauty contests, Thai curries and *phàt thai* would always walk away with the crown. They are flashier, sexier and have stronger PR campaigns. But the real standout of Thai cuisine is a bowl of noodle soup, too simple and honest to shine on stage. This is a dish of subtlety and utility but artistry nonetheless.

Kǔaytǐaw (noodle soup) can get a bad rep because some vendors skimp on the broth and use *lûuk chín plaa* (fishballs), the Asian equivalent to Spam. But when love and mastery create a complex broth combined with quality ingredients, you've tasted perfection.

When it comes to broth, two noodle shops on Th Phra Athit (Map pp286–7), on either side of Soi Chana Songkhram, serve *kǔaytǐaw néua* (beef noodles); the meat is so silky and tender and the broth so flavourful that you barely need to spice it with the provided condiments.

Sometimes the broth plays a minor role to the floating parts. Noodle vendors at Soi 38 Night Market (see p144) serve handmade *bà-mìi* (egg noodles) so delicate that you could cut them with an evil look. Handmade noodles are often served with *kíaw* (stuffed wontons) and *mǔu daeng* (barbecued pork). The noodle seller who sets up near Soi Kasem San 1 (Map pp294–5), across from the National Stadium, is worth the risk of contracting black lung from the nearby traffic.

Foreigners tend to crave pork noodles, but Thais will weep for duck noodles. One well-known duck-noodle vendor (Map pp286–7) is tucked into a little *soi* off Th Chakraphong, near Th Khao San. Look for a Converse shoe sign that marks the entry to the *soi*. Another sign that you might be Thai is a preference for *yen taa foh* (noodles in a red sauce of pickled squid and tofu). These noodles pop up at food stalls in Chatuchak Market (p188).

Jakki (Map pp280–1; ☎ 0 2245 0849; 1/35-36 Soi 7, Th Ratchawithi 7; mains 50-150B; ☽ 11am-2.30pm), just off the Victory Monument roundabout (look for the red and yellow awning), does a bowl of dumpling soup with wontons so big that chasing after them is like bobbing for apples; deep fried dumplings are another speciality and a favourite bulk order for cabinet meetings.

the local Hindu communities' strict vegetarianism, meat eaters are segregated into their own dining area (even though the kitchen doesn't have the same division).

TH SUKHUMVIT

Th Sukhumvit is Bangkok's international avenue running through the immigrant community of Little Arabia, past the girlie bars around Nana, and skirting the well-heeled Thai and executive expat neighbourhoods further east. You wouldn't come to Sukhumvit to eat Thai, but you would come for everything else: from hummus to burgers. Except for the restaurants in Little Arabia and a few notables, you'll be happier with your food hunting if you travel to the higher-numbered *soi* beyond Soi Asoke. Many restaurants in lower Sukhumvit cater largely to the sex-tourist market.

AL HUSSAIN Map pp296-7   Indian $
75/7 Soi 3/1; mains 100-200B; ☽ 11am-midnight; Skytrain Nana
Monopolising the corner of compact Little Arabia, Al Hussain is a covered outdoor café with a range of premade Muslim curries and rice dishes. A helpful server will

emerge out of the crowd of diners to scoop from whatever vat has caught your eye. Across the street are several hookah restaurants where Middle Eastern gentlemen bubble away the afternoon.

ANA'S GARDEN Map pp296-7   Thai $$
☎ 0 2391 1762; 67 Soi 55, Th Sukhumvit; mains 200-300B; ☽ 5am-midnight; Skytrain Thong Lor
Garden restaurants, like fluorescent-lit night markets, are quintessential Thai dining. A homage to olden times, Ana's lush garden of broad-leafed palms and purring fountains also attractively masks Bangkok's stifling concrete. Cosy wooden tables quickly fill up with plates of spicy hot Thai food and sweating beer glasses. A crowd fits well into these spaces, big enough for heated debates and tall tales.

BAN-YAH FITNESS CENTRE
Map pp296-7   Chinese $
☎ 0 2662 2887; Soi 29, Th Sukhumvit; mains 50-150B; ☽ 11am-10pm; Skytrain Asoke
Between the beer and the fried Chinese doughnuts, living in Bangkok can erode the resolve of every Mister Goodbody's healthful habits. Attached to a Chinese qi gong centre, this simple café injects nutri-

tion back into the act of eating. The menu is entirely in Chinese but the handy photos act as a Rosetta stone. Item £A3 is a tasty vegetarian stir-fry with 'one-thousand year old eggs' and chilled tofu, £A2 is marinated cucumber salad with garlic and £C14 is deep-fried spare ribs, a tasty departure from roughage overload. Black-skinned chicken, believed to enhance fertility, is item £D1 and accompanied by an unappetising photo that looks like Nessie. The sign out front reads 'Thai & Chinese massage'.

BED SUPPERCLUB

Map pp296-7 International $$$

☎ 0 2651 3537; 26 Soi 11, Th Sukhumvit, set menu 1000B; ☻ 3 seatings per evening; Skytrain Nana
This is eating entertainment: beds instead of tables, club music instead of clinking silverware, and black lights instead of candles. Before the food arrives you sit cross-legged watching projections of video art and the white-clad servers shuffling through the shadows. With so many distractions, the food could take a back seat, but despite the unconventional posture, it is anything but supine. The changing menu combines New American dishes with Asian accents. The ingredients match better than many of the short-term couples in attendance. Keep groups small and flexible (for the yoga-style dining), aim for the less busy weeknights and, whatever you do, dress up.

BEI OTTO Map pp296-7 German $$$

☎ 0 2262 0892; 1 Soi 20, Th Sukhumvit; mains 300-500B; ☻ 6-11pm Mon-Sat, 11.30am-2.30pm Sun; Skytrain Phrom Phong
Amid speeding motorcycle taxis and hulking pushcarts, this cute Bavarian-style cottage is as out of place as Dorothy's hurricane-blown house when it lands in Oz. Claiming a Bangkok residence for nearly 20 years, Bei Otto's major culinary bragging point is its pork knuckles, reputedly the best in town, a comfortable bar of German beers and an attached bakery with magnificent breads.

BOURBON ST BAR & RESTAURANT

Map pp296-7 American $$

☎ 0 2259 0328; 29/4-6 Soi 22, behind Washington Theatre; mains 150-300B; ☻ 10am-2am; Skytrain Asoke & Phrom Phong
If it was bourbon or its kin that put you to bed last night, you'll need Bourbon St's all-

day breakfasts as an eye-opener. Eggs any style and crispy bacon work like voodoo charms to dispel hangovers. Other Crescent City creations pad the menu along with a salsa that could stand up with pride back on the Rio Grande.

CABBAGES & CONDOMS

Map pp296-7 Thai $$

☎ 0 2229 4611; Soi 12, Th Sukhumvit; mains 150-200B; ☻ 11am-10pm; Skytrain Asoke
'Be fed and be sheathed' is the motto of the restaurant outreach programme of the Population & Community Development Association (PDA), a sex education/AIDS prevention organisation. The restaurant cooks with vegetables familiar to Westerners, such as celery and tomatoes, to create sufficiently complex flavours for those 'wading' into Thai food. Dishes such as *yam wún sên* (mung-bean noodle salad) provide a source of raw vegetables. Instead of after-meal mints, diners receive packaged condoms, and all proceeds go towards PDA educational programmes in Thailand.

CREPES & CO Map pp296-7 French $$

☎ 0 2653 3990; 18/1 Soi 12, Th Sukhumvit; mains 140-280B; ☻ 9am-midnight; Skytrain Asoke
This cute cottage creperie, another 50m down the same *soi* as Cabbages & Condoms, is everyone's favourite weekend brunch date. Crepes of all kinds, brunch classics and a nice selection of Mediterranean mains are sailed into garden-view tables by Breton-attired servers. Morocco and other French colonies are honoured with seasonal menus.

INTERNATIONAL FASHION PLATES

- Bed Supperclub (p155) Futuristic chic with top-notch international fare.
- Eat Me Restaurant (p136) Bangkok's favourite cosmo maven.
- C'yan & Glow (p135) Nouveau Mediterranean amid polished minimalism.
- Reflections Bar & Restaurant (p145) Thai goes candy-cane pop.
- Maha Naga (p143) A cocoon of Moroccan exotica and fusion food.

Eating

TH SUKHUMVIT

DOSA KING Map pp296-7 Indian-Vegetarian $$
☎ 02 6511651; 265/1 Soi 19, Th Sukhumvit; mains 150-250B; 🕑 11am-11pm; Skytrain Asoke
You don't have to get all 'dhal-ed' up to dine on tasty Indian food at this home-away-from-home restaurant. Although a spiffy look would put you in league with the sari-wrapped mamas and clubbing teenagers. Divine renditions of the south Indian speciality, dosas (a thin, stuffed crepe), adorn the tables like ancient parchment scrolls.

GIUSTO Map pp296-7 Italian $$$
☎ 0 2258 4321; Soi 23, Th Sukhumvit; mains 320-480B; 🕑 5pm-midnight; Skytrain Asoke
Nouveau Italian cuisine is hand crafted in this chic glass-encased dining room. The menu is boarding-school Italian, sweetbread appetisers and ornate seafood mains, all of which tally up to the price of a burger back home.

GOVINDA Map pp296-7 Italian Vegetarian $$
☎ 0 2663 4970; Soi 22, Th Sukhumvit; mains 150-300B; 🕑 6-11pm; Skytrain Phrom Phong
Mock meat catches Roman fever at this vegetarian Italian restaurant. The brick-kiln oven gestates colourful and creative pizzas. Salads and pastas also add more variety to a vegetarian's stir-fry routine. The restaurant is near the mouth of the *soi* in the shopping complex, before Larry's Dive Shop.

GREAT AMERICAN RIB COMPANY
Map pp296-7 American $$
☎ 0 2661 3891; 32 Soi 36, Th Sukhumvit; mains 165-400B; 🕑 11.30am-11.30pm; Skytrain Thong Lor
The name might suggest suburban malls, but this barbecue joint would make a rancher tip her hat. Big plates of slow-cooked meat create a map of the American south: pulled pork from the Carolinas, Memphis-style ribs and slathered Texas-style chicken. The menu may be American but the setting and the clientele is totally Thai with outdoor picnic tables, chilli-laced sauces and lots of birthday celebrations. Mexican Mondays smuggle another spice-loving cuisine into Thailand.

GREYHOUND CAFÉ
Map pp296-7 International $$
☎ 0 2664 8663; 2nd fl, Emporium Shopping Centre, btwn Soi 22 & 24, Th Sukhumvit; mains 100-250B; 🕑 11am-10pm; Skytrain Phrom Phong
Eating to be seen is on many Bangkok menus, but Greyhound still sets the pace. You could crawl into the techno soundtrack of the sleek dining room, but everyone knows that the best seats are along the main pedestrian hallway – the better to view and be viewed. Greyhound's hybrid menu is like many of its patrons: cosmopolitan with a cultural identity hand-picked from across the globe.

JE-NGOR Map pp296-7 Thai-Chinese $$
☎ 0 2258 8008; Soi 20, Th Sukhumvit; mains 150-300B; 🕑 lunch & dinner; Skytrain Phrom Phong
Bangkok's version of Martha Stewart, Je-Ngor (the owner's Chinese nickname) built a food empire from a food sideline. She first started collecting fans with her steamed dumplings, which she sold to friends during the Chinese Vegetarian Festival. Today there are six branches of her Thai-Chinese seafood restaurants, all run by near and distant relatives. Of her many talents, *sôm-tam puu dawng* (papaya salad with preserved crab), *puu phàt phrík thai dam* (stir-fried crab with black pepper) and deep-fried fishballs keep her well enthroned. Deep-fried *phèuak hì-má* (snow taro) is a good predinner snack that is rarely seen on Bangkok menus.

KALAPAPREUK ON FIRST
Map pp296-7 Thai & International $$
☎ 0 2664 8410; 1st fl, Emporium Shopping Centre, Soi 24, Th Sukhumvit; mains 150-300B; 🕑 11am-10pm; Skytrain Phrom Phong
When the Thai society types give their cooks a day off, they wander over to this airy café in the Emporium mall for regional Thai specialities. The recent returnees come for views of the park and Western-style cakes, a favourite culinary import in Thailand.

KUPPA Map pp296-7 International $$$
☎ 0 2663 0450-4; 39 Soi 16, Th Sukhumvit; mains 200-500B; 🕑 Tue-Sun; Skytrain Asoke
For Bangkok's ladies who lunch, Kuppa is a regular weekend appointment. Creating the mood of a living room, Kuppa transports the cosmopolitan crowd to brunches they thought would be abandoned with a Bangkok post. The menu is adept and commendable, nailing tricky white sauce pastas and funky pumpkin-feta pizzas. Take a cab, if you don't have driver to deliver you here.

LA PIOLA Map pp296-7 — Italian $$$

☎ 0 2250 7270; sub soi btwn Soi 11 & Soi 13, Th Sukhumvit; set menu 1170B; 6-10pm Tue-Sat; Skytrain Nana

What a charming Italian eatery you are. La Piola outgrew its petite basement digs and has moved into a more ample setting. Every imaginable language assembles in this sunny yellow space to begin the feasting. There is no menu; the only choice you make is what to drink. Three courses, including antipasto, three pasta mains and dessert, will effortlessly appear while the crowd is serenaded with Italian karaoke. You'll leave unimaginably full and drunk with flavours.

LE BANYAN Map pp296-7 — French $$$

☎ 0 2253 5556; 59 Soi 8, Th Sukhumvit; mains 400-900B; 6.30-9.30pm Mon-Sat; Skytrain Nana

Sukhumvit's trendy diners demand change every six months: new menu, new décor, new chef, anything to chase away restaurant boredom. But for the monogamous eaters who value experience, this classy French restaurant proves its wisdom with formal efficient service and traditional fare. A lush garden surrounds the charming Ratanakosin house illuminated with candles and gleaming wine glasses. The house speciality is pressed duck, but the silken and seared foie gras steals the show.

MAHA NAGA Map pp296-7 — International $$$

☎ 0 2662-3060; Soi 29, Th Sukhumvit; mains 300-700B; 6pm-midnight; Skytrain Phrom Phong

Maha Naga spirits diners away to a fantasy world of exotic Asian and Arabic interiors and courtyard fountains. Such an intoxicating setting, surrounded by Bangkok's beautiful people, is sufficient distraction from the lacklustre Thai-Western fusions. It is the perfect indulgence for form-over-function diners.

MOODY'S Map pp296-7 — Lebanese $$

Soi 5, Th Sukhumvit; mains 100-200B; 11am-midnight; Skytrain Nana

These zesty Mediterranean dishes – light and refreshing feta and olive salads, fluffy pita bread, musky lamb chops and creamy hummus – soothe a tender, bread-deprived tummy. Breaking with the Arabic tradition, Moody's serves beer to oblige the imbibing infidels. Sit out on the porch to watch the dolled-up hostess bar girls across the street eat their way through their earning.

NASIR AL-MASRI RESTAURANT

Map pp296-7 — Egyptian $

☎ 0 2253 5582; 4/6 Soi 3/1, Th Sukhumvit; mains 80-120B; 10am-4am; Skytrain Nana

You can't miss this blinding silver temple to Egyptian food. The fruity perfume from the nearby sheesha smokers scents the predinner atmosphere, until the sensory banquet arrives – sesame-freckled flatbread, creamy hummus and flawlessly fried falafels.

PIZZERIA BELLA NAPOLI

Map pp296-7 — Italian $$

☎ 0 2259 0405; 3/3 Soi 31, Th Sukhumvit; mains 150-400B; 6pm-1am Mon-Fri, noon-5pm Sat & Sun; Skytrain Phrom Phong

An eclectic and boisterous crowd gulps down glasses of red wine and gooey and garlicky wood-fired pizzas in this cosy Napolese outpost. Even the plastic *khunyïng* (aristocratic women) seem dressed up in this informal dining room of chequered tablecloths. Don't miss the gelatos and sorbets made from the owner's family recipes.

Courtyard at Maha Naga

RANG MAHAL Map pp296-7   Indian $$

☎ 0 2261 7100; Rembrandt Hotel, Soi 18, Th Sukhumvit; mains 180-280B; ☉ 11am-11pm; Skytrain Asoke

With sky-high dining and an all-you-can-eat buffet, Bangkok really is the 'City of Angels'. Atop the Rembrandt Hotel, Rang Mahal specialises in northern and southern Indian 'royal cuisine' with a popular Sunday buffet.

RUEN MALLIKA Map pp296-7   Thai $$

☎ 02 663 3211; sub-soi off of Soi 22, Th Sukhumvit; ☉ 11am-11pm; mains 200-350B; Skytrain Asoke

Thais have tourists figured out: convert an old teak house into a restaurant and the crowds will come, regardless of the food. But Ruen Mallika improves the formula with exquisite dishes, like dizzyingly spicy *náam phrík* (a thick dipping sauce with vegetables and herbs) and soulful chicken wrapped in banana leaves. The surrounding garden supplies the ingredients for deep-fried flower dish, a house speciality. The restaurant is a little tricky to find; approach from Soi 16 off of Th Ratchadaphisek.

SOI 38 NIGHT MARKET

Map pp296-7   Thai-Chinese $

Soi 38, Th Sukhumvit; mains 30-50B; ☉ 8pm-3am; Skytrain Thong Lor

Night noshing happens with panache at this gourmet night market. Post-clubbers arrive in screaming túk-túk to sneak some post-curfew hooch and chase their liquid courage with handmade noodles and Chinese-style spring rolls.

TAMARIND CAFÉ

Map pp296-7   International Vegetarian $$

☎ 0 2663 7421; 27 Soi 20, Th Sukhumvit; mains 200-250B; ☉ 3pm-midnight Mon-Fri, 10am-midnight Sat & Sun; Skytrain Asoke

Pacific Rim cuisine goes vegetarian at this sleek eatery. Imaginative fresh juices will stave off a cold or transport you to a long-forgotten beach vacation. But many sneak up to the top-floor patio to sip wine and nibble on desserts with the night breezes rustling the potted greenery and the lights of the city twinkling beyond. Tamarind shares space with Gallery F-Stop, which presents rotating photography exhibits,

BREAKING BREAD WITH THE BEAUTIFUL PEOPLE

Like the other City of Angels, Bangkok is filled with models, moguls and media types, all decked out in wearable art and camera-ready poise. And where do these creative gurus break their daily fast? Wherever the comfortably-dressed masses aren't. The fashionable venues change quickly, but everybody who is somebody right now – we can't vouch for tomorrow – socialises at the decidedly uninspired **Au Bon Pain** (Map pp296–7; J Avenue, Soi 55) a concept complex. Location, rather than culinary merit, attracts the movers and shakers who work nearby in design showrooms, production companies and fashion magazine offices. Stop by after office hours to catch the complex in full catwalk swing.

arranged so that visitors can approach the artwork without peering over a fellow diner's shoulder. This is also a wi-fi hot spot.

THONGLEE Map pp296-7   Thai $

☎ 0 2258 1983; Soi 20, Th Sukhumvit; mains 40-70B; ☉ 9am-8pm; closed 3rd Sun of the month; Skytrain Asoke

In any other neighbourhood, Thonglee would be nearly indistinguishable from all the other shopfront wok shops. But Sukhumvit sometimes forgets that it is in Thailand. Instead of being transformed into a massage parlour or visa-wedding service, Thonglee offers a more nutritious service: rice and curries.

VIENTIANE KITCHEN

Map pp296-7   Northeastern Thai $$

☎ 0 2258 6171; 8 Soi 36, Th Sukhumvit; mains 150-250B; ☉ 11am-midnight; Skytrain Thong Lor

A rollicking good upcountry time can be had with only a Skytrain ride to Thong Lor. You'll find all the Isan and Lao 'soul-food' standards, smothered in chilli peppers to give you that bee-stung pout. A *măw lam* (traditional Isan music) band, seating on the floor and rotating fans create an amazing approximation of Isan and a relaxed cultural display, but the hallucinatory spiciness of the food and sweaty bottles of Chang beer might be more to blame. Be sure to tip the band on your way out; no matter the amount, they'll announce to the crowd that it was 1000B.

GREATER BANGKOK

The area around Victory Monument has some interesting food options and is easily accessible on the Skytrain. You'll be sharing stools with local university students and hardly a foreigner in sight.

ANOTAI Map pp278-9   Vegetarian $

☎ 0 2641 5366; 976/17 Soi Lang Phaiyaban; mains 100-200B; ☺ 10am-9pm; subway Rama IX

Hunting for vegetarian restaurants in Bangkok is like foraging for forest mushrooms. It takes a lot of looking. Anotai is a stylish Zen lunch spot for creative pan-Asian dishes, like mouth-popping deep-fried tofu nori and big salads. To get here take the subway to the Rama IX station, then bus or cab to the Rama IX Hospital. Go halfway down the street that runs immediately beside the hospital and turn onto the small alley beside the 'Thailand Ghana Trade Center'. Also look for a small sign in English that says 'Food & Health'. Anotai is in the row of buildings behind the *soi*.

BAAN KLANG NAM Map pp278-9   Thai $$

☎ 0 2292 0175; 3792/106 Soi 14, Th Phra Ram III; mains 200-400B; ☺ 11am-midnight; long-tail boat from Tha Sathon

Near Khlong Toey Port, this rustic wooden house is a favourite of the Thai matriarchs and guests at nearby Montien Riverside. The seafood is a little more expensive here than other riverside restaurants, but so is the quality. Crab, prawns, and whole white fish are among the hits that make people swoon. To avoid traffic and hunting down the dark side road, hire a long-tail boat

from Tha Sathon to arrive at the restaurant's former front door.

BAAN SUAN PAI

Map pp280-1   Thai & International $

☎ 0 2615 2454; Th Phahonyothin; mains 25B; ☺ 11am-9pm; Skytrain Ari

This vegetarian food centre offers a garden's bounty. Everything is strictly vegetarian, even lacking the ubiquitous fish sauce. Most plates offer the choice of three stir-fries, but there's also sushi and noodles. Don't miss the handmade ice cream of such exotic flavours as passionfruit, lemon grass and lotus root. Buy coupons from the woman at the desk, right by the door. The coupons are printed with Thai numbers only, but the denominations are colour-coded as follows: green, 5B; purple, 10B; blue, 20B; red, 25B. The restaurant is just past the petrol station before Soi 4.

PICKLE FACTORY

Map pp280-1   International $$

☎ 0 2246 3036; 55 Soi 2, Th Ratchawithi; mains 160-250B; ☺ 5.30-11.30pm; Skytrain Victory Monument

The Pickle Factory occupies a 1970s-vintage Thai house that looks like it stayed in the '70s, complete with indoor sofa-seating and a swimming pool. The menu includes Western dishes such as Chiang Mai sausage pizzas, smoked chicken wings and stuffed mussels, as well as Thai mango salads. Take a taxi or the long, dreary walk and the threat of *soi* dogs might drive you away empty handed.

REFLECTIONS BAR & RESTAURANT

Map pp278-9   Pan Asian $$

☎ 0 2270 3340; 81 Soi Ari, Th Phahonyothin; mains 150-300B; ☺ 11am-11pm; Skytrain Ari

This is a fantastically kitschy kitchen of retro candy-cane colours, bulbous mod furnishings and outdoor patios. While most new restaurants get *faràng* worked up into a boil, Reflections has done the same to Thai menu-crawlers. The options ramble from Chinese seafood, to Thai standards, to Japanese sushi and is a welcome touch of style for the hole-in-the-wall fans. The attached hotel lobby-bar is a favourite of the neighbourhood's indie creatives.

THAI RESTAURANTS FOR THE FIERY & THE TAME

- Ana's Garden (p140) A garden setting for sweating out all that chilli.
- Ban Khun Mae (p131) Simple and straightforward for beginners.
- Baan Khanitha (p135) Attentive to ambience and cautious eaters.
- Vientiane Kitchen (opposite) Down-home zing with a Thai honky-tonk band.
- Khrua Nopparat (p128) A happy marriage between adventurous and predictable.

FORAGING OFF THE BEATEN TRACK

Hop on the Skytrain heading north of central Bangkok for a food-tourist outing. The restaurants in these mainly Thai neighbourhoods favour more regional dishes from the rural northeast: field-hand food. Soi Ari, off Th Phahonyothin, has become quite a food magnet: the day market at the mouth of the *soi* sells tasty fried chicken and other takeaway treats. For sit-down meals cross the street to the Isan restaurant. Th Rang Nam (Map pp280–1) off Th Phayathai is another grazing option.

RIVER BAR CAFÉ Map pp278-9   Thai $$
☎ 0 2879 1747; 405/1 Soi Chao Phraya, Th Ratcha-withi, Thonburi; mains 180-300B; ☼ 5pm-midnight; taxi only

Go to a few restaurants listed in this book and you'll begin to wonder where all the Thais go. Good question. Thais don't eat out as a hobby but out of necessity, meaning that most frequent a favourite food stall or small décor-less restaurant often cheaper or better than fussing with a home-cooked meal. What would qualify as 'going out' for Westerners is 'celebrating a birthday' for Thais. Well-entrenched in the birthday circuit, this riverside restaurant is a modern glass box full of stylish Thais and nightly, if cheesy, music.

TALAT AW TAW KAW
Map pp278-9   Thai $
Th Kampangphet; mains 30-60B; ☼ 10am-5pm; subway Kamphoeng Pet

Across the street from Chatuchak Market, Aw Taw Kaw is one of Bangkok's biggest fruit and agricultural markets. But that isn't why it pops up on message boards

as *the* best place to eat in the city. For the self-styled food hunters, Aw Taw Kaw is all about the food vendors that occupy the southern section of the pavilion. If you're in the neighbourhood, it is a great concentration of *khànŏm jiin*, curries and more, safely secluded from traffic. On the other hand, there's nothing out here that doesn't pop up on street corners all over the city. To get here, use the Kamphoeng Pet subway station and exit on the opposite side from Chatuchak.

TEE SUD ISAAN INTER
Map pp280-1   Thai & International $
☎ 0 2245 3665; 4/11-12 Th Rang Nam, Th Phaya-thai; mains 80-150B; ☼ 10am-11pm; Skytrain Victory Monument

In any other neighbourhood, this would be a Lonely Planet backpacker staple. But this is a Thai neighbourhood with a sprink-ling of NGO and teacher types who can't afford more central abodes. The resulting clientele is a model of multiculturalism: Westerners with Westerners, Thais with Thais, Thais with Westerners, a Sikh couple, the combinations are endless. The Thai university students come for 'inter' (international) food, and the *faràng* who have gone native dive into homey Isan dishes.

VICTORY POINT Map pp280-1   Thai $
Th Phahonyothin & Th Ratchawithi; mains 30-60B; ☼ 6pm-midnight; Skytrain Victory Monument

In Bangkok, the best meals are always in unlikely places. Far from the foreign forces of inner Bangkok, Victory Point can be as provincial as it wants to be with a squat village of concrete stalls lit in neon and a mix of super casual and super delicious food vendors.

Ententertainment

Entertainment

Bangkok's nightlife scene has seen good times and bad times and lots of times in between. The city first landed on the global scene with its love-you-long-time venues for R&Ring servicemen during the Vietnam War and for airline flight crews on Asian 'layovers'. The girlie-bar scene still thrives, drawing in lonely hearts from across the globe. The majority of residents, though, are bar-hopping yuppies whose watering holes look a lot like London or New York. For a good stretch, Bangkok was poised for nightlife stardom. The discos were big, the drugs were plentiful and the parties raged till dawn. But the Thaksin administration decided in 2001 that Singapore, not Gomorrah, was a better role model and started tucking the city into bed at a respectable hour, imposing a 1am closing time. Being nocturnal, Bangkok has yet to adjust to the curfew. Bars and clubs don't fill up until a precious hour before closing time discharges thirsty patrons out on to the street. After-hours speakeasies are transient but now more popular than the once thriving bar business. Disappointed partiers joke that Singapore and Malaysia are better weekend spots these days than their beloved, anything-goes Bangkok.

The good news is that everything old is new again. Good old Th Khao San is still doing what it does best: an outdoor street party with beer guzzlers and freaky exhibitionists. What used to be an insulated traveller cocoon is now more popular with the locals, and not just with the sensitive cross-cultural types, but with the urban hipsters who make the *faràng* (Westerners) look provincial.

Lower Th Sukhumvit is still a men's playground dominated by the hostess and go-go bars at Soi Cowboy and Nana Entertainment Plaza. Women might want to venture to upper Th Sukhumvit where a more diverse expat and yuppie crowd sips wine and fancy cocktails.

Th Silom has a number of contrasting night-crawling options, including the go-go-bar-cum-tourist-bazaar of Patpong, relaxed English-style pubs and unpretentious dance clubs.

Royal City Avenue (RCA), a suburban nightclub zone, has been given a shot of adrenaline with the inner-city restrictions. Blocks and blocks of clubs thump out their constantly changing themes: hip-hop one month, dance-trance the next. The crowd is young and Thai but intrepid foreigners are making the late-night pilgrimage.

TOP 10 DRINKING & CLUBBING SPOTS

- Ad Here the 13th (p152) Rockin' house band, cheap brews and friendly regulars fit like a good pair of jeans.
- Club Astra (p156) The latest club darling.
- Cheap Charlie's (p150) A good front-loading spot before club-cruising.
- Q Bar (p157) Urban chic delivers Bangkok from the backwater.
- Saxophone Pub & Restaurant (p154) Great live music every night.
- Th Khao San (opposite) Always packed with freaks, hipsters and performers.
- Tawan Daeng German Brewhouse (p154) Don't cross an ocean to hang with tourists; go where the Thais go.
- Opera Riserva Winetheque (p151) Unpretentious wine cellar.
- Wong's Place (p152) Long live holes in the wall with cheap beer and epic tunes.
- Moon Bar at Vertigo (p150) Drink in the scenery from this sky-high bar.

Wong's Place (p152)

DRINKING

Bangkok's watering holes cover the spectrum from English-style pubs to trendy fashion cases. A laundry list of beverages is available, though prices on alcohol are relatively more expensive than, say, cab rides or street food. A beer at the night market could cost double the price of the meal itself. Because food is so integral to any Thai outing, most bars have tasty dishes that are absent-mindedly nibbled between toasts. Bars don't have cover charges, but they do strictly enforce closing time at 1am, sometimes earlier if they suspect trouble from the cops.

BACCHUS WINE BAR Map pp294-5

☎ 0 2650 8986; 20/6-7 Soi Ruam Rudi, Th Ploenchit; Skytrain Ploenchit

Bangkok's hi-so (socialite) crowd has developed a serious grape crush and stylish spots like Bacchus have rushed to the tippling fountain. The interior is *très* mid-20th century with exposed brick walls, floating stairs, and sculpture seating. But alas the VIPs click their high heels to the private top floor with a see-through ceiling, far removed from the tourists and *faràng* in the commoners' section.

BAGHDAD CAFÉ Map pp286-7

Soi 2, Th Samsen; ferry Tha Phra Athit, ordinary bus 15, 30 & 53

Just over Khlong Banglamphu is this sardine-tight sheesha bar for puffing pungent fruit tobacco on Arabic water pipes and chatting with your neighbours about distant lands. A nice divergence from the Arabic tradition is that alcohol is sold right alongside.

BARBICAN BAR Map pp290-1

☎ 0 2234 3590; 9 Soi Thaniya, Th Silom; ☽ 6pm-1am; Skytrain Sala Daeng, subway Silom

If you ever feel down about life in sweaty Bangkok, go directly to the Barbican. Where else could you suck down a few cocktails with friends from Thailand, Singapore and

TH KHAO SAN

The tourist strip of Banglamphu's Th Khao San (Map pp286–7) and the surrounding streets are one big, multicultural party with every imaginable outlet for swilling and socialising. Shirtless Euros guzzle big Beer Changs while draped around the closest stable body. Mixed Thai-*faràng* couples sip cocktails at bars converted from VW buses. Groups of underaged Thai hipsters parade from one end of the street to another dreaming of being club legal. Even high-society Thais occasionally join the parade with a visit to more civilised bars.

There are dozens of indoor options, if you tire of watching the street action from a sidewalk beer stall. Here is a brief cross-section:

Arise (☎ 0 1750 0591; Th Rambutri) Thai indie favourite for live music.

Buddy Bar (☎ 0 2629 4477; Th Khao San) Clean and cool colonial-themed bar for folks who find Bangkok too dirty.

Cave (Th Khao San) A Thai 'kitchen' club with tables arranged around a stage hosting folk and pop bands, but there's also an indoor climbing wall for the sober and the sloppy.

deep (☎ 0 2629 3360; 329/1-2 Th Rambutri) Very stylish Thai crowd of tiny punksters and whisky-set bulldogs.

Hippie de Bar (Th Khao San) Retro décor, pool tables and chill DJs.

Lava Club (☎ 0 2281 6565; 249 Th Khao San) Moody basement lounge spinning all the electronica genres.

Molly Bar (☎ 0 2629 4074; 108 Th Rambutri) Mellow sidewalk beer garden for audible conversations.

Shamrock Irish Pub (2nd fl, Centre Khao San, Th Khao San) Loud live bands and cheap Guinness.

Silk Bar (☎ 0 2281 9981; 129-131 Th Khao San) An open-air cocktail bar for the visiting Sukhumvit entourage crowd.

Susie Pub (☎ 0 2282 4459; 108/5-9 Th Rambutri) Before Khao San was a hip place for Thais to hang out, Susie was a local outpost for university students to play pool and drink in candy pop.

Th Khao San is between Th Chakraphong and Th Tanao, off Th Ratchadamnoen Klang; take the river ferry to Tha Phra Athit, or air-con bus 511 and 512, or ordinary bus 2 and 82.

SOI RAMBUTRI

A visible sigh can be heard as people cross from raucous Th Khao San to quieter Soi Rambutri (Map pp286–7). The VW cocktail bus continues the raging soundtrack of Th Khao San, and **Bangkok Bar**, next door to Sawadee Guesthouse, shoehorns in teeny-bopper Thais. Then things mellow around **Dong Dea Moon**, on the 2nd-floor bar portion of a Korean restaurant. From your privileged perch you can heckle the penny-pinching commoners below or enjoy good tunes and free games of pool. Around the corner you can still catch a guesthouse showing a pirated movie, an old backpacker tradition that is dying out as budgets get bigger.

You'll find Soi Rambutri behind Wat Chana Songkhram off Th Chakraphong; take the river ferry to Tha Phra Athit, or ordinary bus 15, 30 and 53.

Norway, and then stumble out to find a line of Thai women dressed like cheap prom dates reciting 'Hello, massage' in faulty Japanese? In bizarre Bangkok, of course.

BULL'S HEAD & ANGUS STEAKHOUSE Map pp296-7

☎ 0 2259 4444; Soi 33/1, Th Sukhumvit; ⏰ 6pm-midnight; Skytrain Phrom Phong

This is a beautiful galleried bar that's well suited to imagining foggy London nights. Happy hours, quiz nights and comedy shows provide much-needed stimulus if your vocabulary is morphing into Tinglish (Thai-English – dropped tenses, swapped 'l's and 'r's).

CHEAP CHARLIE'S Map pp296-7

Soi 11, Th Sukhumvit; ⏰ Mon-Sat; Skytrain Nana

What are all those foreigners doing standing around that wooden shack? If it looks like fun (and it is), grab yourself a stool at this neighbourhood beer stall. Charlie's started out selling cigarettes, graduated to beer and now has a faithful following of local characters who can spin yarns out of dental floss.

To find it, look for the 'Sabai Sabai Massage' sign on a sub-soi (lane) off Soi 11.

DIPLOMAT BAR Map pp294-5

☎ 0 2690 9999; Conrad Bangkok, 87 Th Withayu; Skytrain Ploenchit

Young sophisticates toast their good fortune and good looks at Bangkok's future leaders' training ground. The bubbly and the grapey spirits are raised in grand toasts while the diva-led lounge band serenades. Those who are unmatched by bottle's end traipse over to 87, the hotel's dance club, to seal the deal on the night's bed warmer. With two nips and tucks in the last year, 87 looks doomed to be replaced by yet another media-generating model.

JOOL'S BAR & RESTAURANT Map pp296-7

☎ 0 2252 6413; Soi 4, Th Sukhumvit; ⏰ 11am-midnight; Skytrain Nana

You can turn your nose up at the Nana girlie-bar scene or curiosity can propel you to the fringes. Jool's offers a comfortable peek into this other world. Lots of sexpats take a breather here for a good romp with some beer buddies. The drunkest always gets to sit in the captain's chair and everyone else gathers around the u-shaped bar for cross-fire conversations.

MOON BAR AT VERTIGO Map pp292-3

☎ 0 2679 1200; Banyan Tree Hotel, Th Sathon Tai; ⏰ weather permitting; subway Lumphini

Sky bars have completely obsessed the city; every year there is a new platform reaching for the heavens. Now nearly forgotten, the restaurant Vertigo and the attached Moon Bar started the trend. From ground level, the elevator delivers you to the 59th floor, where you weave your way through dimly lit hallways, bowing attendants and narrow sets of stairs, emerging to the roar of Bangkok traffic far, far below and a view that will literally take your breath away. Come dressed up at sunset and grab a coveted seat to the right of the bar for more impressive views.

NANG NUAL RIVERSIDE PUB Map pp284-5

☎ 0 2223 7686; Trok Krai, Th Mahachak; ⏰ 4pm-midnight; ferry Tha Saphan Phut or Tha Ratchawong

Is it a bar or a restaurant? This outdoor riverside deck is a quintessential example of Thai sànùk (fun). Groups of friends gather around the whisky set and plates of kàp klâem (drinking food) to watch the river and the night flow by. If you hit this spot at the right time, the bar's blaring pop music will be competing for valuable air space with the Muslim call to prayer from the temple across the river. Equally impressive is the golden sunset bathing Bangkok's mountain range of skyscrapers.

OPERA RISERVA WINETHEQUE

☎ 0 2258 5601; 53/3 Soi 39, Th Sukhumvit; ✹ 5.30pm-1am; Skytrain Phrom Phong

The Italian version of a beer cellar, this low-key wine bar is more for the conversationalist than the sensationalist. You can describe your hankering – something light and dry, not too sweet – and the affable and ample host Roberto can find a suitable match from South Africa, Italy or France.

O'REILLY'S IRISH PUB Map pp290-1

☎ 0 2632 7515; 62/1-2 Th Silom, cnr Soi Thaniya; ✹ 11am-1am; Skytrain Sala Daeng, subway Silom

Bangkok's version of Cheers, O'Reilly's welcomes the professionals with happy-hour specials and is a convenient meeting spot for friends cruising the Silom scene. The Irish-themed bar is a little too shiny and frigidly cooled to be anything but canned, but location is a close second to authenticity.

PHRANAKORN BAR Map pp286-7

☎ 0 2282 7507; 58/2 Soi Damnoen Klang Tai (btwn Th Ratchadamnoen Klang & Trok Sa-Ke) ✹ 6pm-midnight; ferry Tha Phra Athit, air-con bus 511 & 512, ordinary bus 2 & 82

A well-kept secret that Lonely Planet has finally sniffed out, Phranakorn is just steps away from Th Khao San but worlds removed. Students and arty types make this a home away from hovel with eclectic décor, gallery exhibits and, the real draw, a rooftop terrace for beholding the old district's majesty.

SHIP INN Map pp296-7

9/1 Soi 23, Th Sukhumvit; ✹ 11am-midnight; Skytrain Asoke

Just around the corner from Soi Cowboy, Ship Inn provides a mature embrace for a quiet drinking crowd. The bar is as well stocked as a ship captain's quarters, and the music is at a conversation-friendly volume.

TOWER INN SKY GARDEN Map pp290-1

Soi 9, Th Silom; ✹ 6pm-midnight; Skytrain Chong Nonsi

Finding a sky-top bar in this city is easy. Finding one where budget travellers can afford to be is another matter. Luckily there is the poor-man's beer garden on the 19th floor of the Tower Inn. You're not going to impress the *Wallpaper* readers here, but down-to-earth types can ogle the garden green or peep into the surrounding office towers. Even the outdated '80s soundtrack is becoming cool again.

WATER BAR Map pp280-1

☎ 0 2642 7699; 107/3-4 Th Rangnam, Th Phayathai; Skytrain Victory Monument

Every new arrival should learn the whisky-set routine, a drinking tradition more at

---

NIGHTLIFE ANTHROPOLOGIST

Honestly, Bangkok's nightlife is never going to measure up to the world-class cities, but the night-crawling characters are a lot easier to gain access to in Bangkok than the exclusive clubs in New York City.

The cross-section of nightspots and night owls that a foreigner might encounter can be divided into three genres: hi-so, *dèk naew* (trendies), and lo-so. The high-society types split their time between Bangkok and Europe and have pioneered Bangkok's fascination with wine, London lounge, midcentury minimalism and international cuisine. The usual tastes of the rich and famous.

Younger and fashion-fearless are *dèk naew* (Thai for 'trendy child'). The scene can range from arty and creative to pop and parody. The emergence of Bakery Music (see p36) and other alternative labels was funded by the buying power of *dèk naew*, and the '80s fashion revival sprouted amid Siam Square's hipsters before it hit the equivalent neighbourhoods in San Francisco. But for two years now, the rage has been ghetto fabulous: oversized sports jerseys, cockeyed baseball caps, gang-colour bandanas. These imported fashions are for the rich only – rap's true rags-to-riches accomplishment.

At the bottom of the feeding chain are the lo-sos ('low society' as opposed to 'high society'), the ordinary middle class who prefer Thai rock to international electronica and drink whisky sets instead of gin and tonics. Lat Phrao, Pattanakan and other suburban neighbourhoods are where the 'real' Thais live and party. But places like Tawan Daeng German Brewhouse (p154) and sometimes Th Khao San attract average Thais doing average Thai things.

CLUBS WITH A PULSE?

Parts of Bangkok suffer from the urban version of attention deficit disorder and a hyperactive public-relations machine. Media tycoons in Los Angeles might buy themselves jets and tropical islands, but their counterparts in Bangkok entertain themselves with restaurants and nightclubs that dominate social calendars until a competing venture steals away the social climbers. Feeding the frenzy are the nightlife rags that make the newest hotspot sound like Grand Central station. But when you arrive for the fabled body crush all you find is a ghost town, where servers outnumber patrons. Arrived too early? Have the crowds moved on? Hello (echo)?

First, Bangkok is excessively fickle, but it is also resourceful. The professional night owls stay on the scene not because they are making executive salaries with plenty to spare for expensive cocktails (even white-collar labour in Thailand is cheap), but because they work the promotions circuit, a busy weekly calendar of bar anniversaries, art openings, wine tastings and launch parties. Every free party is accompanied by a Thai ceremony: photographers clicking pics of the VIPs and socialites. For commercial liquor promos, there is usually a fashion show: four or five nervous models sprint though the crowd and everyone oohs and aahs.

Many of the events are 'invite' only, but often that's a relative term. To join the booze moochers, dress in your urban best and scour for leads in the entertainment press, such as the monthly *Thailand Tatler*, *Metro: Magazine* and *BKK Magazine*. *Guru*, the weekly entertainment insert in the *Bangkok Post*, covers events in the under-25 world. Party promoters **Dude Sweet** (www.dudesweet.org) work around the clock to fill funky spaces with warm bodies.

home at Thai family gatherings than in flash hotels. At this misnomered bar, just a short walk from Victory Monument, the Sang Som set (Thai whisky with Coke, soda and ice) still reigns as the tipple of choice. The attentive waitress will keep your glass filled to the right proportions (three fingers whisky, a splash of coke, the rest soda) after which you should offer up a toast and drain the night away.

WONG'S PLACE Map pp292-3

27/3 Soi Sri Bamphen, off Soi Ngam Duphli, Th Phra Ram IV; subway Lumphini

An institution reborn, Wong's Place is a time warp into the backpacker world of the early 1980s. The eponymous owner died several years ago, but a relative has removed the padlock and picked up where Wong left off. No-one goes until after midnight, when they're too drunk to realise that they really need to go home. Never mind, Wong's is like home, with an honour system at the bar and a rocking music library. (Don't tell the men in brown, but Wong's usually stumbles past the curfew.)

LIVE MUSIC

As Thailand's media capital, Bangkok is the centre of the Thai music industry, packaging and selling pop, crooners, *lûuk thûng* (Thai country music) and the recent phenomenon of indie bands. Music is a part of almost every Thai social gathering. The

matriarchs and patriarchs like dinner with an easy-listening soundtrack, typically a Filipino band and a synthesizer. Patrons will write a request on a piece of paper and pass them up to the stage.

Dedicated bars throughout the city feature blues and rock bands, but are lean on live indie performances. An indigenous rock style, *phleng phêua chii-wít* (Songs for Life) makes appearances at country-and-western bars filled with buffalo horns and pictures of Native Americans. The shopfront bars on Th Phra Athit are a centre for Thai folk, typically a squeaky guitar and a solo singer. The audience always knows all the words.

Up-and-coming garage bands occasionally pop up at free concerts where the young kids hang out: Santichaiprakan Park (Th Phra Athit), Th Khao San and Siam Square. There are also music festivals, like Noise Pop and Fat Festival (p13), that feature the new breed.

For a schedule of live shows, check out **Eastbound Downers** (www.eastbound-downers .com), a promo site for indie bands, and **Bangkok Gig Guide** (www.bangkokgigguide.com), a comprehensive schedule of shows across the city.

AD HERE THE 13TH Map pp286-7

13 Th Samsen; ⏰ 6pm-midnight; ferry Tha Phra Athit, ordinary bus 15, 30 & 53

Next door to Khlong Banglamphu, this cramped neighbourhood joint features a soulful house band that plays at 10pm nightly. Their version of 'Me and Bobby

McGee' will make you swear Janis Joplin has been reincarnated. Everyone knows each other, so don't be shy about mingling.

AD MAKERS Map pp294-5
☎ 0 2652 0168; 51/51 Soi Lang Suan, Th Ploenchit; ☯ 5.30pm-midnight; Skytrain Chitlom
This brick box has a homely atmosphere of good times and good friends. A lot of patrons mix drinking and eating – two great Thai pursuits. The house band is a dying breed who still does a heartfelt 'Hotel California' as well as Thai folk and other classic rock standards.

BAMBOO BAR Map pp290-1
☎ 0 2236 0400; Oriental Hotel, Soi 38, Th Charoen Krung; ☯ noon-1am; Skytrain Saphan Taksin, ferry Tha Oriental
The romantic image of rubber-plantation barons and colonial mansions are a little out of place in Bangkok's history, but Bamboo Bar, in the historic Oriental Hotel, exudes enough bygone-era charm that modern imperialists are anachronistically content. Internationally recognised jazz bands hold court within a brush stroke of the audience to set a mellow lounge mood.

BROWN SUGAR Map pp292-3
☎ 0 2250 1825; 231/20 Th Sarasin; ☯ 6pm-midnight; Skytrain Ratchadamri
Not to be overlooked is the strip of music bars along Th Sarasin near Lumphini Park,

Live music at Ad Here the 13th (opposite)

including this small jazz club. With a Crescent City informality, Brown Sugar gives inspired performances that are more bebop and brass than the city's usual smooth jazz. On Sunday nights, the high-powered musicians touring the luxury hotels assemble here for impromptu jam sessions.

DALLAS PUB Map pp294-5
☎ 0 2255 3276; 412/1 Soi 6, Siam Square; ☯ 5pm-midnight; Skytrain Siam
American honky-tonks live on in the Thai-country bar. Just across the street from the Novotel hotel, this locals' spot has a rustic wooden interior filled with buffalo horns and Wild West paraphernalia – the aesthetic of the Songs for Life genre, a musical protest movement from the 1980s. Come before 9pm for the acoustic bands whose soulful ballads coax crowd singalongs, eyes closed tight in solidarity. Follow the alley to the narrow stairs to reach the bar.

HARD ROCK CAFE Map pp294-5
☎ 0 2254 0830; Soi 11, Siam Square; ☯ 11am-midnight; Skytrain Siam
It gets lonesome in Siam Square after dark, but this global giant, part of the Hard Rock empire, gives night owls yet another place to expand their T-shirt collection. The guitar-shaped bar features the full range of cocktails and a small assortment of local and imported beers. The crowd is a changing parade of Thais, expats and tourists, and there's live music from 10pm.

LIVING ROOM Map pp296-7
☎ 0 2653 0333; Sheraton Grande Sukhumvit, 250 Th Sukhumvit; ☯ 9pm-midnight; Skytrain Asoke
The power-broker bar of the Sheraton Grande presents highball jazz. Studio-perfected musicians of international calibre put a sizzle into the men's club aesthetic of classic cocktails, complimentary nuts and hushed conversation.

NORIEGA'S Map pp290-1
☎ 0 2233 2813; Silom Soi 4, Th Silom; ☯ 6pm-1am; Skytrain Sala Daeng, subway Silom
If Soi 4's cliquish party could be likened to the grown-up version of a public school cafeteria, then Noriega's would be the misanthropic misfit. All the way at the end of the *soi*, where the neon doesn't shine, Noriega's doesn't play the techno game,

153

preferring the raw noise of rotating blues bands. The scene is the unofficial head-quarters of Bangkok's Hash House Harriers (see p166).

SAXOPHONE PUB & RESTAURANT Map pp280-1

☎ 0 2246 5472; 3/8 Th Phayathai; ⏰ 6pm-midnight; Skytrain Victory Monument

Don't leave town without a visit to this venerable music club. Whether you're a beer-toast distance from the band or perched in the 2nd-floor alcove, Saxophone's intimate space draws the crowd into the laps of great jazz and blues musicians. The sounds are smooth and mellow on your traffic-weary ears. The music changes each night – jazz during the week, and rock, blues and beyond on weekends. There are well-loved reggae-fusion sessions on Sunday night.

TAWAN DAENG GERMAN BREWHOUSE Map pp278-9

☎ 0 2678 1114; 462/61 Th Narathiwat Ratchana-kharin, cnr Th Phra Ram III; ⏰ 5pm-midnight; taxi

Sick of hanging out with bitter expats and clueless tourists? The Thais are all hanging out in this village-sized brew house. The food is tasty, the house-made brews very drinkable and the nightly stage shows pull the crowd into a singalong. Most people come for the Wednesday performance of Fong Nam (see p38). Music starts at 8.30pm.

TH PHRA ATHIT Map pp286-7

Northwest of Th Khao San, bordering the river; ⏰ 6pm-1am; ferry Tha Phra Athit, ordinary bus 15, 30 & 53

Some of the steam that fuelled Th Phra Athit's arty resurrection has dissipated recently, but the street still retains a few closet-sized bars where bohemian Thais mix and mingle with whisky sets and acoustic singalongs. The strip of bars cluster around the block directly in front of the ferry pier.

TOKYO JOES Map pp296-7

☎ 0 2662 5637; 9-11 Siwaporn Plaza, Soi 24, Th Sukhumvit; ⏰ 5pm-1am; Skytrain Phrom Phong

This narrow bar, reminiscent of a railroad car, is like church on Sunday, a house of

worship for blues and jazz. Real regulars, mainly journos and other word-workers, warm the booths here swapping news of their own bands. On Sunday nights, the locally famous Soi Dogs takes the pulpit. ROL Jazz Trio and Georgia from Ad Here also fill the chalkboard schedule. The blues bands lean more toward Stevie Ray Vaughn than the Mississippi Blind Boys, encouraging the crowd to transform from perfect strangers into best buds.

WITCH'S TAVERN Map pp296-7

☎ 0 2391 9791; 306/1 Soi 55, Th Sukhumvit; ⏰ 6pm-1am; Skytrain Thong Lor

You have to trek out to Soi 55 (Soi Thong Lor) to find truly Thai places, even if they are masquerading as something else. This spacious place claims to be an English pub, but it comes closer to a hotel lobby geared towards groups of down-to-earth Thai professionals. Jazz and folk bands start up around 8.30pm and at 10.30pm the house cover band takes to the stage, accepting requests from the audience. Ballads get the biggest rounds of applause.

CLUBBING

Bangkok's disco scene has morphed along with prevailing trends. Gone are the stadium dance halls of the 1990s, replaced by intimate lounges with cool décor. Electronica still rules the evening soundtrack, but hip-hop is now the golden groove. Or at least that's what the nightclubs call 50 Cent and other radio rap acts, a far cry from the heady melodies of hip-hop stateside. Next month, it might be electro, and back to techno before you even know it. Who can say, really?

The closing-time restrictions have hurt the club scene the most, since dance-floor courage comes from wee hours and ingestible substances, long since scrubbed out by police who occasionally conduct urine tests on clubbers. Some of the recklessness is gone, but the young teenyboppers still get disastrously drunk.

What used to be a rotating cast of hotspots has slowed to a few standards on the *soi* off Sukhumvit, Silom and RCA. Clubs in 'entertainment zones' specially designated areas, are supposed to qualify for a 2am closing time, but the police often show up as early as 1am. You'll need ID to prove you're legal (20 years old); they'll card even the

Entertainment

CLUBBING

grey hairs. Cover charges are around 600B and usually include a drink. Most places don't begin filling up until midnight.

To keep the crowds from growing bored, the nightclubs host weekly theme parties and visiting DJs that ebb and flow in popularity. To get an idea of current happenings around town, check the online blogs: **Nocturnal Remission** (nocturnalremission.com), **Bangkok Spins** (www.bangkokspin.com), **Drunk Is Better** (www.drunkisbetter.com) or the entertainment press. Another rule of thumb is the cover charge: if it is more than 200B, the crowd will be mainly *faràng*.

70'S BAR Map pp292-3
☎ 0 2253 4433; 231/6 Th Sarasin; no cover; ⏰ 6pm-1am; Skytrain Chitlom

A little too small to be a club proper, this retro-themed bar spins all the hits from the Me generation in the ultimate Me city. The location is a good staging ground for working up a sweat and then drying off at Brown Sugar (p153), next door.

BED SUPPERCLUB Map pp296-7
☎ 0 2651 3537; 26 Soi 11, Th Sukhumvit; cover 500-600B; ⏰ 8pm-1am; Skytrain Nana

Yup, that's it there, the building that looks like a space alien pod. Inside the shell is a futuristic set liberally borrowing from *2001: A Space Odyssey*, but the laws of gravity still apply. As the name suggests, there are beds for lounging with your friends, and supper is served in a separate restaurant (p141). Tourists and expats are Bed's bread and butter, but yuppie Thais make an appearance on Tuesday hip-hop nights.

PARTY LIKE A BUTTERFLY

If you're having commitment issues, try these streets for a club buffet.

You're probably already there, but **Th Khao San** (p149) has become so diverse lately that you don't really have to leave to get a good dose of Bangkok nightlife.

A young crowd flocks to **Royal City Avenue** (RCA; Map pp278–9; an extension of Rama IX), a district of loud, flashy bars that was once a Thai teen playground but has now diversified for all ages. **Ratchadaphisek Soi 4** (Map pp278–9) has sprouted a recent growth of teenybopper clubs to capitalise on its designation as an entertainment zone.

The party spills out on to the sidewalks of *soi* near Patpong off Th Silom. **Soi 4** (Map pp290–1) is a boisterous carnival of blaring techno, parading drag queens, muscle boys, and a lot of exhibitionism. Tapas is one of the saner options along the row.

A string of café-bars south of **Chatuchak Park** on Th Kampaengphet (Map pp278–9) wind up the night as the weekend market is winding down.

Ekkamai (Map pp296–7; Soi 63, Th Sukhumvit) is Bangkok cool, but the bars change so frequently it is hard for a clunky guidebook to keep up. Check the nightlife rags for leads.

CAFÉ DEMOC Map pp286-7
☎ 0 2622 2571; 78 Th Ratchadamnoen Klang; no cover; ⏰ 8pm-1am Tue-Sun; air-con bus 511 & 512, ordinary bus 2 & 82

Up-and-coming DJs present their turntable dexterity at this unpretentious club. Hip-hop, break beat, drum 'n' bass and tribal fill the night roster, but only special events fill the audience. Keep a watch for the monthly appearance of local wax artists, DJ Spydamonkee and DJ Dragon.

Dancing in Club Astra (p156)

CLUB ASTRA Map pp278-9

☎ 0 9497 8422; RCA, block C; cover charge 250B;
🕐 6pm-2am Wed, Fri & Sat; subway Rama IX

A bold newcomer, Astra adds international-strength music to the pop-leanings of RCA. Special club nights are heavily promoted among backpacker circles, but all of Bangkok's expats are buzzing about the quality tunes and sound system. If Astra is empty, cruise the strip for a dozen other options that are popular with homie-wannabes, plastic pretties in handkerchief miniskirts, and more recently, the poised and polished.

DANCE FEVER Map pp278-9

☎ 0 2247 4295; 71 Th Ratchadaphisek; 🕐 9pm-2am; subway Thailand Cultural Centre

Las Vegas ain't got nothing on Dance Fever's neon extravaganza. Thai pop thunders across the cavernous dance hall with lights spinning maniacally and throngs of Thai twenty-somethings. Pound an extra round of stiff drinks to join in with the bouncing bodies.

LUCIFER Map pp290-1

☎ 234 6902, 76/1-3 Soi Patpong 1; cover 150B;
🕐 9pm-1am; Skytrain Sala Daeng, subway Silom

Meet the Miltonian side of Lucifer: a fun-loving hedonist. Nestled in the heart of Patpong, Lucifer kicks off the night with a few travellers who wander in from the night market. But the hardcore techno, pulsating black light and hired dancing girls bring together the tipsy band of misfits. By 11pm, the crowd shifts to a younger, prettier persuasion with serious dance-floor know-how. Another wave of recruits arrives at hook-up time.

GAY & LESBIAN BANGKOK

Bangkok's male-gay nightlife is out and open with bars, discos and *kàthoey* cabarets, but nightspots for Thai lesbians (*tom-dee*) aren't as prominent or as segregated.

The city's most stylish gays mix with the beautiful people at whatever watering hole is elite enough for their attention. Eat Me (p136) is a gracious dinner date. Most gay foreign men find themselves at one of the bars or dance clubs that line Soi 2 (Map pp292–3) and Soi 4 (Map pp290–1) off Th Silom; the Thai clientele are typically money boys (boyfriends for hire) rather than Thais on an even footing. A more local crowd of students hangs out on the *soi* around Ramkhamhaeng University on Th Ramkhamhaeng (Map pp278–9) near the Lamsalee intersection. The lesbian scene is much more low-key. Many hang out in the art bars along Th Phra Athit (Map pp286–7), including Hemlock (see p127). Soi Ari (Map pp278–9) off Th Phahonyothin is emerging as an arty hang-out for gays and *tom-dee*. Utopia (p247), the well-known gay information provider, has recently released *Utopia Guide to Thailand*, covering gay-friendly businesses in 18 Thai cities, including Bangkok.

Babylon Bangkok (Map pp292–3; ☎ 0 2679 7984; 50 Soi Nantha, near Soi 1/Atakanprasit, Th Sathon; 🕐 10am-11pm) is a four-storey gay sauna that has been described as one of the top 10 of its kind in the world. Facilities include a bar, roof garden, gym, massage room, steam and dry saunas, and spa baths. The spacious, well-hidden complex also has accommodation.

Telephone (Map pp290–1; ☎ 0 2234 3279; 114/11-13 Soi 4, Th Silom) is perennially popular but very cruisy. It is a conversation bar sporting tables equipped with telephones so that patrons can 'ring' each other.

Always packed, the **Balcony** (Map pp290–1; ☎ 0 2235 5891; www.balconypub.com; 86-88 Soi 4, Th Silom) is a lively bar with dancing and karaoke inside and chill-out tables on the terrace.

Massive with the younger crowd, **DJ Station** (Map pp292–3; ☎ 0 2266 4029; www.dj-station.com; 8/6-8 Soi 2, Th Silom) has pounding dance music, flamboyant costume parties and *kàthoey* cabaret at 11pm.

Near Chatuchak Weekend Market, **ICY** (Map pp278–9; ☎ 0 2272 4775; Th Kamphaengphet) is a long-running bar that is consistently loud, crowded and very local.

Near the end of the soi, **ICK Pub** (Map pp278–9; ☎ 0 1442 9472; Soi 89/2, Th Ramkhamhaeng) is a poster child for Ramkhamhaeng's student hangouts full of bubble-gum pop music and late-night schedules.

Sa-Ke Coffee Pub (Map pp286–7; ☎ 0 9748 0212; Trok Sa-Ke, cnr Th Tanao & Th Rachadamnoen Klang) is at the Khok Wua intersection. 'Sa-gay' is a bopping scene just steps from Th Khao San.

Folks claim that **Freeman** (Map pp292–3; ☎ 0 2632 8032; sub-soi off Soi 2, Th Silom) is Bangkok's best *kàthoey* cabaret (11.30pm).

Lesbian-owned **Vega Cafe** (Map pp296–7; ☎ 0 2258 8273; Soi 39, Th Sukhumvit; 🕐 Mon-Sat) pours some of the stiffest drinks in the city and hosts supping *tom-dee*.

NARCISSUS Map pp296-7

☎ 0 2261 3991; 112 Soi 23, Th Sukhumvit; cover
500B; ⏰ 9am-1am; Skytrain Asoke
In keeping with its name, Narcissus is one
of the city's most ostentatious clubs. It
doesn't see as much action as it did in years
past, but the whole city turns up when
Paul Oakenfold graces this palace with his
presence.

Q BAR Map pp296-7

☎ 0 2252 3274; 34 Soi 11, Th Sukhumvit; cover
400-500B; ⏰ 9am-1am; Skytrain Nana
In club years, Q Bar is fast approaching
dinosaur age but still rules the techno-
rati with slick industrial style. Sunday
theme parties and celebrity DJs pack in
the crowds. Detractors complain that the
dance floor is monopolised by working
girls and pot-bellied admirers but still Q is
queen with showboating cocktail slingers.
It boasts perhaps Thailand's largest range
of drinks – 27 types of vodka and 41 brands
of whisky/bourbon. Absinthe even resides
somewhere behind the bar.

SPEED Map pp290-1

☎ 0 9890 8441; Soi 4, Th Silom; ⏰ 6pm-2am;
cover 100B; Skytrain Sala Daeng, subway Silom
Dark enough to blot out inhibitions, Speed
has throttled Soi 4 into a serious hip-hop
and R&B following. The sensible admission
price lures in the baht-lean young ones on
weekends.

ZANTIKA Map pp278-9

☎ 0 2711 5887; 235/11 Soi 63 (Ekamai), Th
Sukhumvit; ⏰ 8pm-1am; Skytrain Ekamai
All Thai-style discos may look the same:
neon lights, stage shows and whisky sets.
But Zantika can hold its liquor and its pedigree. The crowd is top-shelf Thai jet-setters,
children of politicians, and *lûuk khrêung*
(half-Thai, half-*faràng*) models. Even the
moneyed Thais like their drinks affordable
and their disco music deafening.

GO-GO BARS

It is no secret that Bangkok makes male
fantasies come true. From the hostess bars
where pretty young things play flirty drinking games, to the party-favour strip clubs
and massage parlours with 'happy endings',
Bangkok as a sexual playground is both a

novelty and a way of life. New male arrivals
generally either dive in and never resurface
or receive the proper aversion therapy to
keep the scene at curiosity distance.

Looming large in the visitors' imagination is the notorious Patpong district of
ping-pong and 'fuckey' shows. Along two
narrow *soi* (Soi Patpong 1 and Soi Patpong
2, off Th Silom, Map pp290–1), blaring
neon bars with poetic names such as King's
Castle, Supergirls and Pussy Galore cater
mainly to a gawking public (both male and
female) with circuslike sexual exploits.

The gay men's equivalent of Patpong
can be found on nearby Soi Thaniya, Soi
Pratuchai and Soi Anuman Ratchathon,
where bars feature go-go dancers and live
sex shows.

A more direct legacy of the Vietnam
R&R days is **Soi Cowboy** (Map pp296–7; btwn
Soi 21 & Soi 23, Th Sukhumvit), a strip
of hostess and go-go bars targeted at the
consumer, not the curious.

A three-storey complex, **Nana Entertainment
Plaza** (Nana; Map pp296–7; Soi 4/Nana Tai,
Th Sukhumvit) attracts expats and sex tourists for topless dancing and strip shows.
Nana Plaza comes complete with its own
guesthouses, used almost exclusively by
Nana Plaza's female bar workers for illicit meetings. The 'female' staff at Casa-
nova consists entirely of Thai transvestites
and transsexuals; this is a favourite stop
for foreigners visiting Bangkok for sex re-
assignment surgery.

Asian tourists – primarily Japanese, Tai-
wanese and Hong Kong males – flock to
the Ratchada entertainment strip, part of
the Huay Khwang district (Map pp278–9),
along wide Th Ratchadaphisek between Th
Phra Ram IX and Th Lat Phrao. Lit up like
Las Vegas, this stretch of neon boasts huge,
male-oriented, massage, snooker and karaoke and go-go complexes with names like
Caesar's Sauna and Emmanuelle, which are
far grander in scale.

THEATRE & DANCE

When it comes to high art, the city's heyday
has passed with the dismantling of the royal
court. Today Thai preservationists cling to
the classical dance dramas, with little government funding or appreciation, as the
city races to be more modern than it was
the day before. Truthfully, you are more

likely to see more authentic Thai dance at a provincial temple fair than in the country's capital, despite the numerous tourist shows. There are some companies performing Western arts and interesting fusions of the two cultures' traditions. But the number of arts venues are abysmally small compared to more profitable and less cultural businesses. The city's daily newspapers and monthly magazines maintain a calendar of cultural events.

Performances are typically advertised in the *Bangkok Post* or online at www.bang kokconcerts.org. Reservations are recommended for events. Tickets can be purchased through Thai Ticket Master (www.thai ticketmaster.com).

JOE LOUIS PUPPET THEATRE Map pp292-3

☎ 0 2252 9683; www.joelouis-theater.com; Suan Lum Night Bazaar, 1875 Th Phra Ram IV; tickets 600B; ☺ shows 7.30pm & 9.30pm; subway Lumphini

The ancient art of Thai puppetry (*lákhon lék*) was rescued by the late Sakorn Yangkhiawsod, more popularly known as Joe Louis, in 1985. Joe's children now carry on the tradition. His puppet creations are controlled by three puppeteers and can strike many human poses. Modelled after the characters in the epics Ramayana and *Phra Aphaimani,* the puppets perform nightly within this air-conditioned theatre, conveniently located in the Suan Lum Night Bazaar.

NATIONAL THEATRE Map p288

☎ 0 2221 0171; Th Ratchini; tickets 40-80B; air-con bus 503, 508 & 512, ordinary bus 47 & 53

The backbone of Bangkok's classical dance tradition, the National Theatre temporarily closed for renovations in December 2005. The theatre has been in decline recently and municipal plans have even slated the building for destruction. Information as to when the theatre will reopen was unavailable at the time of writing.

PATRAVADI THEATRE Map p288

☎ 0 2412 7287; www.patravaditheatre.com; Soi Wat Rakhang, Thonburi; tickets 300-800B; ☺ shows 7pm Fri-Sun; cross-river ferry from Tha Chang to Tha Wat Rakhang

Across the road from Supatra River House, Patravadi is Bangkok's leading modern-

dance venue. A stylish open-air theatre, Patravadi is the brainchild of Patravadi Mejudhon, a famous Thai actress and playwright. The dance troupe performance is a blend of traditional Thai dance and modern choreography, music and costume. This is also the primary venue for the Bangkok International Fringe Festival, held in April/May.

SIAM NIRAMIT Map pp278-9

☎ 0 2649 9222; www.siamniramit.com; 19 Th Thiam Ruammit; tickets 1500B; ☺ 8pm; subway Thailand Cultural Centre

A cultural theme park, the enchanted kingdom transports visitors to a Disney-fied version of ancient Siam with a technicoloured stage show depicting the Lanna Kingdom, the Buddhist heaven, and Thai festivals. Elaborate costumes and sets are guaranteed to be spectacular both in their grandness and their indigenous interpretation. It is popular with tour groups.

SIAM OPERA Map pp294-5

6th fl, Siam Paragon; Skytrain Siam

The bold new Siam Paragon shopping centre is also boldly marching into the high-arts business with a top-floor opera house. Plans have the new venture rivalling famous opera houses across the globe, but at the time of writing firm details were not yet available.

GET THEE SOME CULTURE

Bangkok's cultural centres extend an open invitation to the entire city for monthly art exhibits, film screenings, stage performances and annual festivals.

Alliance Française Bangkok (Map pp292–3; ☎ 0 2670 4200; www.alliance-francaise.or.th; 29 Th Sathon Tai)

Goethe Institut (Map pp292–3; ☎ 0 2287 0942; 18/1 Soi Goethe, off Soi 1/Atakanprasit, Th Sathon Tai; ☺ 8am-4.30pm Mon-Fri) Also hosts Bangkok Poetry slams and Christmas Art Fair.

Japan Foundation (Map pp296–7; ☎ 0 2260 8560; www.jfbkk.or.th; 10th fl, Serm-Mit Tower, Soi 21, Th Sukhumvit; ☺ 9am-7pm Mon-Fri, 9am-5pm Sat)

Neilson Hays Library Rotunda Gallery (Map pp290–1; ☎ 0 2233 1731; 195 Th Surawong; ☺ hours vary)

SHRINE DANCING

Although scheduled performances are grand, lasting memories are often unscripted and the serendipity of catching a shrine dance is unforgettable, like spotting a rainbow. If you hear the din of drums and percussion from a temple or shrine, follow the sound to see traditional *lákhon kâe bon* (shrine dancing). At Lak Meuang (p75) and Erawan Shrine (p98), worshippers commission costumed troupes to perform dance movements that are similar to classical *lákhon*, but more crude, as they are specially choreographed for ritual purposes.

THAILAND CULTURAL CENTRE Map pp278-9

☎ 0 2247 0028; www.thaiculturalcenter.com; Th Ratchadaphisek, btwn Th Thiam Ruammit & Th Din Daeng; subway Thailand Cultural Centre

Bangkok's primary performing arts facility, the Thailand Cultural Centre is the home of the Bangkok Symphony Orchestra and hosts the International Festival of Dance & Music in September. Occasionally, classical dance performances, regional Thai concerts, like *lûuk thûng* (Thai country music) and Khorat Song, cycle through the yearly calendar.

An exciting newcomer is the **Bangkok Opera** (www.bangkokopera.com), which performs at the cultural centre and at the Queen Sirikit Convention Centre. The opera's founder is the accomplished novelist, Somtow Sucharitkul (better known by his pen name SP Somtow), who has adapted many Thai legends and Buddhist stories to the stage. One recent composition was based on the ghost story of the devoted wife, Mae Nak, who died in childbirth but returned after death to terrorise the villagers. European operas are also presented and reviews have touted the company as invigorating a tradition that is losing favour among modern audiences. The opera company is in negotiations with the new Siam Opera (opposite) for future seasons.

On performance days, a free shuttle picks up passengers from the subway's exit 1.

DINNER THEATRE

Another option for viewing Thai classical dance is through a dinner theatre. Most dinner theatres in Bangkok are heavily pro-moted through hotels to an ever-changing clientele, so standards are poor to fair. They can be tolerably worthwhile if you accept them as cultural tourist traps.

SALA RIM NAM Map pp290-1

☎ 0 2437 3080; Oriental Hotel, Soi 38, Th Charoen Krung; tickets 1800B; ◷ dinner & show 7-10pm; Skytrain Saphan Taksin, ferry Tha Oriental

The historic Oriental Hotel hosts a dinner theatre in a sumptuous Thai pavilion located across the river in Thonburi. Free shuttle boats transfer guests across the river from the hotel's dock. The price is well above average, reflecting the means of the hotel's client base.

SILOM VILLAGE Map pp290-1

☎ 0 2234 4448; mains 150-350B; Th Silom; ◷ 6-10pm; ferry Tha Oriental

More relaxed than most dinner shows, Silom Village delivers comfort, accessibility and decent dinners. Picky eaters swear by the crispy pork and cashew chicken, and the demonstrations of Thai dance and martial arts strike one 'to do' off the itinerary.

SUPATRA RIVER HOUSE Map p288

☎ 0 2411 0305; 266 Soi Wat Rakhang, Thonburi; dishes 150-300B; ◷ dinner shows 8.30-9pm Fri & Sat; restaurant shuttle from Tha Maharat

This stylishly restored teak house garners the famous dual-temple view of Wat Arun as well as the Grand Palace. An outdoor stage hosts dance performances by graduates of the affiliated Patravadi Theatre. The food and service, however, are hit and miss.

KÀTHOEY CABARET

Somewhere between touristy and strange, Bangkok's *kàthoey* cabarets feature musical gender-bending. Convincing ladies (*kàthoey*, or ladyboy) take to the stage with elaborate costumes, MTV-style dance routines and rehearsed lip-synching to pop hits. **Calypso Cabaret** (Map pp294–5; ☎ 0 2261 8937; www.calypsocabaret.com; 1st fl, Asia Hotel, 296 Th Phayathai; tickets 1000B; ◷ shows 8.15pm & 9.45pm) and **Mambo Cabaret** (Map pp296–7; ☎ 0 2259 5715; Washington Sq, Th Sukhumvit, btwn Soi 22 & Soi 24; tickets 600-800B; ◷ shows

8.30pm & 10pm) do family- and tourist-friendly shows of pop and Broadway camp. The gay club **Freeman** (Map pp292–3; ☎ 0 2632 8032; sub-soi between Soi 2 and Soi Thaniya, Th Silom; cover 200B; ☺ shows 11.30pm) has shows that are a little racier.

CINEMAS

To offset the uncomfortable humidity, Bangkok's cinemas offer more than just a movie screening: they pamper. These high-tech, well-air-conditioned palaces offer VIP decadence (reclining seats and table service) in addition to the familiar fold-down seats and sticky floors.

All movies are preceded by the Thai royal anthem, during which everyone is expected to stand respectfully.

Releases of Hollywood movies arrive in Bangkok's theatres in a timely fashion. But as home-grown cinema grows, more and more Thai films, often subtitled in English, fill the roster. Bangkok also hosts several annual film festivals, including the International Film Festival in January (see p11).

At the cinemas listed here, English movies are subtitled in Thai rather than dubbed. Ticket prices range from 100B to 180B for regular seats and up to 500B for VIP seats. You can find movie listings and reviews in the *Nation, Bangkok Post, Metro,* **Movie Seer** (www.movieseer.com) and **Thai Cinema** (www.thaicinema.org).

Alliance Française Bangkok (Map pp292–3; ☎ 0 2670 4200; www.alliance-francaise.or.th; 29 Th Sathon Tai) French film series at the French cultural centre.

EGV (Map pp294–5; ☎ 0 2812 9999; www.egv.com; Siam Discovery Center, 6th fl, Th Phra Ram I; Skytrain Siam) Bangkok's poshest venue for mainstream movies.

Goethe Institut (Map pp292–3; ☎ 0 2287 0942; 18/1 Soi Goethe, off Soi 1/Atakanprasit, Th Sathon Tai) German film series at the German cultural centre.

House (Map pp278–9; ☎ 0 2641 5177; www.houserama.com; 3rd fl, UMG Cinema, RCA, Th Phra Ram IX) Bangkok's first art house showing avant-garde flicks.

Lido Multiplex (Map pp294–5; ☎ 0 2251 1265; btwn Soi 2 & Soi 3, Th Phra Ram I, Siam Square; Skytrain Siam) Arty and independent movies.

Major Cineplex (Map pp294–5; ☎ 0 2515 5810; 7th fl, Central World Plaza, Th Ratchadamri; Skytrain Chitlom) All the amenities and mainstream hits.

Scala Multiplex (Map pp294–5; ☎ 0 2251 2861; Soi 1, Th Phra Ram I, Siam Square; Skytrain National Stadium) Last of the old-style theatres in the heart of Siam Square.

SF Cinema City (Map pp294–5; ☎ 0 2268 8888; www.sfcinemacity.com; 7th fl, Mahboonkrong Centre, Th Phra Ram I; Skytrain National Stadium) Multiplex showing Hollywood blockbusters.

SFV (Map pp296–7; ☎ 0 2260 9333; 6th fl, Emporium Shopping Centre, Th Sukhumvit, cnr Soi 24) Creature comforts and varied screenings.

Sport, Health & Fitness

Sport, Health & Fitness

Although the climate is not conducive to exercise, Bangkokians like to work up a sweat doing more than just climbing the stairs to the Skytrain station. All the popular Thai sports are represented in the capital city: from the top-tier *muay thai* (Thai boxing) matches to a pick-up game of *tàkrâw* (Siamese football) at a construction site. The various foreign expat communities get together for friendly games of whatever back-home sport goes well with drinking. Gyms, yoga studios and parks are common spots to strengthen muscles being boiled away by tropical temperatures. Thais also consider traditional massage an integral component of health, so you can always pay someone else to do all the work. In tandem with the massage tradition are new spa facilities that will help you compete with all the pretty people in the City of Angels.

WATCHING SPORT

Thailand's indigenous sports are acrobatic tests of strength. In the case of *muay thai,* the sport is followed with as much devotion as football is in Western countries. During an important match, every TV in the city is tuned in, and resulting cheers and jeers echo from inside homes and shops. International games are played at the superstadiums in Bangkok; watch the *Bangkok Post* for upcoming matches.

MUAY THAI (THAI BOXING)

The best of the best fight at Bangkok's two boxing stadiums: Lumphini Stadium (Sanam Muay Lumphini; Map pp292–3; Th Phra Ram IV; subway Lumphini) and Ratchadamnoen Stadium (Sanam Muay Ratchadamnoen; Map pp286–7; Th Ratchadamnoen Nok; air-con bus 503, ordinary bus 70). Lumphini Stadium will move, when construction is completed, to a new location on Th Nang Linchee in Sathon (Map pp278–9; ☎ 0 2282 3141).

Tickets at both stadiums have soared to 1000B for 3rd class, 1500B for 2nd class and 2000B for ringside seats. Be aware that these admission prices are more than double what Thais pay, and the inflated price offers no special service or seating. At Ratchadamnoen Stadium, foreigners are sometimes corralled into an area with an obstructed view. Feeling warm and fuzzy already? If you are mentally prepared for the jabs from the promoters, then you'll enjoy the real fight.

Muay thai *(Thai boxing)* at Lumphini Stadium

There is much debate about which seats are better. Ringside gives you the central action, but gambling is prohibited and the crowd is comprised of subdued VIPs. The 2nd-class seats are filled with backpackers and numbers-runners who take bets from the die-hard fans in 3rd class. Akin to being in a stock-exchange pit, hand signals communicating bets and odds fly between the 2nd- and 3rd-class areas. The 3rd-class area is the rowdiest section. Fenced off from the rest of the stadium, most of the die-hard fans follow the match (or their bets) too closely to sit down. If you need more entertainment than two men punching each other, then the crowd in the 3rd-class seats will keep you amused.

Fights are held throughout the week. Ratchadamnoen hosts matches on Monday at 5pm and 9pm, Wednesday and Thursday at 6pm, and Sunday at 5pm. Lumphini hosts matches every Tuesday and Friday at 6pm, and on Saturday at 5pm and 8.30pm. Aficionados say the best-matched bouts occur on Tuesday nights at Lumphini and Thursday nights at Ratchadamnoen. There are eight to 10 fights of five rounds each.

There are English-speaking 'staff' outside the stadium who will practically tackle you upon arrival. Although there have been a few reports of scamming, most of these assistants help steer visitors to the foreigners' ticket windows and hand out a fight roster; they can also be helpful in telling you which fights are the best match-ups. (Some say that welterweights, between 61.2kg and 66.7kg, are the best.) To keep everyone honest, however, remember to purchase tickets from the ticket window, not from a person outside the stadium.

The Isan restaurants on the north side of Ratchadamnoen stadium are well known for their *kài yâang* (grilled chicken) and other northeastern dishes, something of a fight-night tradition.

TÀKRÂW

Once known as 'Siamese football', traditional *tàkrâw* players stand in a circle and keep the ball airborne by kicking it soccer-style. Points are scored for style, difficulty and variety of kicking manoeuvres. A common variation on *tàkrâw*, which is used in school and college or international competitions, is played with a volleyball net, using the same rules as in volleyball except

that only the feet and head are permitted to touch the ball.

Pick-up games are played throughout the city: on a cleared construction site, on Th Khao San or in the parks. The most reliable spots to see the rattan ball in action are at **Lumphini Park** (Map pp292–3; Th Phra Ram IV; Skytrain Ratchadamri, Saladaeng, subway Silom, Lumphini) and **National Stadium** (Map pp280–1; ☎ 0 2214 0120; Th Phra Ram I; Skytrain National Stadium) where more seasoned players do aerial pirouettes, spiking the ball over the net with their feet. One option has players kicking the ball into a hoop 4.5m above the ground (basketball without hands or a backboard!).

HEALTH & FITNESS

Something about the humidity melts away muscle tone. But you'll find many ways to stay trim and toned at Bangkok's array of sports facilities. The weather can be a barrier to outdoor fitness, but early mornings and late evenings provide enough relief from the direct sun for the exercise nuts. Also remember that the Land of Smiles believes whole-heartedly in pampering with a host of traditional and new-fangled spa treatments.

SPAS & MASSAGE

According to traditional Thai healing, the use of herbs and massage should be part of a regular health and beauty regimen, not just an excuse for pampering. The variations on this theme range from storefront traditional Thai massage to an indulgent spa 'experience' with service and style. Recently, spas have begun to focus more on the medical than the sensory.

Although it sounds relaxing, traditional Thai massage *(nûat phaen boraan)*, will seem more closely related to *muay thai* than to shiatsu. It is based on yogic techniques for general health involving pulling, stretching, bending and manipulating pressure points. If done well, a traditional massage will leave you sore but revitalised.

Full-body massages will usually include camphor-scented balms or herbal compresses, while 'oil massage' is usually code for 'sexy massage'. Sightseeing aches and pains can usually be treated effectively with a quick foot massage.

Finding a Thai traditional massage parlour (as opposed to the sexy massage parlours) is easy; they are everywhere and they all look the same, with front-window massage beds and colourful reflexology charts on the walls. A simple errand in a massage neighbourhood means you must run the gauntlet chorus of 'Hello, massage?' The demand for massage is so high that quality can be inconsistent – the only thing 'ancient' about some places is the age of the masseur. Even worse is the massage social hour, where soap operas or parlour gossip get more attention than you do. The going rate for a traditional massage is around 300B per hour and foot massages start at 200B.

BANYAN TREE SPA Map pp292-3
☎ 0 2679 10052; www.banyantree.com; Banyan Tree Hotel & Spa, 21/100 Th Sathon Tai; from US$140; subway Lumphini

This hotel spa delivers modern elegance and world-class pampering. The womb-like spa rooms look out over a silent and peaceful vision of Bangkok from on high. Thai, Swedish and Balinese massages, body scrubs using aromatic oils and herbs with medicinal properties, and beauty treatments comprise the spa's offerings. Many visitors, especially newlyweds, purchase 'spa vacation' packages that include accommodation and spa treatments.

BUATHIP THAI MASSAGE Map pp296-7
☎ 0 2251 2627; 4/13 Soi 5, Th Sukhumvit; 1hr massage 270B, foot 250B; ☽ 10am-midnight; Skytrain Nana

On a small sub-soi behind the Amari Boulevard Hotel, this tidy shopfront has a professional masseur whose focused concentration could melt metal.

MARBLE HOUSE Map pp296-7
☎ 0 2651 0905; 3rd fl, Ruamchit Plaza, 199 Th Sukhumvit; 2hr traditional massage 400B, oil 1000B, foot 300B; ☽ 10am-midnight; Skytrain Sala Daeng

Marble House is on the level, even though the surrounding area is knee-deep in 'friendly' massages. Tucked away on the sleepy 3rd floor of Ruamchit Plaza, the Th Sukhumvit location sees fewer happenstance visitors and has a more affable staff than the branch on Soi Surawong (Map pp290–1; ☎ 0 2235 3519, 37/18-19 Soi Surawong, Th Surawong).

NAKORNTHON THAI MEDICAL SPA Map pp278-9
☎ 0 2416 5454; www.nakornthonhospital.com; 12th fl, Nakornthon Hospital, Th Phra Ram II; access by taxi

The wellness centre of this Bangkok hospital has opened up a traditional Thai medicine wing, combing spa therapy with ancient Thai techniques. The primary practice is the use of tamrub thong, which uses the application of gold leaf and herbs to rejuvenate skin and restore collagen. Other treatments focus on nutritional evaluations and aromatherapy to ensure the balance of the body's essential elements: earth, wind, water and fire.

ORIENTAL SPA Map pp290-1
☎ 0 2439 7613; www.mandarinoriental.com; Oriental Hotel, 48 Soi 38, Th Charoen Krung; from US$200; Skytrain Saphan Taksin, ferry Tha Oriental

Set in a traditional teak home, the spa at the Oriental Hotel offers a full range of massage and health treatments, including a 40-minute 'jet-lag massage' designed to reset your body clock. Privacy is the spa's main strength, with individuals' and couples' suites (shower, massage tables and steam room). The Oriental counts international celebrities among its clients. The spa complex is located across the river on the banks of Thonburi, but can be reached via ferry from the hotel pier.

PIROM SPA: THE GARDEN HOME SPA Map pp296-7
☎ 0 2714 9620; www.piromspa.com; 78 Soi 1, Th Sukhumvit; à la carte services from 800B, packages from 2800B; Skytrain Ploenchit or Nana

Using techniques from northern Thailand, where the women are renowned for their good looks, this spa offers an array of aromatherapy options, hydrotherapy baths, body wraps, facials and Thai massage. Pirom is set in a '60s-style house near Bumrungrad International hospital.

RASAYANA RETREAT Map pp296-7
☎ 0 2662 4803; www.rasayanaretreat.com; 41/1 Soi Prommit off Soi 39, Th Sukhumvit; Skytrain Phrom Phong

The latest generation of spa facilities, Rasayana combines basic beauty and massage treatments with holistic healing techniques, such as detoxification, colonic irrigation and hypnotherapy.

RUEN-NUAD MASSAGE & YOGA Map pp290-1

☎ 0 2632 2663; 42 Th Convent, Th Silom; ⏰ 10am-10pm; 1hr traditional massage 350B, foot 350B; Skytrain Sala Daeng, subway Silom

Just the right mix of old and new, Ruen-Nuad is set in a charming converted wooden house with partitioned massage stations, creating a mood of pampering and privacy typical of spa facilities, but at parlour prices.

SKILLS DEVELOPMENT CENTER FOR THE BLIND

☎ 0 2583 7327; 78/2 Soi 1, Th Tiwanon, Pak Kret; 1½-hr massage 100-150B; ferry Tha Pak Kret

This outreach centre north of central Bangkok trains the blind in the ancient techniques of Thai traditional massage, developing what many people consider to be expert masseurs. Although the massage might be memorable, getting out here is the primary adventure. Take the Chao Phraya Express (p241) north to Tha Nonthaburi, where you will connect to a Laem Thong boat (5.45am to 5.45pm) to Tha Pak Kret. From the pier, hire a motorcycle taxi to take you to the Skills Development Center (one way 10B). You'll need a little Thai to pull this off, but Pak Kret villagers are pretty easy-going and willing to listen to foreigners massacre their language.

WAT PHO THAI TRADITIONAL MASSAGE SCHOOL Map p288

☎ 0 2221 2974; 2 Th Sanam Chai; 1hr Thai massage 270B, foot 250B; ⏰ 10am-6pm; ferry Tha Tien

The school affiliated with Wat Pho is the primary training centre for Thai traditional massage. The *sălaa* (pavilions) within the temple complex are once again open for massage. If you'd like an air-conditioned room, go to the massage training centre closer to the river.

SPORTS CLUBS & GYMS

Bangkok is a gym town, reflecting international trends in fitness. Most large hotels have gyms and swimming pools, as do many large condos and residential complexes. Most residents join facilities either near their work or home to avoid traffic complications. The city's parks are also popular morning and evening work-out zones, with joggers (or, to be more accurate, shufflers), aerobics classes, football players and cyclists. Various groups of expats get together for pick-up games of their beloved sports.

BRITISH CLUB Map pp290-1

☎ 0 2234 0247; www.britishclubbangkok.org; 189 Th Surawong; Skytrain Sala Daeng, subway Silom, Samyan

Open to citizens of Australia, Canada, New Zealand and the UK, or to others by invitation, the British Club's sports facilities include a pool, a golf driving range and squash and tennis courts. The British Club also sponsors indoor football games.

CALIFORNIA WOW Map pp290-1

☎ 0 2631 1122; www.californiawowx.com; cnr Th Convent & Th Silom; Skytrain Sala Daeng, subway Silom

Part of the 24-Hour Fitness network, this spot is more like a disco than a gym. Heart-pounding techno escaping onto the street suggests more serious sweating than what you find inside. Exercise equipment looks out onto Th Convent, providing ogling opportunities from both sides of the fishbowl.

CLARK HATCH PHYSICAL FITNESS CENTRE Map pp294-5

☎ 0 2718 2000; www.clarkhatchthailand.com; 4th fl, Amari Watergate Hotel, 1880 Th Phetburi; ordinary bus 77, khlong taxi Tha Pratunam

This top-class facility offers weight machines, aerobics classes, a pool, sauna and massage. There are nine other locations throughout town.

NATIONAL STADIUM Map pp280-1

☎ 0 2214 0120; Th Phra Ram I; Skytrain National Stadium

This stadium hosts the national soccer team practices (watch for the crowds assembled around the Skytrain station) as well as providing the public with access to swimming facilities, tennis courts and gyms.

RED BULL X PARK Map pp290-1

☎ 0 2670 8080; Th Sathon Tai, opposite Evergreen Laurel Hotel; ⏰ 10am-9pm; Skytrain Chong Nonsi, subway Lumphini, Silom

A skate and BMX park for those daredevils into extreme sports.

Sport, Health & Fitness

HEALTH & FITNESS

GOLF

Success in business goes hand-in-hand with success in golf, so finding well-tended courses in Bangkok is a snap. Most courses are outside the central city and require a car. Green fees range from 450B to 3000B, and it is customary to tip caddies 200B. The website **Thai Golfer** (www.thaigolfer.com) rates Bangkok's courses. Some courses are closed on Monday, while others are open at night for cooler tee times.

A few noteworthy courses include **Bangkok Golf Club** (☎ 0 2501 2828; 99 Th Tiwanon, Pathum Thani), **Panya Hills Golf Course** (☎ 0 3834 9001; 159/1 Th Sansuk-Bangpra, Chonburi), **President Country Club** (☎ 0 2988 7555; www.president.co.th; 42 Mu 8, Th Suwintawong, Lumtoyting Nongjok) and **Subhaphruek** (☎ 0 2317 0801; Km 26, Th Bang Na-Trat; ☒ closed Monday).

JOGGING & CYCLING

Lumphini Park and Sanam Luang both host early-morning and late-evening runners. Bangkok has several Hash groups, meeting for weekly runs through the outskirts of Bangkok. These include Bangkok Hash House Harriers (men only), Bangkok Monday Hash (mixed) and the Harriettes (mixed). The Bangkok Hash House Mountain Bikers meet monthly on Sunday afternoon for a 20km to 30km mountain-bike ride on the outskirts of Bangkok or overnight trips. For contact numbers, check the Sports section of the *Bangkok Post* every Saturday or visit www.bangkokhhh.com.

Jogging through Lumphini Park (p109)

MEDICAL HOLIDAY

If health-care costs back home are exceeding your rent payments, consider hopping on a plane to Thailand. Bangkok's hospitals are on par with Western facilities and cover all the bases – dentistry, nips and tucks, corrective surgeries or sex changes – for less than the price at home.

At the top of the list, **Bumrungrad International** (Map pp296–7; ☎ 02 667 1000; www.bumrungrad .com; 33 Soi 3, Th Sukhumvit; Skytrain Nana) is a US-managed and -accredited hospital with five-star service catering mainly to foreigners. **BNH Hospital** (Map pp292–3; ☎ 02 632 0550; www.bnhhospital.com; Th Convent) is also well regarded for general medicine.

Dental Hospital (☎ 02 2260 5000; 88/88 Soi 49, Th Sukhumvit) is a private dental clinic with fluent English-speaking dentists. **Bangkok Dental Spa** (Map pp296–7; ☎ 02 651-0807; 27 Methawattana Building, 2nd floor, Soi 19, Th Sukhumvit) combines oral hygiene with spa services (foot and body massage).

Medical spas combining alternative therapies, massage and detoxification have taken 'the cure' one step further. See p163 for recommendations.

TENNIS

Some gyms have tennis courts, and the following options are also open to the public: **Central Sports Club Tennis Court** (Map pp292–3; ☎ 0 2213 1909; 13 Soi 1, Th Sathon Tai) and **Santisuk Tennis Courts** (Map pp296–7; ☎ 0 2391 1830; btwn Soi 36 & Soi 38, Th Sukhumvit).

YOGA & PILATES

It is hard to believe that Thais need to be any more relaxed, but the urban routine has spawned a host of yoga studios. Of the many to choose from, three centrally located studios are the two branches of **Absolute Yoga** (www.absoluteyogabangkok .com), in **Lang Suan** (Map pp294–5, ☎ 0 2652 1333, 14th floor, Unico Building, Soi Lang Suan) and **Thong Lor** (Map pp296–7, ☎ 0 2381 0697, 21st floor, 55th Plaza, Soi Thong Lor 2, Th Sukhumvit) and **Yoga Elements Studio** (Map pp294–5; ☎ 0 2655 5671; www.yogaelements.com; 29 Vanissa Bldg, 23rd fl, Th Chitlom). Pilates is offered at **Pilates Studio** (Map pp294–5; ☎ 0 2650 7797; www.pilatesbangkok.com; 888/58-9 Mahatun Plaza, Th Ploenchit).

Shopping ■

Shopping

Shopping in Bangkok revolves around the unlikely duo of glamour malls and pedestrian markets, which work in tandem to separate customers from their baht. The entertainment value of shopping is most obvious at the midday markets selling office workers a little bit of lunch and a lot of inedibles.

Throughout the city, the offerings range from necessities and indulgences to oddities and junk. Items on offer, in order of consumption, include clothes, bearing real and fake pedigree, as well as other designer knock-offs such as bags and accessories, then handicrafts, textiles, art and antiques.

Bargaining is part of the culture at markets and small family-run shops where prices aren't posted. When engaging in this ancient sport, remember it requires finesse rather than force. The best approach is one of camaraderie. If you're interested in buying, ask the vendor the price and then ask if they could lower it. You can then counter with a lower

SHOPPING TREASURE MAP

The city's intense urban tangle sometimes makes orientation a challenge in finding intimate shops and markets. Like having your own personal guide, *Nancy Chandler's Map of Bangkok* tracks all sorts of small, out-of-the-way shopping venues and markets, as well as dissecting the innards of the Chatuchak Weekend Market (p188). The colourful map is sold in bookshops throughout the city.

sum that will tug the return offer closer to a comfortable range. Figures are sometimes volleyed back and forth at this point, but stay calm and cool. It is poor form to haggle over a difference of 10B. Prices aren't negotiable when a price is posted.

Thais are generally so friendly and laid-back that some visitors are lulled into a false sense of security, forgetting that Bangkok is a big city with untrustworthy characters. While your personal safety is rarely at risk in Thailand, you may be unwittingly charmed out of an unfair amount of cash. See p254 for more information about scams.

Shopping Areas

The area around Siam Square has the greatest concentration of shopping malls for designer and department-store goods. Street markets for souvenirs and pirated goods can be found on Th Khao San, Th Sukhumvit and Th Silom.

Opening Hours

Most family-run shops are open from 10am to 7pm daily. Street markets are either daytime (from 9am to 5pm) or night-time (8pm to midnight). Note that streetside vendors are barred by city ordinance to clutter the sidewalks on Mondays, but do so brilliantly every other day. Shopping centres are usually open from 10am to 10pm.

BEST SHOPPING OPTIONS IN BANGKOK

- Chatuchak Weekend Market (p188) Commando-style shopping for wow-factor junkies and stylish scores.
- Mahboonkrong (MBK; p181) Just all around air-con fun with good buys in teenage gear, mobile phones and wacky odds and ends.
- River City Complex (p185) The best one-stop shop for antiques.
- Sampeng Lane (p179) Only the goods are modern in this ancient market.
- Pantip Plaza (p182) Bangkok's tech nation for legit and not-so-legit computer software.
- Th Khao San Market (p170) The best spot to pick up a backpacker-hippie uniform.

Antique shop at River City Complex (p185)

KO RATANAKOSIN

Because of the district's holy status, the attendant shops specialise in the ancient arts of health, safety and fortune. Locals come to inspect sacred amulets and pick up Thai traditional medicines.

AMULET MARKET Map p288 Outdoor Market

Several small soi off Th Maharat, across from Wat Mahathat; ☙ 8am-6pm; ferry Tha Chang, air-con bus 503, 508 & 512, ordinary bus 47 & 53

Catholics with their parade of saints and protective medals will recognise a great kinship with this streetside amulet market. Ranging in size, *phrá khrêuang* (amulets) come in various classes, from rare objects or relics (such as antlers or tusks, or dentures from famous abbots) to images of Buddha or famous monks embossed in bronze, wood or clay. Itinerant dealers spread their wares on blankets along the broken pavement across from the temple, and more permanent shops proliferate into the sunless *soi* heading towards the river. Taxi drivers, monks and average folks squat alongside the displays inspecting novel pieces in the manner of practiced jewellers. Mixed in with certain of the amulets are pulverised substances: dirt from a special temple, hair from a monk or powerful herbs.

When the serious collectors aren't perusing the market, they are flipping through the various amulet newspapers that discuss noteworthy specimens. While money changes hands between vendor and customer, both use the euphemism of 'renting' to get around the prohibition of selling Buddhas.

TRADITIONAL MEDICINE

SHOPS Map p288 Health Supplies

Lining Th Maharat, from Thammasat University to Wat Pho; ☙ 9am-8pm; ferry Tha Chang, air-con bus 503, 508 & 512, ordinary bus 47 & 53

Bangkok's commercial medicine cabinet occupies the riverside thoroughfare of Th Maharat. Packaged up in plastic pill bottles bearing an unsmiling photo of a trusted authority, commercial formulas combine various herbal ingredients – such as galangal, lemon grass, star anise and other flavourings used in various Thai dishes – to target a specific disease or to promote general wellness. Lemon grass is perhaps the most versatile of the common herbal medicines and is employed to treat aches and pains, colds and as an antibacterial agent. It is also used in combination with other aromatics to make massage lotions for kneading sore muscles and dispersing stagnant energy along the body's meridians.

Shops carrying massage supplies cater to practitioners and to students at the nearby Wat Pho massage training school. Keep an eye out for the dumpling-shaped herbal compresses heated and pressed onto the body during sessions of Thai herbal massage.

BANGLAMPHU, THEWET & DUSIT

Banglamphu has wash-and-wear fisherman pants, hip purses and T-shirts, faux dreadlocks and loads of souvenir-quality Thai handicrafts. This is also the place to find secondhand books, pirated CDs and luggage for the trip home. Prices are low, sizes are big and colours suit the Western eye. Th Khao San has also expanded into the silver business with souvenir-grade baubles sold in bulk to DIY-importers.

BANGLAMPHU MARKET

Map pp286-7 Outdoor Market

Th Chakraphong; ☙ 9am-6pm Tue-Sun; ferry Tha Phra Athit, air-con bus 511 & 512, ordinary bus 2 & 82

Spread out over several blocks, the Banglamphu market attracts a no-nonsense crew of street vendors selling snacks, handbags, bras, pyjamas, night-blooming jasmine flower buds *(phuang malai)* and other essentials for the Thai housewife. You many never come here on purpose, but passing through invariably leads to a purchase or at least a warm fuzzy feeling towards daily Thai life.

BO-BE MARKET Map pp280-1 Outdoor Market

Th Krung Kasem; ☙ 9am-6pm; khlong taxi Tha Bo-Be, air-con bus 511

This isn't the place to come for odds and ends, but for big garbage bags full of wholesale clothing. Among the A-to-Z supply is army and camping gear, polyester catastrophes, old-lady bras and high-fashion finds in itty-bitty sizes.

CHAROEN CHAIKARNCHANG SHOP

Map pp286-7   Religious

☎ 0 2222 4800; 87 Soi Nava, Th Bamrung Muang; air-con bus 508

This is easily the largest and most impressive religious shop in the area. The workshop at the back produces gigantic bronze Buddha images for wats all over Thailand. You are unlikely to be in the market for a big Buddha, but looking is fun and who knows when you'll need to do a great deal of merit-making.

NITTAYA CURRY SHOP

Map pp286-7   Food

☎ 02 282 8212; 136-40 Th Chakraphong; ☷ 10am-7pm; ferry Tha Phra Athit, air-con bus 511 & 512, ordinary bus 2 & 82

Nittaya is famous throughout Thailand for her high-quality curry pastes. In fact, most curry batches rely in some way on her base preparations, which are sealed tightly for easy transport. Pick up a couple of canisters for your own pantry or peruse the snack and gift sections where visitors from the provinces load up on certain specialities for friends back home. The store is also an interesting immersion into the neighbourhood's daily shopping habits: motorcycle taxi drivers stop in with a list to fill for the wife and grandmas teeter in to pick up a few odds and ends.

PASSPORT Map pp286-7   Books

☎ 0 2629 0694; 142 Th Phra Athit; ☷ noon-6pm; ferry Tha Phra Athit, ordinary bus 15, 30 & 53

This quirky little shop is a good friend to have. The affable owners are the new breed of Banglamphu creatives: well-read, slightly nonconformist and devoted to the artistic Thai temperament.

The store specialises in yet another trend in Bangkok: graphic-art books from small independent publishers. Typhoon Books is one of the scene's leaders, thanks in part to the publishing house's famous editor, Thai novelist Prabda Yoon, and the overseas success of Wisut Ponnimut's graphic novel, *everybodyeverything*. The titles are mainly Thai but book voyeurs aren't confined by language. Browse the titles, strike up a conversation or just steep in the intellectual atmosphere in the 2nd-floor café.

RIM KHOB FAH BOOKSTORE

Map pp286-7   Books

☎ 0 2622 3510; Democracy Monument, 78/1 Th Ratchadamnoen Klang; ☷ 10am-6pm; air-con bus 511 & 512, ordinary bus 2 & 82

Without having to commit loads of suitcase space, you can sample an array of slim scholarly publications from the Fine Arts Department on Thai art and architecture. The academic texts in English have also been joined by your standard-issue travel books and region-specific titles.

SUKSIT SIAM

Map pp286-7   Books

☎ 0 2225 9531; 113-5 Th Fuang Nakhon; ☷ 10am-6pm; air-con bus 508, khlong taxi Tha Phan Fah

Opposite Wat Ratchabophit, this bookshop specialises in books on Thai progressive politics, especially those representing the views of Sulak Sivaraksa, a leading Thai social critic and Nobel Peace Prize nominee. *Khun* Sulak advocates for socially engaged Buddhism as a form of *dhamma* practice. Many Thai leaders in grass-roots, nongovernmental organisations (NGOs) were inspired by *Khun* Sulak's opinions and received educational training through the affiliated Santi Pracha Dhamma Institute (Peace, People, and Justice Institute). The shop also has mainstream titles on Thailand and Asia in both English and Thai.

TAEKEE TAAKON Map pp286-7   Handicrafts

118 Th Phra Athit; ☷ 10am-5pm Mon-Sat; ferry Tha Phra Athit, ordinary bus 15, 30 & 53

This atmospheric shop has gorgeous textiles from Thailand's main silk-producing areas, especially northern Thailand, as well as high-quality souvenirs and interesting postcards not widely available elsewhere.

TH KHAO SAN MARKET

Map pp286-7   Outdoor Market

Th Khao San; ☷ 10am-2am Tue-Sun; ferry Tha Phra Athit, air-con bus 511 & 512, ordinary bus 2 & 82

The main guesthouse strip in Banglamphu is a day-and-night shopping bazaar, selling everything but the baby and the bath water. Cheap T-shirts, hip purses, wooden elephants, fuzzy puppets, bootleg CDs, hemp clothing, fake student-ID cards, knock-off

(Continued on page 179)

1 Long-tail boat in a khlong (canal; p72) 2 The Lingam Shrine (p98) of Nai Lert Park 3 Statues and furniture inside Jim Thompson's House (p97) 4 Lighting candles at Erawan Shrine (p98)

1 Strip clubs (p157) along Soi Patpong 1 2 A handler and his king cobra at the Queen Saovabha Memorial Institute (Snake Farm; p109) 3 Afternoon tea in the Author's Lounge at the Oriental Hotel (p133) 4 Locals and visitors relaxing in Lumphini Park (p109)

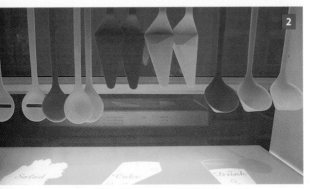

1 *Bed Supperclub (p155)*
2 *Window display of home décor store Propaganda, in the Emporium (p187)* **3** *BTS Skytrain (p242) leaving Nana station*

1 Food stall at Chatuchak Weekend Market (p188) **2** Victory Monument (p114) **3** Clothing and embroidered bags for sale at the Patpong Night Market (p185) **4** Terracotta pottery by the Mon craftspeople of Ko Kret (p113)

1 Monks collecting alms at a merit-making ceremony as part of the Songkran Festival (lunar new year; p12) **2** Lak Meuang (p75)
3 Brass band in Sanam Luang during the Songkran Festival (p12)
4 Royal portraits for sale

1 *Túk-túks in procession begin the Songkran Festival (p12)* **2** *Muay thai (Thai boxing; p19)* **3** *Flying kites in Sanam Luang (p76)* **4** *CD warehouse in the Siam Discovery Center (p183)*

1 Dancers at Erawan Shrine (p98)
2 Bar staff at work, Sirocco (p138)
3 Statue at Silpakorn University
(p77) 4 Performers at the Joe Louis
Puppet Theatre (p158), Suan Lum
Night Bazaar

1 *Royal summer palace, Bang Pa-In (p218)* **2** *Fire twirlers, Rayong, Ko Samet (p223)* **3** *Bangkok skyscrapers*

designer wear, souvenirs, corn on the cob, orange juice. You name it, they've got it.

Do a test run on CD purchases to make sure you didn't buy a dud copy. Most vendors will exchange skipping CDs, but ask beforehand.

THAI NAKORN   Map pp282-3   Handicrafts

☎ 0 2281 7867; 79 Th Prachathipathai; ☻ Mon-Sat; air-con bus 511 & 512

This shop has been in business for 70 years and often fills commissions from the royal family for nielloware and silver ornaments. Silver-moulded cases and clutches, ceremonial bowls and tea sets are among the offerings. The shop assistants might be a little nervous to use English, so you can browse in peace without being followed.

THEWET FLOWER MARKET

Map pp282-3   Plants & Flowers

Th Krung Kasem, off Th Samsen; ☻ 9am-6pm; ferry Tha Thewet

If you have any outdoor space to call your own, you should join in the city-wide fascination with container gardening. This quiet daytime market sells all the basics, from ferociously trimmed bougainvilleas to coconut-shell pots of orchids. Now all you have to do is add water.

CHINATOWN

The Phahurat and Chinatown districts have interconnected markets selling tonnes of fabrics, clothes and household wares, as well as wholesale shops for every imaginable bulk item. There are also a handful of places selling gems and jewellery. See p121 for a suggested walking route through one small sliver of this district.

JOHNNY'S GEMS   Map pp284-5   Gemstones

☎ 0 2224 4065; 199 Th Fuang Nakhon, cnr Th Charoen Krung; ☻ 9.30am-6pm Mon-Sat; air-con bus 508, ordinary bus 56

A long-time favourite of Bangkok expats, Johnny's Gems is a reliable name in an unreliable business. The namesake founder has since passed away, but his son carries on the spick-and-span reputation, primarily in rubies and emeralds in both fun and serious designs.

NAKHON KASEM   Map pp284-5   Outdoor Market

Th Yaowarat & Th Chakrawat; ☻ 8am-8pm; ferry Tha Saphan Phut

Cooking equipment, spare electronic parts, and other bits you didn't know could be resold are available at this open-air market. During looser times, this was once known as the Thieves' Market, selling the fruits of the five-finger discount.

PAK KHLONG MARKET

Map pp284-5   Flowers

Th Chakkaphet & Th Atsadang; ☻ 24hr; ferry Tha Saphan Phut

The bright displays of baby roses, delicate orchids and button carnations are endless. Pak Khlong is also a big vegetable market. Go late at night when the post-drinking crowd arrives to squander their undrinkable baht. There are plans to redevelop this market into a tourist attraction, but thankfully the municipal government hasn't ruined it yet.

TALAT PHAHURAT

Map pp284-5   Outdoor Market

Th Phahurat & Th Triphet, across from Old Siam Plaza; ferry Tha Saphan Phut

If it sparkles, then this market has it. Talat Phahurat purveys boisterous Bollywood-coloured textiles, traditional Thai dance costumes, tiaras, sequins, wigs and other accessories to make you look like a cross-dresser or a *măw lam* (traditional Isan music) performer, or both. Amid the colour spectacle are also good deals on machine-made Thai textiles and children's clothes.

SAMPENG LANE   Map pp284-5   Outdoor Market

Soi Wanit 1, Th Ratchawong; ☻ 8am-8pm; ferry Tha Ratchawong

Sampeng Lane is a narrow artery running parallel to Th Yaowarat and bisecting the

Lotus flowers for sale at Pak Khlong Market

HOT ON THE TRAIL

Walk into a store, any store, in Bangkok and you'll be followed by a sales assistant from rack to rack. They smile, you smile. 'Would you like to look, madame?' They open up the display case remark how lovely and then follow you to the next shiny object. This is the definition of service in a Thai store, not a countermeasure against shoplifting. A sales assistant who doesn't stay glued to a customer's elbow isn't doing a good job. Even in the Western-style department stores you may be overwhelmed with such attention. You can kindly decline help, which will gain you a few feet of breathing room.

commercial areas of Chinatown and Phahurat. The Chinatown portion of Sampeng is lined with wholesale shops of hair accessories, pens, stickers, household wares and beeping flashing knick-knacks. As the *soi* enters Phahurat, the shops morph into a fabric centre and many stores here are operated by Sikh merchants. In the vicinity of Th Chakrawat, gem and jewellery shops abound. Weekends are horridly crowded, and it takes a gymnast's flexibility to squeeze past the pushcarts, motorcycles and other roadblocks.

SAPHAN PHUT NIGHT BAZAAR

Map pp284-5   Outdoor Market

Th Saphan Phut; 🕐 **8pm-midnight Thu-Tue; ferry Tha Saphan Phut**
On either side of the Memorial Bridge (Saphan Phra Phuttha Yot Fa), this night market has loads of cheap clothes, late-night snacking and a lot of people-watching. As Chatuchak Weekend Market becomes more design oriented, Saphan Phut has filled the closets of the fashion-forward, baht-challenged teenagers.

SIAM SQUARE, PRATUNAM & PLOENCHIT

Bangkok is hoping to position itself as a regional shopping hub, elbowing into the circle with Singapore and Hong Kong. So far the luxury malls are a major draw for tourists primarily from Asia and the Middle East, who find the price tags less colossal

than at home. Though the bargains aren't as clear for Westerners, Thailand's emerging fashion designers present a much-needed alternative to ethno-chic. The futuristic shopping malls cluster near the intersection of Th Phra Ram I and Th Phayathai and further west at Th Ratchadamri. Crossing Khlong Saen Saeb leads to Pratunam (Water Gate) district, where a daily open-air bazaar fuels home-grown import/exports. From teeny-boppers to high-rollers, everyone has a favourite centre for window shopping and impulsive splurges.

Keep an eye out for end-of-season and pay-day sales as well as the city-wide sales spree in June.

CENTRAL DEPARTMENT STORE

Map pp294-5   Shopping Centre

☎ 0 2655 7777; Th Ploenchit; 🕐 10am-9pm; **Skytrain Chitlom**
Central is a modern Western-style department store with locations throughout the city. This flagship store is the largest and snazziest of all the branches.

The ground floor carries all the big names in cosmetics with a gang of eager perfume spritzers and sales agents. At the time of writing, Central was planning an expansion of the cosmetics department to include a new natural spa centre, and a 'denim bar' (carrying limited-edition designer jeans from the likes of Evisu, Take Two and Gabba).

Foreigner-sized clothing is one of the shop's strengths. The helpful sales staff will bluntly steer you to slimming colours and relatively huge sizes to fit your sturdy frame.

CENTRAL WORLD PLAZA

Map pp294-5   Shopping Centre

Cnr Th Phra Ram I & Th Ratchadamri; 🕐 **10am-10pm; Skytrain Chitlom**
A major renovation will soon provide much-needed life support to this ailing shopping centre. Most of the warm bodies congregate in the newly expanded Isetan and Zen department stores. The former ice-skating rink has been transformed into a learning library, known as **Thai Knowledge Park** (TK Park; ☎ 0 2250 7620; www.tkpark.or.th; 6th fl), part of a government initiative to cultivate reading and learning habits in children. The library also has Internet access, science demos and creativity classes (mainly in Thai).

Taxi drivers still know the plaza by its former name: World Trade Centre.

ERAWAN BANGKOK

Map pp294-5   Shopping Centre
Th Ploenchit; ⊙ 10.30am-8.30pm; Skytrain Chitlom
Just as the honeymoon period with Gaysorn (below) is coming to end, Bangkok's high society has found a new stomping ground: the shopping wing of the Erawan Hotel. Luxury matrons occupy the 1st floor, while street-smarts chill on the 2nd floor. The top floor is a dedicated wellness centre, should conspicuous consumption prove hazardous to your health. The ladies who lunch can often be found in the ground-floor Urban Kitchen or the 2nd-floor Erawan Tea Room.

GAYSORN PLAZA

Map pp294-5   Shopping Centre
Cnr Th Ploenchit & Th Ratchadamri; ⊙ 10am-10pm; Skytrain Chitlom
A *haute couture* catwalk, Gaysorn has spiralling staircases, all-white halls and bundles of top-name designers. The 2nd floor is a crash course in the local fashion industry. Start with the originals, Fly Now and Senada Theory, and then visit the young fabric wizards; you'll find boudoir-inspired flounces at Stretis and a little bit of everything at Fashion Society, an umbrella store for smaller labels.

Stores on the 3rd floor offer the same level of sophistication for your home. Triphum has mother-of-pearl inlaid cabinets, lacquerware scripture chests and other high-quality Asian reproductions. Just a few doors away, Ayodhya sells more modern home décor in Thai-inspired colours. Ayodhya designer ML Pawinee Santisiri is well known for her water hyacinth products. NV Aranyik preserves traditional Thai craftsmanship. Thann Native sells Thai spa products and hip textiles designed by Beyond Living, a local design house that outfits boutique hotels with hand-woven rugs and colourful cushions.

Gaysorn spares shoppers from sullying themselves amid the street-level chaos with a covered walkway attached to the Skytrain station.

MAHBOONKRONG (MBK)

Map pp294-5   Shopping Centre
Cnr Th Phra Ram I & Th Phayathai; ⊙ 10am-10pm; Skytrain National Stadium, ordinary bus 47
This shopping mall is quickly becoming one of Bangkok's top attractions. Half of the city filters through the glass doors on weekends, stutter-stepping on the escalators, stuffing themselves with junk food or making stabs at individualism by accessorising their mundane school uniforms with high slits or torturous heels. Dozens of backpackers also make the pilgrimage from the main avenue off Th Khao San, accosting shy Thais for bus directions to MBK (pssst, take bus 47 from in front of the lottery building).

A market-stall energy, knock-off goods and proximity to Siam Square make MBK one of the most vibrant shopping centres in Bangkok. You can buy everything you need here: mobile phones, accessories, shoes, name brands, wallets, purses, T-shirts. The middle-class Tokyu department store also sells good quality kitchenware.

The ground floor is often filled with vendors selling knock-off Lacoste shirts or other casual-wear name brands. Stalls of oil painters transform family photographs into mantelpiece canvases (the same can be done of the masters as well).

On the 4th floor, the digital age becomes a produce market. A confusing maze of stalls sells all the components to send you into the land of cellular – a new phone, a new number and a SIM card. Even if you don't need to be reached, walk through to observe the chaos and the mania over phone numbers. Computer print-outs displaying all the available numbers for sale turn the phone numbers game into a commodities market. The luckier the phone number, the higher the price; upwards of

Shopping

SIAM SQUARE, PRATUNAM & PLOENCHIT

FROM NYMPH TO JUMBO

In your home town you may be considered average or even petite, but based on the Thai measuring stick you're an extra large, clearly marked on the tag as 'LL' or worse still, 'XL'. If that batters the body image, then skip the street markets where you'll bust the seams from the waist up, if you can squirm that far into the openings. Only street vendors on Th Khao San accommodate foreign women's natural endowments in the shoulders, bust and hips. If you're larger than a US size 10 or an Australian/UK size 12, you strike out altogether. Men will find that they outsize Thai clothes in length and shoulder width, as well as shoe sizes. For formal wear, many expats turn to custom orders through tailors. For ready-to-wear, Emporium, Central and Robinson department stores carry larger sizes.

DRESSED TO THE NINES

Don't be fooled by the fashion aesthetics promoted by the tourist brochures and hotel lobbies. Within Bangkok's city limits, modern, not traditional, costumes rule the street-side runways that would make Milan feel underdressed. European labels are hotly pursued by fashionistas, but local labels are turning heads both here and abroad.

Local fashion houses, like Fly Now, Senada Theory and Greyhound, are frequent attendees to London and Paris fashion weeks. Fly Now started as a ladies' boutique in 1983 and has expanded across the city with wearable art. Greyhound raced onto the scene in 1980 as a men's wear line and has since expanded to suit the fairer sex. The various lines are urban hip and amorphically Asian. The addition of the Greyhound Café (p142) in the Emporium shopping mall helped define Greyhound's lifestyle image with the global elite. Of the maturing new-wave designers, Senada Theory flirts most closely with ethnic chic, but succeeds in producing couture.

Established designers have stores in Gaysorn and the Emporium, while younger ready-to-wear designers open little boutiques in Siam Square or Chatuchak Market. Even Th Khao San is beginning to show more home-grown design. The government is keen to promote Bangkok's garment industry and the city now hosts two fashion weeks: the biannual Bangkok Fashion Week (see p18) and Elle Fashion Week in November. More ambitious plans have yet to materialise and critics point out that Thailand still lacks skilled craftspeople and high-end fabrics. But for now the raw enthusiasm makes stunning window dressing.

thousands of dollars have been paid for numbers composed entirely of nines, considered lucky in honour of the current king, Rama IX, and because the Thai word for 'nine' is a homophone for 'progress'. Double digits bring a modicum of good fortune.

MARCO TAILORS Map pp294-5   Tailor
☎ 0 2252 0689; Soi 7, Siam Square; 🕙 10am-5pm Mon-Fri; Skytrain Siam

Dealing solely in men's suits, Marco has a wide selection of banker-sensibility wools and cottons. They require at least two weeks and two fittings.

NARAYANA PHAND Map pp294-5   Souvenirs
☎ 0 2252 4670; 127 Th Ratchadamri; 🕙 10am-8pm; Skytrain Chitlom

Souvenir-quality handicrafts are given fixed prices and comfortable air-conditioning at this government-run facility. You won't find anything here that you haven't already seen at all of the tourist street markets, but it is a good stop if you're pressed for time or spooked by haggling.

PANTIP PLAZA
Map pp294-5   Computer Equipment
☎ 0 2656 5030; 604 Th Phetburi; 🕙 10am-10pm; Skytrain Phayathai

There are two likely places a fella might find bliss in Bangkok: Pantip or Nana. Ladies out there should hope their men opt for Pantip, a multistorey computer and electronics warehouse. Shiny, new hardware isn't really Pantip's speciality, but grey-market goods

are. Techno freaks will find pirated software and music, gear for hobbyists to enhance their machines, flea-market-style peripherals and other odds and ends. Up on the 6th floor is **IT City** (☎ 0 2656 5030), a reliable computer megastore that gives VAT refund forms for tourists.

PENINSULA PLAZA
Map pp294-5   Shopping Centre
Th Ratchadamri; 🕙 10am-10pm; Skytrain Chitlom

Well-to-do ladies make regular visits to Peninsula Plaza's helmet-sculpting hair salons and big-is-beautiful jewellery stores as well as silk shops specialising in matriarch styles. On the 2nd floor is a famous midday restaurant, Lunch Time, with a daily menu written in Thai on a blackboard and wholesome dishes that hired help know how to make.

PRATUNAM CENTRE
Map pp294-5   Shopping Centre
Cnr Th Phetburi & Th Ratchaprarop; 🕙 10am-8pm; khlong taxi Tha Pratunam, Skytrain Chitlom

Hoping to become the second MBK, Pratunam Centre has targeted the bargain-happy teenagers and young workers by offering cheaper Chinese imports. The basement level specialises in silver products and consumer goods. Local handicrafts and speciality items are sold on the 1st and 2nd floors. Many of these goods are part of the government-sponsored initiative, One Tambon One Product (OTOP), which promotes handicrafts from Thai villages to cultivate local economic development. There are also plans for a modelling studio and training centre for star-struck teens – ambition to be a model is the Thai equivalent of wanting to be a rapper. Chinese and IT products get a 3rd-level billing.

PRATUNAM MARKET

Map p294-5   Outdoor Market

Cnr Th Phetburi & Th Ratchaprarop; ⏲ **9am-midnight; khlong taxi Tha Pratunam, Skytrain Chitlom**

This market is so sensory that it seemingly creates another time zone and its own climate. A smaller version of Chatuchak, Pratunam Market has a plethora of practical items, such as mobile phone socks, cheap clothes, luggage, market-lady sarongs, bulk toiletries and souvenirs.

The market occupies the trok neighbourhood behind the shopfronts on the corner of Th Phetburi and Th Ratchaprarop. Near Sois 1, 3, and 4 and heading toward Phetburi are seamstress shops with clickety-clack machines making some of the clothes that will go on sale at nearby stalls or putting sequins on *mǎw lam* and *lûuk thûng* (Thai country music) costumes. To take a break, wander some of the *soi* off Th Phetburi for a sampling of this eclectic working-class neighbourhood.

PROMENADE ARCADE

Map pp294-5   Shopping Centre

Nai Lert Park, Th Withayu; ⏲ **10am-5pm; khlong taxi Tha Withayu, Skytrain Ploenchit**

A low-key but worthy stop, Promenade Arcade shelters many of Bangkok's influential décor designers. On the 2nd floor, Narandha features the creations of ML Rojanatorn Na Songkhla (nicknamed Candy); she uses the unlikely ingredient of enamel in her designs, and a new line features waist-long necklaces made out of a string of colourful silk orchids. Sakul Intakul, the acclaimed floral designer, displays his flower vessels (that's a 'vase', kiddo) that bring couture to home arrangements. His floral sculptures can also be seen in the Sukhothai Hotel (p203).

SIAM CENTER & SIAM DISCOVERY

CENTER Map pp294-5   Shopping Centre

Cnr Th Phra Ram I & Th Phayathai; ⏲ **10am-10pm; Skytrain National Stadium, Siam**

These linked shopping malls are surprisingly subdued – almost comatose compared

to frenetic MBK. Thailand's first shopping centre, Siam Center was built in 1976 but hardly shows its age and is getting yet another nip and tuck to siphon some money away from MBK.

In the attached Siam Discovery Center, the ground floor sports all the preppy brand names.

The 4th floor continues to be a primary outpost for the Thai design scene. Panta creates modern furnishings and *objets d'art* out of uniquely Asian materials such as water hyacinth and bamboo. Bangkok-based French designer Gilles Caffier's store 2 Gilles Caffier sells hand-beaded vases, palm-wood chopsticks and other Asian-esque interiors that have landed his designs in Alain Ducasse's restaurant. The only Southeast Asian branch of Habitat, the European décor outlet, is on this floor. Nearby is a branch of Asia Books, which carries a wide selection of design magazines, Thai fiction titles and new guidebooks.

Doi Tung-Mae Fah Luang (5th fl) is a royally funded crafts shop selling handmade cotton and linen from villages formerly involved with poppy production. The styles range from vintage chic to ethnic comfort.

Siam Discovery Center

The 5th floor of Siam Discovery Center is dedicated to children's toys, fashions and baby gear. CD Warehouse has listening stations for getting up-to-date on Thai pop and hip-hop (move over Snoop, here comes Thaitanium).

SIAM PARAGON Map pp294-5   Shopping Centre
☎ 0 2658 3000; Th Phra Ram I, near Th Phayathai; Skytrain Siam
This megamall gobbled up the old Siam Intercontinental Hotel gardens and threw up a gleaming glass complex that has struck competitive fear into the existing malls. With a 15-million-baht price tag, Bangkok's latest greatest mall epitomises the city's fanaticism for the new, the excessive and absurd slogans. This 'peerless' venue is the largest mall in Southeast Asia, sprawling over 500,000 sq metres, and is a showcase for luxury retailers such as Van Cleef & Arpels, Mikimoto and Roberto Cavalli, who

have not yet had a pedestal in the country. Sony Thai will also parade its latest gadgets to Thai gear heads. Even more audacious than the retail sections are Siam World, a spectacular aquarium, an IMAX theatre and the 6th-floor Siam Opera Theatre.

SIAM SQUARE Map pp294-5   Shopping Centre
Th Phra Ram I, near Th Phayathai; Skytrain Siam
It doesn't look like much, just an ageing open-air shopping area divided into 12 *soi*, but Siam Square is ground zero for teenage culture in Bangkok. Pop music blares out of tinny speakers and gangs of hipsters in various costumes ricochet between fast-food restaurants and closet-sized boutiques. **DJ Siam** (Soi 4) carries all the Thai indie (such as Modern Dog) and Japanese pop (J-pop) albums you'll need to speak 'teen'. Small shops peddle pop-hip styles along Soi 2 and Soi 3, but most styles require a barely-there waist. Centerpoint

---

BUYER BEWARE

The disparity between the Thai baht and foreign currencies often clouds the view of otherwise eagle-eyed shoppers. Do your homework and approach each expensive transaction with a healthy amount of scepticism.

Antiques

Real Thai antiques are rare and costly and reserved primarily for serious collectors. Everything else is designed to look old and most shopkeepers are happy to admit it. Reputable antique dealers will issue an authentication certificate. Contact the **Department of Fine Arts** (☎ 0 2226 1661) to obtain a required licence for exporting religious images and fragments, either antique or reproductions.

Gems & Jewellery

Thailand is one of the world's largest exporters of gems and ornaments, but the scams are more ubiquitous than the bargains. Don't buy goods from a shop that claims to have a 'one-day' sale or wants you to deliver uncut gems to your home country for resale (see p254).

Reputable dealers don't pay commissions to túk-túk drivers but are known by customer referrals. Most are members of the Jewel Fest Club, established jointly by the Tourist Authority of Thailand (TAT) and the **Thai Gem Jewellery Traders Association** (www.thaigemjewelry.com). When you purchase from a member shop, a certificate detailing your purchase will be issued and a refund is guaranteed (less 10% to 20%) if you're unhappy. A list of members offering government guarantees is available from TAT, or visit the association's website for buying information.

The latest trend is to open a gem 'museum', charging a hefty admission price, with an attached jewellery store. Proceed with caution.

Tailor-Made Clothes

Tailors are as prolific as massage parlours in Bangkok and so are the scams. Workmanship and fabric quality ranges from shoddy to excellent.

A good tailor doesn't have to advertise; their reputation precedes them in the well-dressed circles of the diplomatic corps. Commission a few small pieces from a reputable shop (one that doesn't have hawkers out the front) before committing to high-cost items and know your fabrics before being duped by synthetics.

(Soi 7) plugs in on weekends with concerts from the latest bands, b-boys and perky models. Finish off a Siam Square tour with a stop at a photo-sticker booth to give the bunny-ears to posterity.

UTHAI'S GEMS

Map pp294-5   Gems & Jewellery

☎ 02 253 8582; 28/7 Soi Ruam Rudi, Th Ploenchit; ☎ by appointment; Skytrain Ploenchit

You need to make an appointment to see Uthai's gem shop, in the upscale embassy neighbourhood. His fixed prices and good service make him a popular choice among expats.

RIVERSIDE & SILOM

Savvy shoppers with larger wallets prowl these streets looking for quality collector items. Fine silks, museum-quality antiques and not-so-perfect pirated goods are all easily accessible at the various shopping malls or street markets.

JIM THOMPSON

Map pp290-1   Thai Silk

☎ 0 2235 8930; 149/4-6 Th Surawong; 9am-6pm; Skytrain Sala Daeng, subway Silom

The surviving business of the international promoter of Thai silk, Jim Thompson sells colourful silk handkerchiefs, place mats and wraps. The styles and motifs attract older, conservative tastes. There are also other branches at Jim Thompson's House (p97), the Emporium and a factory outlet (Soi 93, Th Sukhumvit).

MAISON DES ARTS

Map pp290-1   Handicrafts

☎ 0 2233 6297; 1334 Th Charoen Krung; Mon-Sat; ferry Tha Oriental

Thailand has the oldest bronze-working tradition in the world. This factory produces bronze flatware, tableware and collector pieces. Prices are fixed. Make sure any items you buy are silicon-coated, otherwise they'll tarnish.

NIKS/NAVA IMPORT EXPORT

Map pp290-1   Cameras

☎ 0 2233 2288; 166/4-5 Th Silom; 11am-4pm Mon-Fri; Skytrain Chong Nonsi

On the corner of Soi 12, Niks sells all types of professional equipment, including Nikon, Mamiya and Rollei.

ORCHID PRESS

Map pp290-1   Books

☎ 0 2930 0149; www.orchidbooks.com; Silom Galleria, Th Silom; 10am-8pm; Tha Oriental, Skytrain Chong Nonsi

The venerable Asiana publisher Orchid Press now has a Bangkok showroom. Titles span the region from academic to glossy art books.

ORIENTAL PLACE

Map pp290-1   Shopping Centre

Soi Oriental, 30/1 Th Charoen Krung; 10.30am-7pm; ferry Tha Oriental, Skytrain Saphan Taksin

In front of the Oriental Hotel, this up-market complex has several good, if pricey, antique shops, specialising in antique silks, religious artefacts and curios. A branch of the royally funded Chitlada Shop sells indigenous handicrafts from rural areas of Thailand.

PATPONG NIGHT MARKET

Map pp290-1   Outdoor Market

Soi Patpong 1 & Soi Patpong 2, Th Silom; nightly; Skytrain Sala Daeng, subway Silom

You'll be faced with the competing distractions of strip clubbing or shopping on this infamous street. True to the street's illicit leanings, pirated goods make a prominent appearance even amid a wholesome crowd of families and straight-laced couples. Bargain with determination as first-quoted prices here tend to be astronomically high.

RIVER CITY COMPLEX

Map pp290-1   Shopping Centre

Th Yotha, off Th Charoen Krung; 10am-9pm, many shops close Sun; ferry Tha Si Phraya

Near the Royal Orchid Sheraton Hotel, this multistorey centre is an all-in-one stop for old-world Asiana. Several high-quality art and antique shops occupy the 4th floor, including Pailin Gallery, which deals in collectables from the Ayuthaya era, and Hong Antiques, with 50 years of experience in decorative pieces. Acala is a gallery of unusual Tibetan and Chinese artefacts. Old Maps & Prints offers one of the best selections of one-of-a-kind, rare maps and illustrations, with a focus on Asia. Shipping is easy to arrange and bargaining is advisable.

Shopping

RIVERSIDE & SILOM

SILOM VILLAGE TRADE CENTRE

Map pp290-1   Handicrafts

Soi 24, Th Silom; ☺ 10.30am-7pm; ferry Tha Oriental
Behind the Silom Village, this arcade of
compact shops sells souvenir-quality repro-
duction antiques, including teak carvings,
textiles and ceramics. The pace is relaxed
and rarely crowded. Artisan's has Thai-style
furniture, altar tables and wooden decorations. Gems Garden sells *khon* (masked
dance-drama) masks.

SOI LALAI SAP Map pp290-1   Outdoor Market

Soi 5, Th Silom; ☺ 9am-8pm; Skytrain Sala Daeng,
subway Silom
The 'money-dissolving *soi*' has a number of
vendors selling all sorts of cheap clothing,
watches and housewares during the day.
Thai secretaries in their polyester suits and
clunky heels make up the backbone of the
clientele, so expect a lot of Thai kitsch. Gap
knock-offs mysteriously find their way to
this market.

SUAN LUM NIGHT BAZAAR

Map pp292-3   Outdoor Market

Cnr Th Withayu & Th Phra Ram IV; ☺ 6pm-
midnight; subway Lumphini
Better than Chatuchak? Not really, but
fun, nonetheless. This night market has
thousands of stalls selling modern Thai
souvenirs, handicrafts and a few antiques.
There are several outdoor beer gardens
with glitzy stage shows. The government-
backed venture was just starting to find its
groove when it was announced that a new
mall would take its place. At the time of
writing, details were slim on how much of
the night bazaar would survive.

SUNNY CAMERA Map pp290-1   Cameras

☎ 0 2236 8365; 144/23 Th Silom; ☺ 10am-6pm;
Skytrain Chong Nonsi
For a wide range of camera models and
brands, you could try Sunny Camera. There
are other branches on the 3rd floor of **Mahboonkrong** (MBK; ☎ 0 2217 9293) and at
Th Charoen Krung (☎ 0 2235 2123; 1267-
1267/1 Th Charoen Krung).

TAMNAN MINGMUANG

Map pp290-1   Handicrafts

☎ 0 2231 2120; 3rd fl, Thaniya Plaza, Th Silom;
☺ 10am-9pm; Skytrain Sala Daeng, subway Silom
As soon as you step through the doors of
this museumlike shop, the earthy smell of
dried grass and stained wood rush to meet
you. Rattan, *yan lipao* (a type of vine) and
water hyacinth are woven into delicate
silklike patterns, mimicking the traditional
pottery crafts of celadon and *benjarong* (a
type of hand-painted pottery). These are
exquisite pieces that will outlast flashier
souvenirs available streetside.

THAI HOME INDUSTRIES

Map pp290-1   Handicrafts

☎ 0 2234 1736; 35 Soi 38, Th Charoen Krung;
☺ 10am-5pm; ferry Tha Oriental
You never know what you'll find here
or what is really for sale, but wandering
around the dusty building, a former monks'
quarters, feels like discovering an old attic.
On a recent visit, the display cases absent-
mindedly presented cotton farmer shirts,
bronzeware and some wood carvings. But
we were only admiring all the old stuff and
labels that date way back.

TH SUKHUMVIT

Supplies for the recently arrived expat can
be found at the shops that line the never-
ending Th Sukhumvit. Furniture, clothes
and household knick-knacks hang out on
upper Sukhumvit, while tourist souvenirs
centre around Soi 11. Reputable tailors have
low-key presences in this neighbourhood.

ALMETA Map pp296-7   Silk

☎ 0 2204 1413; www.almeta.com; 20/3 Soi 23, Th
Sukhumvit; ☺ 11am-7pm; Skytrain Asoke
Thailand is famous for its hand-woven silks
but most peddle ghastly colours preferred
by the government officials. Almeta is one

of the few that speaks gen-X with subtle silks dyed to match raw sugar or lotus blossoms. Unlike Chinese silk, hand-woven Thai silk is nubby, almost linenlike in texture. There are also silk sofa pillows and other exotic wedding-gift ideas.

EMPORIUM SHOPPING CENTRE

Map pp296-7   Shopping Centre
622 Th Sukhumvit, cnr Soi 24; ⊙ **10.30am-11pm; Skytrain Phrom Phong**
Part retail therapy, part surrogate home, the Emporium is filled with all the luxuries expats need to pretend they never left their mother country. The ground floor is filled with Euro fashion labels, like Prada, Miu Miu and Chanel. The 2nd floor is more casual, with home-grown contenders like Soda, which has slipped punk into *haute* wear; image-maker Greyhound and kitschy-cool gifts and home décor by Propaganda. Staid Jim Thompson even gets a face-lift with its branch here.

On the 3rd floor, Kinokuniya is the brainiac in the family with serious English and Japanese titles, including children's books. Thai crafts and Thai-arcana can be found on the 4th floor in the new Exotique Thai centre. Kid's stuff and entertainment can be found on this level as well. You can smell the *khànŏm* (Thai desserts) as you ascend to the 5th floor food centre.

More impressive than the resident fashionistas is the newly opened **Thailand Creative & Design Center** (☎ 0 2664 8448; 6th fl), a design museum with an attached gift shop selling cool souvenirs from various exhibits. A recent

Shopping for clothes in Greyhound, Emporium Shopping Centre

show on Isan inspired T-shirts bearing logos 'I Love Nakohn Ratchasima' – take that NYC.

H1 Map pp296-7   Shopping Centre
988/7 Soi 55, Th Sukhumvit; Skytrain Thong Lor to red bus
Thong Lor has sprouted several high-end concept malls, each cornering a different niche of the rich-and-famous market. The most serious of the newcomers, H1 is a village of modular glass cocoons slightly suggestive of old-fashioned Thai housing estates. The beautiful things on display are mid-century revivals, when furniture was sleek and futuristic. Geo sells household décor and gifts, including Beyond Living's décor products. Bansheer Books fills its shelves with art and design books that continue to fuel the city's design revolution. Although H1 opened with much ado, the two anchor restaurants have already exhausted their 15 minutes of fame and the sophisticated space is convent quiet.

L'ARCADIA Map pp296-7   Antiques
☎ 02 259 9595; 12/2 Soi 23, Th Sukhumvit; ⊙ 9am-10pm; Skytrain Asoke
The buyer at L'Arcadia has a sharp eye for collectibles from Myanmar, Cambodia and Thailand, including Sukhothai cabinets, cute red-lacquer containers, Khmer-style sandstone figures and carved, wooden temple decorations. If you simply can't resist that Burmese lounge chair, the shop can arrange to have it shipped home.

NANDAKWANG Map pp296-7   Handicrafts
☎ 0 2258 1962; 108/3 Soi 23, Soi Prasanmit, Th Sukhumvit; Skytrain Asoke
To properly outfit a modern bohemian, you'd need to head up to arty Chiang Mai. Luckily, this Chiang Mai–based store has a Bangkok satellite selling its home-spun chic purses, high-quality woven cotton clothing and household wares (tablecloths, napkins etc). The earnest stuffed animals would make a nice gift for the young ones. There is a branch in Siam Discovery Center (3rd floor).

PLAYGROUND!

Map pp296-7   Shopping Centre
☎ 0 2714 7888; www.playgroundstore.co.th; 818 Soi 55, Th Sukhumvit; Skytrain Thong Lor to red bus
Compared to put-together H1, Playground is the sister heading to rehab. This concept

LOCAL BUYS

Right, you've got gems, silks and elephants on your Bangkok shopping list, but there are loads of local buys that won't make your home look like a beachfront souvenir shop:

Beyond Living – Colourful and textured woven rugs, cushions and handbags draw inspiration from natural Thai materials and handicraft traditions with a distinctly modern flair. Available at Gaysorn (p181) and Geo at H1 (p187).

Harnn & Thann – Smell good enough to eat with these botanical-based spa products: lavender massage lotion, rice-bran soap and jasmine compresses. Products are all natural, rooted in Thai traditional medicine, and stylish enough to share space with brand-name beauty products. Available at Gaysorn (p181).

Mr P Lamp – Thai designer Chaiyut Plypetch dreamed up Propaganda's signature character, the devilish Mr P, who appears in anatomically cartoonish lamps and other products. Available at Siam Discovery Center (p183) and Emporium (p187).

Niwat Cutlery – Born out of the ancient sword-making traditions of Ayuthaya Province, the NV Aranyik company, a family-owned business, produces distinctively Thai cutlery. Available at Gaysorn (p181).

Zebra Stainless Steel Kitchenware – This 40-year-old company based in Rayong scooped out a market niche with its high-quality Chinese soup spoons. It has since expanded into nesting bowls, Thai-style lunchboxes and soup pots that would cost a fortune for comparable quality back home. It's available at department stores and housewares markets.

mall is street-smart cool in a neighbour-hood not alternative enough to get it. Graffiti art, J-pop vinyl dolls, manja: Bangkok now speaks the über-hip language of New York City's Lower East Side. The hulking building balances commerce on the periphery with large central spaces dedicated to street- and pop-art exhibits or performance spaces. In the scattered shopping zones, you'll find jeans by the Thai label Medium-Rare, Kit-Ti's ethnic-cool jewellery and outrageously Victorian whimsies. In the bookstore section, keep an eye out for notebooks by Hoog, a Thai graphic designer whose owl drawings are a spoof on his nickname and reminiscent of the character used to teach Thai schoolchildren the corresponding letter in the alphabet.

RASI SAYAM Map pp296-7   Handicrafts

☎ 0 2262 0729; 82 Soi 33, Th Sukhumvit; Skytrain Asoke, Phrom Phong

Street souvenirs ain't got nothing on Rasi Sayam's tasteful *objets d'art*. Wall-hangings, *benjarong*, basketry and pottery are made specifically for this shop by handicraft villages.

TH SUKHUMVIT MARKET

Map pp296-7   Outdoor Market

Th Sukhumvit btwn Soi 2 & Soi 12, Soi 3 & Soi 15; 🕑 11am-10.30pm; Skytrain Nana

Good morning, sleepy head. Never fear about gifts for back home, the street ven-dors will offer you faux Fendi handbags, soccer kits (Becks, Giggsy and Zidane dominate), watches, sunglasses and jewellery to name a few. You'll also find stacks of nudie DVDs, Chinese throwing stars, penis lighters and other questionable gifts for your high-school-aged brother.

GREATER BANGKOK

Markets really capture the hubbub of Bangkok and the big drawcard out here is the renowned Chatuchak Weekend Market.

CHATUCHAK WEEKEND MARKET

Map pp278-9   Market

Th Phahonyothin; 🕑 8am-6pm Sat & Sun; Skytrain Mo Chit, subway Kamphoeng Pet

Imagine if all the city markets, with their green shade umbrellas and narrow walk-ways, were fused together in one great big market-style concentration camp. Now add in a little artistic flair, a climate like a sauna, the energy of bargaining crowds and you've got a rough sketch of Chatuchak (also spelled 'Jatujak' or nicknamed 'JJ'). More than 15,000 stalls cater to hundreds of thousands of visitors during the two days when the market is in full operation (other days, only certain portions are open).

Everything is sold here, from live chickens and snakes to vintage fans and *măw lam* CDs. Once you're deep in the bowels, it will seem like there is no order and no escape, but Chatuchak is arranged into sections: crafts, clothing, plants, pets and more. Nancy Chandler's map (see the boxed text, p168) has a handy breakdown and there are posted maps within the complex. An information centre and several ATMs with foreign-exchange booths near the Chatuchak Park offices, near the northern end of the market's Soi 1, Soi 2 and Soi 3. Come early to beat the heat and the crowds and watch your valuables carefully, as sticky fingers love JJ too.

In years past Chatuchak was more of a working-class market, selling housewares and gravel. But Bangkok has become more self-assured, and the weekend market has moved towards boutique. Young designers and artists cut their teeth in these little stalls, hoping to graduate to more permanent space. Reflecting the city's obsession with mid-century revival, there are lots of design-wise products, vintage gear, Eames-inspired furniture and atomic-age colours.

Clothing dominates most of the market, starting in Section 8 and continuing through the even-numbered sections to 24. Stalls sell the usual ethnic garb, army surplus and

Th Sukhumvit branch of Asia Books (below)

other modest and immodest duds. In Section 5 funky secondhand clothes get a minor role, featuring grease-monkey work shirts with sewn-on name labels. Tourist-sized clothes and textiles are in Sections 10 and 8.

Section 7 is becoming an arty bastion with little galleries and knick-knack stalls. More traditional arts and crafts, like musical instruments, hill-tribe crafts, religious amulets and antiques, hang out in Section 25 and 26. Sections 2 and 3 are also filled with nifty décor shops and cafés.

Across from the southern side of the market on Th Kampaengphet 2 is a strip of stores

BONDING WITH BOOKS

For new books and magazines, Asia Books and Bookazine have extensive selections and several branches throughout the city.

Asia Books

Central World Plaza (Map pp294–5; ☎ 0 2255 6209; 3rd fl, Central World Plaza, Th Ratchadamri)

Emporium Shopping Centre (Map pp296–7; ☎ 0 2664 8545; 3rd fl, Emporium Shopping Centre, Th Sukhumvit)

Peninsula Plaza (Map pp294–5; ☎ 0 2253 9786; 2nd fl, Peninsula Plaza, Th Ratchadamri)

Siam Discovery Center (Map pp294–5; ☎ 0 2658 0418; 4th fl, Siam Discovery Center, Th Phra Ram I)

Th Sukhumvit (Map pp296–7; ☎ 0 2651 0428; 221 Th Sukhumvit, btwn Soi 15 & Soi 17)

Thaniya Plaza (Map pp290–1; ☎ 0 2231 2106; 3rd fl, Thaniya Plaza, Th Silom)

Bookazine

Siam Square (Map pp294–5; ☎ 0 2255 3778; 286 Th Phra Ram I, btwn Soi 3 & Soi 4, opposite Siam Center)

Silom Complex (Map pp290–1; ☎ 0 2231 3135; 2nd fl, Siam Complex, cnr Th Silom & Th Phra Ram IV)

Th Sukhumvit (Map pp296–7; ☎ 0 2655 2383; Nailert Bldg, Th Sukhumvit btwn Soi 3 & Soi 5)

New titles are also available from Kinokuniya at the Emporium (see p187). Art books can be found at Passport (p170) and Rim Khob Fah Bookstore (p170). Politicos should trot over to Suksit Siam (p170).

Used titles are easy to find in Banglamphu, but are rare elsewhere. If you're tied to New Bangkok, try **Elite Used Books** (Map pp296–7; ☎ 0 2258 0221; 593/5 Th Sukhumvit at Soi 33/1; Skytrain Phrom Phong) or **Dasa Book Cafe** (Map pp296–7; ☎ 0 2661 2993; Th Sukhumvit btwn Soi 26 & Soi 28).

selling traditional wood furniture, vintage fans and phonographs and other treasures of yore. Keep an eye out for water hyacinth rugs, every condo dweller's dream accent.

Lots of Thai-style eating and snacking will stave off Chatuchak rage (cranky behaviour brought on by dehydration or hunger). Food stalls are set up between Sections 6 and 8. Close to the market office are several air-con restaurants. As evening draws near, cross Th Kampaenphet 2 to the cosy whisky bars that keep nocturnal hours. Lots of musicians start to sprinkle the market with the twang of guitars as the sun begins to lose its heat.

In the mornings, Aw Taw Kaw Market sets up opposite the south side of Chatuchak Weekend Market, selling organic-ally grown (no chemical sprays or fertilisers) fruits and vegetables. See p146 for food options here.

Operated by the Asoke Foundation, the vegetarian restaurant near the weekend market is one of Bangkok's oldest. It's open only on weekends from 8am to noon and is an adventure to find. Cross the footbridge above Th Kampaengphet, heading away from the market, and towards the southern end of Th Phahonyothin. Take the first right onto a through street heading into the car park, and walk past the nightclubs and bars. Turn right, and you'll see a new block of buildings selling bulk food stuff. The restaurant is at the end of this strip. Prices are ridiculously low (around 10B per dish) and you buy tickets at the front desk.

Sleeping

Sleeping

Despite Bangkok's international reputation as an insomniac, you'll need a place to bed and bathe. Since accommodation is spread across the city, it is best to pick a neighbourhood and then a hotel. Your choices are modern Sukhumvit, the business centre around Silom, the scenic riverside, the backpacker enclave of Banglamphu, the shopping district around Siam Square, or boisterous Chinatown. The closer you are to your inner-city destination, the less time you'll spend in traffic.

Each neighbourhood specialises in a certain budget range. The greatest concentration of cheapies is in Banglamphu. Th Silom and Th Sukhumvit cater mainly to midrange and top-end budgets. Interesting options in the low end of the midrange can be found in Siam Square and Chinatown.

And what kind of slumber does the City of Angels offer? There won't be any unpleasant surprises in the top-end category. Bangkok has all the luxury-class models, from historic to chic, with five-star service and exotic elements like fresh orchids and staff in shimmering silk uniforms. Most rooms in top-enders have exceptional city views, and the tropically landscaped pool is suspended many storeys above the ground. All the necessities for savvy travellers are in place: gyms, business centres and a spa. Most lobbies are outfitted with wi-fi, but rooms only offer high-speed cable. Rates usually include breakfast. Executive floors with all the privileges offer equally privileged views. Special perks are listed in the individual reviews. Please note that luxury hotels typically quote their rates in US dollars, a holdover from the Asian currency crisis.

It isn't until you strip down to the midrange hotels that inconsistency becomes apparent. They all have the look of a hotel in the West – a door attendant, uniformed desk clerks and a well-polished lobby – but without the predictability. Unexpected quirks include dated décor or worn-out baths or beds. For some reason curtains and bathrooms age worse than a has-been rock star. Most rooms have TV (with a few international channels), refrigerator, minibar, phone and a desk. Internet access is not always available. Swimming pools and complimentary breakfasts are noted in the review.

At the bottom of the range, listed in the Cheap Sleeps section, are the backpackers' old friends: guesthouses and cheap hotels. Sometimes you'll find a converted family house with only the basics: a bed, a light and four walls with a fan and shared bathroom (typically a cold-water shower).

TOP BANGKOK SLEEPS

After looking into every hotel room that would let us in, here is a purely subjective list of the best the city has to offer.

- Best Business Options – Swiss Lodge (p203) and Four Seasons Hotel (p199)
- Best for Modern Sophistication – Sukhothai Hotel (p203) and Peninsula Hotel (p204)
- Best for Classical Thai – Baan Thai (p205), Oriental Hotel (p204), Old Bangkok Inn (p194) and Ibrik Resort (p194)
- Best Hip Options – Reflections Rooms (p209), Conrad Bangkok (p199) and the Metropolitan (p202)
- Best for Families – Pathumwan House (p200) and Amari Watergate (p199)

Apartment at the Metropolitan (p202)

PRICE GUIDE

$$$	over 3000B a night
$$	800–3000B a night
$	under 800B a night

LONGER-TERM RENTALS

Staying in Bangkok for longer than a week? Consider a serviced apartment with weekly and monthly rates. These include furniture, daily cleaning services, linens, a kitchenette and direct-dial telephones, all included in the basic rent. Usually an on-site business and fitness centre and in-room Internet access are also available.

Where there is one executive residence, there are many, so the accommodation listed here are a cross section of what's available. In the heart of Silom's business district, Siri Sathorn Executive Residence (p202) is a fashionable option. In the embassy district, Natural Ville (p200) is as charming as its leafy residential street. If you need central and affordable, check out Pathumwan House (p200), near Siam Square.

In addition to these options, check the 'Property Guide' in the *Bangkok Post* on Thursday for rental advertisements and listings, or the following online resources: www.bangkokapartments.info, bangkok.craigslist.org or www.mrroomfinder.com.

> ### BOOK ACCOMMODATION ONLINE
>
> For more accommodation reviews and recommendations by Lonely Planet authors, check out the online booking service at www.lonelyplanet.com. You'll find the true, insider lowdown on the best places to stay. Reviews are thorough and independent. Best of all, you can book online.

BANGLAMPHU & KO RATANAKOSIN

Banglamphu, which includes the backpacker ghetto of Th Khao San, is a well-padded landing zone for jet-lagged travellers. It is fairly easy to find a cheap place to crash at short notice, just show up and start hunting, as most cheapies don't take reservations. The midrange hotels take reservations and often offer better rates for advance bookings.

The neighbourhood can be sliced into three distinct personalities centred around the following streets: Th Khao San, Soi Rambutri/Th Phra Athit and Th Samsen.

Once synonymous with cheap backpackers, Khao San has upgraded its image – sort of – and certainly its prices. It is still the familiar neon strip of raucous enthusiasm with the attendant souvenirs, touts and raucous soundtrack, but now there are real 'date' restaurants and barely twenties travelling with robust credit cards. Many of the bare-bones digs that gave Khao San its dirtbag reputation have been replaced by highrises with air-con and a lift. In fact, Th Khao San is no longer the bargain it used to be. As options go upscale, prices across the board creep higher. Savvy budgeters should shop around for the latest makeover or newcomer luring new business with cut-rate promotions. Or better yet, step off the street to find better value.

Along the smaller street of Soi Rambutri and the river-facing Th Phra Athit is a more mature scene than that of the rambunctious Khao San. The creature comforts of the hotels are greater, less techno music invades your temporary address and outdoor parties adhere to the Cinderella curfew of midnight. This area is within walking distance of Tha Phra Athit, where you can catch express boats to major historical sites along the river.

Across Khlong Banglamphu, Th Samsen runs parallel to the river heading north to Thewet. The small *soi* that branch off the road at regular intervals shelter a few family-run guesthouses amid a typical village world of thick-hipped mothers, freshly bathed babies and neighbours shuffling off to the nearest shopkeeper to buy sundries. Accommodation options in this area are true basics with fans and shared cold-water bathrooms.

BHIMAN INN Map pp286-7   Hotel $$

☎ 0 2282 6171; www.bhimaninn.com; 55 Th Phra Athit; r 900-1500B; ferry Tha Phra Athit, ordinary bus 15, 30 & 53; ✗ ▣

Goodbye old guesthouse, hello new boutique. Although the word is used generously, Bhiman gives comfort with sips of style – a vast improvement on its frumpy sister, Viengtai Hotel (p195). The fortress façade yields to chequerboard hallways. Smokers and nonsmokers are segregated by floor, with more space given to the fire-breathers. The standard rooms are swallowed by the bed, but green-tiled bathrooms make bath-time fun.

BOWORN BB Map pp286-7   Guesthouse $$

☎ 0 2629 1073; www.bowornbb.com; 335 Th Phra Sumen; r 600-900B; ferry Tha Phra Athit, air-con bus 511 & 512, ordinary bus 2 & 82; ⌨

Cultural chameleons will love this antique neighbourhood of green-and-yellow shophouses and flip-flop-clad families with hardly a sign of tourist incursions. Boworn has bland but clean concrete rooms with bathrooms and a fresh coat of paint. The mattresses are too lean for folks who have developed creaks, but the rooftop enjoys temple views and breezes and the downstairs café provides a convenient shot of joe.

BUDDY LODGE Map pp286-7   Hotel $$

☎ 0 2629 4477; www.buddylodge.com; 265 Th Khao San; d 1800-2200B; ferry Tha Phra Athit, air-con bus 511 & 512, ordinary bus 2 & 82; ⌨ ⌨

Smack dab on Khao San, this boutique hotel has proven that even an old travellers' ghetto can be gentrified. Buxom rooms are dressed up like a tropical manor with terracotta-tiled floors and wood-panelled walls. The result is a romantic retreat with all the modern amenities.

IBRIK RESORT Map p288   Hotel $$$

☎ 0 2848 9220; www.ibrikresort.com; 256 Soi Wat Rakhang, Th Arun Amarin, Thonburi; d 4000B; Thonburi; ferry Tha Wang Lang; ⌨

Only three rooms big, this itty-bitty resort offers style and privacy for the average professional. Virginally white, the rooms are minimal but cosy in a traditional wooden house and perfect for a romantic getaway

that won't feel forced. Price includes breakfast. There is also a sister property in town on Th Sathon (Map pp290–1; ☎ 0 2211 3470; 235/16 Th Sathon Tai).

LAMPHU HOUSE Map pp286-7   Guesthouse $

☎ 0 2629 5861; www.lamphuhouse.com; 75-77 Soi Rambutri, Th Chakraphong; d from 580B; ferry Tha Phra Athit, ordinary bus 15, 30 & 53; ⌨

A refreshing oasis, Lamphu House creates a mellow mood with its hidden location and breezy, smartly decorated rooms. This used to be a hospital in another era and the spirit of cleanliness remains today. Some rooms have balconies overlooking the green courtyard.

OLD BANGKOK INN Map pp286-7   Hotel $$

☎ 0 2629 1785; www.oldbangkokinn.com; 609 Th Phra Sumen; d 2100B; air-con bus 511 & 512, ordinary bus 2 & 82, khlong taxi Tha Phan Fah; ⌨ ⌨

This atmospheric shophouse was once a humble noodle house. Now it is a boutique hotel pleasingly decorated in colours that will evoke visions of desserts: crème caramel walls, dark cocoa furnishings and persimmon silk bedspreads. You might call it 'cottage-style cosy' or, more honestly, cramped; nonetheless, it is better suited for the nimble. The 1st-floor Lemongrass room has a small shady patio; but the 2nd-floor Rice room has high ceilings and a little more wiggle room. All rooms have Internet-ready computer terminals. Price includes breakfast. If you stay elsewhere, at least stop by the café for a cup of old-world charm.

MANGO LAGOON

Map pp286-7   Guesthouse $

☎ 0 2281 4783; 30 Soi Rambutri; d 600-700B; ferry Tha Phra Athit, ordinary bus 15, 30 & 53; ⌨

Have your Tivas sprouted mushrooms from your dank cell? Claim sunshine at Mango Lagoon, a multidecker motel-style building with windows overlooking the neighbours' corrugated roofs and napping cats. The rooms are almost full-fledged hotel rooms with carpet that hasn't yet turned stale, real furniture, and a TV that might threaten Khao San's tradition of showing communal movies. Despite all this, you still get the Thai budget shower-over-the-toilet combo. The front courtyard offers a pleasant palm garden and café.

Guest room at Old Bangkok Inn (opposite)

NEW WORLD HOUSE APARTMENTS & GUEST HOUSE Map pp286-7   Hotel $$

☎ 0 2281 5596; www.newworldlodge.com; Th Samsen; d 1400B; ferry Tha Phra Athit, ordinary bus 15, 30 & 53; 🍴

Muslim families, provincial Thais and even some long-term English teachers make New World a short-term global village. Plus the neighbourhood is a treat: instead of dodging tailors and orange-juice sellers, you hop around kids on oversized bikes, badminton games and freshly laundered babies. Some rooms have balconies overlooking the somewhat scenic Khlong Banglamphu.

ROYAL HOTEL Map pp286-7   Hotel $$

☎ 0 2222 9111-26; fax 0 2224 2083; cnr Th Ratchadamnoen Klang & Th Atsadang; d 1600B; air-con bus 511; 🍴 🚇

This is the third-oldest hotel in Bangkok and it's just a short walk from the famous sites in Ko Ratanakosin. Despite repeated attempts, we've never seen beyond the marble lobby, but former guests have described it as a conveniently located but ageing monarch. Price includes breakfast. Most taxi drivers know this hotel as the 'Ratanakosin' (as the Thai sign on top of the building reads), not as the Royal.

THAI COZY HOUSE Map pp286-7   Guesthouse $

☎ 0 2629 5870; www.thaicozyhouse.com; 111/1-3 Th Tani; d 750B; ferry Tha Phra Athit, air-con bus 511 & 512, ordinary bus 2 & 82; 🍴

Making inroads into a frontier for *faràng*, this newcomer is eager to usher in the backpackers with so many extras (TV and fridge) that the rooms shrink beyond cosy. The busy market just beyond the front door will be a challenge for big backpacks and gentle giants, but those who travel light might find the daily squeeze an entertaining hurdle.

THAI HOTEL Map pp286-7   Hotel $$

☎ 0 2282 2831; www.thaihotel.cc; 78 Th Prachatipatai; s/d 1250/1450B; ordinary bus 9, 12 & 56; 🍴 🖥 🚇

A reliable midranger, Thai Hotel has modern standards and an ageing but reserved atmosphere. A complimentary shuttle bus runs to the area's attractions. Next door, an open-air Chinese coffee shop makes the best *kaafae yen* (iced Thai coffee) in the city.

VIENGTAI HOTEL Map pp286-7   Hotel $$

☎ 0 2280 5434; www.viengtai.co.th; 42 Th Rambutri; d 1850-2000B; ferry Tha Phra Athit, air-con bus 511 & 512, ordinary bus 2 & 82; 🍴 🚇

Before Th Khao San was 'discovered', this was a basic Chinese-style hotel in a neighbourhood minding its own business. Over the last decade or so the Viengtai has continually renovated its rooms and raised its prices until it now sits solidly in the midrange. With conservative hotel décor, Viengtai doesn't offer much in the way of personality, but peace and comfort are givens. Plus those Lucy-and-Desi twin beds are charmingly old fashioned.

CHEAP SLEEPS

For budget travellers happy to forfeit cleanliness, privacy and quiet for the sheer thrill of paying close to nothing, monastic 150B to 250B rooms can still be found amid the upwardly mobile options. Try Soi Damnoen Klang and Trok Mayom, two little alleys that run parallel to Khao San where small wooden houses are divided into even smaller rooms. Other budget options squat around Th Samsen over Khlong Banglamphu.

CHAI'S HOUSE Map pp286-7   Guesthouse $
☎ 0 2281 4901; 49/4-8 Soi Rongmai; s/d from 160/275B; ferry Tha Phra Athit, air-con bus 511 & 512, ordinary bus 2 & 82; ✕
Quickly losing ground to gimmicks, Chai's is refreshingly simple: a family-run guesthouse in an old wooden house with golden polished floors, shared bathrooms and a

REACHING FOR FEWER STARS

For some international travellers, stars matter: not the celestial or celebrity kind, but the shorthand system used to rank hotel quality. The more stars, the better the quality, and the higher the price tag.

But connoisseurs of thrift prefer the remedial-reader version of hotels, the three- or even two-star special. These places usually post lists of rules in every room forbidding durian, gambling and ammunitions. Remember this is a family place, not a bus station. And the surviving thumbprints on the wall are a testament to Thailand's extreme heat and abstinence from bleach. Every lower-starred hotel also has a prominently displayed grandfather clock, considered more modern than the porcelain thrones in the bathroom.

Just like the ritzy places, though, service is a priority: a bellboy guards the front door and the staff will outnumber the potted plants in the lobby. Just don't ask anyone to read a map; it will be twisted and turned upside down until it looks like an origami crane.

pretty café out front. This is luxury for early birds (a 1am curfew is required of guests). To get here from Soi Rambutri, take a right on the soi running beside Baan Sabai.

KC GUEST HOUSE
Map pp286-7   Guesthouse $
☎ 0 2282 0618; 64 Trok Kai Chae, Th Phra Athit; d 250-500B; ferry Tha Phra Athit, air-con bus 511 & 512, ordinary bus 2 & 82; ✕
Sometimes escaping the tourist ghetto can feel like swimming against the tide. This sweet family-run spot casts a lifeline between tourist amenities and Thai life. The simple rooms are thoughtfully spotless and freshly painted. There is an old backpacker camaraderie in the reading library and plant-shaded café.

PRAKORP'S HOUSE
Map pp286-7   Guesthouse $
☎ 0 2281 1345; fax 0 2629 0714; 52 Th Khao San; s/d 150/250B; ferry Tha Phra Athit, air-con bus 511 & 512, ordinary bus 2 & 82
One of the last old-style guesthouses on Th Khao San, Prakorp's is an old wooden house set back from the road. There are five simple rooms in the old house, giving visitors a real dose of what life was like a hundred years ago. Rooms in the new building aren't as nice or as much a trip to the past.

PRASURI GUEST HOUSE
Map pp286-7   Guesthouse $
☎ /fax 0 2280 1428; Soi Phrasuli; s 250B, d 380-500B; ferry Tha Phra Athit; air-con bus 511 & 512, ordinary bus 2 & 82
Venturing outside Th Khao San, follow Th Din So into a neighbourhood of family-run storefronts. At the first soi (Soi Phrasuli), hang a right to reach this guesthouse. Instead of the usual crowd of sunburnt Europeans, Prasuri's downstairs restaurant is crowded with Thai schoolchildren on a lunch break. Despite the din of secondary-school gossiping, the rooms are quiet and clean and all have bathrooms.

RAJATA HOTEL Map pp286-7   Hotel $
☎ 0 2281 8977; 46 Soi 6, Th Samsen; s/d 360/480B; ferry Tha Phra Athit, air-con bus 506, ordinary bus 53; ✕
Along this soi, there are several 'no-tell' motels designed for hourly visitors who need

lots of privacy (note the interior car park). Of the strip, Rajata is the best with crisp, clean sheets, no stale-smoke smell and a lingering retro Los Angeles style. Backpackers who don't want to be bothered with comparing travel notes make up a good portion of the clientele.

VILLA GUEST HOUSE

Map pp286-7 · Guesthouse $

☎ 0 2281 7009; 230 Soi 1, Th Samsen; s/d 250/500B; ferry Tha Phra Athit, air-con bus 506, ordinary bus 53

This old teak house occupies a cosy garden amid the village life of Soi 1. Instead of the noise of traffic, Villa wakes up to the sound of roosters crowing or stiff-broomed sweeping and the smells of mesquite cooking fires. Like a dusty old book, Villa is full of stories lurking in dark corners and among the shabby-chic furniture. With only 10 rooms (all with shared bathroom and fan), Villa is often full and recommends making reservations.

THEWET & DUSIT

The district north of Banglamphu near the National Library is known as 'Thewet' (pronounced acrobatically enough to tongue-tie nontonal speakers). Guesthouses line the *soi* side of Th Si Ayuthaya popular with Asia-savvy budgeters. This is a lovely, leafy area with a morning market, a busy neighbourhood temple and easy access to the river ferry. The only drawbacks are that downtown Bangkok is many traffic jams away and the street is prone to flooding during the rainy season.

The surrounding neighbourhood of Dusit has a few large package-tour hotels.

SHANTI LODGE Map pp282-3 · Guesthouse $

☎ 0 2281 2497; Th Si Ayuthaya; d 600B; ferry Tha Thewet, ordinary bus 53 & 30;

Nobody does affordable chic like Shanti Lodge, where a rambling wooden house with a maze of artfully decorated air-con rooms crouches above a blissed-out garden café downstairs. But that's not all, there is yet another signature: the staff. Year after year, visit after visit, the faces might change but all have mastered the ice-queen routine. Some travellers like it, others ignore it, but consider yourself warned.

TRANG HOTEL Map pp282-3 · Hotel $$

☎ 0 2282 2141; www.trang-hotel.co.th; 99/1 Th Wisut Kasat; d from 2700B; ordinary bus 30, 49 & 53;

This is a subdued midrange option popular with families. Rooms with all the mod cons radiate from an interior pool courtyard and a shady outdoor sitting area. The hotel's landscaping blocks out the traffic-choked main road.

The location is a plus for visitors bound for the nearby UN offices, but a drawback for sightseers as the only public-transport options are the public buses or a lengthy walk to the nearest river-ferry pier.

CHEAP SLEEPS

BANGKOK INTERNATIONAL YOUTH HOSTEL Map pp282-3 · Hostel $

☎ 0 2282 0950; www.hihostels.com; 25/2 Th Phitsanulok; dm 70-120B; r 250-350B; ferry Tha Thewet, ordinary bus 16 & 509;

East of Th Samsen is the Bangkok branch of this international network. Loyalty to the network puts many first-timers at ease even if the rooms are cramped and tired, and the location is dull and far flung. One plus is the friendly common area of good-natured early risers, many in town for English-teaching stints or language study.

SRI AYUTTAYA GUEST HOUSE

Map pp282-3 · Guesthouse $

☎ 0 2282 5942; Soi Thewet, Th Si Ayuthaya; d 300-600B; ferry Tha Thewet, bus 53 & 30;

Sri Ayuttaya has romantic air-con rooms with pretty hardwood floors, exposed brick and other stylish touches. Avoid the front rooms, which have built-in wake-up calls from the street's motorcycles. The fan rooms are more basic.

TAEWEZ GUESTHOUSE

Map pp282-3 · Guesthouse $

☎ 0 2280 8856; www.taewez.com; 23/12 Soi Thewet, Th Si Ayuthaya; d with 200-400B; ferry Tha Thewet, bus 53 & 30;

The caboose in this street's guesthouse chain, Taewez is more basic, but it's well loved by repeat visitors and long-term layabouts for one simple reason: it is cheap and clean. The air-con room is in fact one of the best deals in town, but the fan rooms aren't as smart.

CHINATOWN

Many visitors venture into this neighbourhood in search of a little more cultural immersion than can be found in the overpublicised Khao San. Chinatown's hotels are unexciting high-rise buildings outfitted to suit the aesthetic tastes of visiting Chinese families: lobbies of mirrors and faux gold. But the rates and rooms communicate in the international language for 'value'. The Indian district known as Phahurat is less expensive and caters to low-end business travellers from the subcontinent.

There are several budget choices in the area around Bangkok's main train station, Hualamphong, for early morning getaways. Watch your pockets and bags around the Hualamphong area.

BURAPHA HOTEL Map pp284-5   Hotel $
☎ 0 2213 5459; fax 0 2226 1723; 160/14 Th Charoen Krung; d 550-600B; ferry Tha Saphan Phut, air-con bus 507 & 508, ordinary bus 73; 🅿
On the western edge of Chinatown, Burapha has nice simple rooms and is popular with do-it-yourself exporters hitting the Sampeng Lane wholesale shops. You'll share the cramped elevator with huge plastic bags filled with goods en route to foreign soil. The hotel segregates its guests by nationality: the Westerners get one floor, Indians another and Chinese yet another.

GRAND CHINA PRINCESS
Map pp284-5   Hotel $$
☎ 0 2224 9977; www.grandchina.com; 215 Th Yaowarat; s/d 2000/2200B; ferry Tha Ratchawong, air-con bus 507, ordinary bus 73; 🅿
Literally in the heart of Chinatown, this multistorey matron is popular with the shark-fin loving crowd and has acceptable rooms buoyed by great views of Banglamphu. The top floor has a panoramic rotating restaurant to make your dreams of gaudy Asia complete.

KRUNG KASEM SRIKUNG HOTEL
Map pp284-5   Hotel $
☎ 0 2225 0132; fax 0 2225 4705; 1860 Th Krung Kasem; d 550B; ordinary bus 25, 35 & 53, subway Hualamphong; 🅿 🅿
Southwest of Hualamphong train station, this high-rise has clean, sizable rooms.

THE NOSE KNOWS

Top-end and some midrange hotels have smoking and nonsmoking floors. If you've got a nose for stale cigarette smoke, which has amazing endurance in the tropics, state your preference at the time of booking.

Exterior rooms pick up a lot of street noise but also garner a killer view of the circulating traffic around the train station.

NEW EMPIRE HOTEL Map pp284-5   Hotel $
☎ 0 2234 6990-6; fax 0 2234 6997; 572 Th Yaowarat; d 580-650B; ferry Tha Ratchawong, air-con bus 507, ordinary bus 73; 🅿
Near the Th Charoen Krung intersection and a short walk from Wat Traimit, New Empire has a central Chinatown location and pleasant 'deluxe' rooms. The standard rooms are home to many long-term Chinese Thai who use the common hallway as a living room for visiting, smoking and hanging up laundry.

RIVER VIEW GUEST HOUSE
Map pp284-5   Guesthouse $
☎ 0 2234 5429; fax 0 2237 5428; 768 Soi Phanurangsi, Th Songwat; d 450-800B; ferry Tha Si Phraya, ordinary bus 36 & 93; 🅿
River View has an awesome and affordable location in the Talat Noi area, between Silom and Chinatown, steps from the river. The fan rooms have the best view, but neither category is exceptionally clean. And if your room is too depressing, there is always the rooftop bar-restaurant to buoy your spirits.

River View is a tough one to find. Heading north on Th Charoen Krung from Th Si Phraya, take a left on to Th Songwat (before the Chinatown Arch), then the second left onto Soi Phanurangsi. You'll start to see signs at this point.

CHEAP SLEEPS
TT GUEST HOUSE
Map pp284-5   Guesthouse $
☎ 0 2236 2946; fax 0 2236 3054; 516-518 Soi Sawang, Th Maha Nakhon; d without bath 250-280B; ordinary bus 36 & 93
In a locals' neighbourhood, this family-run guesthouse is an easy walk to the train sta-

tion. Step through the gate into a shaded courtyard that is perfect for sipping coffee and thumbing through the newspaper. The rooms are clean with a few touches to stave off blandness. To get here from Th Phra Ram IV, follow Th Maha Nakhon underneath the expressway, turn left on Soi Sawang and follow it all the way to the end past the machine shops and deep-fry woks.

SIAM SQUARE & PRATUNAM

As central as Bangkok gets, this area is conveniently located on the Skytrain near shopping centres and loads of high-rise chains. In the midrange zone, a devoted cast of túk-túk and taxi drivers throng the entrances of hotels zealously pouncing on every map-toting victim. If you're a pedestrian wanderer, you'll be happier at a smaller hotel that is less of a target. Soi Kasem San 1, off Th Phra Ram I, has a cluster of nice guesthouses for the early-to-bed, early-to-rise travellers.

AMARI WATERGATE Map pp294-5   Hotel $
☎ 0 2653 9000; www.amari.com/watergate; 847 Th Phetburi; r US$100-250; Skytrain Chitlom, khlong taxi Tha Pratunam; 🅿 🖵 🖭
Right in the centre of Bangkok's Pratunam district, this chain hotel has large rooms, great views and is well situated for easy access to shopping centres and markets. The only trouble is it's a little bit of a hike to the nearest Skytrain station.

ASIA HOTEL Map pp294-5   Hotel $$
☎ 0 2215 0808; www.asiahotel.co.th; 296 Th Phayathai; s/d from 2500/3000B; Skytrain Ratchathewi; 🅿 🖭
Often a first stop for those new to Asia, this hotel is a reliable stand-by, but nothing to write home about. The superior and deluxe rooms have recently had a makeover, but the standard rooms need to hurry up and graduate. The lobby pantomimes luxury with faux chandeliers and polished granite floors, and a constant tide of guests fills the chamber with an ambient roar. It's connected by a covered walkway to the Skytrain station.

BANGKOK CITY INN Map pp294-5   Hotel $$
☎ 0 2253 5372; fax 0 2253 774; 43/5 Th Ratchadamri; r from 1200B; khlong taxi Tha Pratunam, Skytrain Chitlom; 🅿
A two-star poster child, Bangkok City Inn is luxury compared to a guesthouse but a flophouse compared to others. The twin beds are surprisingly comfortable, the baths are adequate, the air-con units wheezy, the staff large if not especially helpful. But to land a bed so close to the shopping centres that you can see their neon signs is a budgetary feat. Price includes breakfast.

Taxis have a tough time finding this place; it is in-between Khlong Saen Saeb and Big C, set back a few *soi* into the old shopping arcade.

CONRAD BANGKOK Map pp294-5   Hotel $$$
☎ 0 2690 9999; www.conradhotels.com; All Seasons Place, 87 Th Withayu; from US$175; Skytrain Ploenchit; 🅿 🖵 🖭
Contemporary but respectable, the Conrad is aimed at road warriors and jet-setters born after the baby boom. Thai silks and rust and ochre earth tones transform the rooms into minispas. Here the humble water closet has been transformed into fully fledged entertainment with an adjustable TV and in-room speakers, deep-soak tubs, rain-dispensing shower heads and a peek-a-boo window. The corner rooms aren't as impressive as all the buzz. The old-school cocktail lounge is a favourite with local cosmopolitans.

FOUR SEASONS HOTEL
Map pp294-5   Hotel $$$
☎ 0 2250 1000; www.fourseasons.com; 155 Th Ratchadamri; d from US$200; Skytrain Ratchadamri; 🅿 🖵 🖭
This is classic Thai architecture, with a spectacular traditional mural descending a grand staircase and neck-craning artwork on the ceiling. The lobby is library quiet despite the perpetual photo-op in front of the central mural. It should be noted, however, that rooms are almost dinosaur conservative and some are situated around an outdoor (un-air-conditioned) courtyard. Guests complain that the price tag doesn't match the product, while others counter that this is the only luxury hotel with in-room massages for late-night arrivals.

GRAND HYATT ERAWAN

Map pp294–5   Hotel $$$

☎ 0 2254 1234; www.bangkok.hyatt.com; 494 Th Ratchadamri; d from US$170; Skytrain Chitlom; �︎ 🖥 🚾

Inside this venerable hotel is a jungle atrium that erases urban fatigue. Rooms have hi-tech gadgets, such as reading lights that pull out of the wall and in-room temperature controls. European-style tubs with tall shower heads make the bathrooms fully functional. The rooms in the rear of the hotel overlook the prestigious Bangkok Royal Sports Club racetrack.

HOLIDAY MANSION HOTEL

Map pp294–5   Hotel $$

☎ 0 2255 0099; fax 0 2253 0130; 53 Th Withayu; s/d 2500/2700B; Skytrain Ploenchit; 🚫 🚾

One of the most affordable options for this high-powered district, the Holiday Mansion is a solid choice. The hulking concrete building has a pleasant interior courtyard pool and huge rooms, some of which have been recently renovated. The shops in front were recently replaced with an inviting bar and lounge, adding considerable charm to what was otherwise a rather plain affair. Price includes breakfast.

INTERCONTINENTAL BANGKOK

Map pp294–5   Hotel $$$

☎ 0 2656 0444; www.intercontinental.com, 973 Th Ploenchit; d from US$150; ste from US$250; Skytrain Chitlom; 🚫 🖥 🚾

This modern scraper is an upscale business option with all the extras to make leisure visitors content. The standard rooms have huge beds, marble bathrooms, separate bath and shower (tall enough for over-sized foreigners) and a work desk. Then there are the Club rooms that occupy dizzying heights and have their own reception room with complimentary nibbles.

NATURAL VILLE

Map pp294–5   Serviced Apartment $$$

☎ 0 2250 7000; www.naturalville.com; 61 Soi Lang Suan, Th Ploenchit; daily 3300B, per month 80,000-115,000B; Skytrain Ploenchit; 🚫 🖥 🚾

This swish spot fits right in with elegant Langsuan and its diplomatic neighbours. The one-bedroom apartments (75 sq metres) are big enough for you to spread

your wings in the City of Angels. The 52-sq-metre room is a little tight and warrants a nimble occupant. But all in all the monthly and even daily rates should wash away homesickness.

NOVOTEL BANGKOK ON SIAM SQUARE Map pp294–5   Hotel $$$

☎ 0 2209 8888; www.accorhotels.com; Soi 6, Siam Square; d from 4800B; Skytrain Siam; 🚫 🖥 🚾

Another convenient spot for business or leisure, Novotel is among Siam Square's shopping malls and a short hustle to the Skytrain station. This smart hotel is so familiar that you might forget you've travelled over an ocean or a continent. Rooms look exactly like high-end hotels back home.

PATHUMWAN HOUSE

Map pp294–5   Hotel $$

☎ 0 2612 3580; fax 0 2216 0180; 22 Soi Kasem San 1, Th Phra Ram I; d daily 1000-1400B, monthly 24,000-40,000B; Skytrain National Stadium; 🚫

Tucked back in the crook of the *soi*, this friendly high-rise is mainly a long-term hotel but lots of dailies cycle through after striking out elsewhere. Rooms are a decent size with a minibar and a generous bed. Standard rooms fringe a dark interior courtyard. Your comings and goings will be announced by a collection of chirping caged birds. The downstairs restaurant does one of the best brewed coffees in town.

RENO HOTEL Map pp294–5   Hotel $$

☎ 0 2215 0026; fax 0 2215 3430; 40 Soi Kasem San 1; d from 900B; Skytrain National Stadium; 🚫 🚾

This Vietnam War veteran is now an R&R option for the new millennium, where you can rest in simple rooms and recreate beside the pool. Any day now the smart retro look of the lobby is going to creep up the stairs and into the barracklike rooms. Then this will be a real war hero. Price includes breakfast.

SWISSÔTEL NAI LERT PARK

Map pp294–5   Hotel $$$

☎ 0 2253 0123; www.nailertpark.swissotel.com; 2 Th Withayu; d from US$200; Skytrain Ploenchit; 🚫 🖥 🚾

Aiming for the *Wallpaper* crowd, the newly renovated Nai Lert Park is a collision of styles, from the 1980s atrium to the chic modular rooms. But no matter how many shiny spangles they hang from the ceiling, the real draw is the jungle garden and shaded pool providing an instant remedy for jet lag.

VIP GUEST HOUSE/GOLDEN HOUSE

Map pp294-5   Hotel $$

☎ 0 2252 9535; www.goldenhouses.net; 1025/5-9 Th Ploenchit; d 1300B; Skytrain Chitlom; ✗
The shiny lobby of this small inn leads to rooms with mammoth-sized beds, parquet floors and a pleasant absence of the usual low-grade mistakes. The bathrooms, however, don't have tubs, only showers. VIP is down a little alley near the TOT office. Price includes breakfast.

CHEAP SLEEPS

A-ONE INN Map pp294-5   Guesthouse $

☎ 0 2215 3029; www.aoneinn.com; 25/13-15 Soi Kasem San 1; d 500-750B; Skytrain National Stadium; ✗
A small family operation, A-One has cosy and clean rooms with hardwood floors. Robin Hood, the resident dog who sports various T-shirts, now has partial ownership of the downstairs Internet café. A-One is also a wi-fi hotspot.

BED & BREAKFAST INN

Map pp294-5   Guesthouse $

☎ 0 2215 3004; Soi Kasem San 1; s/d 400/500B; Skytrain National Stadium; ✗
At the time of writing, Bed & Breakfast Inn was getting a cacophonous renovation, which might mean bigger and better rooms than before. Price includes breakfast.

WENDY HOUSE Map pp294-5   Guesthouse $$

☎ 0 2214 1149; www.wendyguesthouse.com; Soi Kasem San 1; d from 800-1000B; Skytrain National Stadium; ✗
This cheery place has small but well-scrubbed rooms and tiled baths. Rates have steadily climbed with the recent addition of a daily breakfast, so Wendy is slightly less than its former superb value. There are also a few too many rooms smelling of stale cigarettes (you can always ask for a better ventilated one). The desk staff are genuinely sweet and the well-lit lobby has daily newspapers, Internet access and informal swap talks.

SILOM, LUMPHINI & SATHON

A cluster of stylish high-end hotels occupy busy Th Sathon, near embassy row and several international office buildings.

From stylish to spinster, the hotels in Bangkok's primary business district are anything but carbon copies. Mainly business travellers, airline staff and other Bangkok vets stay in this area, but many first-time tourists come for the proximity to Patpong Market, Suan Lum and the river.

Parts of Silom are well served by Skytrain, which is a relief because traffic crawls day and night. Cars move faster along Sathon's multilane corridor lined by embassies and stylish hotels.

There are a few winners in the otherwise depressing backpacker haunt around Soi Ngam Duphli. As usage increases, any day now the convenient subway stop is going to bring big changes to this forgotten zone.

BANGKOK CHRISTIAN GUEST HOUSE

Map pp292-3   Guesthouse $$

☎ 0 2233 2206; www.bcgh.org; 123 Soi Sala Daeng 2, Th Convent; s/d/tr 1100/1500/1800B; Skytrain Sala Daeng, subway Silom; ✗
This Christian guesthouse is steps away from Patpong's strip clubs, proving that vice and morality are constant companions. The rooms are institutional but adequate and family-style meals provide fellowship as well as sustenance. A small outdoor playground is available. Price includes breakfast.

BANYAN TREE HOTEL

Map pp292-3   Hotel $$$

☎ 0 2679 1200; www.banyantree.com; Thai Wah II Bldg, 21/100 Th Sathon Tai; d US$180-350, ste US$900-1100; subway Lumphini; ✗ ▢ ▣
In a sleek wafer of a skyscraper, the Banyan Tree has translated the mood of a spa into a hotel, with the fragrance of gardenias, stairways in woodland colours and a sunken lobby next to a languid fountain-and-rock garden. The suites are magnificent, with separate work and sleep areas, two TVs and deep bathtubs. Families complain that all the stylish stairs aren't a good match for strollers and toddlers.

DUSIT THANI Map pp292-3   Hotel $$$

☎ 0 2200 9000; www.dusit.com; 946 Th Phra Ram IV; d US$210-300; Skytrain Sala Daeng, subway Silom; ⊠ ⊡ ⊡

Dusit Thani defined Bangkok glamour in the 1970s when it reigned as the city's tallest skyscraper. Much to everyone's shock, this conservative old gal has recently gone under the knife to be redesigned in the global Zen trend. Despite the identity crisis, this venerable hotel has an impressive tiered lobby encircling a lush garden and a buzz of excitement as Thais in their finest arrive and depart for wedding banquets or conferences.

FOR YOU RESIDENCE

Map pp290-1   Hotel $$

☎ 0 2635 3900; www.foryouresidence.com; 839 Th Silom; d 1400B; ferry Tha Oriental, Skytrain Chong Nonsi; ⊠

A classic example of Tinglish, this creatively named hotel is straightforward value with clean, nondescript rooms. It is a relative newcomer in the area and still scrubs in the corners.

LA RÉSIDENCE HOTEL

Map pp290-1   Hotel $$

☎ 0 2233 3301; residence@loxinfo.co.th; 173/8-9 Th Surawong; d 1700B; ste 2700B; Skytrain Chong Nonsi; ⊠

'Boutique' translates well into Thai. La Résidence is a charming boutique inn with playfully and individually decorated rooms. The standard room is very small and fittingly decorated like a child's bedroom with lavender and green tiling. The next size up is more mature and voluptuous, with blood-red walls and modern Thai motifs. The overall effect is casual sophistication for folks who feel itchy in corporate chains.

METROPOLITAN Map pp292-3   Hotel $$$

☎ 0 2625 3333; www.metropolitan.como.bz; 27 Th Sathon Tai, d from US$240; subway Lumphini; ⊠ ⊡

Young and trendy, the Metropolitan has been crowned Bangkok's *it* place for more than two years running. The techno-cool lobby leads to sleek modern rooms with white-on-black contrasts. This used to be the old YMCA building and the ghost of hostels past is still apparent in the cramped City rooms, where minimalist becomes torturous. But the bathroom is big enough for rock-star primping and the suites are more humane. No need to rush off to Sukhumvit to see the beautiful people: they'll come to you thanks to the two in-house restaurants (C'yan and Glow, p136) and the members-only bar (Met Bar).

MONTIEN HOTEL Map pp290-1   Hotel $$$

☎ 0 2233 7060; www.montien.com; 54 Th Surawong; s/d 3000/4000B; Skytrain Sala Daeng, subway Silom; ⊠ ⊡ ⊡

The old guard of Thai hotels, Montien receives patronage from the diplomatic corps as well as government functions. From the rooms on the south wing, you can get a view of blazing Patpong. This is not the height of fashion or luxury, but the desk staff is kind and the costumed door attendants are on the ball.

PAN PACIFIC Map pp292-3   Hotel $$$

☎ 0 2632 9000; www.panpacific.com; 952 Th Phra Ram IV; r from US$245; Skytrain Sala Daeng, subway Silom; ⊠ ⊡

Right at the mouth of Silom, Pan Pacific packages subdued luxury for the well-mannered elite. The atrium lobby starts on the 23rd floor and peers into Lumphini Park. The hallways are in an eternal twilight that soothes after Bangkok's sensory assault. The rooms are understated, almost forgettable, refreshingly spared from the modern trends. Superior rooms have a convenient dressing alcove between the bed and bathroom for those modest mouses.

SIRI SATHORN EXECUTIVE RESIDENCE

Map pp292-3   Serviced Apartment $$$

☎ 0 2266 2345; www.sirisathorn.com; 27 Soi Sala Daeng 1, Th Silom; daily from US$130, per month studio 65,000B, 1 bedroom 75,000-85,000B; Skytrain Sala Daeng, subway Silom; ⊠ ⊡ ⊡

Affiliated with the Sukhothai Hotel, this boutique executive residence offers stylish city roosts in the heart of the Silom business district. With great views, the accommodation feels more like an apartment; they even lack that sterile hotel smell. Studios are 57 sq metres and bedrooms are 60 to 95 sq metres.

SOFITEL SILOM BANGKOK

Map pp290-1   Hotel $$$

☎ 0 2238 1991; www.sofitel.com; 188 Th Silom;
r US$180; Skytrain Chong Nonsi; 🅿 🛗

Coffee and liqueur colours add a spike of
cool to this otherwise suburban-minded
hotel. Floor space in the standard rooms is
usurped by a colossal king-sized bed piled
high with a soft and fluffy duvet. Suites
allow for more energetic pacing. The 37th
floor V9 wine bar is currently riding the
citywide grape crush with city views and
affordable prices.

SUKHOTHAI HOTEL

Map pp292-3   Hotel $$$

☎ 0 2287 0222; www.sukhothai.com; 13/3 Th
Sathon Tai; d US$190, ste US$300; subway Lumphini; 🅿 🛗 🛗

Many luxury hotels try so hard to emulate
the West that they end up looking like
empty flatteries. Not the Sukhothai. This
one digs deep into the region's architectural heritage to capture a uniquely Thai
modernism. Named after Thailand's ancient
capital, the hotel evokes walking mandalas
of colonnaded antechambers and exterior
ponds of floating Buddha figures and brick
stupas. The rooms have lovely hardwood
floors and reasonably sized bathrooms.

SWISS LODGE Map pp290-1   Hotel $$$

☎ 0 2233 5345; www.swisslodge.com; 3 Th Convent; d 4000-5000B; Skytrain Sala Daeng, subway
Silom; 🅿 🛗 🛗

With only 57 rooms, Swiss Lodge is an
intimate inn with large-scale amenities.
Rooms are new, showers are tall, beds are
comfortable and the staff is on the mark.
Soundproof windows further enhance the

A pond outside Sukhothai Hotel

attraction for people doing business along
this busy corridor. Price includes breakfast.

TOWER INN Map pp290-1   Hotel $$

☎ 0 2237 8300-4; www.towerinnbangkok.com;
533 Th Silom; s/d 2000/2500B; Skytrain Chong
Nongsi; 🅿 🛗

There is so much going for this multistorey
hotel that it is hard to admit its weaknesses.
The pros are the location, top-floor beer
garden and glass-enclosed elevator with
street views. In the con category are the
inconsistent rooms that vary from average
to depressing. Want to feel good about this
showdown? Secure a powerful discount.

TRIPLE TWO SILOM Map pp290-1   Hotel $$$

☎ 0 2627 2222; www.tripletwosilom.com; 222 Th
Silom; r 4000B; Skytrain Chong Nonsi; 🅿

An old Silom shophouse has been tapped
by the contemporary-conversion wand to
create a new and improved boutique. Pan-
Asian styles tip-toe through modern colours
and old-timey photographs. The limited
number of rooms brings an intimacy that
nearby hotels can't provide. A swimming
pool and fitness centre are available for
guests at the sister property, the Narai Hotel.

CHEAP SLEEPS

MALAYSIA HOTEL Map pp292-3   Hotel $

☎ 0 2286 3582; fax 0 2287 1457; 54 Soi Ngam
Duphli; s 598-688B, d 698-788B; subway Lumphini;
🅿 🛗

This place was once Bangkok's most famous
budget travellers' hotel, but now it is more
popular as a gay pick-up scene. The superior
rooms, though, are cheery and cheap.

NIAGARA HOTEL Map pp290-1   Hotel $

☎ 0 2635 0676-85; 26 Soi 9, Th Silom; d 680B;
Skytrain Chong Nonsi; 🅿

From the outside, Niagara looks like another
shady no-tell motel, with a well-hidden car
park for midday breaks, but it's one of the
best bargains in Silom. The rooms are immaculate with gleaming white bathrooms
(the shower curtains are brand-spanking
new) and cleanliness even extends to the
regular changing of air-con filters, an otherwise foreign concept. The rock-hard bed is
graced with a plush comforter and a fresh
coat of paint brings cheer to the institutional

setting. A dubious perk is the three channels of 24-hour pornography.

PENGUIN HOUSE Map pp292-3 *Guesthouse $*
☎ 0 2679 9991; 27/23 Soi Sri Bamphen; r per night 750B, 2-night minimum; subway Lumphini
This new guesthouse has rooms big enough for a ping-pong game and real furniture with a hint of décor. Rooms in the back of the house will be quieter than streetside, and there are a couple of interior rooms that sleep two couples. Weekly and monthly rates are also available.

SALA THAI DAILY MANSION
Map pp292-3 *Guesthouse $*
☎ 0 2287 1431; sub-soi off Soi Sri Bamphen; d 300-500B; subway Lumphini
The youthful exuberance of this long-running guesthouse has begun to wane and the once social common spaces are now collecting piles of papers and bottles. But the basic rooms (shared bathrooms) are still clean and cheap. There is a small sitting area with a TV on the 3rd floor and a breezy rooftop terrace. Try the other guesthouses next door if Sala Thai doesn't suit you.

RIVERSIDE

A necklace of famous luxury hotels encircle the rim of the mighty Mae Nam Chao Phraya. This is romantic Bangkok, where old colonial buildings wilt under the elements and twinkling fairy lights reflect in the water. There are few real cheapies along the riverside, but we have listed the one that passes the mould-free test.

ORIENTAL HOTEL Map pp290-1 *Hotel $$$*
☎ 0 2659 9000; www.mandarinoriental.com; 48 Soi 38, Th Charoen Krung; d from US$250, ste from US$500; ferry Tha Oriental;
The 128-year-old Oriental Hotel is one of the most famous hotels in Asia and continues to cultivate respect as one of the region's best luxury hotels. The management prides itself on highly personalised service – once you've stayed here the staff will remember your name, what you like to eat for breakfast, even what type of flowers you'd prefer in your room.

Then there's the hotel's effervescent history of English tea and steamer travel. The original Author's Wing is a Victorian gingerbread confection with sepia-toned photographs of King Chulalongkorn. The rooms and suites in this wing are dedicated to the famous writers who bedded and penned in the Oriental (see the boxed text, below).

The modern River Wing, built in 1976, and the Tower, built in 1958, are the more imposing buildings, noticeable from the river, with contemporary Thai decorations, spacious bathrooms and river terraces. The Garden Wing retains the most old-fashioned glamour with parquet floors and drippy chandeliers.

PENINSULA HOTEL Map pp290-1 *Hotel $$$*
☎ 0 2861 2888; www.bangkok.peninsula.com; 333 Th Charoen Nakhon; d from US$200, ste from US$420; private ferry dock near the Oriental Hotel;
The Peninsula is world class, with all the international accolades to prove it. The lobby

FROM LITERATI TO GLITTERATI

Now a famous grand dame, the Oriental Hotel started its career as the seafarers' version of a Th Khao San guesthouse. The original owners, two Danish sea captains, traded the nest to Hans Niels Andersen, the founder of the formidable East Asiatic Company. Andersen transformed the hotel into a civilised palace of grand architecture and luxury standards. He hired an Italian architect, S Cardu, to design what is now the Author's Wing, which was the city's most fantastic building not constructed by the king.

The rest of the hotel's history relies on its famous guests. A Polish-born sailor named Joseph Conrad stayed here in 1888. The hotel brought him good luck: he got his first command on the ship *Otago*, from Bangkok to Port Adelaide, which in turn gave him ideas for several early stories. W Somerset Maugham stumbled into the hotel with an advanced case of malaria. In his feverish state, he heard the German manager arguing with the doctor about how a death in the hotel would hurt business. Maugham's overland Southeast Asian journey is recorded in *Gentleman in the Parlour: A Record of a Journey from Rangoon to Haiphong,* which gave literary appeal to the hotel. Other notable guests have included Noel Coward, Graham Greene, John le Carré, James Michener, Gore Vidal and Barbara Cartland. Some modern-day writers claim that an Oriental stay will overcome writer's block.

is poised and polished, an Asian-esque temple of squared black marble hallways and confident power players. Being on the Thonburi side of the river, the Peninsula faces Bangkok's best view of glowing skyscrapers. The tastefully decorated rooms and suites boast oversized executive work desks, private fax numbers, lots of techie gizmos and sweeping views of the city. The affiliated golf course and country club are also first rate.

ROYAL ORCHID SHERATON

Map pp290-1   Hotel $$$

☎ 0 2266 0123; www.starwoodhotels.com; 2 Soi Captain Bush, Th Si Phraya; d from US$150; ferry Tha Si Phraya; 🍴 🖳 🔁

Expansive and busy, the Sheraton is an equal-opportunity chameleon, easily morphing from business to leisure. Every room commands a river view, and the crisp, efficient service makes the guests feel like royalty. For discerning Asiana collectors, the hotel is next door to the River City shopping complex (p185).

Plant boxes decorate the façade of the Shangri-La Hotel

SHANGRI-LA HOTEL

Map pp290-1   Hotel $$$

☎ 0 2236 7777; www.shangri-la.com; 89 Soi Wat Suan Phlu, Th Charoen Krung; d from US$200, ste from US$300; ferry Tha Oriental, Skytrain Saphan Taksin; 🍴 🖳 🔁

The Shangri-La strives for an understated New Asia aesthetic with a lobby sheathed in floor-to-ceiling windows facing a tropical garden and the river beyond. It's within the luxury sphere, yet families won't feel like bulls in a china shop. The Krung Thep wing has terraces overlooking the river and is closer to the Skytrain than the main wing.

CHEAP SLEEPS
NEW ROAD GUESTHOUSE

Map pp290-1   Guesthouse $

☎ 0 2237 1094; fax 0 2237 1102; 1216/1 Th Charoen Krung; d 600B; ferry Tha Si Phraya 🍴

Sandwiched between the luxes, New Road is a friendly cheapie with clean, tiled rooms and compact bathroom. A comfortable downstairs sitting area collects all the guests in front of the communal TV.

TH SUKHUMVIT

Staying in this area puts you in the newest, most cosmopolitan part of Bangkok: modern, frivolous, international and frenetic. South of Soi Asoke (Soi 21) is the main tourist sector where you will encounter the offspring of the 1960s R&R days: sex tourism. North of Soi Asoke, the girlie bars begin to dissipate and are replaced with package-tour hotels. With the strengthening of the economy, the building boom has sprung to life once again, and each empty lot is rushing to fill its void with another condo skytower.

With the arrival of the Skytrain and the subway, you can now leapfrog over or under Sukhumvit's endless traffic jam to the long-distance bus stations as well as the train station.

BAAN THAI Map pp296-7   Hotel $$$

☎ 0 2258 5403, 0 2661 4051; www.thebaanthai .com; 7 Soi 32, Th Sukhumvit; r from US$265; Skytrain Phrom Phong, Thong Lor; 🍴 🖳 🔁

For Jim Thompson House fans, now there is a lodging equivalent – this former royal

THE PERILS OF ONLINE BOOKING   Karla Zimmerman

Neon bikinis: that's odd, we thought, as our taxi drove out of the snarled traffic on Th Sukhumvit and up to our hotel. The building across the street was bursting with women clad in glowing skimp-wear. German oom-pah songs wafted through the air, and advertisements for 'bratwursts' covered menu boards at the surrounding restaurants.

Yes, we were jet-lagged, having just spent 21 hours to reach Bangkok, and it was the middle of the night, when strange things tend to happen. But bratwursts and fluorescent bikinis?

We entered the hotel lobby, where Western men and young Thai women nuzzled on all the available couches. That's when the light bulb popped over our heads, and we realised our situation: the room we'd booked on the Internet – a room of 'luxurious comfort' with 'teakwood decorations and cable TV' – was located in a de facto brothel. We'd arrived at the Nana Entertainment Plaza.

A quick amble around the hotel grounds brought us to bars like Hollywood Strip (Pool! Shows! Girls! Darts!), Carnival (GoGo Girls, Girls, Girls!) and G-Spot (250 Girls Upstairs!). The latter's dancers made the neon-bikini group look practically Amish by comparison.

Despite the distraction of drinking one's beer and eating one's *phàt thai* in venues where most of the patrons were getting hand jobs, we appreciated our unplanned bite of this classic slice of Bangkok. Next time, though, we'll be more careful when booking online. While a hotel that touts 'easy access, 24 hours' can't be faulted for false advertising, it's wise to remember that words have multiple meanings.

palace has been converted into a 22-room luxury retreat. At the end of a brick *soi,* well shielded from modernity, Baan Thai is an idyllic garden of classical Thai houses, with peaked triangular roofs and trapezoidal frames. Every room smells of polished wood and is decorated with rich Thai silks. You could spend your entire stay here padding around all the cosy corners or sampling the wellness and spa features.

BANGKOK BOUTIQUE HOTEL

Map pp280-1   Hotel $$
☎ 0 2261 2850; www.bangkokboutiquehotel.com; 241 Soi Asoke, Th Sukhumvit; r from 2900B; subway Phetburi; ✸ ▯
Hip and modern, Bangkok Boutique Hotel has pioneered the outer reaches of Asoke with minimalist flair, and perhaps too much of it. The rooms are cramped and bare with new-fangled foam-core beds leaving only a sliver of floor space. Even in the farthest-flung room, some street noise from churning Asoke may creep in at all hours. The one plus is that a multitude of offices is nearby, making this boutique the closest bed for business. Price includes breakfast.

DAVIS   Map pp296-7   Hotel $$$
☎ 0 2260 8000; www.davisbangkok.net; Soi 24, Th Sukhumvit; d from US$100; Skytrain Phrom Phong, subway Sirikit Centre; ✸ ▯ ▩
The coolly sophisticated Davis is a peach of a place. Rooms are decorated in a global

sampling of regal themes: a Raj's palace, a Kyoto hermitage or a Burmese plantation. Born for the pages of *Architectural Digest,* the detached Thai wood villas are polished to a burnished gold, with deep sleigh beds and big sunny windows arranged around a private lap pool and garden.

FEDERAL HOTEL   Map pp296-7   Hotel $$
☎ 0 2253 0175; federalhotel@hotmail.com; 27 Soi 11, Th Sukhumvit; d from 950-1200B; Skytrain Nana; ✸ ▩
Club Fed, as the Pattaya crowd calls it, was once an R&R stop for American GIs and remains a Soi 11 fixture thanks to its honest rates, frangipani-lined swimming pool and time-warped coffee shop. Upstairs rooms are a bargain for the neighbourhood and have sunny windows and comfortable, if dated, furnishings. The ground levels, however, should be avoided as these occasionally flood in the rainy season and aren't worth the price.

JW MARRIOTT BANGKOK

Map pp296-7   Hotel $$$
☎ 0 2656 7700; www.marriott.com/bkkdt; 4 Th Sukhumvit at Soi 2; d from US$175, ste from US$275; Skytrain Nana; ✸ ▯ ▩
By far the best of Sukhumvit's business breed, JW Marriott pours an elixir of comfort and luxury for its international guests. A glass curtain separates you from the harsh tropical elements outside, and the

towering black-and-gold lobby creates the illusion of stepping inside a giant's lacquered wardrobe. Rooms get the royal treatment with king-sized beds, and the executive club has all the complimentary this and thats.

MAJESTIC GRANDE Map pp296-7 Hotel $$$
☎ 0 2262 2999; www.majesticgrande.com; 12 Soi 2, Th Sukhumvit; r from 5000B; Skytrain Nana; 🛇 🛋

The newborn sister property of Majestic Suites has location, style and good-value promotional rates. The lobby is a white echo-chamber hallway, better suited for high-heeled sashays to and fro than for tête-à-têtes. But once beyond the severe foyer, rooms and bathrooms are generous and sunny. A sauna and spa accompany the small swimming pool area should you need to augment your daily sweating.

MAJESTIC SUITES Map pp296-7 Hotel $$
☎ 0 2656 8220; www.majesticsuites.com; 110-110/1 Th Sukhumvit btwn Soi 4 & Soi 6; s/d 1165/1500B; Skytrain Nana; 🛇

Love-for-money is prevalent in this part of Th Sukhumvit, but Majestic's hermetically sealed rooms deliver privacy and quiet. The hotel is small and friendly and rooms that face Sukhumvit have a bird's-eye view of the street's traffic-snarled grandeur. Gym and pool facilities are available at the new sister property Majestic Grande (above).

PARK AVENUE @ 22 Map pp296-7 Hotel $$
☎ 0 2262 0000; www.hotelparkavenue.com; 30 Soi 22, Th Sukhumvit; r from 2700B; Skytrain Phrom Phong; 🛇 🛋

A palette of cocoa and black brings a splash of global Zen to Soi 22. Not quite the Park Avenue of international repute, this large hotel does a convincing job of acting like an intimate boutique. Bathrooms are pint sized. Price includes breakfast.

ROYAL ASIA LODGE & PARADISE
Map pp296-7 Hotel $$
☎ 0 2251 5514; www.royalasialodge.com; 91 Soi 8, Th Sukhumvit; d 1190B; ste 1400B; Skytrain Nana; 🛇 🛋

At the residential end of a typical Sukhumvit *soi*, petite Royal Asia has quiet, comfortable rooms well removed from the area's

constant hustle and bustle. The rooms are a little musty and the bathrooms are truly Thai (a shower means watering the whole room), but the desk staff are a spirited cheerleading squad of friendly greetings and chit-chat. A free shuttle service provides transport to Th Sukhumvit.

ST JAMES HOTEL Map pp296-7 Hotel $$
☎ 0 2261 0890; www.amari.com; 18 Soi 26, Th Sukhumvit; r from 2000B; Skytrain Phrom Phong; 🛇 🖳 🛋

Part of the Amari empire, the St James is a medium-sized number popular with Japanese businessmen. The lobby is a Zen waiting room of clean lines overlooking an attached garden of steroid-pumped house plants. Rooms are straightforward, with king-sized beds the most extravagant feature; the deluxe rooms get a desk. Bathrooms are true water closets (shut the door and there's the water).

SHERATON GRANDE SUKHUMVIT
Map pp296-7 Hotel $$$
☎ 0 2649 8888; www.sheratongrandesukhumvit .com; 250 Th Sukhumvit; r from US$165; Skytrain Asoke; 🛇 🖳 🛋

Competing with the Conrad and the Grand Hyatt Erawan to be the inner-city queen, the Sheraton relaxes corporate luxury travellers into cooing infants. Rooms come with either a city or lake view, the bathtubs are great and the sky-high pool is a jungle oasis.

SWISS PARK HOTEL Map pp296-7 Hotel $$
☎ 0 2254 0228; fax 0 254 0375; 155/23 Soi 11/1, Th Sukhumvit; s/d 1500/1700B; Skytrain Nana; 🛇

From the outside, Swiss Park looks like yet another sexpat flophouse. But this soot-stained tower is a diamond amid cubic zirconias. Buxom, sunlit executive rooms boast clean, presentable space with unintentionally retro furnishings and polished floors.

WESTIN GRANDE SUKHUMVIT
Map pp296-7 Hotel $$$
☎ 0 2651 1000; www.westin.com/bangkok; 259 Th Sukhumvit at Soi 19; r US$110-200; Skytrain Asoke; 🛇 🖳 🛋

Westin leads Sukhumvit's business pack with executive-strength rooms and a sky-high lobby. Unlike the rock-hard beds found in most Thai hotels, the Westin presents the trademarked 'Heavenly' beds, which are, as the name suggests, divinely soft and cosy. Bathrooms have separate bathtubs and showers with shower heads that are tall enough for the big-boned milk-fed crowd.

CHEAP SLEEPS

ATLANTA Map pp296-7   Guesthouse $
☎ 0 2252 6069, 0 2252 1650; fax 0 2656 8123; 78 Soi 2 (Soi Phasak), Th Sukhumvit; d from 700B; Skytrain Nana, Ploenchit; ⊠ ⊑
The oldest hotel in the Th Sukhumvit area, the Atlanta enjoys cultlike status with return budget travellers who shun the Banglamphu 'tourist' scene. The mid-century lobby, with its old-fashioned writing desks and a grand-entrance staircase, has been perfectly preserved from the days of pill-box hats and white gloves. And the jungle-landscaped pool provides those economy-class contortionists with opportunities for first-class lounging. The rooms have recently been gussied up with a new coat of paint, although the bathrooms could still use some work. The Atlanta

also sternly enforces a policy barring sex tourists.

This hotel was started as the Atlanta Club in the 1950s by Dr Max Henn, a former secretary to the Maharajah of Bikaner and owner of Bangkok's first international pharmacy.

MIAMI HOTEL Map pp296-7   Hotel $
☎ 0 2253 0369; fax 0 2253 1266; 2 Soi 13, Th Sukhumvit; d 750B; Skytrain Nana; ⊠ ⊑
This laissez-faire joint has changed very little since the days when the GIs ran wild in Bangkok, and it shows in the lumpy beds and rustic bathrooms. But the down-and-out charm has earned this place mythic status among folks who have spent too many hungover weekends watching war movies on TV or who claim to be collecting material for a 'novel'. Discounts are given for long-term stays should you join these lounge lizards.

SUK 11 Map pp296-7   Hostel $
☎ 0 2253 5927; www.suk11.com; sub-soi off Soi 11, Th Sukhumvit; dm 250B, s 450-500B, d 600-700; Skytrain Nana
Sukhumvit's primary outpost of backpacker culture, Suk 11 is tucked down a little

Lobby of the Atlanta

sub-*soi* off Soi 11, where you'll instantly feel that you've found a calm oasis amid the concrete jungle. The garden-guarded sitting area of rustic wooden furnishings is serenaded by tranquil tunes and maintains a postbeach after-glow. The upstairs rooms have been transformed from a bland shophouse into a funky Thai-style tree house with plank walkways and terracotta accents.

GREATER BANGKOK

If you're staying outside central Bangkok, choose a place near the Skytrain for zippy commutes. Options in Thonburi are less accessible but more local.

ARTISTS PLACE Map pp280-1   Guesthouse $

☎ 0 2862 0056, 0 2862 0074; artistsplace@hotmail.com; 63 Soi Thiam Bunyang, off Soi Krung Thonburi 1, Th Krung Thonburi; d 350-380B; Skytrain Saphan Taksin to bus 106

A whole lot of personality awaits you at this quirky spot in Thonburi. Charlee is your host and resident artist and staying at his home hardly feels like a business transaction. The rooms are basic but the space is inviting, with a rooftop sitting area and an artist's studio space. It is tricky to find, so call for help.

BANGKOK MARRIOTT RESORT & SPA

Map pp278-9   Hotel $$$

☎ 0 2476 0022; fax 0 2476 1120; 257/1-3 Th Charoen Nakhon; d from US$100, ste from $200; hotel shuttle boat from Tha Sathon & Tha Oriental; 🖾 🖳 🖳

Set amid the lushest landscaped gardens by the river, the Marriott Resort & Spa really is a place where you can get away from it all. Because it's situated downriver from the main action, it gives you the perfect excuse not to leave the divine poolside area.

REFLECTIONS ROOMS

Map pp278-9   Hotel $$

☎ 0 2270 3344, 0 2270 3359; www.reflections-thai.com; 81-83 Soi 7, Th Phahonyothin; d 2050-2600B; Skytrain Ari; 🖾 🖳 🖳

Well ain't you a treat amid all these soot-stained concrete boxes. All dolled up in visions of kitsch, Reflections is the best thing Bangkok has cooked up since lunch. Local designers were each assigned a room (30 in all) and all proceeded to go to town with brushes of whimsy, urbanity and straight-up cool. Reflections uses Starbucks sizing for its rooms: small is really big and large is really large. Browse the website to get a sneak preview of the rooms.

SLEEPING IN TRANSIT

By the time you read this, Bangkok may have finally opened its new Suvarnabhumi Airport and the **Novotel Suvarnabhumi Airport Hotel** (www.accorhotels-asia.com; Th Rachathewi, Bang Pli, Samut Prakan; d from 3600B), which is scheduled to open as this book goes to print, will be the closest option for airport lodging. But because deadlines are so very flexible for government contracts, we've provided options for good old Bangkok International Airport at Don Muang.

Amari Airport Hotel (Map pp278–9; ☎ 0 2566 1020; www.amari.com; 333 Th Choet Wutthakat; r US$200-350; 🖾 🖳) Directly across from Don Muang airport, this well-appointed hotel picks up most of the airport trade. If you're in transit, day-use rooms start at US$85.

Rama Gardens Hotel (Map pp278–9; ☎ 0 2561 0022; fax 0 2561 1025; 9/9 Th Vibhavadi Rangsit; r 2300-3500B; 🖾 🖳) Rama Gardens whisks transiting travellers away from the sterility of airport canisters to a tranquil garden setting. Rooms in the new deluxe wings are large with deep-soak tubs. Price includes breakfast. Shuttle buses make the 10-minute drive between the airport to pick-up and deliver guests.

We-Train International House (Map pp278–9; ☎ 0 2967 8550-4; www.we-train.co.th; 501/1 Muu 3, Th Dechatungkha, Sikan, Don Muang; dm 200B, r 740-1000B; 🖾 🖳) This quiet place 3km from the airport is run by the Association for the Promotion of the Status of Women, a nongovernment organisation that promotes women's rights and safety. The institutional hotel has nice rooms with bathroom, air-con and phone, plus a large pool and coffee shop. The best way to get here is by taxi (about 70B) from the front of the Amari Hotel, across the footbridge from the airport. Male guests are also welcome.

THAI HOUSE
Guesthouse $$

☎ 0 2903 9611; www.thaihouse.co.th; 32/4 Mu, 8 Tambon Bang Meuang, Bang Yai, Nonthaburi; s/d 1400B/1600B

This traditional Thai home, surrounded by fruit trees and river music, has been converted into a guesthouse far from Bangkok's urban snarl. The reception is warm and the setting old-fashioned Siam. There are no worries about searching for food: cooking courses are taught on the premises. Price includes breakfast. From Tha Chang, take a public boat to Bang Yai in Nonthaburi via Khlong Bangkok Noi. Once you reach the public pier in Bang Yai, charter a boat to Thai House's own pier – all the boat pilots know it.

Sleeping

GREATER BANGKOK

Excursions

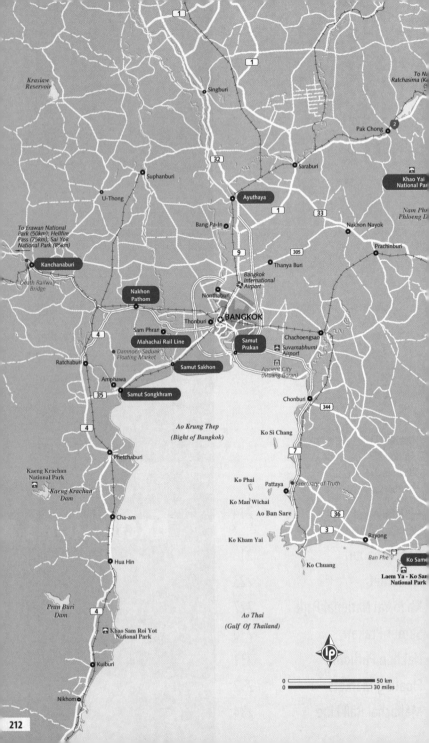

Excursions

Once you've forgotten what peace and quiet feels like, point yourself in either direction outside the capital to see the gentle side of Thailand. Overnight and day trips are all easily reached by public transport and give an interesting look at provincial Thailand, where fashion is dictated by the market racks, business signs aren't in English and children might be surprised to see a foreigner. In addition to their tourist attractions, these towns revolve around the local food markets – from the daytime produce markets for kitchen basics and takeaway food to the night markets for socialising and dining. Bangkok's outlying areas also have many theme parks and animal attractions that will entertain children sick of humouring their parents.

NATURE

Swim out of Bangkok's concrete bowl to fresh air, night-critter music and open vistas. Forested limestone ranges to the west and northeast are criss-crossed by swollen waterfalls in the wet season and stalked by jungle creatures when humans aren't looking.

To the northeast, the Dangrek Mountains geographically fuse Thailand and Cambodia and break the fertile central plains around Bangkok. Claiming this wooded landscape is **Khao Yai National Park** (p227), one of Thailand's biggest and best preserves. Its mountainous monsoon forests dress and undress with the comings and goings of the seasons and claim hundreds of resident species. Visitors can take quick dips into nature while staying at a nearby resort, playing golf and touring start-up wineries. But tree-huggers can fully commune with thick forests at rustic park shelters. Spotting the big game is rare, but waterfalls occupy the majority of nature-trippers' itineraries. Thais make quick in-and-out tours of cascades in between eating episodes. The Thais' penchant for fun is even more evident when mixed with fresh air and natural splendour.

West of Bangkok, limestone hills rise out of the sun-parched land like a great ruined city. **Kanchanaburi** (p218) is the best base for exploring this area of waterfalls, caves and tropical jungle. Bike rides will take you past shaggy fields of sugar cane being harvested by hand and lovingly tended spirit houses guarding uninhabited woods. Organised tours take visitors on whirlwind outings by land, water and rail. Incongruous with the peaceful natural setting is Kanchanaburi's unfortunate role in WWII as the site of a Japanese-run prisoner of war (POW) camp for Allied soldiers. Through this dramatic landscape the POWs were forced to build a supply railway. The remaining memorials to the men who died are touching examples of humanity's shared struggle against violence.

CULTURE

Thailand's heroic ancient capital, **Ayuthaya** (p214) is a Unesco World Heritage Site and a major pilgrimage site for anyone interested in Thai history. The remaining red-brick temples, which resisted the Burmese siege in the 18th century, are now resisting the pull of gravity. It is hard to imagine today, but this modern city of temple ruins was once a golden city that bewitched European traders in the heyday of the Asian trade route. Ayuthaya is also a popular spot for the celebration of Loi Krathong (see p217). Nearby Bang Pa-In, a royal summer palace, is a surviving homage to the world's architectural styles that convened near this port city.

The Ancient City, an architectural museum in **Samut Prakan** (p230), has reproduced Thailand's great monuments into a tastefully arranged park. Explorable by bicycle, the peaceful grounds and impressive structures will inspire further-flung excursions throughout the country.

Nakhon Pathom (p231) is believed to be the country's oldest city, as borne out by the presence of the world's tallest Buddhist monument, Phra Pathom Chedi, whose original structure dates to the 6th century.

Outside the capital, village life is still tied to the *khlong* (canals) and rivers that knit the land to the sea. Home stays and **floating markets** (p232) are among the tourist-ready routes for paddling into this world. The famous floating market at **Damnoen Saduak** (p232), although very touristy, makes for an easy journey to the riverine hinterlands. After a brief spin through the floating market, long-tail boats can also cruise the surrounding canals, which serve as primary arteries for their inhabitants.

BEACHES

With its emerald seas, languid breezes and blonde strips of sand, **Ko Samet** (p223) is an easy weekend getaway for urban warriors. Small bungalows dot the various bays, which are connected by footpaths traversing rocky outcrops. You can claim a piece of sand and watch the day expire, dine at beachside barbecues and listen to the music of the hidden insects.

JOURNEYS

Although slow going, the train to **Kanchanaburi** (p218) passes a steady parade of green fields, modest wooden huts, melancholy water buffalo and tiny villages seemingly swallowed up by the surrounding countryside. If you take the train beyond Kanchanaburi to Nam Tok, you travel over portions of the railway constructed by Allied POWs during their imprisonment in the Japanese forced-labour camp.

The galloping rhythm of the **Mahachai Rail Line** (p234) will take you straight to nowhere. The destinations, a string of gulfside towns where fish smells instead of smog fill the air, aren't nearly as interesting as watching the kids and grandmas struggle in and out of the train's metal canisters as the nearby jungle tries to gobble up the tracks.

AYUTHAYA

พระนครศรีอยุธยา

Ayuthaya, the lost city, the fallen city, the resurrected city. This mild-mannered modern town cocoons a dazzling past. Built at the confluence of three rivers (Chao Phraya, Pa Sak and Lopburi), this island city was the seat of the Siamese kingdom and dominated the region for 400 years. It was courted by foreign interests and extended its control deep into present-day Laos, Cambodia and Myanmar (Burma). Perhaps its strength derived from its auspicious namesake, Ayodhya (Sanskrit for 'unassailable' or 'undefeatable'), the home of Rama in the Indian epic Ramayana.

Such an immortal name invited disaster. European companies conspired with and against each other to control trade with Ayuthaya. In the late 17th century, a Greek advisor to King Narai even plotted an unsuccessful coup. But it was the Burmese who, after several attempts, eventually conquered and destroyed the city in 1767 astride their battle-trained elephants. The surviving Thai army fled south to re-establish control in Thonburi.

The famed capital suffered greatly at the hands of the invading Burmese army. Many of the city's temples were levelled, and the sacred Buddha figures were decapitated as if they were enemy combatants. Although Thailand's Fine Arts Department has done extensive restoration work on the ancient capital, it is still rare to find an unscarred Buddha amid Ayuthaya's ruins.

What Ayuthaya lacks in preservation it makes up for with its rich history. This was no place for obscure kings cloaked in untranslatable myths; Ayuthaya was a cosmopolitan centre complete with well-documented political intrigue. Its proximity to Bangkok allows for a day's shot of culture and history with a painless return home.

Getting a handle on the religious and historical importance of the temples is difficult without some preliminary research. **Ayuthaya Historical Study Centre** has informative, professional displays that paint a clear picture of the ancient city. Also purchase the Ayuthaya pamphlet for sale at Wat Phra Si Sanphet's admission kiosk for post-ruins reading. Other museums in town include **Chao Sam Phraya National Museum**, which features a basic roundup of Thai Buddhist

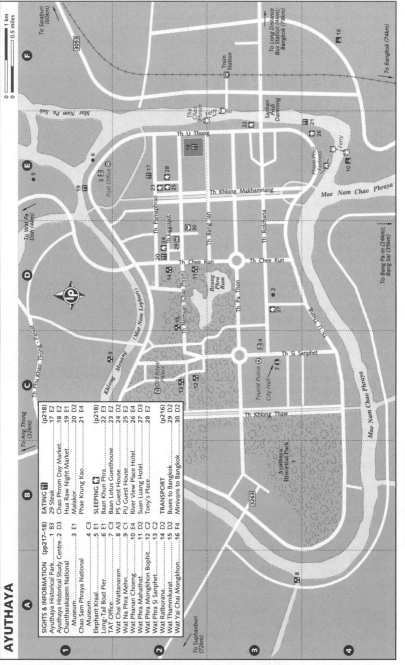

www.lonelyplanet.com

AYUTHAYA

sculpture with an emphasis on Ayuthaya pieces, and **Chantharakasem National Museum**, which is a museum piece in itself. Chantharakasem was built by the 17th king of Ayuthaya, Maha Thammaracha, for his son Prince Naresuan, who later became one of Ayuthaya's greatest kings and ruled from 1590 to 1605. Among the exhibits is a collection of gold treasures from Wat Phra Mahathat and Wat Ratburana.

AYUTHAYA HISTORICAL PARK

The Ayuthaya Historical Park is separated into two geographical districts. Ruins 'on the island', in the central part of town west of Th Chee Kun, are best visited on bicycle or motorbike; those 'off the island', opposite the river from the centre, are best visited on an evening boat tour. You can also take a bicycle across the river by boat from the pier near Phom Phet fortress, inside the southeast corner of the city centre.

On the Island

Wat Phra Si Sanphet was once the largest temple in Ayuthaya and was used as the royal temple-palace by several kings. Built in the 14th century, the compound contained a 16m standing Buddha coated with 250kg of gold, which was melted down by the Burmese conquerors. It is mainly known for the *chedi* (stupas) erected in the Ayuthaya style, which has come to be identified with Thai art more than any other style. The adjacent **Wat Phra Mongkhon Bophit**, which dates to the 1950s, houses a huge bronze seated Buddha, the largest in Thailand.

Ancient stone chedi *(stupa) at Wat Phra Si Sanphet*

Wat Phra Mahathat, on the corner of Th Chee Kun and Th Naresuan, has one of the first *prang* (Khmer-style tower) built in the capital. One of the most photographed sites in Ayuthaya is a Buddha head engulfed by

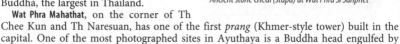

TRANSPORT

Distance from Bangkok 85km

Direction North

Travel Time Two hours by bus; 1½ hours by train

Bus 1st-class air-con (72B) and 2nd-class air-con (61B) buses depart Bangkok's Northern & Northeastern Bus Terminal (also called Mo Chit; Map pp278–9) to Th Naresuan in Ayuthaya every 20 minutes between 5am and 7pm. On Th Naresuan in Ayuthaya, a minivan service shuttles passengers to and from Bangkok's Northern & Northeastern Bus Terminal (65B, every 20 minutes from 5am to 5pm).

Train North-bound trains leave from Bangkok's Hualamphong station (Map pp284–5) roughly every 30 minutes between 6.20am and 9.30am, and 6pm and 10pm. The 3rd-class fare is 20B. From Ayuthaya's train station, the quickest way to reach the city is to walk straight west to the river, where you can take a short ferry ride (3B) across to Tha Chao Phrom. Alternatively, a túk-túk to any point in old Ayuthaya should be around 30B to 40B. You can also take the train from Bangkok's Don Muang airport to Ayuthaya (20B to 40B) roughly every hour from 6am to 9am and 3pm to 10pm.

Boat Many boat companies in Bangkok offer scenic boat tours to Ayuthaya; see p72 for more information.

Getting Around Guesthouses rent bicycles for 50B per day or motorcycles for 250B per day; túk-túk tours cost 200B per hour.

LOI KRATHONG: GIVING THANKS TO THE RIVER

Ayutthaya holds one of the country's largest Loi Krathong festivals (a lunar holiday held on the full moon of the 12th lunar month, usually November), in which small boats are launched into waterways in honour of the river goddess. This is a perfect opportunity to give your *kràthong* (small lotus-shaped floats made from banana leaves and topped with incense, flowers, coins and candles) a more provincial send-off far from Bangkok's stinky canals.

Ayutthaya's celebrations vary from quiet, family-friendly events to rollicking live music shows. A full army of food vendors covers every available corner. The highlight of the festival is the launching of *kràthong* out into the junction of the Lopburi and Pa Sak rivers. *Kràthong* can be purchased at the pier, or you can make your own from materials for sale. Thai tradition says that any couple who launch a *kràthong* together are destined to be lovers – if not in this lifetime then the next.

Other events include outdoor stages offering *lí-keh* (folk plays with dancing and music), Thai pop, cinema and *lákhon chaatrii* (dance-drama) all at the same time – the din can be deafening! Fireworks are also a big part of the show.

At the **Bang Sai Royal Folk Arts & Crafts Centre** (☎ 0 3536 6252; 24km west of Ayutthaya; admission 100B) and at **Bang Pa-In** (see p218) festivities centre on traditional costumes and handmade *kràthong*.

---

fingerlike tree roots. Across the road, **Wat Ratburana** contains *chedi* and murals that are not quite as dilapidated.

Neighbouring **Wat Thammikarat** features overgrown *chedi* ruins and lion sculptures.

Off the Island

Southeast of town on Mae Nam Chao Phraya, **Wat Phanan Choeng** was built before Ayutthaya became a Siamese capital. The temple's builders are unknown, but it appears to have been constructed in the early 14th century, so it's possibly Khmer. The main *wíhăan* (central sanctuary) contains a highly revered 19m sitting Buddha image from which the wat derives its name. The temple is dedicated to Chinese seafarers involved in the Thai-Chinese trade route during Ayutthaya's heyday, and on weekends it is crowded with Buddhist pilgrims from Bangkok who pay for lengths of saffron-coloured cloth to be ritually draped over the image.

The ruined Ayutthaya-style tower and *chedi* of **Wat Chai Wattanaram**, on the western bank of Mae Nam Chao Phraya, have been restored. Photographers favour this spot at sunset.

Wat Yai Chai Mongkhon is southeast of the town proper, and can be reached by white-and-green minibus 6. It's a quiet place built in 1357 by King U Thong and was once famous as a meditation centre. The compound contains a very large *chedi*, and a community of *mâe chii* (Buddhist nuns) resides here.

North of the city, the **Elephant Kraal** is a restoration of the wooden stockade once used for the annual roundup of wild elephants. A huge fence of teak logs planted at a 45-degree angle enclosed the elephants. The king had a raised observation pavilion for the thrilling event.

North of the old royal palace *(wang lŭang)* grounds is a bridge to **Wat Na Phra Mehn**. This temple is notable because it escaped destruction in the 1767 Burmese capture, though it has required restoration over the years. The main *bòt* (central chapel) was built in 1546 and features fortresslike walls and pillars. During the 18th-century Burmese invasion, Burma's King Along Phaya chose this site to fire a cannon at the palace; the cannon exploded and the king was fatally injured, thus ending the sacking of Ayutthaya. The *bòt* interior contains an impressive carved wooden ceiling and a splendid 6m-high sitting Buddha in royal attire. (The figure's ornate clothing is an artistic characteristic unique to the Ayutthaya period; other representations of Buddha typically depict monastic robes.) Inside a smaller *wíhăan* behind the *bòt* is a green-stone, European-pose (sitting in a chair) Buddha from Ceylon, said to be 1300 years old. The walls of the *wíhăan* show traces of 18th- or 19th-century murals.

Information & Sights

Ayutthaya Historical Park At many of the ruins a 30B admission fee is collected from 8am to 6.30pm.

Ayutthaya Historical Study Centre (☎ 0 3524 5124; Th Rotchana; adult/student 100/50B; 9am-4.30pm Mon-Fri, 9am-5pm Sat & Sun)

Chantharakasem National Museum (☎ 0 3525 1586; Th U Thong; admission 30B; 9am-4pm Wed-Sun) Northeast corner of town.

Chao Sam Phraya National Museum (☎ 0 3524 1587; Th Rotchana & Th Si Sanphet; admission 30B; 9am-4pm Wed-Sun)

BANG PA-IN
บางปะอิน

This postcard-perfect palace lies just 24km south of Ayuthaya. A hodgepodge of international architectural styles reflects the eclectic tastes of Rama IV (King Mongkut; r 1851–68) and his son and heir Rama V (King Chulalongkorn; r 1868–1910), who both used the residence as a retreat from the summer rains. The winged-eaved Thai-style pavilion, the ornate Chinese-style Wehat Chamrun Palace and a Swiss chalet mansion (the preferred residence of Rama V) are all on display. A flamboyant lookout tower (Withun Thatsana) gave the king fine views over the gardens and lakes.

Bang Pa-In can be reached by blue săwngthăew (pick-up truck, 13B, 45 minutes) from Ayuthaya's Chao Phrom Market (Map p215) on Th Naresuan. From Bangkok there are buses (50B) every half-hour from the Northern & Northeastern Bus Terminal (Mo Chit; Map pp278–9). You can also reach Bang Pa-In by two morning trains from Bangkok (3rd class, 12B). Tour groups love Bang Pa-In, so try to visit later in the day.

Chao Phraya Express Boat (☎ 0 2623 6001; tour 430B; 8am-5.30pm) does a tour every Sunday from Tha Maharat (Map p288) in Bangkok to Bang Pa-In and Bang Sai's Royal Folk Arts & Crafts Centre.

Long-tail boat trip (2hr evening trip 500B) You can complete a semicircular tour of the island and see some of the less accessible ruins, which include Wat Phanan Choeng and Wat Chai Wattanaram, as well as river life. PU Guest House arranges tours or you can hire a boat at the pier.

Tourist Authority of Thailand (TAT; ☎ 0 3524 6076; 108/22 Th Si Sanphet; 9am-5pm) Now occupying a larger facility, TAT provides maps, bus schedules and information about Loi Krathong festivities.

Eating

29 Steak (Th Pamaphrao; dishes 35-90B; 3.30-11pm) When slathered with chilli sauce, steak is given a lifetime visa to Thai culinary circles, judging by the local clientele.

Hua Raw Night Market & Chao Phrom Day Market (Th U Thong) These markets are the highlight of Ayuthaya noshing.

Malakor (Th Chee Kun; dishes 50-100B) Opposite Wat Ratburana, this restaurant is located in a two-storey wooden house with a charming dinnertime view of the dramatically lit temple. It has Westernised Thai dishes, plus an excellent selection of coffees.

Phae Krung Kao (Th U Thong; dishes 60-100B; 10am-2am) On the southern side of the bridge, this floating restaurant is so popular that Thai locals even rouse their geriatric grandmas for a night out.

Sleeping

Keep an eye out for the newest guesthouse in town for better quality and promotional rates.

Baan Khun Phra (☎ 0 3524 1978; 48/2 Th U Thong; dm/s/d 150/250/350B) This genteel old teak house is the most atmospheric place in town with a prime riverfront location and breezy rooms. There is also a four-bed dorm. Rooms come with ceiling fans and shared bathroom.

Baan Lotus Guest House (☎ 0 325 1988; 20 Th Pamaphrao; r 300B) A restored teak house with simple rooms overlooking a lotus pond.

PS Guest House (☎ 0 6334 7207; 23/1 Th Juggrapot; d 120-180B) On a back road parallel to Th Naresuan and off Th Chee Kun, this quirky place has odd-sized rooms in a two-storey house surrounded by a quiet neighbourhood. The manager and staff speak English well. Bathrooms are shared.

PU Guest House (☎ 0 3525 1213; 20/1 Soi Thaw Kaw Saw, off Th Naresuan; d from 300B) At the end of the soi, this well-run spot has massive amounts of tourist information, clean rooms with varying amenities, and a friendly café.

River View Place Hotel (☎ 0 3524 1444; 35/5 Th U Thong; d from 2800B;) Great river views, as the name suggests, and spacious rooms; book through an agent for discounts.

Suan Luang Hotel (☎ /fax 0 3524 5537; Th Rotchana; d 500-600B;) This five-storey hotel has passable air-con rooms with fridge, TV and private bathrooms. The hotel functions as a training facility for students doing tourism majors at the neighbouring Rajabhat University.

Tony's Place (☎ 0 3525 2578; Soi Thaw Kaw Saw, off Th Naresuan; d 180-450B) Tony's is a sprawling establishment with an energetic party atmosphere and busy patio restaurant and bar. Rooms are dependable, and some have balconies.

KANCHANABURI
อ.เมืองกาญจนบุรี

Leafy Kanchanaburi (pronounced 'kan-cha-na-buri') is a refreshing retreat from city life. It is gingerly embraced by craggy limestone mountains and groomed with sugar-cane plantations. Riverside guesthouses specialise in the art of relaxing after a day of sightseeing in the scenic countryside. In fact, Kanchanaburi provides a better retreat into provincial Thailand than over-stimulated Ayuthaya.

The peaceful setting belies the town's tragic role in WWII as a Japanese-run POW camp. Many soldiers were worked to death building the now-notorious Death Railway, immortalised in the famous war-era book and movie that were set on the River Kwai (Mae Nam Khwae). Many visitors come here specifically to pay their respects to the fallen POWs at the Allied cemeteries and to photograph the otherwise unspectacular bridge. You can set your watch by the arrival of the package tourist buses, carrying Chinese or Japanese tourists, blazing through the major war sites before hurrying off to the nearby sapphire mines.

Don't be fooled by Kanchanaburi's sleepy daytime demeanour. The tranquil river blazes through the night with all-night disco and karaoke barges popular with van tours from Bangkok. Out-of-tune crooners and shoddy stereo systems disrupt the calm that many travellers are hoping to find at guest-houses along the riverside. Sometimes Asia needs a mute button.

Kanchanaburi was originally established by Rama I (King Buddha Yodfa; r 1782–1809) as a first line of defence against the Burmese who, it was commonly believed, might use the old invasion route through the Three Pagodas Pass on the Thai–Burmese border. The pass is still a popular smuggling route into Myanmar today.

During WWII, the Japanese used Allied POWs to build the **Death Railway** along this same invasion route, though in reverse, along Mae Nam Khwae Noi (Small Kwai River) to the pass. Carving a rail bed out of the 415km stretch of rugged terrain was a brutally ambitious plan

TRANSPORT

Distance from Bangkok 130km

Direction West

Travel Time 1½ to three hours

Bus Regular buses leave from the Southern Bus Terminal (Map pp278–9) in Thonburi (air-con 100B, every 20 minutes until 7pm) to Kanchanaburi's bus station off Th Saengchuto.

Train Kanchanaburi is a stop on the scenic but slow Bangkok Noi–Nam Tok line. The train leaves from Bangkok Noi station (Map p288) in Thonburi twice a day (7.45am and 1.50pm, 30B) and stops at Kanchanaburi's train station, just off Th Saengchuto. To return to Bangkok, there is one morning and one afternoon departure.

Getting Around Kanchanaburi is very accessible by bicycle; you can hire bikes at most guesthouses (50B per day). For areas outside of town, rent a motorcycle (150B to 200B per day) from the Suzuki dealer near the bus terminal. Săamláw within the city cost 30B a trip. Regular săwngthăew (5B) cruise Th Saengchuto, but be careful you don't accidentally charter one all for yourself.

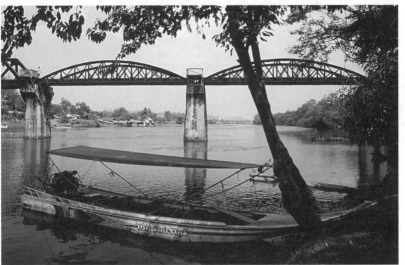

Death Railway Bridge (p221) across Mae Nam Khwae, Kanchanaburi

intended to meet an equally remarkable goal of providing an alternative supply route for the Japanese conquest of Myanmar and other countries to the west. Japanese engineers estimated that the task would take five years. But the railway was completed in a mere 16 months entirely by forced labour, either captured Allied soldiers or Burmese and Malay prisoners, with minimal machines and nutrition. A Japanese brothel train inaugurated the line.

Close to 100,000 labourers died as a result of the hard labour, torture or starvation; 16,000 of them were Western POWs, mainly from Britain and the Netherlands. The POWs' story

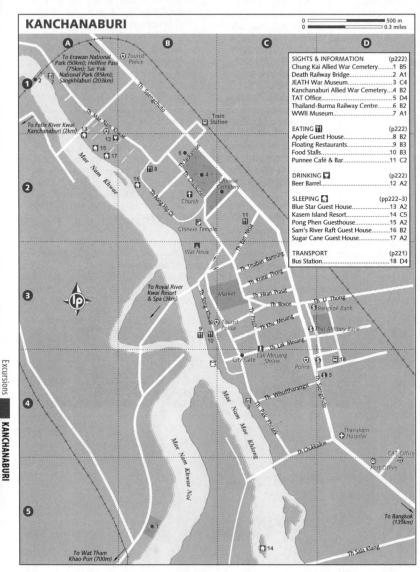

KANCHANABURI

SIGHTS & INFORMATION	(p222)
Chung Kai Allied War Cemetery	1 B5
Death Railway Bridge	2 A1
JEATH War Museum	3 C4
Kanchanaburi Allied War Cemetery	4 B2
TAT Office	5 D4
Thailand-Burma Railway Centre	6 B2
WWII Museum	7 A1

EATING	(p222)
Apple Guest House	8 B2
Floating Restaurants	9 B3
Food Stalls	10 B3
Punnee Café & Bar	11 C2

DRINKING	(p222)
Beer Barrel	12 A2

SLEEPING	(pp222–3)
Blue Star Guest House	13 A2
Kasem Island Resort	14 C5
Pong Phen Guesthouse	15 A2
Sam's River Raft Guest House	16 B2
Sugar Cane Guest House	17 A2

TRANSPORT	(p221)
Bus Station	18 D4

was chronicled in Pierre Boulle's book *The Bridge on the River Kwai* and popularised by a movie based on the book.

Perhaps because of the catchy title, the **Death Railway Bridge** across Mae Nam Khwae is one of Kanchanaburi's most popular attractions, despite its rather unspectacular appearance (yup, that's a bridge). Actually the structure that has posed for a million tourist snapshots is a postwar reconstruction; the original was bombed in 1945 by Allied planes after it had been in use for 20 months. Only the curved portions of the bridge are original.

Not an essential stop, the **WWII Museum** next to the bridge has a picture-postcard view of the bridge as well as an odd assortment of war and peace memorabilia.

As for the Death Railway, only a small portion remains, as much of the original track was carted off by Karen and Mon tribespeople for use in the construction of local buildings and bridges. A railway line travels part of the original route from Kanchanaburi west to the village of Nam Tok, across Mae Nam Khwae. Trains depart Kanchanaburi at 10.50am for the two-hour trip to Nam Tok, where you'll have a 20-minute layover before the last departure back to Kanchanaburi.

Before you trek out to the Death Railway Bridge, get a little history under your belt at the **Thailand-Burma Railway Centre** and the Kanchanaburi Allied War Cemetery. Exhibits outline Japanese aggression in Southeast Asia during WWII and Japan's plan to connect Rangoon (Yangon), in Myanmar, with Bangkok via rail for transport of military supplies. Across the street from the centre, the **Kanchanaburi Allied War Cemetery** is the final resting place of only a small portion of the total number of prisoners who died during the construction of the railway. Lovingly tended, the cemetery is a touching gift from the Thai people to the countries whose citizens died on their soil.

Another less visited cemetery, **Chung Kai Allied War Cemetery**, is a short and scenic bike ride from central Kanchanaburi. As in the more visited cemetery in town, the Chung Kai burial plaques carry names, military insignia and short epitaphs for Dutch, British, French and Australian soldiers.

If you still have emotional energy, the **JEATH War Museum** is a heartfelt testament to the atrocities of war. The museum operates in the grounds of a local temple and has reconstructions of the bamboo huts that were used by the POWs as shelter. The long huts contain various photographs taken during the war, drawings and paintings by POWs, maps, weapons and other war memorabilia. The acronym JEATH represents the fated meeting of Japan, England, Australia/America, Thailand and Holland at Kanchanaburi during WWII.

Viewing the bridge and museums doesn't quite communicate the immense task of bending the landscape with human muscle. A better glimpse comes from a visit to **Hellfire Pass Memorial**, an Australian-Thai Chamber of Commerce memorial dedicated to the POW labourers, 75km north of Kanchanaburi. A crew of 1000 prisoners worked night and day for 12 weeks to cut a pass through the mountainous area dubbed Hellfire Pass. Nearly 70% of the crew died in the process. A memorial museum and walking trail remembers their work and lives.

The limestone hills surrounding Kanchanaburi are famous for their temple caves, an underground communion of animistic spirit worship and traditional Buddhism. Winding arteries burrow into the guts of the caves past bulbous calcium deposits and altars for reclining or meditating Buddhas, surrounded by offerings from pilgrims. An easy bike ride from town, **Wat Tham Khao Pun** is one of the closest cave temples, and is safe to visit despite its tragic past. This temple was the site of the 1995 murder of a British tourist by a drug-addicted monk living at the wat. Kanchanaburi residents, like the rest of Thailand, were mortified by the crime, and many now refer to the cave as 'Johanne's Cave' in memory of the victim.

KANCHANABURI KNOWLEDGE

Try as you might, you will find few Thais who have ever heard of the River Kwai. The river over which the Death Railway trundled is pronounced locally like 'quack' without the '-ck'. If spelled phonetically, 'Kwai' should be 'Khwae'. In the mispronounced river live *plaa yĩisòk*, the most common edible fish in this area and the model for the city's attractive fish-shaped street signs.

The monk was defrocked and sentenced to death (commuted to life imprisonment without parole by the king in 1996).

There are several other temples with various tourist attractions: monks tending tigers or floating nuns. Tour operators usually include a stop at whichever spot has the most inquirers.

Northwest of Kanchanaburi town is the area's natural playground. **Erawan National Park** sports a watery mane of waterfalls visited by locals and tourists for a day trip of photographs, picnics and swimming. **Sai Yok National Park** has more variety: waterfalls, limestone caves, hot springs and accommodation. Tour organisers in Kanchanaburi arrange day outings to these parks on various expeditions: river kayaking, elephant trekking, waterfall spotting and bamboo rafting – you name it, Kanchanaburi has it.

Information & Sights

Chung Kai Allied War Cemetery (admission free; ☺ 7am-6pm) Three kilometres from the TAT office. From Th Lak Meuang, take the bridge across the river through picturesque corn and sugar-cane fields until you reach the cemetery on your left.

Death Railway Bridge Two kilometres from town. Best visited by bicycle, following the river north. You can also travel over the bridge by train en route to Nam Tok (see the boxed text, p219).

Erawan National Park (☎ 0 3457 4222; admission 200B; ☺ 8am-4pm)

Hellfire Pass Memorial (Rte 323; ☺ sunrise-sunset)

JEATH War Museum (Th Pak Phraek; admission 30B; ☺ 8.30am-6pm) The war museum is at the end of Th Wisuttharangsi (Visutrangsi), near the TAT office. The common Thai name for this museum is *Phíphítháphan Songkhram Wát Tâi* (Wat Tai War Museum).

Kanchanaburi Allied War Cemetery (Th Saengchuto; admission free; ☺ 7am-6pm) It's just around the corner from the riverside guesthouses, or you could catch a săwngthăew or orange minibus 2 anywhere along Th Saengchuto going north – the fare is 5B.

Sai Yok National Park (admission 200B)

TAT office (☎ 0 3451 1200; Th Saengchuto; ☺ 8.30am-4.30pm) Provides a great provincial map with information about trips outside Kanchanaburi, as well as bus and train schedules. It's near the bus terminal.

Thailand-Burma Railway Centre (☎ 0 3451 0067; 73 Th Jaokannun; adult/child 60/30B; ☺ 9am-5pm)

Wat Tham Khao Pun (admission by donation; ☺ 7am-4pm) This temple is about 4km from the TAT office and 1km southwest of the Chung Kai cemetery across the railroad tracks and midway up the hill. It's best reached by bicycle.

WWII Museum (Th Mae Nam Khwae; admission 30B; ☺ 9am-6pm) Near the Death Railway Bridge; best reached by bicycle.

Eating & Drinking

Apple Guest House (☎ 0 3451 2017; Th Rong Hip Oi; dishes 50-120B; ☺ 8am-10pm) This guesthouse restaurant introduces newcomers to Thai food without being condescending. Both the *kaeng mátsàmàn* (Muslim-style curry) and *phàt thai* (rice noodles stir-fried with egg, tofu and peanuts) are highly recommended.

Beer Barrel (Th Mae Nam Khwae; ☺ 6pm-midnight) Deep in a thicket of trees, this mazelike bar of gigantic wooden tables is a soothing elixir after a day of doing nothing.

Floating restaurants (Th Song Khwae; dishes 100-200B; ☺ 6-11pm) Down on the river are several large floating restaurants where the quality of the food varies but it's hard not to enjoy the atmosphere. Most cater to Thais out for a night of drinking and snacking.

Food stalls (Th Song Kwae; dishes 30-60B; ☺ 6-11pm) Opposite the floating restaurants are some restaurants that are just as good but less expensive. This is where the bus drivers grab a meal while waiting for their tour groups to return.

Punnee Café & Bar (☎ 0 3451 3503; Th Ban Neua; dishes 50-180B) A local legend, Punnee serves decent Western breakfast and advertises the coldest beer in town. Lots of information on Kanchanaburi is available here.

Sleeping

The most scenic places to stay are the floating guesthouses along the river, but these are also the loudest, thanks to the nightly disco and karaoke barges. A pair of good earplugs and a night of imbibing will help to block out the bass sounds. A săamláw (three-wheeled pedicab) or motorcycle taxi from the bus or train stations to the river area and most guesthouses should cost from 20B to 30B.

Blue Star Guest House (☎ 0 3451 2161; off Th Mae Nam Khwae; d 150-600B; ⚒) The interior rooms have funky décor with faux stones that line the walls. A wooden boardwalk leads to the interesting options of A-frame stilted tree houses reminiscent of an Ewok village.

Kasem Island Resort (☎ 0 3451 3359, in Bangkok 0 2255 3604; d 750-1250B; ⚒ ⚑) Sitting on an island in the middle of Mae Nam Mae Khlong, about 200m from Th Chukkadon, Kasem Island Resort has tastefully designed thatched cottages and house rafts. There are facilities for swimming, fishing and rafting, as well as an outdoor bar and restaurant. The resort has an office near Tha Chukkadon where you can arrange a free shuttle boat out to the island.

Pong Phen Guesthouse (☎ 0 3451 2981; 5 Soi Banglated, Th Mae Nam Khwae; d 230-280B; 🔀) These modern rooms set in a lush garden have more creature comforts than most budget options.

Royal River Kwai Resort & Spa (☎ 0 3465 3297; Th Kanchanaburi-Sai Yok; d from 1400B; 🔀 🖥) Catching the design bug, Royal River sports the global Zen look and a riverside pool amid landscaped grounds 3km from town.

Sam's River Raft Guest House (☎ 0 3462 4231; 48 Th Rong Hip Oi; d 250-350B; 🔀) New and spiffy bamboo rooms with polished wooden floors sit on the river, while cheaper interior rooms escape the noise. The staff is young and sassy.

Sugar Cane Guest House (☎ 0 3462 4520; 22 Soi Pakistan, off Th Mae Nam Khwae; d 250-550B; 🔀) This friendly spot has comfortable rooms on a raft with a wide veranda, as well as bungalows and a riverside restaurant. Raft rooms are all doubles with private bathroom; the expensive rooms have beds with box springs (a rarity in guesthouses).

KO SAMET
เกาะเสม็ด

When ocean breezes and turquoise waters are calling, you don't have to hustle down the peninsula. Only a half a day's journey from Bangkok, Ko Samet has sandy beach coves and an endless expanse of ocean. Plus it is a relatively dry island, making it an excellent place to visit during the rainy season when every other paradise island is under water. Of course, all of this makes it very popular with everyone – Thais, foreigners, even stray dogs – especially on weekends or holidays. If you're plotting a beach getaway, opt for September rather than March.

Ko Samet earned a permanent place in Thai literature when classical Thai poet Sunthorn Phu set part of his epic *Phra Aphaimani* on its shores. The story follows the travails of a prince exiled to an undersea kingdom governed by a lovesick female giant. A mermaid assists the prince in his escape to Ko Samet, where he defeats a giant by playing a magic flute. Today the poem is immortalised on the island by a **mermaid statue** built on a rocky point separating Ao Hin Khok and Hat Sai Kaew.

In the early 1980s, Ko Samet began receiving its first visitors: young Thais in search of a retreat from city life. At that time there were only about 40 houses on the island. Rayong and Bangkok speculators saw the sudden interest in Ko Samet as a chance to cash in on an up-and-coming Phuket and began buying up land along the beaches. No-one bothered about the fact that Ko Samet had been a national marine park since 1981. When *faràng* (Westerners) soon followed, spurred on by rumours that Ko Samet was similar to Ko Samui '10 years ago' (one always seems to miss it by a decade), the National Parks Division stepped in and built a visitors' office on the island, ordered that all bungalows be moved back behind the tree line and started charging admission to the park.

TRANSPORT

Distance from Bangkok 200km

Direction Southeast

Travel Time Four hours

Bus The best way to reach Ko Samet is somewhat roundabout: bus to Rayong, săwngthăew to Ban Phe and boat to the island. Options that seem more direct often take longer and cost more. Air-con buses to Rayong (137B, 3½ hours, every 30 minutes from 5am to 9.30pm) leave Bangkok's Eastern Bus Terminal (Ekamai; Map pp278–9). Buses to Ban Phe (140B), the pier to Ko Samet, leave from Ekamai as well, but the travel time is slower. Guesthouses around Th Khao San often arrange transport that costs more time than money. From Rayong bus station, take a săwngthăew (20B, 30 minutes, every 15 minutes) to Ban Phe (where you catch the boat to Ko Samet).

Boat Boats to Ko Samet leave from Ban Phe's many piers; be sure to buy tickets directly from a boat office at the pier instead of a scammer waiting at the bus station. Most boats go to Na Dan Pier (return 100B), but there are also boats to Ao Wong Deuan (return 120B) and other beaches in high season. Boat schedules vary depending on the season, so prepare to wait an hour or more unless it's very busy. You can also charter a speedboat (1200B to 2000B).

KO SAMET

0 — 1 km
0 — 0.5 miles

To Ban Phe (5km)

Laem Noi Na

To Ban Phe (5km)

To Ban Phe (5km)

Laem Phra

Ao Wiang Wan

Ao Kham

Na Dan Pier

Na Dan

Ao Phrao

Hat Laem Yai

Laem Ya/Ko Samet National Park

Hat Sai Kaew

Ao Hin Khok

Laem Yai

Ao Phai

Ao Phutsa (Ao Thap Thim)

Laem Rua Taek

Ao Nuan

Bamboo Restaurant

Ao Cho

Ao Wong Deuan

Hat Saeng Thian

Ao Thian

Ao Thai (Gulf of Thailand)

Ao Wai

Ao Kiu Na Nai

Ao Kiu Na Nok

Laem Khut

Ao Karang

SIGHTS & INFORMATION	(p226)
Ko Samet Health Centre	1 C2
Mermaid Statue	2 C2
National Park Branch Office	3 B3
National Park Main Office	4 C2
Post Office	5 C2

EATING 🍴	(p226)
Bamboo Restaurant	6 B3
Naga Bungalows	7 C2
Panorama Restaurant	8 B1

SLEEPING 🏠	(pp226–7)
Ao Nuan Bungalows	9 B3
Ao Phai Hut	10 C2
Ao Prao Resort	11 B2
Ao Putsa	12 B3
Le Vimarn Cottages & Dhivarin Spa	13 B2
Lima Coco	14 B2
Lung Dam Resort	15 B4
Malibu Garden Resort	16 B4
Paradee Resort & Spa	17 A6
Ploy Talay	18 C2
Sai Kaew Beach Resort	19 C2
Saikaew Villa	20 C2
Samed Villa	21 B3
Sametville Resort	22 B5
Silver Sand	23 B3
Tok's Little Hut	24 C2
Tub Tim Resort	25 B3
Vongdeuan Resort	26 B4

The timber jetty at Ao Cho, Ko Samet

Except at the admission gate, the regulating hand of the National Parks Division is almost invisible, as many attempts to halt encroachment have been successfully defeated by resort operators or developers. One lasting measure is the ban on new accommodation (except where it replaces old sites), ensuring that bungalows are spread thinly over most of the island.

The northern end of the island is where most of the development is located, but compared to Bangkok even the densest part of Ko Samet seems as sparsely populated as the Australian outback. The further south you go, the less likely you are to be kept awake by a guesthouse disco.

Most boats from the mainland arrive at **Na Dan Pier**, where there is one 7-Eleven and a few Internet shops (without which this could be called 'wilderness'). On the northeastern coast is **Hat Sai Kaew** (Diamond Beach), the most developed stretch of beach on the island and the best place for nightlife. Wealthy Bangkokians file straight into Hat Sai's air-con bungalows with their designer sunglasses and designer dogs.

Around the next headland is a scruffier set of beaches: **Ao Hin Khok**, **Ao Phai** and **Ao Phutsa**, fittingly claimed by backpackers.

A rocky headland crossed by a footpath separates palm-shaded Ao Phutsa from beaches to the south. Quiet **Ao Nuan** and **Ao Cho** (Chaw) have beaches that aren't voluptuous enough to attract crowds.

Immediately to the south is the prom queen of the bunch: **Ao Wong Deuan**, whose graceful stretch of sand supports an entourage of sardine-packed sun-worshippers, screaming jet skis and honky-tonk bars akin to those in Pattaya.

Thai college kids claim **Ao Thian** (Candle-light Beach) for all-night guitar jam sessions. Further south is a castaway's dream of empty beaches and gentle surf, and the starting point for languid walks to the western side of the island to see fiery sunsets.

The only developed beach on the western side of the island is **Ao Phrao** (Coconut Beach), which hosts the island's only luxury resort and moonlights as 'Paradise Beach' to those escaping winter climates.

BEFORE SAMET MEANT ESCAPE

If marketing minds had been involved, Ko Samet would still be known by its old name: Ko Kaew Phitsadan (Vast Jewel Isle), a reference to the abundant white sand. But the island's first cash cow, the cajeput (or *sàmèt*) tree, lent its name to the island as this valuable firewood source grew in abundance here. Locally, the *sàmèt* tree has also been used in boat building.

Excursions **KO SAMET**

SANCTUARY OF TRUTH
ปราสาทสัจจธรรม

Planted on a dramatic promontory overlooking the ocean, the **Sanctuary of Truth** (☎ 0 3836 7229; www.sanctuaryoftruth.com; Soi 12, Th Naklua, Naklua; admission 500B) is a fanciful vision reflecting the creator's intellectual curiosity and religious convictions. Lek Viriyaphan, known widely as Khun Lek, was a thinker and dreamer; most importantly, he was rich and preferred to spend his fortune on grand architectural projects, such as the Ancient City and the Sanctuary of Truth, instead of the pursuits that make the rich filthy. From a distance, the Sanctuary of Truth looks like every other Thai temple but with a million-dollar view. A little closer and the building becomes a visual sermon with each surface covered in woodcarvings based on Khmer, Thai, Chinese and Hindu iconography stacked on top of each other, reaching 20 storeys high.

The sanctuary is near Pattaya, which is accessible from Bangkok's Eastern Bus Terminal for 110B. From Pattaya take a *săwngthăew* to Naklua, a neighbouring town, and disembark at Soi 12. It is a long walk to the end of the *soi* from here and private transport might be advisable.

Information & Sights

Boat trips (per person 600-800B) Several bungalows on the island can arrange boat trips to nearby reefs and uninhabited islands, such as Ko Thalu and Ko Kuti.

Ko Samet Health Centre (☎ 0 3861 2999; btwn Hat Sai Kaew & Na Dan; 8.30am-8pm Mon-Fri, until 4.30pm Sat & Sun) Small public clinic with English-speaking doctors for minor health problems.

National Park entrance gates (Hat Sai Kaew; adult/child 200/100B; dawn to dusk) There's another office on Ao Wong Deuan.

Post office (Ao Hin Khok, next to Naga Bungalows; 8.30am-4.30pm Mon-Fri, 8.30am-noon Sat) Post restante and Internet access.

Eating

Most guesthouses have restaurants, and many offer beachside dining in the evenings.

Bamboo Restaurant (Ao Cho; dishes 80-150B; 8am-10pm) This restaurant offers inexpensive but tasty food and good service.

Naga Bungalows (☎ 0 3865 2448; Ao Hin Khok; dishes 150-200B; 8am-10pm) This guesthouse restaurant has a bakery with warm rolls, croissants and doughnuts in the morning and great sandwiches and pizza throughout

the day. There are plenty of tofu dishes on the menu and weekly buffet meals.

Panorama Restaurant (Moo Ban Talay Resort, Ao Noi Na) City sensibilities serve Asian and Western cuisine instead of grub. West of Na Dan.

Safari Noodle Stand (noodles 30B; lunch & dinner) A mobile noodle shop that plies the road between Na Dan and Ao Phai.

Sleeping

Because of demand, Ko Samet's prices aren't always reflective of amenities. A ramshackle hut starts at 300B, and with air-con this can climb to 800B. Reservations aren't always honoured, so at peak times it is advisable to arrive early, poised for the hunt.

HAT SAI KAEW

Ploy Talay (☎ 0 3864 4212; d 500-800B;) This place is one of the few cheapies in the neighbourhood; the cheapest bungalows should be retired from service.

Sai Kaew Beach Resort (☎ 0 2438 9771-2; r 3600-4800B, bungalow 4800-5500B;) Spick-and-span bungalows, some with private terraces amid a classy beach resort.

Saikaew Villa (☎ 0 3865 1852; d 700-1650B;) A huge complex with the usual grumpy staff and adequate accommodation. Try to get a room away from the noisy generators.

AO HIN KHOK & AO PHAI

Ao Phai Hut (☎ 0 3864 4075; Ao Phai; r 500-1000B) Comfortable bungalows in a pretty garden setting of humming insects and pecking chickens. If you don't like what you see here, follow the road until it becomes a footpath that hugs the shore connecting all the bays to one another.

Samed Villa (☎ 0 3864 4094; Ao Phai; d 600-900B;) Come here for well-maintained, tree-shaded bungalows with large verandas. Smaller units have private bathrooms, and larger units suit families. The best of the bunch have great sea views.

Silver Sand (☎ 0 6530 2417; Ao Phai; d 300-1200B;) This establishment has about 40 comfortable bungalows with their own verandas and some with beach frontage. There is also a beach bar.

Tok's Little Hut (☎ 0 3864 4072; Ao Hin Khok; d 300-800B) This was one of the island's first bungalow operations. There are very simple fan bungalows, and the price is gauged by the room's proximity to the generator.

AO PHUTSA (AO THAP THIM) & AO NUAN

Ao Nuan Bungalows (Ao Nuan; d 200-400B) If you blink you'll miss this beach and the secluded rustic huts scattered about the hillside. They all have shared bathrooms and intermittent electricity. It's a five-minute walk over the headland from Ao Phutsa.

Ao Putsa (☎ 0 3964 4030; Ao Phutsa; d 500–600B) This place has well-worn huts, but some of them are quite close to the water, making them a good beach catch.

Tub Tim Resort (☎ 0 3864 4025; Ao Phutsa; d 500–1500B; 🕸) At the southern end of the beach, Tub Tim has older, smaller bungalows on a shady hillside and newer, more spacious wooden bungalows with sea views and air-con.

AO WONG DEUAN & AO THIAN

Lung Dam Resort (☎ 0 3865 1810; Ao Thian; d 500–1000B) This is good for low-budget romance – the huts are built of scrap and junk, both organic and otherwise. It all looks as if it belonged to some settlement of castaways marooned on a deserted island. During the high season, the restaurant sets up on the beach for drinks under the stars.

Malibu Garden Resort (☎ 0 3864 4020; Ao Wong Deuan; bungalows 1500–3000B; 🕸) This resort has well-built brick or wooden bungalows; the more expensive rooms have a fridge and TV. Breakfast is included. The resort has its own boat to Ban Phe that leaves two to three times a day.

Vongdeuan Resort (☎ 0 3865 1777; Ao Wong Deuan; bungalows 1200–3500B; 🕸) This is the best of Ao Wong Deuan, and is quite extravagant by Ko Samet standards. Most bungalows are teak-style houses with front-row beach seating.

OTHER EASTERN BEACHES

Paradee Resort & Spa (☎ 0 2438 9771-2; www.samedresorts.com; Ao Kiu Na Nok; villa 15,000B; 🕸 🖳) Oh la la, Samet has gone upscale with this well-padded private spot. Beachfront villas adore a pretty stretch of sand and sport modern Thai design and so many extras that you don't need to leave. A private speed boat from Ban Phe can also be arranged, of course.

Sametville Resort (☎ 0 3865 1681; Ao Wai; d 800–1500B; 🕸) Sametville is very private and offers a fine combination of upscale accommodation and isolation. Transport here can be arranged from Ban Phe piers.

AO PHRAO

Ao Prao Resort (☎ 0 2438 9771-72; www.samedresorts.com; chalets 5200–10,800B; 🕸 🖳) The oldest luxury lodging on Samet has been surpassed by younger models, but the private seclusion and all the bells and whistles still earn their keep. Ao Prao Divers, at the resort, provides diving, windsurfing, kayaking and boat trips.

Le Vimarn Cottages (☎ 0 2438 9771-2; www.samedresorts.com; d 8000–10,500B; 🕸 🖳 🖳) The new luxe option, Le Vimarn is manicured tranquillity with elegant and modern rooms. There are loads of facilities, including the lavish **Dhivarin Spa** (☎ 0 3864 4104-7).

Lima Coco (☎ 0 3865 1377; d 2500–10,000B; 🕸) Formerly the Dome Bungalows, this bungalow village is built on the hillside and has a few midrange options worth investigating.

KHAO YAI NATIONAL PARK

อุทยานแห่งชาติเขาใหญ่

Cool and lush, Khao Yai National Park is an easy escape into the primordial jungle. The 2168-sq-km park spans five forest types, from rainforest to monsoon, and is the primary residence of elephants, gibbons, tropical birds and audible yet invisible insects. Like a diligent baker, the jungle wakes up with the dawn, making a different kind of morning noise than the city sounds: chirping insects, hooting monkeys, whooping macaques and anonymous shrieks and trills. Khao Yai is a major birding destination with large flocks of hornbills and several migrators, including the flycatcher from Europe. Caves in the park are the preferred resting place for wrinkle-lipped bats. In the grasslands, batik-printed butterflies dissect flowers with their surgical tongues.

The park has several accessible trails for self-tours but birders or animal trackers should consider hiring a jungle guide to increase their appreciation of the environment and to spot more than the tree-swinging

TRANSPORT

Distance from Bangkok 196km

Direction Northeast

Travel Time Three hours

Bus From Bangkok's Northern & Northeastern Bus Terminal (Mo Chit; Map pp278–9), take a bus to Pak Chong (ordinary/air-con 90/150B, every 30 minutes from 5am to 10pm). From Pak Chong, take a săwngthăew (15B, from 6am to 5pm) to the entrance gate of the park.

Getting Around There is no transportation within the park, but hitchhiking is generally safe and acceptable within the park boundaries. From the entrance gate you'll have to walk or flag a passing car for a ride to the visitors' centre, but folks are happy to oblige.

KHAO YAI NATIONAL PARK

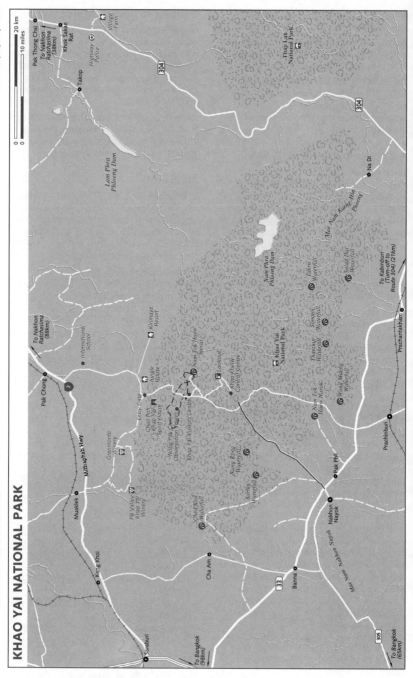

gibbons and blood-sucking leeches (the rainy season is the worst time for leeches). In total, there are 12 maintained trails criss-crossing the entire park, which makes walking end to end troublesome. Access to transport is often another reason why a tour might be more convenient for some, although Thai visitors with cars are usually happy to pick up pedestrians.

A two-hour walk from the park headquarters leads to the **Nong Pak Chee observation tower**, which is a good spot for watching early-morning insect-feeding birds, thirsty elephants and sambar deer. Spotting the park's reclusive tigers and elephants isn't as common as adoring the frothy waterfalls that drain the peaks of the Big Mountain. The park's centrepiece is **Nam Tok Haew Suwat** (Haew Suwat Falls), a 25m-high cascade that is a roaring artery in the rainy season. **Nam Tok Haew Narok** (Haew Narok Falls) is its larger cousin with three pooling tiers and a towering 150m drop.

Nam Tok Haew Suwat (Haew Suwat Falls), Khao Yai National Park

Bordering the southern perimeter of the park, **Nakhon Nayok province** is being developed as an adventure-sport destination. Canoeing and kayaking trips float down the tame Mae Nam Nakhon Nayok while rafting trips spin-cycle down the more rambunctious Kaeng Hin Phoeng.

The cool highlands around Khao Yai are also home to a nascent **wine industry**. These have been dubbed the 'New Latitude' wines because grapes do not normally grow between Thailand's 14th and 18th parallels. Village Farm, PB Valley Khao Yai Winery and GranMonte are a few of the wine makers that are managing to coax shiraz and chenin blanc grapes from the relatively tropical climate.

Information & Sights

The best time to visit the park is in the dry season (December to June), but during the rainy season river rafting and waterfall spotting will be more dramatic. Most guesthouses and lodges arrange jungle treks and rafting tours.

GranMonte (☎ 0 3622 7334; www.granmonte.com; 52 Th Phausak-Kudla) Small winery that provides tastings and tours.

Khao Yai Visitors Centre (☎ 0 3731 9002; admission 200B; ☼ 8am-6pm) Topographical maps, hiking advice, and jungle guides can be arranged at this centre within the park.

Nong Pak Chee observation tower Reservations need to be made at the visitors' centre.

PB Valley Khao Yai Winery (☎ 0 3622 7328; www .khaoyaiwinery.com; 102 Moo 5, Phaya Yen, Pak Chong; tastings 150B; winery day tour 600B; ☼ 7.30am-4.30pm)

TAT Central Region Office 8 (☎ 0 3731 2282; tatnayok@tat.or.th; 182/88 Moo 1, Th Suwannason, Nakhon Nayok) Official information centre for adventure tours in Nakhon Nayok province.

Eating & Sleeping

Golf courses and upscale resorts ring the perimeter of the park. Pak Chong is the primary base-camp town, but Nakhon Nayok and Prachinburi are beginning to develop more low-key options. Most guesthouses will provide jungle tours and transport to the park. There are restaurants within the park and the towns surrounding the park have lively night markets.

Cabbages & Condoms Resort (☎ 0 3622 7065; www .pda.or.th; 98 Moo 6, Phaya Yen, Pak Chong; d 2000-5000B) This resort, with a hotel ambience, is the sister facility of the Bangkok restaurant (p141) with the same name that supports a great cause: HIV/AIDS education and prevention.

Jungle House (☎ 0 4429 7307; www.junglehousehotel .com; 21/5 Th Thanarat; Km 19.5, Pak Chong; d 400-1000B) An old favourite with lots of extras to keep kids entertained. Loft rooms encourage monkeylike agility.

Kirimaya (☎ 0 4442 6000; www.kirimaya.com; 1/3 Moo 6, Th Thanarat, Pak Chong; r 7000-10,000B; 🌐 🛏) Contemporary villas and crisp décor soak up a view of the Big Mountain (Khao Yai).

Palm Garden Lodge (☎ 0 9989 4470; www.palmgalo .com; Prachinburi; r 400-650B; 🌐) Woodsy gardens and rustic bungalows keep you in touch with nature. The

lodge is 7km south of the southern entrance, near Ban Kon Khuang on Hwy 33, and arranges park tours.

Park Lodging (☎ 0 2562 0760, Khao Yai Visitors Centre) Within the park, there are three types of accommodation: villas sleeping 12 people (3500B), longhouse dorms (30B per person, sleeps up to 30 people) and camping (40B per person).

Village Farm (☎ 0 3622 6393; www.villagefarm.co.th; Tambon Thasamakee, Wan Nam Kheo, Khorat; d 2000-6400B) A vineyard and resort combines creature comfort with farm living. Restored teak villas are cradled in 32 hectares of farmland.

SAMUT PRAKAN
อ.เมืองสมุทรปราการ

Of all the daytrip destinations outside of Bangkok, Samut Prakan makes the sweaty bus ride worth it. The town is located at the mouth of Mae Nam Chao Phraya, where it empties into the Gulf of Thailand and is often referred to as Pak Nam. But it isn't the working port you've come to see, but the outlying attractions.

The **Ancient City** (Muang Boran) will challenge preconceptions that Thailand is infested with soot-stained concrete buildings, dusty roads and screaming motorcycles. Billed as the world's largest open-air museum, the Ancient City covers more than 80 hectares of peaceful countryside scattered with 109 scaled-down facsimiles of many of the kingdom's most famous monuments. The grounds are shaped to replicate Thailand's general geographical outline, with the monuments located accordingly.

Visions of Las Vegas and its corny replicas of world treasures might spring to mind, but the Ancient City has architectural integrity and is a preservation site for classical buildings and art forms. It's a great place for long, undistracted bicycle rides (rental from the admission office is 50B), as it's usually quiet and never crowded. There is lots of open space for picnics, if you want to pick up some food from the market in central Samut Prakan, or you can enjoy a leisurely meal of *sôm-tam* (spicy salad) in an open-air pavilion, catching cool breezes and listening to the rhythm of the mortar and pestle mixing your dish's ingredients.

Samut Prakan Crocodile Farm & Zoo has more than 30,000 crocs who spend their time wallowing in mud. It also harbours elephants, monkeys and snakes. The farm has trained-animal shows, including croc wrestling and elephant performances, and the reptiles get their dinner between 4pm and 5pm.

TRANSPORT

Distance from Bangkok 30km

Direction South

Travel Time Two hours

Bus Ordinary bus 102 (5.50B) and air-con buses 508 and 511 (20B) ply regular routes between central Bangkok's Th Sukhumvit and Pak Nam (central Samut Prakan). The bus station in Samut Prakan is located on Th Srisamut in front of the harbour and the market. Note where the Bangkok bus drops you off because Samut Prakan has very few streets signs in Roman script. If traffic is horrendous, consider catching the Skytrain's Sukhumvit line to On Nut station and then catching the aforementioned buses on the road heading out of Bangkok; you can catch the Skytrain at On Nut heading back into Bangkok as well.

Getting Around Săwngthǎew and minibuses to the town's attractions are usually parked nearby. The Ancient City is 3km from central Samut Prakan on the Old Sukhumvit Hwy; take a green minibus 36 (6B), which passes the entrance to the Ancient City; nervous types should sit on the left side of the bus to watch for the 'Muang Boran' sign. To return to town, cross the main highway and catch a white săwngthǎew 36 (6B). To reach the crocodile farm from central Samut Prakan, take the blue săwngthǎew S1 or S80 (10B); this will go directly to the gate.

Information & Sights

Ancient City (☎ 0 2323 9253; www.ancientcity.com; Old Sukhumvit Hwy; adult/child 300/200B; ☾ 8am-5pm)

Samut Prakan Crocodile Farm & Zoo (☎ 0 2703 4891; adult/child 300/200B; ☾ 7am-6pm)

NAKHON PATHOM
อ.เมืองนครปฐม

On most days, Nakhon Pathom is a typical provincial Thai town, merely sleepwalking through its daily chores. It is one of the oldest towns in Thailand and the entryway for Buddhist missionaries from India. Nakhon Pathom's ancient history is most evident in the town's crowning jewel: Phra Pathom Chedi, one of the world's largest *chedi* (stupas). After taking a few quick photos of the temple, most visitors head off to sites elsewhere.

Inside the Phra Pathom Chedi

But during the town's annual festivals, Nakhon Pathom kicks up its heels for a full dose of Thai fun: eating, dancing, socialising and general merriment. All the luscious tropical fruits grown in the province are brought to Phra Pathom Chedi for the agricultural fair (during Chinese New Year in January/February). The annual temple fair (typically held in November at Phra Pathom Chedi) is a mainstay of any Thai childhood and a good spot to see classical dance and theatre *in situ*.

Occupying the centre of town is the 120m **Phra Pathom Chedi**, the world's tallest Buddhist monument. The original structure, which is buried within the massive orange-glazed dome, was erected in the early 6th century by the Theravada Buddhists of Dvaravati, but in the early 11th century the Khmer king, Suryavarman I of Angkor, conquered the city and built a Brahman *prang* over the sanctuary. The Burmese of Bagan, under King Anuruddha, sacked the city in 1057 and the *prang* lay in ruins until Rama IV had it restored in 1860. There's a Chinese temple attached to the outer walls of the *chedi*, next to which outdoor *lí-keh* (folk plays with dancing and music) are sometimes performed. On the

TRANSPORT

Distance from Bangkok 56km

Direction West

Travel Time One hour

Bus From Thonburi's Southern Bus Terminal (Map pp278–9), air-con buses 997 and 83 (40B) depart for Nakhon Pathom throughout the day. To return to Bangkok, catch one of the idling buses from Th Phayaphan on the canal side of the road, a block from the train station. Bus 78 from Nakhon Pathom to Damnoen Saduak floating market (p232) depart from southeast of Phra Pathom Chedi.

Train Express and rapid trains (20B to 40B) leave Bangkok's Hualamphong station (Map pp284–5) in the morning (7.45am and 9.20am) and more frequently between 1pm and 7pm. Ordinary trains (20B) leave from Thonburi's Bangkok Noi station (Map p288) at 7.45am and 1.50pm. For an afternoon return, Hualamphong-bound trains depart at 5.15pm and 7.00pm, and one Bangkok Noi–bound train departs at 4.20pm.

THEME PARKS

Just outside Bangkok are theme park playgrounds delivering large doses of pachyderm dances and cultural shows. It is easier to sign on with a tour operator than to try to reach these sights independently.

Dream World (☎ 0 2533 1946; www.dreamworld-th.com; Km 7 Rangsit-Nakorn Nayok, Thanya Buri; combination tickets 1000-1200B; ☺ 10am-5pm Mon-Fri, 10am-7pm public holidays) No-excuses fun park with roller coasters, paddle boats, stunt shows, go-carts and an artificial snow world.

Rose Garden Aprime Resort (☎ 0 3432 2588; www.rose-garden.com; Km 32 Th Phetkasem, Sam Phran, Nakhon Pathom; ☺ cultural show at 2.45pm) A little more grown-up, this theme park resort features a Thai cultural village with demos of handicrafts, dancing, traditional ceremonies (including weddings) and martial arts. There's also a resort hotel, swimming pools, tennis courts, elephant rides and a golf course, as well as a namesake rose garden (with 20,000 bushes).

Samphran Elephant Ground & Zoo (☎ 0 2295 2938; www.elephantshow.com; Km 30 Th Phetkasem, Sam Phran; adult/child 450/250B; ☺ 8am-6pm) A kilometre from the Rose Garden is a 9-hectare zoo with elephant roundups and crocodile shows. On Labour Day (1 May), the annual Elephant Queen Parade is held for heavy-set women who can display the girth and the elegance of the elephant.

Siam Park (☎ 0 2919 7200; www.siamparkcity.com; 99 Th Serathai, Khannayao; adult/child 500/400B; ☺ 10am-6pm Mon-Fri, 9am-7pm Sat & Sun) A water park with artificial waves, giant water slides and a flow pool. There is also an amusement park, small zoo and playground.

eastern side of the monument, in the *bòt*, is a Dvaravati-style Buddha seated in a European pose similar to the one in Wat Na Phra Mehn (p217) in Ayuthaya. It might, in fact, have come from Phra Mehn.

The wat surrounding the *chedi* enjoys the kingdom's highest temple rank, Ratchavorama-havihan, one of only six temples so honoured in Thailand. The ashes of Rama VI (King Vajiravudh; r 1910–25) are interred in the base of the Sukhothai-era Phra Ruang Rochanarit, a large standing Buddha image in the wat's northern *wíhǎan*.

Sights & Eating

Day market (btwn train station & Phra Pathom Chedi; ☺ 6am-4pm) Keep an eye out for *khâo lǎam* (sticky rice and coconut steamed in a bamboo joint), which is reputed to be the best in Thailand. There are many good, inexpensive food vendors and restaurants in this area too.

Phra Pathom Chedi Museum (admission 30B; ☺ 9am-4pm Wed-Sun) In the grounds of the *chedi*, this museum contains interesting Dvaravati sculpture.

Rathchaphruek (Th Ratchadamnoen, near Soi 5; dishes 100B) Located directly west of Phra Pathom Chedi, this open-air restaurant (no Roman-script sign) has a pleasant setting with good, medium-priced Thai food.

Tang Ha-Seng (71/2-3 & 59/1-2 Th Thesa; dishes 50B) This is an old, reliable stand-by, located east of the *chedi*, that does inexpensive Chinese meals. There's no Roman-script sign.

FLOATING MARKETS

ตลาดน้ำ

Pictures of the floating markets *(tàlàat náam)* with the wooden canoes pregnant with fruits have defined the official tourist profile of Thailand for more than 20 years. The imagery is beautiful but utterly fictional. Roads and motorcycles have moved daily errands onto dry ground. An updated version of the floating market would show row upon row of souvenir stands lining the canals and boatloads of tourists glued to their cameras. The floating fruit vendors are still there, but the piles of exotic colours have diminished to a few lacklustre, overpriced bunches of bananas.

The most famous of the breed is the **Damnoen Saduak Floating Market**. The 100-year-old market is now essentially a floating souvenir stand filled with package tourists. But beyond the

TRANSPORT

Damnoen Saduak

Distance from Bangkok 65km

Direction Southwest

Travel Time Two hours

Bus Air-con buses 78 and 996 (72B) go direct from Thonburi's Southern Bus Terminal (Map pp278–9) to Damnoen Saduak every 20 minutes, beginning at 6.30am. Most buses will drop you off at a pier along the *khlong,* where you can hire a boat directly to the floating market. The regular bus stop is in town just across the bridge. A yellow såwngthåew (5B) does a frequent loop between the floating market and the bus stop in town.

Don Wai Market

Distance from Bangkok 50km

Direction Southwest

Travel Time 1½ hours

To reach Don Wai Market, see Rose Garden Aprime Resort, p234.

Amphawa Market

Distance from Bangkok 55km

Direction Southwest

Travel Time Two hours

To reach Amphawa Market, take a Samut Songkhram–bound (61B) bus from Thonburi's Southern Bus Terminal (Map pp278–9) and transfer to Amphawa-bound blue bus (10B) to Talat Nam Amphawa. Long-tail boats can also be hired from Samut Songkhram's pier. Alternatively, you can take a bus from Thonburi all the way to Amphawa (66B).

Tha Kha Floating Market

Distance from Bangkok 55km

Direction Southwest

Travel Time Two hours

Tours can be organised through Baan Tai Had Resort (below)

market, the residential canals are quite peaceful and can be explored by hiring a boat for a longer duration. South of the floating market are several small family businesses, including a Thai candy maker, a pomelo farm and a knife crafter.

Not technically a swimmer, **Don Wai Market** claims a riverbank location in Nakhon Pathom province, having originally started out in the early 20th century as a floating market for pomelo and jackfruit growers and traders. More popular with Thai tourists, Don Wai specialises in edible souvenirs like *pèt phá-lór* (five-spice stewed duck).

The **Amphawa Floating Market**, about 7km northwest of Samut Songkhram, convenes in front of Wat Amphawa. There are other floating markets nearby that meet in the mornings on particular lunar days, including **Tha Kha Floating Market**. Tha Kha convenes along an open, breezy *khlong* lined with greenery and old wooden houses.

Information & Sights

Amphawa Floating Market (Talat Náam Amphráwaa; 4pm-9pm Fri-Sun)

Baan Tai Had Resort (☎ 0 3476 7220; www.baantaihad .com; 1 Moo 2, Th Tai Had, Samut Songkhram) Rents

kayaks and organises trips for exploring the Amphawa and Tha Kha markets.

Bike & Travel (☎ 0 2990 0274; www.cyclingthailand .com) This tour company organises bike trips to Damnoen Saduak and the surrounding villages.

Damnoen Saduak Floating Market (Khlong Damnoen Saduak; ☻ 7am-noon) You can hire a boat from any pier that lines Th Sukhaphiban 1, which is the land route to the floating market area. The going rate is 250B per person per hour.

Damnoen Saduak Tourist Information Office (Th Sukhaphiban 1; ☻ 9am-5pm) This office, across from the floating market, can organise transport to access outlying canal sites if you want a two- to three-hour tour. It also arranges for home stays and other canal trips.

Don Wai Market (Talat Don Wai; 6am-6pm) The market can be reached via river tour or hired long-tail boat.

Rose Garden Aprime Resort (☎ 0 3432 2588; www .rose-garden.com; Km 32 Th Phetkasem, Sam Phran, Nakhon Pathom) Organises trips along the Tha Chin river taking in the Don Wai Market and the riverside orchid farms.

Tha Kha Floating Market (2nd, 7th & 12th day of waxing & waning moons, 7am-noon weekends)

MAHACHAI RAIL LINE
สายรถไฟมหาชัย

Commuters, but few tourists, know about this rail spur linking Thonburi with a string of gulfside towns scented with the fishy perfume of the sea. The journey through the woods and villages and into the busy market towns is a pleasant, pointless trip for sating the lust to wander.

The adventure begins when you take a stab into Thonburi looking for the **Wong Wian Yai train station** (Map pp280–1; Th Taksin; bus 37). Just past the traffic circle (Wong Wian Yai) is a fairly ordinary food market that camouflages the unceremonious terminal of this commuter line.

Only 15 minutes out of the station and the city density yields to squatty villages where you can peek into homes and shops selling colourful plastic packages or a shot of rice whisky for the morning commute. Further on palm trees, small rice fields and marshes filled with giant elephant ears and canna lilies crowd the tracks, tamed only briefly by little whistle-stop stations.

The wilderness and backwater farms evaporate quickly as you enter Samut Sakhon, popularly known as Mahachai because it straddles the confluence of Mae Nam Tha Chin and Khlong Mahachai. It is a bustling port town, several kilometres from the Gulf of Thailand and the end of the first rail segment.

Mahachai has a few religious attractions on the outskirts of town. A few rusty cannon pointing towards the river testify to the town's crumbling fort, built to protect the kingdom from sea invaders. Before the 17th century, the town was known as Tha Jiin (Chinese Pier) because of the large number of Chinese junks that called here.

Jao Mae Kuan Im Shrine at Wat Chawng Lom is a 9m-high fountain in the shape of the Mahayana Buddhist Goddess of Mercy, and it is popular with regional tour groups. The colourful image, which pours a perpetual stream of water from a vase in the goddess's right hand, rests on an artificial hill into which a passageway is carved, leading to another Kuan Im shrine.

A few kilometres west of Samut Sakhon, further along Hwy 35, is the Ayuthaya-period **Wat Yai Chom Prasat**, which is renowned for the intricately carved wooden doors on

TRANSPORT

Distance from Bangkok 28km to Samut Sakhon; 74km to Samut Songkhram

Direction Southwest

Travel Time One hour to Samut Sakhon, two hours to Samut Songkhram

Train Trains leave Thonburi's Wong Wian Yai station (Map pp280–1) roughly every hour starting at 5.30am to Samut Sakhon. You'll need to leave Thonburi before 8.30am in order to do the trip entirely by train. There are four departures (7.30am, 10am, 1.30pm, 4.40pm) from Samut Sakhon to Samut Songkhram. The 3rd-class train costs 10B for each leg. To return there are two afternoon departures (11.30am and 3.30pm) from Samut Songkhram to Samut Sakhon, which has hourly departures to Thonburi until 7pm.

Bus If you get a late start, you can always return to Bangkok by bus. In both Samut Sakhon and Samut Songkhram the train station is a five-minute walk from the bus terminal. Regular buses from Samut Sakhon (72B) and Samut Songkhram (61B) arrive at the Southern Bus Terminal (Map pp278–9) in Thonburi. Both cities have bus service to Damnoen Saduak (p232).

its *bòt*. You can easily identify the wat from the road by the tall Buddha figure standing at the front.

Don't forget that the rail journey isn't over yet. In fact, the most interesting segment is yet to come. From the Mahachai station, work your way along the road that runs parallel to the train tracks through a dense market of rubber fishermen boots and trays of tentacled seafood to reach the harbour pier.

The harbour is clogged with water hyacinth, which forms floating islands for fish-hunting cranes and bug-chasing birds. Just beyond are the big wooden fishing boats, bursting with the day's catch and draped like a veiled widow with fishing nets. Boarding the ferry, you have to jockey for space with the motorcycles that cross back and forth, driven by school teachers and errand-running housewives.

Once on the other side, take a right at the first intersection, follow it all the way through the temple and past the drying fish racks to the train tracks and turn right to reach the station. This is Ban Laem, from which trains continue on to Samut Songkhram.

Ban Laem is a sleepy little station that keeps up a convincing charade that no one has ever come or gone from here. The ghost world is suddenly awoken when the rattling metal snake rolls in. Beyond the city, the wilderness is so dense that it seems the surrounding greenery might engulf the train tracks, so that the middle of nowhere stays that way. The illusion that concrete has forgotten this place is suddenly broken when civilisation once again emerges as you enter the bustling city of Samut Songkhram. In between train arrivals and departures, market stalls set up directly on the tracks hiding the back-door entrance.

Samut Songkhram, commonly known as Mae Klong, lies along a sharp bend in Mae Nam Mae Klong, just a few kilometres from the Gulf of Thailand. Owing to flat topography and abundant water sources, the area surrounding the provincial capital is well suited to the steady irrigation needed to grow guava, lychee and grapes. A string of artificial sea-lakes used in the production of salt fill the space between Mae Klong and Thonburi.

The capital is a fairly modern city with a large market area between the train line and bus terminal. **Wat Phet Samut Worawihan**, in the centre of town near the train station and river, contains a renowned Buddha image called Luang Phaw Wat Ban Laem – named after the *phrá sàksìt* (holy monk) who dedicated it, thus transferring mystical powers to the image.

At the mouth of Mae Nam Mae Klong, not far from town, is the province's most famous tourist attraction: a bank of fossilised shells known as **Don Hoi Lot**. These shells come from *hǎwy làwt* (clams with a tubelike shell). The shell bank is best seen late in the dry season when the river surface has receded to its lowest level (typically April and May). Many seafood restaurants popular with city folk have been built at the edge of Don Hoi Lot.

Wat Satthatham, 500m down the road from Don Hoi Lot, is notable for its *bòt* constructed of golden teak and decorated with 60 million baht worth of mother-of-pearl inlay. The inlay completely covers the temple's interior and depicts scenes from the *Jataka* (stories from the Buddha's lives) above the windows and the Ramakian below.

King Buddhalertla (Phuttha Loet La) Naphalai Memorial Park, a 10-minute walk from Amphawa Floating Market (p233), is a museum housed in a collection of traditional central Thai houses set on four landscaped acres. Dedicated to Rama II (King Buddha Loetla; r 1809–24), a native of the Amphawa district, the museum contains a library of rare Thai books, antiques from early-19th-century Siam and an exhibition of dolls depicting four of Rama II's theatrical works *(Inao, Manii Phichai, Ramakian, Sang Thong)*. Behind the houses is a lush botanical garden and beyond that is a dramatic-arts training hall.

Pinsuwan Benjarong Complex is a small factory that produces top-quality *benjarong*, traditional five-coloured Thai ceramics. Here you can watch craftspeople painting the ornate floral patterns for which *benjarong* is known.

FLIGHT OF THE FIREFLIES

Drop off the tourist trail with a home stay in Samut Songkhram's riverside villages. Local families provide spare space on the floor protected by a mosquito net for sleeping and feed you like a long-lost child. In the morning, visitors join the residents in making morning offerings to the monks. Like imprecise clockwork, the noodle vendor paddles through the neighbourhood. At night long-tail boats zip through the sleeping waters to watch the star-like dance of the fireflies. Baan Song Thai Plai Pong Pang (☎ 0 3475 7333, in Amphawa district) organises home stays and has been recognised for ecotourism excellence.

Information & Sights

Don Hoi Lot (Samut Songkhram) To get to Don Hoi Lot you can hop into a sǎwngthǎew in front of Somdet Phra Phut-talertla Hospital at the intersection of Th Prasitwatthana and Th Thamnimit; the trip takes about 15 minutes. Or you can charter a boat from the Mae Klong Market pier (thâa tàlàat mâe klawng), a scenic journey of around 45 minutes.

Jao Mae Kuan Im Shrine (Wat Chawng Lom, Samut Sakhon; admission 20B; ☽ sunrise to sunset) To get here from the ferry terminal at the harbour end of Th Sethakit (Tha Maha-chai), take a ferry (2B) to Tha Chalong, and from there take a motorcycle taxi (10B) for the 2km ride to Wat Chawng Lom.

King Buddhalertla (Phuttha Loet La) Naphalai Memo-rial Park (Km 63, Route 35, Samut Songkhram; admission 20B; ☽ park 9am-6pm daily, museum 9am-6pm Wed-Sun) To get here from Amphawa Floating Market, walk over the bridge and follow the road through the gardens of Wat Amphawa Chetiyaram. For details on getting to the Amphawa market, see p233.

Pinsuwan Benjarong Complex (☎ 0 3475 1322; Samut Songkhram; ☽ 9am-4pm) You can reach the complex, which is 1km from King Buddhalertla Park, by motorcycle taxi (10B).

Wat Yai Chom Prasat (☽ 9am-6pm; Hwy 35, Samut Sakhon; admission 20B) To reach here from Samut Sakhon, board a westbound bus (3B) heading towards Samut Songkhram. The wat is about a 10-minute ride from the perimeter of town.

Eating

Khrua Chom Ao (☎ 0 3442 2997, Samut Sakhon; dishes 60-200B) This open-air seafood restaurant has a view of the gulf and a loyal local following. It is about a five-minute walk from Wat Chawng Lom, down the road running along the side of the temple opposite the statue of the Chinese goddess Kuan Im.

Khun Toom (☎ 0 6905 0616; Th Jetsada Withee, Samut Sakhon; ☽ 11am-9pm) Impressive seafood and itty-bitty prices; try the hâwy pim thâwt náam plaa (deep-fried shellfish).

Tarua Restaurant (Ferry Terminal Bldg, Th Sethakit, Samut Sakhon; dishes 60-200B) Occupying three floors of the ferry building, this seafood restaurant offers an English-language menu.

Directory

Directory

TRANSPORT

AIR

Bangkok is easily reached by air from an extensive list of cities in Europe, Asia, the USA and Australia. Thailand's national carrier is **Thai Airways International** (THAI; www.thaiair.com), which also operates a number of domestic air routes. Bangkok is one of the world's cheapest cities to fly out of, due to the Thai government's relaxed restrictions on air fares and aggressive competition between airlines and travel agencies.

Airlines – Domestic

Over the last five years or so Thailand has partially deregulated its air routes, which has resulted in several low-fare, no-frills airlines, some of which only lasted a year or two. Listed below are the ones that seem to have staying power.

Bangkok Airways (PG; Map pp296–7; ☎ 0 2265 5555; www.bangkokair.com; Queen Sirikit National Convention Centre, 99 Th Vibhavadi Rangsit)

Nok Air (OX; Map pp278–9; ☎ 1318; www.nokair.com; Bangkok International Airport)

Orient Thai Airlines (OX; ☎ 0 2267 3210, hotline 1126; www.orient-thai.com; 17th fl, Jewelry Trade Center Bldg, 919/298 Th Silom)

PB Air (9Q; Map pp296–7; ☎ 0 2261 0220; www.pbair.com; 17th fl, UBC II Bldg, 591 Soi 33, Th Sukhumvit)

Thai Air Asia (AK; Map pp278–9; ☎ 0 2515 9999; www.airasia.com; Bangkok International Airport)

Thai Airways International (TG; Map pp278–9; ☎ 0 2628 2000; www.thaiair.com; 89 Th Vibhavadi Rangsit)

Airlines – International

Air Asia (AK; Map pp278–9; ☎ 0 2515 9999; www.airasia.com; Bangkok International Airport)

Air Canada (AC; Map pp290–1; ☎ 0 2670 0400; www.aircanada.ca; Suite 1708, Empire Tower, River Wing West, Th Sathon Tai, Yannawa, Sathon)

Air France (AF; Map pp290–1; ☎ 0 2635 1191; www.airfrance.com; 20th fl, Vorawat Bldg, 849 Th Silom)

Air India (AI; Map pp296–7; ☎ 0 2254 3280; www.airindia.com; 12th fl, One Pacific Pl, 140 Th Sukhumvit)

Air New Zealand (NZ; Map pp294–5; ☎ 0 2254 8440; www.airnz.co.nz; 14th fl, Sindhorn Bldg, 130-132 Th Withayu)

American Airlines (AA; Map pp294–5; ☎ 0 2263 0225; www.aa.com; 11th fl, Ploenchit Tower, Th Ploenchit)

Cathay Pacific Airways (CX; Map pp294–5; ☎ 0 2263 0606; www.cathaypacific.com; 11th fl, Ploenchit Tower, 898 Th Ploenchit)

China Airlines (CI; Map pp294–5; ☎ 0 2250 9898; www.china-airlines.com; 4th fl, Peninsula Plaza, 153 Th Ratchadamri)

Garuda Indonesia (GA; Map pp292–3; ☎ 0 2679 7371-2; www.garuda-indonesia.com; 27th fl, Lumphini Tower, 1168/77 Th Phra Ram IV)

Japan Airlines (JL; ☎ 0 2649 9500; www.jal.co.jp/en/; JAL Bldg, 254/1 Th Ratchadaphisek)

KLM Royal Dutch Airlines (KL; Map pp292–3; ☎ 0 2679 1100 ext 2; www.klm.com; 19th fl, Thai Wah Tower II, 21/133-134 Th Sathon Tai)

Lao Aviation (QV; Map pp290–1; ☎ 0 535 3786; 491/1 Ground fl, Silom Plaza, Th Silom)

Lufthansa Airlines (LH; Map pp296–7; ☎ 0 2264 2400; www.lufthansa.com; 18th fl, Q House, Asoke Bldg, 66 Soi 21, Th Sukhumvit)

Malaysia Airlines (MH; Map pp294–5; ☎ 0 2263 0565; www.malaysiaairlines.com; 20th fl, Ploenchit Tower, 898 Th Ploenchit)

Qantas Airways (QF; ☎ 0 2636 1747; www.qantas.com.au; 14th fl, Abdulrahim Pl, 990 Th Phra Ram IV)

Singapore Airlines (SQ; Map pp292–3; ☎ 0 2236 0440; www.singaporeair.com; 12th fl, Silom Center Bldg, 2 Th Silom)

Swiss (LX; ☎ 0 2636 2150; www.swiss.com; 21st fl, Abdulrahim Pl, 990 Th Phra Ram IV)

Thai Airways International (TG; Map pp278–9; ☎ 0 2280 0060; www.thaiair.com; 89 Th Vibhavadi Rangsit)

United Airlines (UA; Map pp294–5; ☎ 0 2253 0558; www.united.com; 14th fl, Sindhorn Bldg, 130-132 Th Withayu)

BOOKINGS ONLINE

Flights, tours and rail tickets can be booked online at www.lonelyplanet.com/travel_services.

CLIMATE CHANGE & TRAVEL

Climate change is a serious threat to the ecosystems that humans rely upon, and air travel is the fastest-growing contributor to the problem. Lonely Planet regards travel, overall, as a global benefit, but believes we all have a responsibility to limit our personal impact on global warming.

Flying and Climate Change

Pretty much every form of motorised travel generates CO2 (the main cause of human-induced climate change) but planes are far and away the worst offenders, not just because of the sheer distances they allow us to travel, but because they release greenhouse gases high into the atmosphere. The statistics are frightening: two people taking a return flight between Europe and the US will contribute as much to climate change as an average household's gas and electricity consumption over a whole year.

Carbon Offset Schemes

Climatecare.org and other websites use 'carbon calculators' that allow travellers to offset the level of greenhouse gases they are responsible for with financial contributions to sustainable travel schemes that reduce global warming – including projects in India, Honduras, Kazakhstan and Uganda.

Lonely Planet, together with Rough Guides and other concerned partners in the travel industry, support the carbon offset scheme run by climatecare.org. Lonely Planet offsets all of its staff and author travel.

For more information check out our website: www.lonelyplanet.com.

Airport

Air services are set to shift to Suvarnabhumi Airport (also known as New Bangkok International Airport), 30km east of Bangkok at Nong Ngu Hao, in the second half of 2006. See www.suvarnabhumiairport.com for the latest information.

At the moment, **Bangkok International Airport** (BKK; Map pp278–9), situated 25km north of the city at Don Muang, is Thailand's main international hub. The busiest airport in Southeast Asia, Bangkok International has two international terminals (Terminal 1 and Terminal 2) and one domestic terminal. Once Suvarnabhumi Airport opens, it is likely that Bangkok International Airport will remain open to serve all domestic airlines except for THAI.

Foreign-exchange booths on the ground floor of the arrival hall and in the departure lounge of both international terminals give a good rate of exchange, so there's no need to wait until you're in the city centre to change money if you need Thai currency. ATMs can also be found in the arrival and departure halls.

Left-luggage facilities (per item up to 24hr 70B, each additional 12hr 70B, maximum 6 months; 🕐 5am-midnight) are available in the departure hall in both terminals.

Public-transport details are still to be finalised for Suvarnabhumi Airport; a rail link with the city is under construction and there will also be an airport bus service.

To reach the city from Bangkok International Airport, choose one of the following options.

AIRPORT BUS

Special airport buses operate from Bangkok International Airport to central Bangkok for 100B, with services every 15 minutes from 5.30am to 12.30am. There's an airport-bus desk on the forecourt between Terminal 1 and Terminal 2, and another in front of the domestic terminal. To catch an airport bus back to the airport, just wait at one of the designated stops, which are signposted with relevant lines indicated, and buy a ticket on board the bus. The buses service the following four routes from the airport:

A-1 To Th Charoen Krung via Pratunam, Th Ratchadamri, Th Silom and Th Surawong.

A-2 To Sanam Luang via Th Phayathai, Th Lan Luang, Th Ratchadamnoen Klang and Th Tanao (close to Th Khao San in Banglamphu). In the reverse direction, it stops on Th Phra Athit.

A-3 To the Phrakhanong district via Th Sukhumvit, including the Eastern Bus Terminal.

A-4 To Hualamphong Railway Station via Th Ploenchit, Th Rama I, Th Phayathai and Th Rama IV, passing Siam Square.

MINIVAN FROM BANGLAMPHU

If you're heading out to the airport from Banglamphu, all the local hotels and guesthouses can book you onto air-con minivans. These vans pick up from hotels and guesthouses and leave every hour on the hour from 4am until 1am (70B to 100B, 1½ hours).

PUBLIC BUS

Cheapest of all are the public buses to Bangkok that stop on the highway in front of the airport, but these are slow and crowded, and conductors usually won't allow you on board with bulky luggage. The fares range from 5B to 17B, depending on the distance and whether the bus is air-conditioned. Ordinary bus 59 passes Th Khao San and the Democracy Monument in Banglamphu. Air-con buses are faster and you might actually get a seat. The following are useful routes:

Bus 4 Th Silom.

Bus 10 Victory Monument, Southern Bus Terminal.

Bus 13 Th Sukhumvit, Eastern Bus Terminal.

Bus 29 Northern Bus Terminal, Victory Monument, Siam Square and Hualamphong Railway Station.

TAXI & LIMOUSINE

For public metered taxis, walk directly to the public-taxi desk on the forecourt in front of Terminal 1 or the domestic terminal. You'll have to join the queue and obtain a receipt from the efficient desk staff, which will include details of where you want to go (in Thai) and the licence-plate number of the cab that will take you (in English).

Cabs booked through this desk always use their meters, but you must also pay a 50B official airport surcharge and reimburse drivers for any charges if you use the city tollway; drivers will always ask your permission to use the tollway.

The taxi touts in the arrivals lounge work for limousine taxi companies, usually with Mercedes or large Toyota sedans, charging flat fares of 400B to 800B to central Bangkok.

TRAIN

The walkway that connects Terminal 1 to the Amari Airport Hotel (p209) also provides access to Don Muang train station, which has trains to Hualamphong Railway Station every 15 minutes or so between 6.06am and 8.07pm (3rd-class ordinary/express 5/30B, one hour). To get to Banglamphu from Hualamphong Railway Station, pick up ordinary bus 53 from the Th Rong Meuang side of the station.

Flight Bookings

FROM ASIA

STA Travel has many branches in Asia, including **Bangkok** (☎ 0 2236 0262; www.statravel.co.th), **Singapore** (☎ 6737 7188; www.statravel.com.sg), **Hong Kong** (☎ 2736 1618) and **Japan** (☎ 03 5391 2922; www.statravel.co.jp). Another resource in Japan is **No 1 Travel** (☎ 03 3205 6073; www.no1-travel.com); in Hong Kong try **Four Seas Tours** (☎ 2200 7777; www.fourseastravel.com).

FROM AUSTRALIA & NEW ZEALAND

Call or visit the websites of the following agencies to locate branches in Australia and New Zealand.

Flight Centre Australia (☎ 131 600; www.flightcentre.com.au); New Zealand (☎ 0800 243 544; www.flightcentre.co.nz)

STA Travel Australia (☎ 1300 360 960; www.statravel.com.au); New Zealand (☎ 0508 782 872; www.statravel.co.nz)

For online bookings in Australia, try www.travel.com.au, and in New Zealand, www.travel.co.nz.

FROM CANADA

Travel Cuts (☎ 866 246 9762; www.travelcuts.com) is Canada's national student travel agency. For online bookings try www.expedia.ca and www.travelocity.ca.

FROM CONTINENTAL EUROPE

Recommended agencies in France:

Anyway (☎ 0892 302 301; www.anyway.fr)

Lastminute (☎ 0899 785 000; www.lastminute.fr)

Nouvelles Frontières (☎ 0825 000 747; www.nouvelles-frontieres.fr)

OTU Voyages (☎ 0155 823 232; www.otu.fr) Student and young person specialist agency.

Voyageurs du Monde (☎ 0892 688 363; www.vdm.fr)

Recommended agencies in Germany:

Expedia (☎ 0180 500 7143; www.expedia.de in German)

Just Travel (☎ 089 747 3330; www.justtravel.de)

Lastminute (☎ 01805 284 366; www.lastminute.de in German)

STA Travel (☎ 06974-303 292; www.statravel.de in German)

One recommended Italian agent specialising in student and youth travel is **CTS Viaggi** (☎ 06 4411166; www.cts.it in Italian).

In the Netherlands try **Airfair** (☎ 0900 7 717 717; www.airfair.nl in Dutch).

Recommended agencies in Spain:

Barceló Viajes (☎ 902 116 226; www.barceloviajes.com in Spanish)

Nouvelles Frontières (☎ 915 474 200)

FROM INDIA
A recommended agency in India is **STIC Travels** (www.stictravel.com); Delhi (☎ 011 2332 0239); Mumbai (☎ 022 2218 1431); Chennai (☎ 044 2433 0211).

FROM THE MIDDLE EAST
Here is a list of recommended agencies.

Al Rais Travels (www.alrais.com; Dubai)

Egypt Panorama Tours (☎ 2 359 0200; www.eptours .com; Cairo)

Orion Tours (☎ 212 232 6300; www.oriontour.com; Istanbul)

FROM SOUTH AMERICA
Here is a list of recommended agencies.

ASATEJ (☎ 0810 777 2728; www.asatej.com in Spanish; Argentina)

IVI Tours (www.ividiomas.com in Spanish; Venezuela)

Student Travel Bureau (☎ 3038 1555; www.stb.com.br in Spanish; Brazil)

FROM THE UK
Discount air travel is big business in the UK. Advertisements for many travel agencies appear in the travel pages of the weekend broadsheet newspapers, in *Time Out*, in the *Evening Standard* and in the free magazine *TNT*.

The following are recommended travel agencies:

Flight Centre (☎ 0870 499 0040; www.flightcentre .co.uk)

Flightbookers (☎ 0870 082 3000; www.ebookers.com)

North-South Travel (☎ 01245 608 291; www.north southtravel.co.uk) Donates part of its profit to projects in the developing world.

Quest Travel (☎ 0870 442 3542; www.questtravel.com)

STA Travel (☎ 0870 630 026; www.statravel.co.uk) For travellers under the age of 26.

Trailfinders (www.trailfinders.co.uk)

Travel Bag (☎ 0870 082 5000; www.travelbag.co.uk)

FROM THE USA
Discount travel agents in the US are known as consolidators (although you won't see a sign on the door saying 'Consolidator'). San Francisco is the ticket consolidator capital of America, but some good deals can be found in Los Angeles, New York and other big cities.

The following agencies are recommended:

Avia Travel (☎ 800-950 2842; www.aviatravel.com)

Cheap Tickets (☎ 312-260 8100; www.cheaptickets.com)

Expedia (www.expedia.com)

Lowestfare.com (www.lowestfare.com)

BOAT
Although many of Bangkok's *khlong* (canals) have been paved over, there is still plenty of transport along and across Mae Nam Chao Phraya and up and down adjoining canals.

The **Chao Phraya Express Boat** (☎ 0 2623 6143; www.chaophrayaboat.co.th) runs between Tha (Pier) Nonthaburi in northern Bangkok and Tha Wat Ratchasingkhon (Map pp278–9) in the south. There are local services every 15 minutes from 6am to 7.55pm daily; fares range from 9B to 13B. At peak times on weekdays there are also express services, which fly yellow or orange flags and stop at fewer stops, charging from 19B to 32B. A special tourist boat runs between Tha Wang Lang (Map p288) and Tha Sathon (Map pp290–1) every 30 minutes between 9am and 3pm; the one-day pass for unlimited travel on this boat costs 100B.

There are also dozens of cross-river ferries, which charge 2B for the crossing and run every few minutes until late at night.

Khlong-taxi boats run along Khlong Saen Saeb (Banglamphu to Bang Kapi), Khlong Phrakhanong (Sukhumvit to Sinakharin University campus), Khlong Bang Luang/ Khlong Lat Phrao (Th Phetburi Tat Mai to Saphan Phahonyothin) and Khlong Phasi Charoen in Thonburi (Kaset Bang Khae port to Saphan Rama I). These boats are mostly used by daily commuters and pull into the piers for just a few seconds – jump straight on or you'll be left behind. Fares range from 8B to 20B.

You can also charter long-tail boats – large enough to seat 20 people – for 500B an hour from Tha Chang (Map p288) and Tha Phra Athit (Tha Banglamphu; Map pp286–7).

BUS

You can save a lot of money in Bangkok by using the public buses, which are run by the **Bangkok Mass Transit Authority** (BMTA; ☎ 184, 0 2246 0973; www.bmta.co.th) – the website has information on all bus routes. Ordinary (nonair-con) buses cost 5B (cream-and-red) or 6B (white-and-blue) for any journey under 10km between 5am and 11pm; from 11pm to 5am all ordinary buses cost 6B.

Cream-and-blue air-con buses cost 9B to 17B, depending on the distance travelled; white-and-pink air-con buses – which are double the length of regular air-con buses – cost a flat 10B. Yellow-and-orange Euro II air-con buses cost between 11B and 21B depending on distance. Small minibuses painted green cost 4.50B, while similar ones plying the *soi* (lanes) are 4B.

Pick up a copy of *Bangkok Thailand* (also known as *Tour 'n Guide Map*), which features all the Bangkok bus routes, at any bookshop.

Be careful with your belongings while riding Bangkok buses. Pickpockets and bag slashers are common on ordinary buses, particularly around the Hualamphong Railway Station area. Some public buses on routes 2, 11, 16, 29, 34, 36, 22, 101, 126 and 136 operate as 'lady-buses' and will carry only women – you can tell straightaway whether a bus is a lady-bus because they're painted all-pink.

CAR & MOTORCYCLE

You'll need to have nerves of steel to drive yourself around Bangkok and we really don't recommend it. The traffic is chaotic, the roads are poorly signposted, and random contraflows mean that you can suddenly find yourself facing a wall of cars coming the other way.

Hire

If you still want to give it a go, all the big car-hire companies have offices in Bang-

kok. Rates start at around 1200B per day for a small car, including basic insurance; personal accident cover is an extra 100B per day. An International Driving Permit and passport are required for all rentals.

A few reliable Bangkok car-rental companies include the following:

Avis Rent-A-Car (☎ 0 2255 5300; www.avisthailand .com; 2/12 Th Withayu) Branches at Bangkok International Airport and Grand Hyatt Erawan Hotel (Map pp294–5).

Budget Car Rental (Map pp278–9; ☎ 0 2203 9200; www.budget.co.th; 19/23 Bldg A, Royal City Ave, Th Phetburi Tat Mai) Also at Bangkok International Airport.

Hertz Th Withayu (☎ 0 2654 1105; M Thai Tower, All Seasons Pl, 87 Th Withayu); Don Muang (Map pp278–9; ☎ 0 2928 1525; Amari Airport Hotel, 333 Th Choet Wuthakat, Si Kan, Don Muang) Also at Bangkok International Airport.

National Car Rental (SMT Rent-a-Car; ☎ 0 2722 8487; http://smtrentacar.com; 727 Th Si Nakharin) Also at Bangkok International Airport.

Parking

Finding a parking space in Bangkok can be a hassle. You can often park on the street for a small fee, but unless you can read Thai road signs this is bit of a gamble. It's usually safer to use the car parks at the big shopping centres or the private car parks in the central business district. Most midrange and top-end hotels offer parking for guests.

SKYTRAIN

The **BTS Skytrain** (*rót fai fáa;* ☎ 0 2617 7300; www.bts.co.th) allows you to soar above Bangkok's legendary traffic jams in air-conditioned comfort. Services are fast, efficient and cheap, although the Skytrain can become busy during the morning and afternoon rush hours.

There are two lines. The Silom line runs from Saphan Taksin station, on the banks of Mae Nam Chao Phraya just past Saphan Taksin (Taksin Bridge), near the intersection of Th Charoen Krung and Th Sathon, to National Stadium station on Th Phra Ram I, next to Siam Square. The Sukhumvit line runs from On Nut, near Soi 77 at the southeastern end of Th Sukhumvit, to Mo Chit, near Chatuchak Weekend Market on Th Phahonyothin. The two lines intersect at Siam station (also called Central), at Siam Square. Plans to extend the existing lines probably won't bear fruit for a few more years.

Fares range from 10B to 40B and trains run from 6am to midnight. Ticket machines take only coins, but change is usually available from window attendants. There are useful one-day (100B) and three-day (280B) passes that allow unlimited transport by Skytrain. If you buy the three-day pass, you'll get a free Bangkok map and guide. Long-term visitors will want to buy a stored-value SkyCard, with refills of 100B (100B minimum, no maximum) available, and valid for two years. For these you must pay a 30B deposit, refunded when you return the used card.

SUBWAY (METRO)

The subway system *(rót fai fáa mahăanákhawn)*, operated by the **Metropolitan Rapid Transit Authority** (MRTA; ☎ 0 2246 5733, 0 2246 5744; www.bangkokmetro.co.th) and nicknamed 'the Metro', opened in August 2004 and is a useful supplementary form of transport, especially for the Ratchada area in northeastern Bangkok, and for Hualamphong Railway Station. The 20km Blue Line goes from Hualamphong Railway Station to Bang Seu and features 18 stations, including four that link up with the Skytrain. Fares cost 14B to 36B depending on distance travelled. The trains run every seven minutes from 6am to midnight, except during peak hours – 6am to 9am and 4.30pm to 7.30pm – when frequency is increased to every five minutes. You can ride the entire line in just 25 minutes from Hualamphong to Bang Seu.

TAXI

Bangkok taxis almost all use their meters, and most have wonderful air-con and working seat belts. You can flag them down anywhere. The meter charge is 35B for the first 2km, then 4.50B per kilometre for the next 10km, 5B per kilometre for 13km to 20km and 5.50B per kilometre for any distance greater than 20km. If traffic is moving slowly, a small per-minute surcharge kicks in. Freeway tolls – 30B to 70B depending on where you start – must be paid by the passenger. Twenty-four-hour 'phone-a-cab' services, **Siam Taxi** (☎ 1161) and **Taxi Radio** (☎ 1681), are available for an additional 20B over the regular metered fare.

During the morning and afternoon rush hours, taxis might refuse to go to certain destinations because of the traffic; if this happens, just try another cab. Around Th Khao San and other tourist areas, some cabbies might try to charge a flat fee – just walk away and find another cab.

From the Southern Bus Terminal, almost every taxi charges a flat fee of 200B to 300B into town.

It is possible to hire a taxi all day for 1500B to 2000B, depending on how much driving is involved.

Motorcycle Taxi

With traffic almost permanently gridlocked in central Bangkok, motorcycle taxis have become the only feasible way to get around during the rush hour. However, taking a motorcycle taxi through the Bangkok traffic is not for the faint-hearted. The kamikaze drivers routinely drive against the flow of traffic and the average journey will involve half a dozen incidents in which you are just millimetres away from a gruesome death. That said, passengers do get helmets in Bangkok and there are good hospitals nearby! Fares range from 10B for a short hop to 60B for a longer cross-town trip – we leave the decision in your hands.

TÚK-TÚK

Called *săamláw khrêuang* by the Thais – túk-túk is 'foreigner talk' – these puttputting little three-wheelers are best for short trips, preferably at night, when the pollution won't sour your alfresco trip as much. They're really worth catching only for the novelty appeal because they're not much cheaper than metered taxis. You have to bargain – about 40B for a short hop is a fair price.

Beware of any túk-túk driver who offers to take you sightseeing for only 10B or 20B an hour. His sole purpose will be to guide you to shady gem or tailor shops hoping for commissions.

PRACTICALITIES

ACCOMMODATION

The Sleeping chapter contains our recommendations for places to stay in the city, arranged by neighbourhood. Reviews are listed alphabetically.

Bangkok hotels enjoy a relatively high occupancy rate year-round, but space can be particularly tight during the two peak seasons, November to March and July to August. Seasonal discounts are occasionally available at top-end hotels in May, June and September only.

Fancier hotels oriented towards business travellers sometimes offer weekend rates that are slightly lower than weekday rates.

Booking Services

For midrange and top-end hotels, discounts of 30% to 50% per night can easily be obtained through many Thai travel agencies. At Bangkok International Airport, in the arrival halls of both the international and domestic terminals, the **Thai Hotels Association** (THA; ☎ 0 2996 7725; www.thaihotels.org) can also arrange discounts. If you're travelling with THAI, ask about special discounts at affiliated hotels.

Web-based booking services also regularly run Internet specials for midrange and top-end hotels. User-friendly booking sites with plenty of options include www.bangkok.com and www.asiatravel.com. For bookings made within 14 days of arrival, www.latestays.com can be very economical.

BUSINESS HOURS

Most government offices are open from 8.30am to 4.30pm on weekdays, but close from noon to 1pm for lunch. In recent years the government has pushed for a 'no lunch closing' policy – you might even see signs posted to this effect – but in reality government employees pay no attention and you will almost surely be disappointed if you expect to get anything done between noon and 1pm.

Regular bank hours in Bangkok are 9.30am to 3.30pm Monday to Friday, but several banks have special foreign-exchange

offices that are open longer hours (generally from 8.30am until 8pm) every day of the week. Note that all government offices and banks are closed on public holidays (see p249).

Commercial businesses usually operate between 8.30am and 5pm on weekdays and sometimes Saturday morning as well. The larger shops usually open from 10am to 6.30pm or 7pm, but smaller shops may open earlier and close later. Hours for restaurants and cafés vary greatly. Some open as early as 8am, others around 11am and still others are open in the evenings only. Some close as early as 9pm and others stay open all night. Bars, by law, can't open before 4pm and must close by 1am.

CHILDREN

Thais love children and in many instances will shower attention on your offspring, who will find ready playmates among their Thai counterparts and a temporary nanny service at practically every stop.

For the most part, parents needn't worry too much about health concerns, although it is worth laying down a few ground rules, such as frequent hand washing, to head off potential medical problems. All the typical health precautions apply (see p247). Children should especially be warned not to play with animals, as rabies is relatively common in Thailand.

Nappies (diapers), formula and other infant requirements are available at Bangkok supermarkets, pharmacies and convenience stores.

Check out Lonely Planet's *Travel With Children* for further advice.

Fun for Kids

Bangkok has plenty of attractions for children. Among the most recommended are the centrally located Dusit Zoo (p90), the Bangkok Doll Factory & Museum (p95), the Children's Discovery Museum (p113) and, on the city's outskirts, Safari World (p114). Queen Saovabha Memorial Institute (Snake Farm; p109), Lumphini Park (p109) and Samphran Elephant Ground & Zoo (p232) are other good options. Most shopping centres offer free children's play centres on their uppermost floors. These areas often have banks of video-game machines off to one side.

CLIMATE

At the centre of the flat, humid Mae Nam Chao Phraya delta, Bangkok sits at the same latitude as Khartoum and Guatemala City, and can be as hot as the former and as wet as the latter.

The southwest monsoon arrives between May and July and lasts into October. This is followed by a dry period from November to May, which begins with lower relative temperatures until mid-February (because of the influence of the northeast monsoon, which bypasses this part of Thailand but results in cool breezes), followed by much higher relative temperatures from March to May.

It usually rains most during August and September, though it can flood in October since the ground has reached full saturation by then. If you are in Bangkok in early October, you may find yourself in hip-deep water in certain parts of the city. An umbrella can be invaluable – a raincoat will just make you hot.

See p11 for recommendations on best times of year to visit.

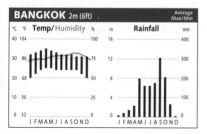

COURSES
Cooking

Amaze your friends back home with your deft preparations of *yam* (hot and tangy salad) and *lâap* (spicy minced-meat salad) after attending a Thai culinary course at one of the following.

Baipai Thai Cooking School (Map pp278–9; ☎ 0 2294 9029; www.baipai.com; 150/12 Soi Naksuwan, Rh Nonsee, Yannawa) A relatively new school offering courses lasting from one to five days.

Blue Elephant Cooking School (Map pp290–1; ☎ 0 2673 9353; www.blueelephant.com/school; 233 Th Sathon Tai) A state-of-the-art teaching kitchen, with options for all-vegetarian menus and choice of either one-on-one cooking classes or group classes.

Oriental Hotel Cooking School (Map pp290–1; ☎ 0 2659 9000); www.mandarinoriental.com; 48 Soi 38, Th Charoen Krung) Plush and famous, this is where visiting celebs typically learn how to turn out a *kaeng khĭaw-wăan* (green curry).

Thai House (☎ 0 2903 9611; www.thaihouse.co.th; Tambon Bang Meuang, Amphoe Bang Yai, Nonthaburi) Popular residential cooking course in a traditional central Thai house about 40 minutes north of Bangkok by boat. The programmes include all meals, one to three nights' accommodation and transfer to and from central Bangkok.

Language

Tuition at most Thai language schools averages around 250B per hour for group classes, more for private tutoring. We recommend the following:

AAA Thai Language Center (Map pp294–5; ☎ 0 2655 5629; www.aaathai.com; 6th fl, 29 Vanissa Bldg, Th Chitlom) Opened by a group of experienced Thai language teachers from other schools, AAA Thai has a loyal following.

American University Alumni (AUA) Language Center (Map pp294–5; ☎ 0 2252 8170; www.auathailand.org; 179 Th Ratchadamri) One of the largest private language-teaching institutes in the world.

Union Language School (☎ 0 2252 8170; union_lang@yahoo.com; 109 Th Surawong) Affiliated with the Christian Church of Thailand, Union's rigorous course offers a balance of structure-oriented and communication-oriented methodologies.

Meditation

Although at times Bangkok might seem like the most unlikely Buddhist city on earth, there are several places where interested foreigners can learn about Theravada Buddhist meditation. Instruction and accommodation are free of charge.

Wat Mahathat (Map p288; ☎ 0 2823 6326; Tha Phra Chan) The International Buddhist Meditation Centre at Wat Mahathat provides meditation instruction several times daily at Section 5, a building near the monks' residences. There is also a special Saturday session for foreigners at the Dhamma Vicaya Hall. Air-con buses 8 and 12 pass near the wat; the nearest Chao Phraya Express pier is Tha Maharat.

World Fellowship of Buddhists (Map pp296–7; ☎ 0 2661 1284; www.wfb-hq.org; Benjasiri Park, Soi 24, Th Sukhumvit) A clearing house for information on Theravada Buddhism as well as dialogue between various schools of Buddhism. The centre hosts meditation classes from 2pm to 5pm on the first Sunday of every month.

Yoga

Bikram Yoga Bangkok (☎ 0 2652 1333; www.bikramyo gabangkok.com; 29/1 14th fl, Soi Lang Suan, Th Ploenchit)

Iyengar Yoga Studio (☎ 0 2714 9924; www.iyengar-yoga -bangkok.com; 3rd fl, Fiftyfifth Plaza, Soi 55, Th Sukhumvit)

CUSTOMS

Thailand prohibits the importation of illegal drugs, firearms and ammunition (unless registered in advance with the Police Department), and pornographic media. A reasonable amount of clothing for personal use, toiletries and professional instruments are allowed in duty-free, as is one still or one movie or video camera with five rolls of still film or three rolls of movie film or video tape. Up to 200g or 250g of tobacco cigarettes can be brought into the country without paying duty. One litre of wine or spirits is allowed in duty-free.

Electronic goods such as personal stereos, calculators and computers can be a problem if the customs officials have reason to believe you're bringing them in for resale. As long as you don't carry more than one of each, you should be OK.

For information on currency import or export, see p252.

Be sure to check the import regulations in your home country before taking or sending back a large quantity of high-value Thailand purchases.

Antiques & Art

When you are leaving Thailand, you must obtain an export licence for any antiques or objects of art you want to take with you. Export licence applications can be made by submitting two front-view photos of the object(s), with no more than five objects to a photo, and a photocopy of your passport, along with the object(s) in question, to the **Department of Fine Arts** (DFA; ☎ 0 2623 6115; 31 Na Phra Lan) at the Bangkok National Museum. Allow three to five days for the application and inspection process to be completed.

Buddhas or other deity images (or any part thereof) to be exported require a permit from the Ministry of Commerce as well as a licence from the DFA. The one exception to this is the small Buddha images (*phrá phim* or *phrá khrêuang*) that are meant to be worn on a chain around the neck. These

may be exported without a licence as long as the reported purpose is religious.

ELECTRICITY

Electric current is 220V, 50 cycles. Electrical wall outlets are usually of the round, two-pin type. Some outlets accept plugs with two flat pins, and some will accept either flat or round pins. Any electrical supply shop will carry adaptors for international plugs, as well as voltage converters.

EMBASSIES

Countries with diplomatic representation in Bangkok include the following:

Australia (Map pp292–3; ☎ 0 2287 2680; 37 Th Sathon Tai)

Cambodia (Map pp292–3; ☎ 0 2254 6630; 185 Th Ratchadamri)

Canada (Map pp292–3; ☎ 0 2636 0540; 15th fl, Abdulra-him Bldg, 990 Th Phra Ram IV)

EU (Map pp294–5; ☎ 0 2255 9100; 19th fl, Kian Gwan House II, 1410/1 Th Withayu)

France Embassy (Map pp290–1; ☎ 0 2266 8250-6; 35 Soi 36, Th Charoen Krung); Consulate (Map pp292–3; ☎ 0 2287 1592; 29 Th Sathon Tai)

Germany (Map pp292–3; ☎ 0 2287 9000; 9 Th Sathon Tai)

India (☎ 0 2258 0300-6; 46 Soi 23, Th Sukhumvit)

Indonesia (Map pp294–5; ☎ 0 2252 3135; 600-602 Th Phetburi)

Laos (Map pp278–9; ☎ 0 2539 6679; 520/1-3 Soi 39, Th Ramkhamhaeng)

Malaysia (☎ 0 2679 2190-9; 33-35 Th Sathon Tai)

Myanmar (Map pp290–1; ☎ 0 2233 2237; 132 Th Sathon Neua)

Netherlands (Map pp294–5; ☎ 0 2309 5200; 15 Soi Tonson)

New Zealand (Map pp294–5; ☎ 0 2254 2530-3; 19th fl, M Thai Tower, All Seasons Pl, 87 Th Withayu)

Singapore (Map pp290–1; ☎ 0 2286 2111; 9th & 18th fl, Rajanakam Bldg, 183 Th Sathon Tai)

South Africa (Map pp292–3; ☎ 0 2253 8473; 6th fl, Park Pl, 231 Th Sarasin)

Switzerland (Map pp294–5; ☎ 0 2253 0156-60; 5 Th Withayu Neua)

UK & Northern Ireland (Map pp294–5; ☎ 0 2305 8333; 1031 Th Withayu)

USA (Map pp294–5; ☎ 0 2205 4000; 120-122 Th Withayu)

Vietnam (Map pp294–5; ☎ 0 2251 5836-8; 83/1 Th Withayu)

EMERGENCY

Ambulance (via Police) ☎ 191

Fire ☎ 199

Police ☎ 191

Tourist Assistance Center ☎ 0 2282 8129

Tourist Police ☎ 1155

GAY & LESBIAN TRAVELLERS

Thai culture is very tolerant of homosexuality, both male and female. The nation does not have laws that discriminate against homosexuals, and the gay and lesbian scene in Bangkok is pretty much out in the open.

Organisations & Publications

Utopia (www.utopia-asia.com/thaibang.htm) is a gay and lesbian website with lots of Bangkok information.

Anjaree Group (☎ 0 2668 2185; anjaree@ hotmail.com; PO Box 322, Ratchadamnoen Post Office, Bangkok 10200) publishes the monthly *AN: Another Way Magazine* (Thai only). The organisation also sponsors various group activities. The **Lesbian Guide to Bangkok** (www.bangkoklesbian.com) is a relatively new source of information on lesbian activities and venues in the city. **LeSLa** (www .lesla.com) started out as a website for Thai lesbians but the site is now Thai/English bilingual; the group meets every Saturday evening at the **Chit Chat Pub** (☎ 0 2719 6419; Soi 85, Th Lat Phrao). **Lesbian Adventures Thailand** (www.lesbianadventuresthailand.com) is an adventure travel company owned and operated by women.

Gay men may be interested in the **Long Yang Club** (☎ 0 2266 5479; www.longyangclub .com), which is a 'multicultural social group for male-oriented men who want to meet outside the gay scene', with branches all over the world. The Thailand chapter hosts various events in Bangkok.

The monthly *Metro* magazine stays abreast of gay and lesbian happenings in the capital.

HEALTH

Travel health depends on your predeparture preparations, your daily health care while travelling and how you handle any medical problem that does develop. While the potential dangers can seem quite frightening, in reality few travellers experience anything more than an upset stomach.

Bangkok and the surrounding regions of central Thailand are entirely malaria free, so you won't need to worry about taking any antimalarial medication if you don't plan to venture beyond that area.

Basic Rules

FOOD

Beware of ice cream that is sold in the street or anywhere it might have melted and been refrozen; if there's any doubt, steer well clear. Raw or undercooked shellfish such as mussels, oysters and clams should be avoided, as should undercooked meat.

If a place looks clean and well run and the vendor also looks clean and healthy, then the food is probably safe. In general, places that are packed with travellers or locals will be fine, while empty restaurants are questionable. The food in busy restaurants is cooked and eaten quite quickly with little standing around, and is probably not reheated.

WATER

All water served in restaurants or to guests in offices or homes in Bangkok comes from purified sources. It's not necessary to ask for bottled water unless you prefer it. Reputable brands of Thai bottled water or soft drinks are generally fine. Try to purchase glass water bottles, however, as these are recyclable (unlike the plastic ones).

Fruit juices are made with purified water and are safe to drink. Milk in Thailand is always pasteurised.

Ice is generally produced from purified water under hygienic conditions and is therefore theoretically safe. The rule of thumb is that if it's chipped ice, it probably came from an ice block (which may not have been handled well), but if it's ice cubes or 'tubes', it was delivered from the ice factory in sealed plastic.

Before You Go

Pack medications in their original, clearly labelled containers. A signed and dated letter from your physician describing your medical conditions and medications, including generic names, is also a good idea. If carrying syringes or needles, be sure to have a physician's letter documenting their medical necessity. If you have a heart condition bring a copy of your ECG taken just prior to travelling.

If you take any regular medication bring double your needs in case of loss or theft. In Bangkok you can buy many medications over the counter without a doctor's prescription, but it can be difficult to find some of the newer drugs, particularly the latest antidepressant drugs, blood-pressure medications and contraceptive pills.

Internet Resources

There is a wealth of travel-health advice on the Internet. For further information, Lonely Planet (www.lonelyplanet.com) is a good place to start. The World Health Organization (WHO; www.who.int/ith) publishes a superb book called *International Travel & Health,* which is revised annually and is available online at no cost. Another website of general interest is MD Travel Health (www .mdtravelhealth.com), which provides complete travel-health recommendations for every country and is updated daily. The Centers for Disease Control and Prevention (CDC; www.cdc.gov) website also has good general information.

Medical Problems & Treatment

In Thailand medicine is generally available over the counter and the price will be much cheaper than in the West. However, be careful when buying drugs, particularly where the expiry date might have passed or correct storage conditions might not have been followed.

AIR POLLUTION

Pollution is something you'll become very aware of in Bangkok, where heat, dust and motor fumes combine to form a powerful brew of potentially toxic air. Air pollution can be a health hazard, especially if you suffer from lung diseases such as asthma. It can also aggravate coughs, colds and sinus problems and cause eye irritation or infections. Consider avoiding very polluted areas if you think they might jeopardise your health, or invest in an air filter.

AVIAN INFLUENZA

In 2004 parts of the capital were quarantined to stop the possible spread of avian influenza (bird flu), but no human infections

occurred in the city. In about a dozen other provinces in Thailand, however, 17 cases of human infection turned up and there were 12 recorded deaths in 2004. In 2005 a further seven cases occurred, two of which were fatal. There have been no known avian flu infections in Thailand since 2005.

According to the WHO, the risk of contracting avian flu is very low. The primary risk of contracting bird flu comes from handling live poultry. Contrary to myth, eating chicken or other poultry does not put one at risk of avian flu infection. Also contrary to much speculation there is no scientific evidence, at present, that the virus has increased its ability to spread easily from one person to another.

HEAT

Bangkok can be hot and humid throughout the year. For most people it takes at least two weeks to adapt to the hot climate. Swelling of the feet and ankles is common, as are muscle cramps caused by excessive sweating. You can prevent these by avoiding dehydration and excessive activity in the heat. Take it easy when you first arrive. Taking salt tablets isn't a good idea (they aggravate the gut), but drinking rehydration solution or eating salty food helps. Treat cramps by stopping activity, resting, rehydrating with double-strength rehydration solution and gently stretching.

Dehydration is the main contributor to heat exhaustion. Symptoms include feeling weak, headache, irritability, nausea or vomiting, sweaty skin, a fast, weak pulse and a normal or slightly elevated body temperature. Treatment involves getting out of the heat and/or sun, fanning the victim and applying cool, wet cloths to the skin, laying the victim flat with their legs raised and rehydrating with water containing a quarter teaspoon of salt per litre. Recovery is usually rapid and it is common to feel weak for some days afterwards.

Heatstroke is a serious medical emergency. Symptoms come on suddenly and include weakness, nausea, a hot, dry body with a temperature of more than 41°C, dizziness, confusion, loss of coordination, seizures and eventually collapse and loss of consciousness. Seek medical help and begin cooling by getting the victim out of the heat, removing their clothes, fanning them and applying cool, wet cloths or ice to their body, especially to the groin and armpits.

Prickly heat is a common skin rash in the tropics, caused by sweat being trapped under the skin. The result is an itchy rash of tiny lumps. Treat it by moving out of the heat and into an air-conditioned area for a few hours and by having cool showers. Creams and ointments clog the skin so they should be avoided. Locally bought prickly-heat powder can be helpful.

HIV & AIDS

Infection with the HIV might lead to acquired AIDS, which is a fatal disease. Any exposure to blood, blood products or body fluids could put the individual at risk. The disease is often transmitted through sexual contact or dirty needles – tattooing, vaccinations, acupuncture and body piercing can potentially be as dangerous as intravenous drug use if the equipment is not clean.

In Thailand around 95% of HIV transmission occurs through sexual activity, and the remainder through natal transmission or through illicit intravenous drug use. HIV/AIDS can also be spread through infected blood transfusions, although this risk is virtually nil in Thailand due to rigorous blood-screening procedures.

HOLIDAYS

Chinese New Year (usually late February or early March) and Songkran (mid-April) are the two holiday periods that most affect Bangkok. For up to a week before and after these holidays, all public transport in or out of the city might be booked up, although during the holidays themselves Bangkok tends to be very quiet (except in Chinatown during Chinese New Year and Th Khao San during Songkran). Because it's peak season for foreign tourists visiting Thailand, December and January can also be very tight.

See p11 for detailed information on individual festivals and holidays. Government offices and banks close down on the following public holidays.

New Year's Day 1 January

Chakri Day (commemorates the founder of the Chakri dynasty, Rama I) 6 April

Coronation Day (commemorates the 1946 coronation of the king and queen) 5 May

Rains Retreat (Khao Phansa; beginning of the Buddhist rains retreat, when monks refrain from travelling away from their monasteries) July (date varies)

Queen's Birthday 12 August

Chulalongkorn Day 23 October

Ok Phansa (end of Buddhist rains retreat) October/November (date varies)

King's Birthday 5 December

Constitution Day 10 December

INTERNET ACCESS

The Internet is easily accessed in Bangkok. Most travellers make use of Internet cafés and free web-based email such as **Yahoo** (www.yahoo.com) or **Hotmail** (www.hotmail.com). For the visitor who needs to log on only once in a while, these are a less-expensive alternative to getting your own account – and it certainly beats lugging around a laptop. The going rate is 1B or 2B per minute, although we've seen a few places where slower connections are available at 0.50B per minute.

Th Khao San (Map pp286–7) has the highest concentration of access points in the city (more than 40 at last count), so if it's choice you want, head there. Other good areas for Internet centres include Th Silom (Map pp290–1), Th Ploenchit and Siam Square (Map pp294–5). Additionally, many Bangkok guesthouses and hotels offer Internet access.

Using Your Laptop

RJ11 phone jacks are the standard in most hotels, though in a few older hotels and guesthouses the phones might still be hard wired. In the latter case you might be able to use a fax line in the office, since all fax machines in Thailand are connected via RJ11 jacks. Some places will allow guests to use the house fax line for laptop modems, provided online time is kept short.

Temporary dial-up Internet accounts are available from several Thai Internet service providers (ISPs). One of the better ones is WebNet, offered by **CSLoxinfo** (www.csloxinfo.cocom). You can buy a block of 12 hours (160B, valid for three months), 30 hours (380B, valid for a year) or 63 hours (750B valid for a year).

Wi-fi (wireless fidelity) is not hard to find in Bangkok. All 40 branches of the Starbucks coffee chain in the city offer wi-fi services. You'll need to buy a prepaid card (one hour 150B, five hours 600B, 20 hours 1500B) to log on. Some bars and cafés offer free wi-fi services. Many top-end, as well as a few midrange hotels also have wi-fi, sometimes for free and sometimes only by prepaying for time. **NetStumbler** (www.net stumbler.com) and **Jiwire** (www.jiwire.com) have fairly comprehensive lists of hot spots, both free and prepay, in Bangkok.

LEGAL MATTERS

In general, Thai police don't hassle foreigners, especially tourists. If anything, they tend to go out of their way not to arrest a foreigner breaking minor traffic laws, taking the approach that a friendly warning will suffice.

One major exception is drug laws. Most Thai police view drug-takers as a social scourge and consequently see it as their duty to enforce the letter of the law; for others it's an opportunity to make untaxed income via bribes. Which direction they'll go often depends on drug quantities; small-time offenders are sometimes offered the chance to pay their way out of an arrest, while traffickers usually go to jail.

Be extra vigilant about where you dispose of cigarette butts and other refuse in Bangkok. The city has a strong antilittering law, and police won't hesitate to cite foreigners and collect fines of 2000B.

If you are arrested for any offence, the police will allow you to make a phone call to your embassy or consulate in Thailand if you have one, or to a friend or relative. There's a whole set of legal codes governing the length of time and manner in which you can be detained by the police before being charged or put on trial, but the police have a lot of discretion. As a foreigner, the police are more likely to bend these codes in your favour than the reverse. However, as with police worldwide, if you don't show respect to the men in brown you will only make matters worse.

Tourist Police

The best way to deal with most serious hassles regarding rip-offs or thefts is to contact the Tourist Police, who are used to dealing with foreigners, rather than the regular Thai police. The Tourist Police maintain a hotline 24 hours a day – dial ☎ 1155 from any phone in Thailand to lodge complaints or to request assistance with regard to personal safety. You can also call this number

between 8.30am and 4.30pm daily to request travel information.

The Tourist Police can be very helpful in cases of arrest. Although they typically have no jurisdiction over the kinds of cases handled by regular cops, they might be able to help with translation or with contacting your embassy.

Visiting Prisoners

If you would like to visit someone who is serving a prison sentence in Bangkok, you should contact the prisoner's Bangkok embassy, tell the consular staff the prisoner's name and ask them to write a letter requesting you be permitted to see that prisoner. The embassy can provide directions to the prison and tell you the visiting hours. Usually visiting is allowed only a couple of days a week. Don't try going directly to the prison without a letter from the prisoner's embassy, as you might be refused entry.

Visiting imprisoned foreigners in Bangkok has become something of a fad. With the resulting increase in inquiries, both embassy and prison staff are tightening up on the release of prisoner information. The Thai corrections system does not accept the Western notion that prisoners should receive visitors with whom they have no previous familial or social connection (exceptions are sometimes made for missionaries).

For the latest information on visitation policies, contact your embassy in Bangkok.

MAPS

A map is essential for finding your way around Bangkok, and there are many competing for your attention. Lonely Planet's comprehensive *Bangkok City Map*, in a handy, laminated, fold-out sheet-map form, includes a walking tour and is fully indexed.

A bus map is the best way to navigate Bangkok's economical bus system. The most popular is the durable *Tour 'n Guide Map (Bangkok Thailand)*, aka the 'blue map', which shows all bus routes and some walking tours. It's regularly updated, but inevitably some bus routes will be wrong, so take care. Other similar maps include the *Bangkok Bus Map*, with lots of sightseeing tips, and *Latest Tour's Map to Bangkok & Thailand* (a 'blue map' clone).

The long-running, often-imitated and never-equalled *Nancy Chandler's Map of*

Bangkok contains information on out-of-the-way places and where to buy unusual things around the city. A new edition is released every year. Another contender on the market, Groovy Map's *Bangkok by Day & Night,* combines an up-to-date bus map, Skytrain and MRTA subway routes, the usual sightseeing features and a short selection of restaurant and bar reviews. Groovy Map also publishes *Roadway Bangkok,* a GPS-derived 1:40,000 driving map of the city that includes all tollways, expressways, roads and lanes labelled in Thai and English.

The free *City Map of Bangkok,* published and distributed by the Tourism Authority of Thailand (TAT), is a folded sheet map on coated stock with bus routes, major hotels, the latest expressways, sightseeing, hospitals, embassies and more. Separate inset maps of popular areas are useful. You can pick it up at the airport TAT desk or at any Bangkok TAT office (see p258).

MEDICAL SERVICES

More than Thailand's main health-care hub, Bangkok has become a major destination for medical tourism, with patients flying in for treatment from all over the world (see p166). In addition to three university research hospitals, the city is home to more than a dozen public and private hospitals, and hundreds of private medical clinics. Bumrungrad International, widely considered the best medical facility in the country, has US accreditation and offers such conveniences as Starbucks and free wi-fi.

The Australian, US and UK embassies maintain up-to-date lists of doctors who can speak English. For doctors who speak other languages, contact the relevant embassy.

Here is a list of Bangkok's better hospitals:

Bangkok Christian Hospital (Map pp290–1; ☎ 0 2634 0560; www.bkkchristianhosp.th.com;124 Th Silom)

Bangkok Hospital (Map pp278–9; ☎ 0 2310 3344; www.bangkokhospital.com; 2 Soi 47, Th Phetburi Tat Mai)

BNH Hospital (Map pp292–3; ☎ 0 2686 2700; www.bnhhospital.com; 9 Th Convent)

Bumrungrad International (Map pp296–7; ☎ 0 2667 1000; www.bumrungrad.com; 33 Soi 3, Th Sukhumvit)

Mission Hospital (Map pp280–1; ☎ 0 2282 1100, www.mission-hospital.org; 430 Th Phitsanulok)

Phyathai Hospital 1 (Map pp280–1; ☎ 0 2640 1111; www.phyathai.com; 364/1 Th Si Ayuthaya)

Samitivej Hospital (Map pp278–9; ☎ 0 2711 8000; www.samitivej.co.th; 133 Soi 49, Th Sukhumvit)

St Louis Hospital (Map pp290–1; ☎ 0 2210 9999; www.saintlouis.or.th; 215 Th Sathon Tai)

Should you need urgent dental care, suggested contacts in Bangkok include the following:

Dental Design Clinic & Lab (☎ 0 2261 9119; www.dentaldesignclinic-lab.com; 20 Dental Design Bldg, Soi 21, Th Sukhumvit)

Siam Family Dental Clinic (Map pp294–5; ☎ 0 2255 6664; www.siamfamilydental.com; 292/6 Soi 4, Siam Square)

Silom Dental (☎ 0 2636 9092; 439/4-5 Th Narathiwat Ratchanakharin)

All of the hospitals above have substantial ophthalmological treatment facilities. The best eye specialist in the city is **Rutnin Eye Hospital** (☎ 0 2639 3399; www.rutnin.com; 80/1 Soi Asoke).

In the Sampeng/Yaowarat district, along Th Ratchawong, Th Charoen Krung, Th Yaowarat and Th Songwat, you will find many Chinese clinics and herbal dispensaries. The **Pow Tai Dispensary** (572-574 Th Charoen Krung) has been preparing traditional Chinese medicines since 1941. **Huachiew General Hospital** (Map pp280–1; ☎ 2223 1351; hch@huachiewhospital.com; 665 Th Bamrung Meuang) is a large medical facility dedicated to all phases of traditional Chinese medicine, along with modern international medicine. The team of licensed acupuncturists at Huachiew are thought to be Thailand's most skilled.

MONEY

The basic unit of Thai currency is the baht. There are 100 *satang* in one baht. Coins come in denominations of 25 *satang*, 50 *satang*, 1B, 5B and 10B. Older coins have Thai numerals only, while newer coins have Thai and Arabic numerals.

Paper currency comes in denominations of 20B (green), 50B (blue), 100B (red), 500B (purple) and 1000B (beige). A 10,000B bill was on the way when the 1997 cash crunch came, and the idea has yet to be revived.

See p21 for more information about the Thai economy.

ATMs & Credit/Debit Cards

Debit cards issued by a bank in your own country can be used at ATMs around the city to withdraw cash (in Thai baht only) directly from your account back home. There are plenty of ATMs and they're easy to find. You can use MasterCard debit cards to buy baht at foreign-exchange desks at either Bangkok Bank or Siam Commercial Bank. Visa debit cards can buy cash through the Thai Farmers Bank exchange services.

Credit cards as well as debit cards can be used for purchases at many shops, hotels and restaurants. The most commonly accepted cards are Visa and MasterCard, followed by Amex and Japan Card Bureau (JCB). To report a lost or stolen card, call the following telephone hotlines in Bangkok.

Amex (☎ 0 2273 5050)

MasterCard (☎ 001 800 11 887 0663)

Visa (☎ 001 800 441 3485)

Bargaining

Items sold by street vendors, in markets and in most shops are flexibly priced – that is, the price is negotiable. The only places where you'll see fixed prices in Bangkok are department stores. If the same kind of merchandise is offered in a department store and a small shop or market, it's a good idea to check the department store price for a point of reference.

Whether at guesthouses or five-star hotels, room rates can sometimes be bargained down, particularly outside Bangkok's peak season, November to March.

Thais respect a good haggler. Always let the vendor make the first offer, then ask 'Is that your best price?' or 'Can you lower the price?' This usually results in an immediate discount from the first price. Now it's your turn to make a counter-offer; always start low, but don't bargain at all unless you're serious about buying. Negotiations continue back and forth until a price is agreed upon – there's no set discount from the asking price, as some vendors start ridiculously high, others closer to the 'real' price.

It helps if you've done your homework by shopping around, and the whole process becomes easier with practice. Keep the negotiations relaxed and friendly, and speak slowly and clearly (but not in a condescending manner). Vendors will almost always give a better price to someone they like.

Changing Money

Banks or legal moneychangers offer the optimum foreign-exchange rates. When buying baht, US dollars are the most readily accepted currency and travellers cheques receive better rates than cash. Generally, British pounds and euros are second to the US dollar in acceptability. As banks charge up to 23B commission and duty for each travellers cheque cashed, you'll save on commissions if you use larger cheque denominations. See p244 for information on bank opening hours.

American Express card holders can get advances in travellers cheques. The Amex agent is **SEA Tours** (Map pp280–1; ☎ 0 2216 5759; 8th fl, Suite 88-92, Payathai Plaza, 128 Th Phayathai).

See the inside front cover for exchange rates. Current exchange rates are printed in the *Bangkok Post* and the *Nation* every day, or you can walk into any Thai bank and ask to see a daily rate sheet.

Exchange Control

By Thai law, any traveller arriving in Thailand is supposed to carry at least the following amounts of money in cash, travellers cheques, bank draft or letter of credit, according to visa category: Non-Immigrant Visa, US$500 per person or US$1000 per family; Tourist Visa, US$250 per person or US$500 per family; Transit Visa or no visa, US$125 per person or US$250 per family. Your funds might be checked by authorities if you arrive on a one-way ticket or if you look as if you're at 'the end of the road'.

There is no limit to the amount of Thai or foreign currency you may bring into Thailand. Upon leaving, you are permitted to take no more than 50,000B per person without special authorisation; exportation of foreign currencies is unrestricted. An exception is made if you are going to Cambodia, Laos, Malaysia, Myanmar or Vietnam, where the limit is 500,000B.

It's legal to open a foreign-currency account at any commercial bank in Thailand. As long as the funds originate from abroad, there are no restrictions on their maintenance or withdrawal.

NEWSPAPERS & MAGAZINES

Two well-respected English-language newspapers are published daily in Thailand and distributed throughout most of the country's provincial capitals: the *Bangkok Post* in the morning and the *Nation* in the afternoon. The *Bangkok Post* is Thailand's oldest English-language newspaper, established in 1946. Both papers publish online. The Singapore edition of the *International Herald Tribune* is widely available in Bangkok.

Published by Bangkok expats, *Untamed Travel* magazine is an entertaining and useful read, with excellent travel information for Thailand and much of the region, alongside well-written and often irreverent stories covering the local and global travel scene. *Bangkok Metro* takes a *TimeOut* approach, heavy with listings on art, culture, cuisine, film and music in Bangkok. The monthly *Le Gavroche* offers news and features on Thailand for the Francophone community.

Popular international magazines are sold in specialist bookshops (see p189).

PHARMACIES

Pharmacies are plentiful in the city, in fact in business areas you'll stumble on one every 100m or so. Most Bangkok pharmacists speak excellent English. If you don't find what you need at the smaller pharmacies, try one of the hospitals listed under Medical Services (p251), as they usually stock a wider range of pharmaceuticals. The hospital pharmacies are open 24 hours; smaller pharmacies usually open around 10am and close between 8pm and 10pm. One nonhospital pharmacy that's open 24 hours is **Foodland Supermarket Pharmacy** (Map pp296–7; ☎ 0 2254 2247; 1413 Soi 5, Th Sukhumvit).

POST

Thailand has a very efficient postal service, and both domestic and international postal rates are very reasonable. Bangkok's **main post office** (Communications Authority of Thailand, CAT; Map pp290–1; Th Charoen Krung) is open from 8am to 8pm on weekdays and from 8am to 1pm on weekends and holidays.

A 24-hour international telecommunications service (including telephone, fax, telex and telegram) is located in a separate building to the right and slightly in front of the main post office building.

The easiest way to reach the main post office is via the Chao Phraya Express, which stops at Tha Muang Khae at the river end of Soi 34, next to Wat Muang Khae, just south of the post office.

Couriers

DHL Worldwide (☎ 0 2658 8000; 22nd fl, Grand Amarin Tower, Th Phetburi Tat Mai)

FedEx (☎ 0 2367 3222; 8th fl, Green Tower, Th Phra Ram IV)

UPS (☎ 0 2712 3300; 16/1 Soi 44/1, Th Sukhumvit)

Packaging

There's an efficient and inexpensive packaging service at the main post office, or you could simply buy the materials at the counter and do it yourself. The parcel counter is open from 8am to 4.30pm on weekdays and from 8.30am to noon on Saturday. When the parcel counter is closed (weekday evenings and Sunday mornings), an informal packing service (using recycled materials) is open behind the service windows at the centre rear of the building.

Branch post offices throughout the city also offer parcel services.

Receiving Mail
POSTE RESTANTE

Bangkok's poste-restante service is reliable, though with the popularity of email these days few tourists use it. When you receive mail, you must show ID, sign your name and write your passport number, the number of the letter and date of delivery in the book provided. The poste-restante counter at the main post office on Th Charoen Krung is open from 8am to 8pm on weekdays and from 8am to 1pm on weekends. Branch post offices throughout Bangkok also offer poste-restante services.

AMERICAN EXPRESS

The Amex agent **SEA Tours** (Map pp280–1; ☎ 0 2216 5759; 8th fl, Suite 88-92, Payathai Plaza, 128 Th Phayathai; ◷ 8.30am-noon & 1-4.30pm Mon-Fri, 8.30-11.30am Sat) will take mail on behalf of Amex card holders. It won't accept courier packages that require your signature.

RADIO

Bangkok has around a hundred FM and AM stations. Some of the Bangkok FM stations feature surprisingly good music programmes with British, Thai and American DJs. Looking for *lûuk thûng* (Thai country) music? Station Luk Thung 90 FM broadcasts classic and new *lûuk thûng* styles. For the Thai alternative, tune into Fat Radio 104.5 FM.

The BBC World Service, Radio Canada, Radio Japan, Radio New Zealand, Singapore Broadcasting Company and Voice of America all have broadcasts in English and Thai over short-wave radio. The frequencies and schedules, which change hourly, are published in the *Bangkok Post* and the *Nation*.

SAFETY

By and large, Bangkok is a very safe place with little street crime to speak of. Beware of crafty pickpockets on public buses, particularly in the area around Hualamphong Railway Station.

Scams

Thais are generally so friendly and laid-back that some visitors are lulled into a false sense of security that makes them vulnerable to scams and con schemes of all kinds. Con artists tend to haunt first-time tourist spots, such as the Grand Palace area, Wat Pho and Siam Square (especially near Jim Thompson's House).

Most scams in Bangkok begin the same way: a friendly Thai male (or, on rare occasions, a female) approaches a lone visitor and strikes up a seemingly innocuous conversation. Sometimes the con man says he's a university student or teacher; at other times he might claim to work for the World Bank or a similarly distinguished organisation. If you're on the way to Wat Pho or Jim Thompson's House, for example, he may tell you it's closed for a holiday or repairs. Eventually the conversation works its way around to the subject of the scam – the better con men can actually make it seem as though you initiated the topic.

The scam itself almost always incorporates gems, tailor shops or card playing. With gems, the victim is invited to a gem and jewellery shop – your new-found friend is picking up some merchandise for himself and you're just along for the ride. Somewhere along the way he usually claims to have a connection in your home country (what a coincidence!) with whom he has a regular gem export-import business. One way or another, the victim is convinced that they can turn a profit by arranging a gem purchase and reselling the merchandise at home. After all, the jewellery shop just happens to be offering a generous discount today.

There are seemingly infinite variations on the gem scam, almost all of which end up with the victim purchasing small, low-quality sapphires and posting them to their home country. Once you return home, of course, the cheap sapphires turn out to be worth much less than what you paid for them. Many have invested and lost virtually all their savings.

Even if you were able to return your purchase to the gem shop in question, chances are slim to none they'd give a full refund. The con artist who brings the mark into the shop gets a commission of 10% to 50% per sale – the shop takes the rest. The Thai police are usually of no help, believing that merchants are entitled to whatever price they can get. The main victimisers are a handful of shops who get protection from certain high-ranking government officials.

At tailor shops the objective is to get you to pay exorbitant prices for poorly made clothes. The tailor shops that do this are adept at delaying delivery until just before you leave Thailand, so that you don't have time to object to poor workmanship. The way to avoid this scam is to choose tailor shops yourself and not offer any more than a small deposit – no more than enough to cover your chosen fabrics – until you're satisfied with the workmanship.

The card-playing scam starts out very similarly to the gem scenario: a friendly stranger approaches the lone traveller on the street, strikes up a conversation and then invites him or her to the house of his relative for a drink or meal. After a bit of socialising, a friend or relative of the con arrives on the scene; it just so happens a little high-stakes card game is planned for later that day. Like the gem scam, the card-game scam has many variations, but eventually the victim is shown some cheating tactics to use with help from the 'dealer', some practice sessions take place and finally the game gets under way. The mark is allowed to win a few hands first, then somehow loses a few, gets bankrolled by one of the friendly Thais, and then loses the Thai's money. Suddenly your new-found buddies aren't so friendly any more – they want the money you lost. Sooner or later you end up cashing in most or all of your travellers cheques or making a costly visit to an ATM. Again the police won't take any action – in this case because gambling is illegal in Thailand and you've broken the law by playing cards for money.

Other minor scams involve túk-túk drivers, hotel employees and bar girls who take new arrivals on city tours; these almost always end in high-pressure sales pushes at silk, jewellery or handicraft shops. In this case greed isn't the ruling motivation – it's simply a matter of weak sales resistance.

Follow the TAT's number-one suggestion: disregard all offers of free shopping or sightseeing help from strangers – they will invariably take a commission from your purchases. You might also try lying whenever a stranger asks how long you've been in Thailand – if it's only been three days, say three weeks! The con artists rarely prey on anyone except new arrivals.

You should contact the Tourist Police if you have any problems with consumer fraud. Call ☎ 1155 from any phone.

TAXES & REFUNDS

Thailand has a 7% value-added tax (VAT) added to many goods and services. Visitors to Bangkok who hold valid Tourist Visas and who depart by air may apply for a VAT refund on purchases made at certain shops and department stores. Refunds are available only at the departure halls of Thailand's international airports, where you must fill out a VAT refund application and present it to customs officers along with the purchased goods and receipts.

Larger hotels will usually add a 10% hotel tax, and sometimes an 8% to 10% service charge as well, to your room bill.

TELEPHONE

The telephone system in Thailand, operated by the government-subsidised but privately owned Telephone Organisation of Thailand (TOT) under the Communications Authority of Thailand (CAT), is efficient if costly, and from Bangkok you can direct-dial most major centres with little difficulty.

The telephone country code for Thailand is ☎ 66. Thailand no longer uses separate area codes for Bangkok and the provinces, and all phone numbers in the country use eight digits (preceded by 0 if you're dialling domestically). When dialling Thailand from outside the country, you must first dial whatever international access code

is necessary, followed by 66 and then the phone number in Thailand.

For directory assistance, dial ☎ 13.

International Calls

To direct-dial an international number from a private phone, simply dial ☎ 001 before the number. For operator-assisted international calls, dial ☎ 100.

A service called Home Country Direct is available at Bangkok's main post office (Map pp290–1), Bangkok International Airport (Map pp278–9), Queen Sirikit National Convention Center (Map pp296–7), Sogo department store (Map pp294–5), the Banglamphu post office (Map pp286–7) and Hualamphong Railway Station (Map pp284–5). Home Country Direct phones offer easy one-button connection to international operators in about 40 countries around the world.

Alternatively you can direct-dial Home Country Direct access numbers from any private phone (most hotel phones won't work) in Thailand. Dial ☎ 001 999 followed by one of the numbers below:

Home Country Direct access numbers

Australia (Optus)	61 2000
Australia (Telstra)	61 1000
Canada	15 1000
Canada (AT&T)	15 2000
Denmark	45 1000
Finland	358 1000
France	33 1000
Germany	49 1000
Israel	972 1000
Italy	39 1000
Japan	81 0051
Korea	82 1000
Netherlands	31 1035
New Zealand	64 1066
Norway	47 1000
Singapore	65 0000
Sweden	46 1000
Switzerland	41 1000
UK (BT)	44 1066
UK (MCL)	44 2000
USA (AT&T)	11 1111
USA – Hawaii	14424
USA (MCI)	12001
USA (Sprint)	13877

Directory

PRACTICALITIES

TOT offers a separate international service to 30 select countries (including Australia, Belgium, Canada, Denmark, France, Germany, Hong Kong, Japan, Malaysia, Singapore, UK and USA), accessed by dialling ☎ 008 first. The TOT service costs less per minute than the corresponding CAT service, so there's no reason to use the 001 route if you have a choice.

Hotels generally add surcharges (sometimes as much as 50% above the CAT rate) for international long-distance calls, so it's always cheaper to call abroad from a CAT telephone office. A useful CAT office stands next to the main post office (Map pp290–1). You can also make long-distance calls and send faxes at the TOT office (Map pp294–5) on Th Ploenchit – but this office accepts cash only, and no reverse-charge or credit-card calls can be made.

Depending on where you are calling, reimbursing someone later for a reverse-charge call to your home country might be less expensive than paying CAT/TOT charges – it is worth comparing rates at source and destination.

Private long-distance phone offices with international service always charge more than the government offices, although their surcharges are usually lower than hotel rates.

Whichever type of phone service you use, the least expensive time of day to make calls is from midnight to 5am (30% discount on standard rates), followed by 9pm to midnight or 5am to 7am (20% discount). You pay full price from 7am to 9pm (this rate is reduced by 20% on Sunday).

If you're calling from someone's private phone, you must dial the international access code (☎ 001) before dialling the country code, area code and phone number you wish to reach.

International Phonecards

ThaiCard, a CAT-issued, prepaid international phonecard, comes in 300B and 500B denominations and allows calls to many countries at standard CAT rates. You can use the ThaiCard codes from either end, eg calling the UK from Thailand or calling Thailand from the UK.

Lenso phonecards cover international phone calls from yellow Lenso International Card phones, wall phones found in airports, shopping centres and in front of some post offices. Cards come in two denominations, 250B and 500B, and are sold in convenience stores and some supermarkets. You can also use most major credit cards with Lenso phones and dial AT&T direct-access numbers (though rates are high). It's the most expensive way to call internationally.

Internet Phone

The cheapest way to call internationally is via the Internet, and many Internet cafés in Bangkok are set up to allow Internet phone calls. Most charge only the regular per-minute or per-hour fees they charge for any other kind of Internet access, if the call itself is a free call. A few charge extra for Internet phone calls, and of course if the call isn't free you will pay for both Internet time and the call – but this is still often less expensive than using CAT.

CAT itself offers the PhoneNet card, which comes in denominations of 300B, 500B and 1000B and allows you to call overseas via Voice over Internet Protocol for a 40% to 86% saving over regular rates. The difference with PhoneNet is that you can call from any phone, ie you don't call from a computer. Quality is good and the rates represent excellent value (only 6B per minute to most countries); refills are available for 300B and 500B. Cards are available from any CAT office or online at www .thaitelephone.com.

Mobile Phones

TOT authorises the use of private mobile phones tuned to GSM networks. If you bring your own mobile phone, roaming is not usually a problem, though it can be quite expensive.

Two cellular operators in Thailand, Orange and DTAC, will allow you to use their SIM cards in an imported phone, as long as your phone isn't SIM-locked. Rates depend on the calling plan you choose, but are typically around 3B per minute anywhere in Thailand. Mobile-phone shops dealing in such cards can easily be found in most shopping centres in Bangkok.

Major hotels in Bangkok can arrange the rental of handsets and SIM cards but it's less expensive to buy a used mobile phone and prepaid SIM card if you're around more than a couple of days. Mahboonkrong

(MBK) shopping centre (p181) is a good place to look for inexpensive used and new mobile phones,

Payphones & Phonecards

There are three kinds of public payphones in Thailand: red, blue and green. The red phones are for local calls, the blue are for both local and long-distance calls (within Thailand), and the green ones are for use with phonecards.

Local calls from payphones cost 1B for three minutes (add more coins for more time), except when calling a mobile phone number, where the rate is 3B per minute. Local calls from private phones cost 3B, with no time limit. Some hotels and guesthouses have private payphones that cost 5B per call. Long-distance rates within the country vary from 3B to 12B per minute, depending on the distance.

For use with the green card phones, domestic TOT phonecards are available at the information counter or gift shops of Bangkok International Airport, major shopping centres and 7-Elevens. TOT phonecards come in 25B, 50B, 100B, 200B and 500B denominations, all roughly the same size as a credit card.

TELEVISION

Thailand has five VHF TV networks based in Bangkok; all but one are government operated. The single private network, ITV, is owned by the current prime minister's family, so even this one cleaves to the government line politically. All telecast a mixture of news, music, documentaries and dramatic series. Some English programming is available – check the TV schedules in the *Bangkok Post* and the *Nation* for details.

Satellite & Cable TV

UBC (www.ubctv.com), the only cable company broadcasting in Thailand, carries six English-language movie channels (censored for language, nudity and violence), four sports channels, imported TV series, three music channels (MTV Asia, Channel V and VH1), CNN International, CNBC, NHK, BBC World Service Television, the Discovery Channel and all the standard Thai networks. You can access further information on UBC's website or in the Bangkok dailies.

Thailand has its own ThaiCom 1 and 2 satellites as uplinks for AsiaSat and as carriers for the standard Thai networks and Thai Sky (TST). The latter includes five channels offering news and documentaries, Thai music videos and Thai variety programmes. Other satellites tracked by dishes in Thailand include China's Apstar 1 and Apstar 2. Additional transmissions from these and from Vietnam, Myanmar and Malaysia are available with a satellite dish.

TIME
Thai Calendar

The official year in Thailand is reckoned from the Western calendar year 543 BC, the beginning of the Buddhist Era, so that AD 2006 is 2549 BE, AD 2007 is 2550 BE etc. All dates in this book refer to the Western calendar.

Time Zone

Thailand's time zone is seven hours ahead of GMT/UTC. Thus, noon in Bangkok is 9pm the previous day in Los Angeles, midnight the same day in New York, 5am in London, 6am in Paris, 1pm in Perth, and 3pm in Sydney and Melbourne. Times are an hour later in countries/regions that are on Daylight Savings Time. See also the World Time Zones map (p276)

At government offices and local cinemas, times are often expressed according to the 24-hour clock, eg 11pm is written as 2300.

TIPPING

Tipping is not normal practice in Bangkok, although they're used to it in expensive hotels and restaurants; don't bother elsewhere. The exception is loose change left from a largish Thai restaurant bill; for example, if a meal costs 288B and you pay with a 500B note, leave the 12B coin change on the change tray. It's not so much a tip as a way of saying 'I'm not so money-grubbing as to grab every last baht'.

TOURIST INFORMATION

Operated by the Bangkok Metropolitan Administration (BMA), the **Bangkok Tourist Division** (BTD; Map pp286–7; ☎ 0 2225 7612; www.bangkoktourist.com; 17/1 Th Phra Athit; ☉9am-7pm) has a friendly and informative staff. As well as stocking a wealth of brochures, maps and event schedules, staff can assist with the chartering of boats at the adjacent pier.

Local bus maps are distributed by a BTD **tourist information booth** (Map pp286–7; ☎ 0 2281 5538) next to the Chana Songkhram police station on Th Chakraphong, close to the corner of Th Khao San. BTD also has counters in Bangkok International Airport, opposite Wat Suthat and Wat Phra Kaew, and at most major shopping centres.

The **TAT main office** (Map pp280–1; ☎ 0 2250 5500; www.tourismthailand.org; 1600 Th Phetburi Tat Mai, Makkasan, Ratchathewi) has useful, well-produced and informative brochures on sightseeing and cultural topics. The **TAT information compound** (Map pp286–7; ☎ 0 2282 9773; Th Ratchadamnoen Nok; ☉ 8am-4.30pm), near the Ratchadamnoen Stadium, is more convenient. The TAT also maintains a 24-hour **Tourist Assistance Center** (☎ 1155) in the compound for matters relating to theft and other mishaps, run by its paramilitary arm, the Tourist Police (see p250).

The TAT also has information desks at Bangkok International Airport in the arrivals area of Terminal 1 (☎ 0 2504 2701) and Terminal 2 (☎ 0 2504 2669); both are open from 8am to midnight.

TAT Offices Abroad

Australia (☎ 02-9247 7549; info@thailand.net.au; Level 2, 75 Pitt St, Sydney, NSW 2000)

France (☎ 01-53 53 47 00; tatpar@wanadoo.fr; 90 Ave des Champs Elysées, 75008 Paris)

Germany (☎ 069-138 1390; tatfra@tat.or.th; Bethmannstrasse 58, D-60311 Frankfurt am Main)

Japan Tokyo (☎ 03-3218 0337; tattky@tat.or.th; South Tower 2F, Room 259, Yurakucho Denki Bldg, 1-7-1 Yurakucho, Chiyoda-ku, Tokyo 100); Osaka (☎ 06-6543 6654; info@tatosacom; Technoble Yotsubashi Bldg 3F, 1-6-8 Kitahorie, Nishi-ku, Osaka 550-0014)

Malaysia (☎ 603-216 23480; sawatdi@po.jaring.my; Suite 22.01, Level 22, Menara Lion, 165 Jalan Ampang, 50450 Kuala Lumpur)

Singapore (☎ 65-235 7901; tatsin@singnet.com.sg; c/o Royal Thai Embassy, 370 Orchard Rd, 238870 Singapore)

UK (☎ 020-7925 2511; 3rd fl, Brook House, 98-99 Jermyn St, London SW1Y 6EE)

USA Los Angeles (☎ 323-461 9814; tatla@ix.netcom.com; 1st fl, 611 North Larchmont Blvd, Los Angeles, CA 90004); New York (☎ 212-432 0433, 1-800 THAI LAND; tatny@tat .or.th; 61 Broadway, Suite 2810, New York, NY 10006)

TRAVELLERS WITH DISABILITIES

Bangkok presents one large, ongoing obstacle course for the mobility-impaired, with its high curbs, uneven pavements and nonstop traffic. Many of the city's streets must be crossed via pedestrian bridges flanked with steep stairways, while buses and boats don't stop long enough to accommodate even the mildly disabled. Rarely are there any ramps or other access points for wheelchairs.

A few of the most expensive top-end hotels make consistent design efforts to provide disabled access to their properties. Other deluxe hotels with high employee-to-guest ratios are usually good about providing staff help where building design fails. For the rest, you're pretty much left to your own resources.

Organisations

Accessible Journeys (☎ 610-521 0339; www.disabil itytravel.com; 35 West Sellers Ave, Ridley Park, Pennsylvania, USA)

Mobility International USA (☎ 541-343 1284; info@miusa.org; PO Box 10767, Eugene, OR 97440, USA)

Society for Accessible Travel & Hospitality (☎ 212-447 7284; www.sath.org; Suite 610, 347 Fifth Ave, New York, NY 10016, USA)

VISAS

The Royal Thai Ministry of Foreign Affairs lists its visa policies at www.mfa.go.th /web/12.php.

Non-Immigrant Visas

The Non-Immigrant Visa is good for 90 days, must be applied for in your home country, costs around US$60 and is not difficult to obtain if you can offer a good reason for your visit. Business, study, retirement and extended family visits are among the purposes considered valid. If you want to stay longer than six months, this is the one to get: you can buy two back-to-back 90-day visas, and when the first expires, leave the country and come back in on the second visa. If you plan to apply for a Thai work permit, you'll need to possess a Non-Immigrant Visa first.

The Non-Immigrant Business Visa (usually abbreviated by immigration officials to 'non-B') allows unlimited entries to Thailand for one year. The only hitch is that you must leave the country at least once every 90 days to keep the visa valid. However, a 90-day non-B can be extended to a full year if you're able to obtain a work permit during the first 90 days.

Tourist Visa Exemption

The Thai government allows 41 nationalities, including those from most European countries, Australia, New Zealand and the USA (see www.mfa.go.th/web/12.php for a detailed list), to enter the country without a visa for 30 days at no charge. Citizens of Brazil, Republic of Korea and Peru may enter without a visa for 90 days.

Without proof of an onward ticket and sufficient funds for their projected stay, any visitor can be denied entry, but in practice your ticket and funds are rarely checked if you're dressed neatly.

A few nationalities must obtain a visa in advance of arrival or they'll be turned back. Check with a Thai embassy or consulate if you plan on arriving without a visa.

Tourist Visas

If you plan to stay in Thailand for more than a month, you should apply for the 60-day Tourist Visa (US$30). One passport photo must accompany all applications.

Transit Visas

Citizens from a list of 14 nations, including the People's Republic of China, Taiwan and several countries in Central and South Asia, can obtain a 15-day Transit Visa (800B). You might be required to show you have 10,000B per person or 20,000B per family to obtain this visa.

Visa Extensions & Renewals

It is possible to extend 60-day Tourist Visas by up to 30 days at the discretion of Thai immigration authorities. You can go to the Bangkok **Immigration Office** (Map pp292–3; ☎ 0 2287 3101; Soi Suan Phlu, Th Sathon Tai) or apply at any immigration office in the country. The fee for extension of a Tourist Visa is 1900B. Bring along one photo and one copy each of the photo and visa pages of your passport. Usually only one 30-day extension is granted.

The 30-day, no-visa stay can be extended for seven to 10 days (depending on the immigration office) for 1900B. You can also leave the country and return immediately to obtain another 30-day stay. There is no limit on how often you can do this, nor is there a minimum interval that you must spend outside the country.

Extension of the 15-day Transit Visa is allowed only if you hold a passport from a country that has no Thai embassy.

If you overstay your visa, the usual penalty is a fine of 500B for each extra day, with a 40,000B limit. Fines can be paid at the airport or in advance at the **Immigration Office** (Room 416, 4th fl, Old Bldg, Soi Suan Phlu, Th Sathon Tai). If you've overstayed only one day, you don't have to pay. Children under 14 travelling with a parent do not have to pay the penalty.

WOMEN TRAVELLERS

Contrary to popular myth, Thailand doesn't receive a higher percentage of male visitors than most other countries. In fact around 40% of visitors are women, a higher ratio than the worldwide average as measured by the World Tourism Organization. The overall increase for women visitors has climbed faster than that for men in almost every year since the early 1990s.

Everyday incidents of sexual harassment are much less common in Thailand than in India, Indonesia or Malaysia, and this might lull women familiar with those countries into thinking that Thailand is safer than it is. However, virtually all incidents of attacks on foreign women in Thailand have occurred outside Bangkok, typically in remote beach or mountain areas. If you're a woman travelling alone, try to pair up with other travellers when moving around at night. Make sure hotel and guesthouse rooms are secure at night – if they're not, demand another room or move to another hotel or guesthouse.

WORK

Bangkok's status as the heart of the Thai economy provides a variety of work opportunities for foreigners, although in general it's not as easy to find a job as in more developed countries. As in the rest of East and Southeast Asia, there is a high demand for English speakers to provide instruction to Thai citizens. This is not due to a shortage of qualified Thai teachers with a good grasp of English grammar, but rather a desire to have native-speaker models in the classroom.

Teaching English

Those with academic credentials such as teaching certificates or degrees in English as a second language will get first crack at the better-paying jobs, such as those at universities and international schools. But there are perhaps hundreds of private language-teaching establishments in Bangkok that hire noncredentialed teachers by the hour. Private tutoring is also a possibility. International oil companies pay the highest salaries for English instructors, but are also quite choosy.

If you're interested in finding teaching work, start with the English-language *Greater Bangkok Metropolitan Telephone Directory* yellow pages. Check all the usual headings – Schools, Universities, Language Schools (nearly a hundred listings in Bangkok alone) and so on.

A website maintained by an English as a foreign language teacher in Bangkok, www .ajarn.com, has tips on where to find teaching jobs and how to deal with Thai classrooms, as well as current job listings.

Volunteering & Other Jobs

Voluntary and paying positions with organisations that provide charitable services in education, development or public health are available for those with the right education and/or experience. Some contacts:

Australian Volunteers International (☎ 03-9279 1788, 1800 331 292; www.australianvolunteers.com; Melbourne, Australia)

US Peace Corps (☎ 800-424 8580; www.peacecorps.gov; Washington DC, USA)

Voluntary Service Overseas Canada (VSO Canada; ☎ 613-234 1364, 1 888 876 2911; www.vsocanada.org; Ottawa, Canada); UK (VSO; ☎ 020-8780 7200; www.vso .org.uk; London, UK)

Volunteer Service Abroad (VSA; ☎ 04-472 5759; www .vsa.org.nz; Wellington, New Zealand)

The UN backs a number of ongoing projects in Thailand. In Bangkok, try calling the following:

Food & Agriculture Organization (☎ 0 2281 7844)

Unesco (☎ 0 2391 0577)

Unicef (☎ 0 2280 5931)

UN Development Programme (☎ 0 2282 9619)

UN World Food Programme (☎ 0 2280 0427)

World Health Organization (☎ 0 2282 9700)

Busking is illegal in Thailand, where it is legally lumped together with begging.

Work Permits

All work in Thailand requires a Thai work permit. Thai law defines work as 'exerting one's physical energy or employing one's knowledge, whether or not for wages or other benefits', so theoretically even volunteer and missionary work requires a permit.

Work permits should be obtained via an employer, who may file for the permit before the employee arrives in-country. The permit itself is not issued until the employee enters Thailand on a valid Non-Immigrant Visa (see p258).

For information about work permits, contact any Thai embassy abroad or check the Ministry of Foreign Affairs website (www.mfa.go.th/web/12.php).

Language

Language

It's true – anyone can speak another language. Don't worry if you haven't studied languages before or that you studied a language at school for years and can't remember any of it. It doesn't even matter if you failed English grammar. After all, that's never affected your ability to speak English! And this is the key to picking up a language in another country. You just need to start speaking.

Learn a few key phrases before you go. Write them on pieces of paper and stick them on the fridge, by the bed or even on the computer – anywhere that you'll see them often.

You'll find that locals appreciate travellers trying their language, no matter how muddled you may think you sound. So don't just stand there, say something! If you want to learn more Thai than we've included here, pick up a copy of Lonely Planet's comprehensive and user-friendly *Thai Phrasebook*.

PRONUNCIATION
Tones

In Thai the meaning of a single syllable may be altered by means of different tones. For example, depending on the tone, the syllable *mai* can mean 'new', 'burn', 'wood', 'not?' or 'not'.

The following chart represents tones to show their relative pitch values:

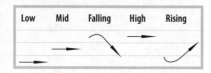

Low	Mid	Falling	High	Rising

The tones are explained as follows:

low tone – 'flat' like the mid tone, but pronounced at the relative bottom of one's vocal range. It is low, level and with no inflection, eg *bàat* (baht – the Thai currency).

mid tone – pronounced 'flat', at the relative middle of the speaker's vocal range, eg *dii* (good); no tone mark is used.

falling tone – sounds as if you are emphasising a word, or calling someone's name from afar, eg *mâi* (no/not).

high tone – pronounced near the relative top of the vocal range, as level as possible, eg *máa* (horse).

rising tone – sounds like the inflection used by English speakers to imply a question – 'Yes?', eg *sǎam* (three).

Consonants

The majority of Thai consonants correspond closely to their English counterparts. The combinations **kh**, **ph** and **th** are all aspirated versions of **k**, **p** and **t** respectively. Aspirated consonants are pronounced with an audible puff of breath. A similar differentiation in English is heard in the 't' in 'pit' and 'tip'.

SOCIAL
Meeting People

Hello.
sà·wàt·dii (khráp/   สวัสดี(ครับ/ค่ะ)
  khâ) (to m/f)
Goodbye.
laa kàwn   ลาก่อน
Please.
kà·rú·naa   กรุณา
Thank you (very much).
khàwp khun (mâak)   ขอบคุณ(มาก)
Yes.
châi   ใช่
No.
mâi châi   ไม่ใช่
I
phǒm/dì·chǎn (m/f)   ผม/ดิฉัน
you
khun   คุณ
Do you speak English?
khun phûut phaa·sǎa   คุณพูดภาษา
  ang·krìt dâi mǎi?   อังกฤษได้ไหม
Do you understand?
khâo jai mǎi?   เข้าใจไหม
I understand.
khâo jai   เข้าใจ
I don't understand.
mâi khâo jai   ไม่เข้าใจ

Could you please ...?
khǎw ... dâi mǎi?
ขอ…ได้ไหม
  repeat that
  phûut ìik thii   พูดอีกที
  speak more slowly
  phûut cháa long   พูดช้าลง
  write it down
  khǐan hâi   เขียนให้

Going Out

What's on ...?
mii à·rai tham ...?
มีอะไรทำ…
  locally
  thǎew thǎew níi   แถวๆนี้
  this weekend
  sǎo aa·thít níi   เสาร์อาทิตย์นี้
  today
  wan níi   วันนี้
  tonight
  kheun níi   คืนนี้

Where are the ...?
... yùu thîi nǎi?
…อยู่ที่ไหน
  clubs
  nai kláp   ไนท์คลับ
  gay venues
  sà·thǎan ban·
    thoeng keh   สถานบันเทิงเกย์
  places to eat
  ráan aa·hǎan   ร้านอาหาร
  pubs
  phàp   ผับ

Is there a local entertainment guide?
mii khûu meu sà·thǎan ban·thoeng
  baw·rí·wehn níi mǎi?
มีคู่มือสถานบันเทิงบริเวณนี้ไหม

PRACTICAL
Question Words

Who?
khrai?   ใคร
What?
a·rai?   อะไร
When?
mêua rai?   เมื่อไร
Where?
thîi nǎi?   ที่ไหน
How?
yàang rai?   อย่างไร

Numbers & Amounts

0	sǔun	ศูนย์
1	nèung	หนึ่ง
2	sǎwng	สอง
3	sǎam	สาม
4	sìi	สี่
5	hâa	ห้า
6	hòk	หก
7	jèt	เจ็ด
8	pàet	แปด
9	kâo	เก้า
10	sìp	สิบ
11	sìp·èt	สิบเอ็ด
12	sìp·sǎwng	สิบสอง
13	sìp·sǎam	สิบสาม
14	sìp·sìi	สิบสี่
15	sìp·hâa	สิบห้า
16	sìp·hòk	สิบหก
17	sìp·jèt	สิบเจ็ด
18	sìp·pàet	สิบแปด
19	sìp·kâo	สิบเก้า
20	yîi·sìp	ยี่สิบ
21	yîi·sìp·èt	ยี่สิบเอ็ด
22	yîi·sìp·sǎwng	ยี่สิบสอง
30	sǎam·sìp	สามสิบ
40	sìi·sìp	สี่สิบ
50	hâa·sìp	ห้าสิบ
60	hòk·sìp	หกสิบ
70	jèt·sìp	เจ็ดสิบ
80	pàet·sìp	แปดสิบ
90	kâo·sìp	เก้าสิบ
100	nèung ráwy	หนึ่งร้อย
1000	nèung phan	หนึ่งพัน
2000	sǎwng phan	สองพัน
10,000	nèung mèun	หนึ่งหมื่น
100.000	nèung sǎen	หนึ่งแสน
1,000,000	nèung láan	หนึ่งล้าน

Days

Monday	wan jan	วันจันทร์
Tuesday	wan ang·khaan	วันอังคาร
Wednesday	wan phút	วันพุธ
Thursday	wan phà·réu·hàt	วันพฤหัสฯ
Friday	wan sùk	วันศุกร์
Saturday	wan sǎo	วันเสาร์
Sunday	wan aa·thít	วันอาทิตย์

Banking

I'd like to ...
yàak jà ...
อยากจะ...

  change money
  lâek ngoen
  แลกเงิน

  change some travellers cheques
  lâek chék doen thaang
  แลกเช็คเดินทาง

Where's the nearest ...?
... thîi klâi khiang yùu thîi nǎi?
...ที่ใกล้เคียงอยู่ที่ไหน

  automatic teller machine
  tûu eh·thii·em
  ตู้เอทีเอม

  foreign exchange office
  thîi lâek ngoen tàang prà·thêt
  ที่แลกเงินต่างประเทศ

Post

Where is the post office?
thîi tam kaan prai·sà·nii yùu thîi nǎi?
ที่ทำการไปรษณีย์อยู่ที่ไหน

I want to send a ...
yàak jà sòng ...
อยากจะส่ง...

  fax
  fàak   แฟกซ์
  parcel
  phát·sà·dù   พัสดุ
  postcard
  prai·sa·nii·yá·bàt   ไปรษณียบัตร

I want to buy ...
yàak jà séu ...
อยากจะซื้อ...

  an envelope
  sawng jòt·mǎi   ซองจดหมาย
  a stamp
  sa·taem   แสตมป์

Phones & Mobiles

I want to buy a phone card.
yàak jà séu bàt thoh·rá·sàp
อยากจะซื้อบัตรโทรศัพท์
I want to make a call to ...
yàak jà thoh pai ...
อยากจะโทรไป...
reverse-charge/collect call
kèp plai thaang
เก็บปลายทาง

I'd like a/an ...
tâwng kaan ...
ต้องการ...

  adaptor plug
  plák tàw
  ปลั๊กต่อ
  charger for my phone
  khrêuang cháat sǎm·ràp thoh·rá·sàp
  เครื่องชาร์จสำหรับโทรศัพท์
  mobile/cell phone for hire
  châo thoh·rá·sàp meu thěu
  เช่าโทรศัพท์มือถือ
  prepaid mobile/cell phone
  thoh·rá·sàp meu thěu bàep jài lûang nâa
  โทรศัพท์มือถือแบบจ่ายล่วงหน้า
  SIM card for the ... network
  bàt sim sǎm·ràp khreua khài kǒrng ...
  บัตรซิมสำหรับเครือข่ายของ...

Internet

Where's the local Internet café?
ráan in·toe·nét yùu thîi nǎi?
ร้านอินเตอร์เนตอยู่ที่ไหน

I'd like to ...
yàak jà ...
อยากจะ...

  check my email
  trùat ii·mehn   ตรวจอีเมล
  get online
  tàw in·toe·nét   ต่ออินเตอร์เนต

Transport

What time does the ... leave?
... jà àwk kìi mohng?
...จะออกกี่โมง

  bus
  rót meh   รถเมล์
  ferry
  reua khâam fâak   เรือข้ามฟาก
  train
  rót fai   รถไฟ

What time's the ... bus?
rót meh ... maa kìi mohng?
รถเมล์...มากี่โมง

  first
  khan râek   คันแรก
  last
  khan sùt thái   คันสุดท้าย
  next
  khan tàw pai   คันต่อไป

Are you free? (taxi)
wâang mǎi?   ว่างไหม

Please put the meter on.
pòet mí·toe dûay | เปิดมิเตอร์ด้วยหน่อย
nòy

How much is it to ...?
pai ... thâo·rai? | ไป...เท่าไร

Please take me to (this address).
khǎw phaa pai ... | ขอพาไป...

FOOD

breakfast
aa·hǎan cháo | อาหารเช้า
lunch
aa·hǎan thîang | อาหารเที่ยง
dinner
aa·hǎan yen | อาหารเย็น
snack
aa·hǎan wâang | อาหารว่าง

Can you recommend a ...
náe·nam ... dâi mǎi?
แนะนำ...ได้ไหม
bar/pub
baa/phàp | บาร์/ผับ
café
ráan kaa·fae | ร้านกาแฟ
restaurant
ráan aa·hǎan | ร้านอาหาร

For more detailed information on food and dining out, see p42 and p123.

EMERGENCIES

It's an emergency!
pen hèt chùk chǒen!
เป็นเหตุฉุกเฉิน
Could you please help me/us?
chûay dâi mǎi?
ช่วยได้ไหม

Call the police/a doctor/an ambulance!
taam tam·rùat/mǎw/rót phá·yaa·baan dûay!
ตามตำรวจ/หมอ/รถพยาบาลด้วย
Where's the police station?
sà·thǎa·nii tam·rùat thîi klâi khiang yùu
thîi nǎi?
สถานีตำรวจที่ใกล้เคียงอยู่ที่ไหน

HEALTH

Where's the nearest ...?
... thîi klâi khiang yùu thîi nǎi?
...ที่ใกล้เคียงอยู่ที่ไหน
chemist
ráan khǎi yaa | ร้านขายยา
doctor/dentist
mǎw/mǎw fan | หมอ/หมอฟัน
hospital
rohng phá·yaa· | โรงพยาบาล
baan

I need a doctor (who speaks English).
tâwng kaan mǎw (thîi phûut phaa·sǎa
ang·krìt dâi)
ต้องการหมอ(ที่พูดภาษาอังกฤษได้)

Symptoms

I have (a) ...
pǒm (m)/dì·chǎn (f) ...
ผม/ดิฉัน...
diarrhoea
pen rôhk tháwng | เป็นโรคท้องร่วง
rûang
fever
pen khâi | เป็นไข้
headache
pùat hǔa | ปวดหัว
pain
jèp pùat | เจ็บปวด

GLOSSARY

baht – Thai currency
BMA – Bangkok Metropolitan Administration
BTS – Bangkok Mass Transit System
CAT – Communications Authority of Thailand
faràng – foreigner of European descent
Isan – *isǎan;* general term for Northeastern Thailand, from the Sanskrit name for the medieval kingdom Isana, which encompassed parts of Cambodia and Northeastern Thailand.
khlong – *khlawng;* canal
MRTA – Metropolitan Rapid Transit Authority, agency responsible for the Metro subway.
rai – Thai unit of measurement (area); 1 rai = 1600 sq metres

Ratanakosin – style of architecture present in the late 19th to early 20th century, which combines traditional Thai and European forms; also known as 'old Bangkok'
reua hǎang yao – long-tail boat
rót fai fáa – BTS Skytrain
rót fai fáa máhǎanákhawn – MRTA subway
soi – *sawy;* lane or small road
TAT – Tourist Authority of Thailand
tha – *thâa;* pier
THAI – Thai Airways International
thanon – *thanǒn* (abbreviated 'Th' in this guide); road or street
TOT – Telephone Organisation of Thailand
trok – *tràwk;* alleyway
wat – Buddhist temple, monastery

Behind the Scenes

THE LONELY PLANET STORY

The story begins with a classic travel adventure: Tony and Maureen Wheeler's 1972 journey across Europe and Asia to Australia. There was no useful information about the overland trail then, so Tony and Maureen published the first Lonely Planet guidebook to meet a growing need.

From a kitchen table, Lonely Planet has grown to become the largest independent travel publisher in the world, with offices in Melbourne (Australia), Oakland (USA) and London (UK). Today Lonely Planet guidebooks cover the globe. There is an ever-growing list of books and information in a variety of media. Some things haven't changed. The main aim is still to make it possible for adventurous travellers to get out there – to explore and better understand the world.

At Lonely Planet we believe travellers can make a positive contribution to the countries they visit – if they respect their host communities and spend their money wisely. Every year 5% of company profit is donated to charities around the world.

THIS BOOK

This 7th edition of Bangkok was researched by Joe Cummings and China Williams, as was the 6th edition. Joe wrote all editions before that. This guide was commissioned in Lonely Planet's Melbourne office and produced in Melbourne by the following:

Commissioning Editor Kalya Ryan

Coordinating Editor Kate Whitfield

Coordinating Cartographer Hunor Csutoros

Coordinating Layout Designer Katie Thuy Bui

Managing Editor Brigitte Ellemor

Managing Cartographer Corinne Waddell

Assisting Editors Barbara Delissen, Helen Yeates, Tim Webb, Lutie Clark, Katie Lynch, Yvonne Byron

Assisting Cartographer Sally Gerdan

Cover Designer Pepi Bluck

Language Content Coordinator Quentin Frayne

Project Manager Chris Love

Special thanks to Bruce Evans for his advice on Thai language matters

Thanks to Suzannah Shwer, Helen Christinis, Glenn van der Knijff, Mark Germanchis, Raphael Richards, David Burnett, Sally Darmody, Celia Wood, Kate McDonald, Laura Jane, Wibowo Rusli, Gerard Walker, Wendy Wright

Cover photographs The 46m reclining Buddha of Wat Pho, Glenn Beanland/Lonely Planet Images (top); Heavy traffic on Th Ratchaprarop, Pratunam, Richard I'Anson/Lonely Planet Images (bottom); Young monks, Adam Pretty/Getty (back).

Internal photographs by Lonely Planet Images, Mick Elmore and Richard I'Anson except for the following: p178 (#1) Claver Carroll; p178 (#2) Kraig Lieb; p216 Lee Foster; p219 Dennis Johnson; p225 Frank Carter; p229 John Elk III. All

images are copyright of the photographer unless otherwise indicated. Many of the images in this guide are available for licensing from Lonely Planet Images: www.lonelyplanet images.com.

THANKS

JOE CUMMINGS

Bangkok brothers, sisters and friends who offered immeasurable support during my research include Korakot Punlopruksa, Kittiwat Ratanadilok Na Phuket, Wannapa Rakkeo, Kaprice Kea, Cameron Cooper, Jim Algie, Aphirum Ratchatawet and Suwannee Emon.

CHINA WILLIAMS

Thanks to my Bangkok crew: Luka, Mason and Sylvie. A heaping helping to Apple and Ong Ang Talay for food recommendations and movie night. And a pat to Sarah Wintle, a great Bangkok pal. Many regards to the kind-hearted tag team at Bangkok Tourist Division and TAT. A big nod goes to my stateside contacts: Bee and Aek for the gig guide. Curtsy to Susan Kepner for the academic side of things. A big *wai* to my hubby for helping me see things I forget to appreciate. Thanks also to Joe Cummings, Kalya Ryan and the smart production team at Lonely Planet.

OUR READERS

Many thanks to the travellers who used the last edition and wrote to us with helpful hints, useful advice and interesting anecdotes:

Philip Ampofo, Chris Bain, David Bitkower, Lennert Christensen, Garry & Joanna Clarke, Robert Cook, Anne Fahey, David Fearn, Barry & Trish Fox, Elke Franke, Julian Hernandez, Christop Holweger, Susan Irwin, Jessie Kutsch, KK Lahiri, Audrey Leeson, Alex Legroux, Mangla Ningomba, Andrzej Nowak, Phanuphong Paothong, Megha Prem, Thomas Rau, Matthew A Rifkin, Ben Sand, Patrice Schneider, Cameron Scott, Lorenzo Sonelli, John Statham

ACKNOWLEDGMENTS

Many thanks to the following for the use of their content:

BTS Route Map © 2004 Bangkok Mass Transit System Public Company Limited

Salvatore Besso's impressions are reproduced from the English translation of the original Italian, titled *Siam and China* by C Matthews, Simpkin, Marshall, Hamilton, Kent & Co Ltd (1914), London

Notes

Index

See also separate indexes for Eating (p273), Entertainment (p274), Shopping (p274) and Sleeping (p275).

Index

Index

273

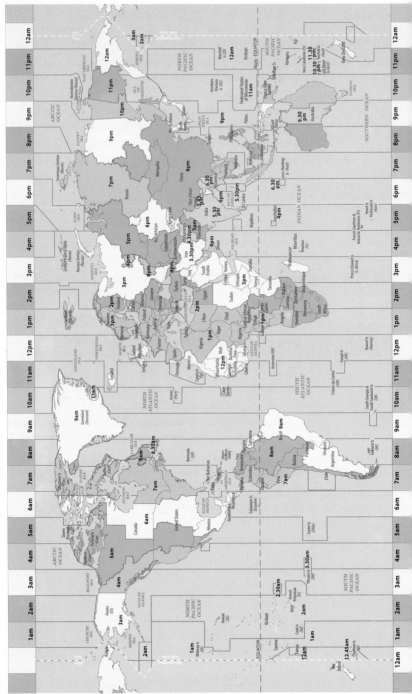

MAP LEGEND

ROUTES

Tollway
Freeway
Primary Road
Secondary Road
Tertiary Road
Lane
Unsealed Road

One-Way Street
Mall/Steps
Tunnel
Walking Tour
Walking Trail
Walking Path

TRANSPORT

Ferry
Monorail
Rail (Underground)

Rail
Bangkok Skytrain

HYDROGRAPHY

River, Creek
Intermittent River

Canal
Water

AREA FEATURES

Airport
Area of Interest
Beach
Building, Featured
Building, Information
Building, Other
Building, Transport

Cemetery, Christian
Land
Mall
Park
Sports
Urban

POPULATION

○ CAPITAL (NATIONAL)
● Large City
● Small City

○ Medium City
○ Town, Village

SYMBOLS

Sights/Activities
Beach
Buddhist
Castle, Fortress
Christian
Hindu
Islamic
Jewish
Monument
Museum, Gallery
Other Site
Ruin
Winery, Vineyard
Zoo, Bird Sanctuary
Eating
Eating

Drinking
Drinking
Café
Entertainment
Entertainment
Shopping
Shopping
Sleeping
Sleeping
Transport
Airport
Bus Station
Cycling, Bicycle Path
General Transport
Taxi Rank

Information
Bank, ATM
Embassy/Consulate
Hospital, Medical
Information
Internet Facilities
Police Station
Post Office, GPO
Telephone
Geographic
Lookout
Mountain
National Park
Waterfall

Maps

SIGHTS & ACTIVITIES (pp112–14, 162–6)
Asia Voyages........................(see 5)
Baipai Thai Cooking School............1 C7
Bangkok University Art Gallery.........2 E7
Children's Discovery Museum...........3 D4
Khlong Prem Prison....................4 D3
Manohra Cruises.....................(see 26)
Menam Riverside Hotel.................5 C7
Nakornthon Thai Medical Spa..........6 A8
Safari World..........................7 F3
Skills Development Center for the
Blind................................8 C2
Tadu Contemporary Art................9 E5

EATING (pp145–6)
Anotai..............................10 D6
Baan Klang Nam......................11 C7
Reflections Bar & Restaurant.........12 D5
Reflections Rooms..................(see 12)
River Bar Café......................13 C5
Talat Aw Taw Kaw....................14 D4

DRINKING (pp149–52)
ICK Pub.............................15 F5
ICY.................................16 D4

ENTERTAINMENT (pp148–60)
Club Astra..........................17 E6
Dance Fever.........................18 D5
House...............................19 E6
Siam Niramit........................20 D5
Tawan Daeng German
Brewhouse...........................21 D7
Thailand Cultural Centre.............22 D5
Zantika.............................23 E6

SHOPPING (pp188–90)
Chatuchak Weekend Market...........24 D4

SLEEPING (pp209–10)
Amari Airport Hotel..................25 E1
Bangkok Marriott Resort & Spa.......26 B7
Rama Gardens Hotel..................27 E2
We-Train International House.........28 E1

TRANSPORT (pp238–43)
Air Asia...........................(see 30)
Budget Car Rental...................29 D6
Budget Car Rental...................30 E2
Eastern Bus Terminal................31 E6
Hertz..............................(see 25)
Hertz..............................(see 30)
Nok Air............................(see 30)
Northern & Northeastern Bus
Terminal...........................32 D4
Southern Bus Terminal...............33 B5
Thai Air Asia......................(see 30)
Thai Airways International...........34 D3

INFORMATION
Bangkok Hospital....................35 D6
Chinese Embassy.....................36 D5
Lao Embassy........................37 E5
Nepal Embassy......................38 E6
Philippines Embassy.................39 D6
Rama IX Hospital....................40 D6
Samitivej Hospital..................41 D6
South Korean Embassy................42 D5
TAT Office.........................(see 24)

0 _____ 5 km
0 _____ 3 miles

5

BANG KAPI
Th Srinakorih
15

Th Lat Phrao

Th Ramkhamhaeng
Hua Mark
Sports Complex
Ramkhamhaeng
University

Th Vibhavadi Rangsit

Ari
12

SI YAN
Th Ratchawithi
Samsen

DUSIT
Chitralada
Palace

Mae Nam Chao Phraya

13

BANGLAMPHU

KO RATANAKOSIN
Wat Arun

CHINATOWN
Wong
Wian Yai

BANGKOK
NOI
Thonburi
(Bangkok Noi)

TALING
CHAN
33
Khlong Bangkok Noi
Th Chaun Santiwong

THONBURI
Khlong Bangkok Yai

Wat
Pak Nam

DAO
KHANONG

BANG
KHUN
THIAN

To Nakhon
Pathom (35km)

To Nakhon
Pathom (32km)

To Kaset Bang
Khue (18km)

Th Phetkasem
Khlong Phasi Charoen

Khlong Dao Khanong

Khlong Samrong (Chai)

6

Th Prakhanong
Khlong Prakhanong

Th Si Nakharin

Th Petchaburi Tat Mai

On Nut

37
Soi 39 (Soi Prachs Uthit)
42
9
17
Th Phra Ram IX
Kamphaeng Phet 7
Royal City Ave
Th Wattanatam
Th Petchaburi Tat Mai
Th Thiam
Ruammit
20
22
40
29
19
Th Phayatham
Th Ratchadaphisek
Suthisan
Pracharat Bamphen
HUAY
KHWANG
18
36
10
16
Thailand
Cultural
Centre
Soi Rong
Phayaban
41
Asoke-Din Daeng
Rama IX
Makkasan Daeng
Th Petchaburi
Th Phra Ram I
Th Phra Ram I
Chalerm Mahanakhon
Expwy
Lumphini
Park
THUNG
MAHAMEK
Hualamphong
See Central Bangkok Map (pp280-1)

KHLONG
TAN
23
38
Ekamai
Soi 63 (Ekamai)
Soi 55 (Thong Lor)
31
Phra
Khanong
39
Th Sukhumvit
Phrom
Phong
Soi 21 (Asoke)

KHLONG
TOEY

PORT
Th Phra Ram IV

21
Th Ratchadaphisek
Wat Chong
Nonsi
Th Narathiwat
Ratchanakharin
TROK
CHAN
Th Chan
Expressway
Th Sathon

THANON
TOK
1
5
Tha
Ratchasinghkhon
Wat
Ratchasinghkhon
26
Th Chalun Nakhon

Th Phra Ram III
Th Sukhawat
Th Taksin

RATBURANA
PHRA
PRADAENG

BANGNA
To Samut Prakan
(3km)

Nam (Chao Phraya)

To Samut
Sakhon (19km)

6

7

Seacon
Shopping
Square
Rama IX
Royal Park

Soi 103 (Soi Udom Suk)
Soi 101

PHRA
KHANONG
Soi 71
Wat
Thammamongkhon

8

To Sinakharin
University (8km);
Chonburi (48km)

To Samut Prakan
(3km)

Skytrain & Station
Subway & Station

279

5 6 7 8

A B C D

1

To Southern
Bus Terminal
(4km)

To Tha
Nonthaburi

Dusit
Park

Th Phra Ram

Th Ratchawithi

Th Samsen

Th Ratchasima

Amphon
Park

Th U Thong Nai

DUSIT

Dusit
Zoo

Chitra
Park

Th Si Ayuthaya

Th Phitsanulok

Saphan Phra
Ram VIII

Th Samphraya

Th Krung Kasem

Th Luk Luang

Th Prachathipatai

Th Wisut Kasat

Th Samsen

See Thewet & Dusit Map (pp282–

Royal
Turf Club

2

Santichaiprakan
Park

Khlong Banglamphu

Banglamphu
Market

BANGLAMPHU

Th Phra Sumen

Th Ratchadamnoen Nok

Th Nakhon Sawan

Th Phra Ram V

Th Phitsanulok

Th Luk Luang

Th Krung Kasem

Khlong Bangkok Noi

Thonburi
(Bangkok Noi)

Saphan
Phra Pin
Klao

Th Phra Pin Klao

Th Chao Fa

Th Phra Athit

Th Chakraphong

Th Tanao

Th Ratchadamnoen Klang

Th Lan Luang

Th Chakraphatdi

To Wat
Suwannaram
(1km)

Th Phra Pin Klao

Th Ratchini

Th Ratchadamnoen Mai

Th Din So

PHRA
NAKHON

Tha Bo-Bae

27

22

Th Phrannok

Thammasat
University

KO
RATANAKOSIN

Sanam
Luang

Th Na Phra Lan

Th Ratchadamnoen Nai

Th Atsadang

Th Tanao

Th Maha Chai

Th Chakraphatdi

Th Bamrung Meuang

25

3

Soi Ma Toom

Th Arun Amarin

Th Mahathat

Th Sanam Chai

Th Kanlaya Namit

Khlong Lawt

ThBotphram

Th Fuang Nakhon

Th Tri Thong

POM PRAP
SATTRU PHAI

Th Luang

Th Wora Chak

Th Yukhon 2

Th Luang

Th Rong Meuang

Th Krung Kasem

Khlong Phadung Krung Kasem

BANGKOK
NOI

Th Thai Wang

See Ko Ratanakosin Map (p288)

Tha
Ratchini

Th Charoen Krung

PHAHURAT

CHINATOWN

Nakhon
Kasem

Th Charoen Krung

Th Maitri

Th Mittraphan

Th Ram VI

Th Charoen

4

Khlong Chueng

Th Wang Doem

Khlong Mon

Th Ban Mo

Th Chakkaphet

Th Triphet

Th Chakkaphet

Khlong Ong Ang

Th Chakrawat

Th Ratchawong

Th Yaowarat

Th Songsawat

Th Charoen Krung

Th Phra Maitri

Th Songwat

Th Tri Thong

Th Charoen Krung

Hualamphong

Hualamphong

12

7

29

Wat
Kalayanamit

Tha
Saphan
Phut

Phra Pokklao
Bridge

SAMPHAN
THAWONG

Th Charoen Krung

5

Tha Pak
Talat
Atsadang

BANGKOK YAI

Khlong Bangkok Yai

Th Wang Doem

Mae Nam Chao Phraya

Th Maha Phrutharam

5

Th Itsaraphap

Th Prachathipok

Th Somdet Chao Phraya

Th Din Daeng

See Chinatown Map (pp284–5)

Th Itsaraphap

BANG

Th Charoen Krung

Th Phayathai – Bangkho

Phayathai

Th Mahesak

Th Surasak

Expswy

Su

6

Th Intharaphitak

Th Intharaphitak

Wong
Wian
Yai

Mittraphab
Hospital

Th Lat Ya

Th Charoen Rat

Soi Rat Ruam Charoen

Th Charoen Nakhon

Th Krung Thonburi

23

Thoet Thai Rd

Talat Wong
Wian Yai

Wong Wian Yai

Wat
Intharam

Th Taksin

Soi Krung
Thonburi

KHLONG SAN

THONBURI

Saphan Taksin

Saphan Taksin

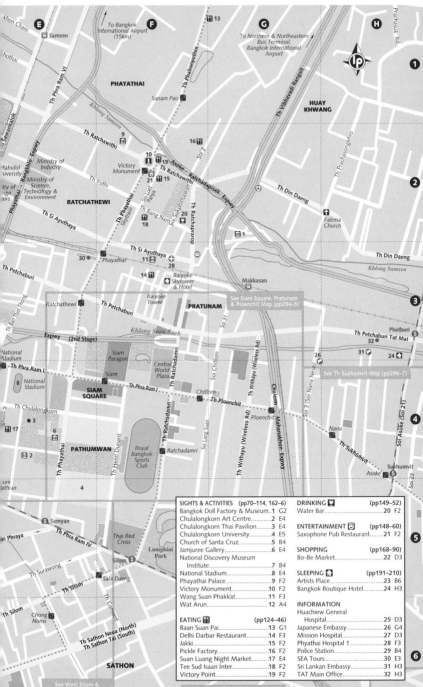

To Bangkok
International Airport
(15km)

To Northern &
Northeastern
Bus Terminal;
Bangkok International
Airport

PHAYATHAI

Sanam Pao

**HUAY
KHWANG**

Th Ratchawithi

Victory
Monument

Asoke - Ratchadapisek Expwy

Th Din Daeng

Fatima
Church

RATCHATHEWI

Th Si Ayuthaya

Th Rang Nam

Th Si Ayuthaya

Th Din Daeng

Phayathai

Klong Samsen

Baiyoke
Skytower
& Hotel

Makkasan

PRATUNAM

Ratchathewi

Th Petchaburi

Khlong Saen Saeb

See Siam Square, Pratunam
& Ploenchit Map (pp294–5)

Baiyoke
Tower

Expwy (2nd Stage)

Th Petchaburi Tat Mai

Phetburi

National
Stadium

Siam
Paragon

Central
World
Plaza

Th Phra Ram I

Nana

See Th Sukhumvit Map (pp296–7)

National
Stadium

**SIAM
SQUARE**

Siam

Th Phra Ram I

Chitlom

Th Chulalongkorn

Th Ploenchit

PATHUMWAN

Royal
Bangkok
Sports
Club

Ratchadamri

Ploenchit

Nana

Th Sukhumvit

Sukhumvit

Asoke

Legend listings:

See West Silom &
Surawong Map (pp290–1)

See Lumphini & Sathon Map (pp292–3)

SATHON

Th Silom

Th Sathon Neua (North)
Th Sathon Tai (South)

Chong
Nonsi

Sala Daeng

Th Surawong

Lumphini
Park

Thai Red
Cross

Samyan

Th Phra Ram IV

THEWET & DUSIT

Tha Saphan
Sang Hee

A

Saphan
Krungthon

B

C

D

Th Sangkhalok

Th Khao

1

Th Ratchawithi

Mae Nam Chao Phraya

Soi 13

2

4

Soi 11

Soi Chaiyot

• Rajabhat
University

Wat
Ratchathiwat

Soi 9

Th Samsen

3

11

Wat Ratchathewet

17

15

19 •

Th Si Ayutthaya

16

National
Library

Soi 12

Tha
Thewet

THEWET

DUSIT

10

Th Krung Kasem

Amp
Pa

4

13

Th Si Ayuthaya

Th Ratchasima

Klong Phadung Kasem

14

5

To Saphan
Phra Ram VIII

Th Luk Luang

Th Phitsanulok

Th Kasem

See Banglamphu Map (pp286–7)

Parusakkawan
Palace

Soi 3

12

Th Krung Kasem

Th Samsen

Soi Thewet 1

Th Prachatipatai

Ministry of
Education
•

Th Ratchadamnoen Nok

6

Th Wisut Kasat

18

Governme
House

SIGHTS & ACTIVITIES	(pp88–91, 162–6)
Abhisek Dusit Throne Hall	1 E3
Ananta Samakhom Throne Hall	2 E4
Ancient Cloth Museum	3 E3
Church of the Immaculate Conception	4 B2
Dusit Zoo	5 F5
HM King Bhumibol Photography Exhibitions	6 E3
Royal Elephant Museum	7 F3
Vimanmek Teak Mansion	8 E3
Wat Benchamabophit	9 E6

EATING	(pp129–30)
In Love	10 A4
Kaloang Home Kitchen	11 A3

SHOPPING	(pp169–79)
Thai Nakorn	12 C5
Thewet Flower Market	13 B4

SLEEPING	(p197)
Bangkok International Youth Hostel	14 C5
Shanti Lodge	15 A3
Sri Ayuttaya Guest House	16 A4
Taewez Guesthouse	17 A3
Trang Hotel	18 B6

INFORMATION	
Fine Arts Department	19 B3

CHINATOWN

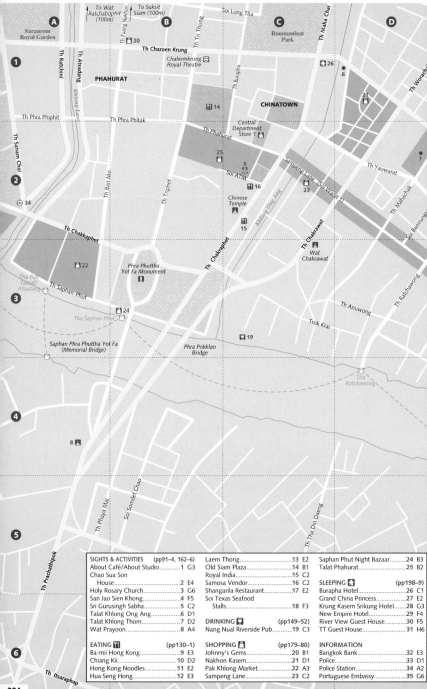

0 ____ 300 m
0 ____ 0.2 miles

E **F** **G** **H**

Th Luang

Th Yukhon 2

Soi Rong
Muang 4 **1**

**POM PRAP
SATTRU PHAI**

Central Hospital

Soi Rong
Muang 3

Th Luang

Th Suapa

Th Mangkon

Th Mangkon

Th Mittaphan

Soi Rong Muang 1

Th Rong Meuang

Th Charat Muang **2**

Wat Mangkon
Kamalawat

Trok Itsaranuphap

Th Matichit

Th Santiphap

Wong Wian
22 Karakada

Th Charoen Muang

11

Th Ratchawong

Th Mangkon

Th Charoen Krung

12

Th Yaowarat

Trok Itsaranuphap

Th Yaowaphanit

Th Phadungdao

Th Phra Ram IV

Th Matichit

Th Charoen Muang **3**

Talat
Kao

9

18

1

28

Hualamphong
Railway Station

Simpeng Lane

(Soi Wanit 1)

**AMPHAN
HAWONG**

2

Th Songwat

Th Songwat

Th Songwat

29

Wat Traimit

Th Traimit

Hualamphong
S

Th Phra Ram IV **4**

Chinatown
Arch

Soi Charoen Phanit

Th Charoen Krung

Th Traimit

Th Kao Lan

Mae Nam Chao Phraya

See West Silom & Surawong Map (pp290–1)

Soi 20

Wat Thawng
Nophakhun

30

4

Soi Charoen Phanit

Talat
Noi

Th Maha Phruttharam

Bangkhlo Expwy

Th Maha Nakhon **5**

Tha Krom Chao
(Harbour
Department Pier)

Harbour
Department

Soi 22

Soi
Sawang

Phayathai

31

3

Th Yotha

35

Somdet Chao Phraya

Th Si Phraya **6**

285

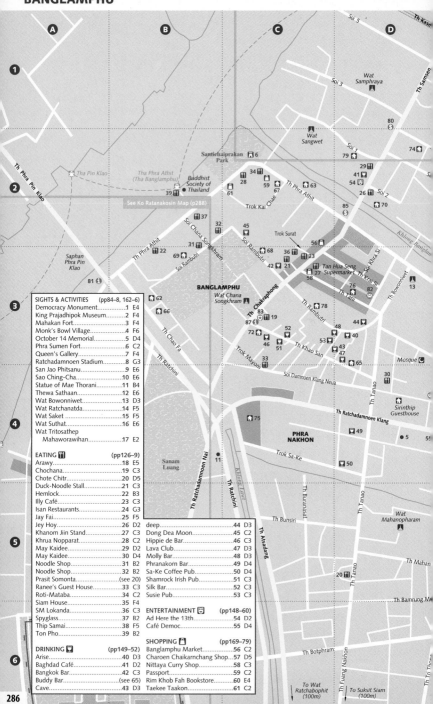

Wat Intharawihan

To Wat
Benchamabophit
(300m)

See Thewet & Dusit Map (pp282–3)

United
Nations

Government House

Trok Bahn Lo

Soi Phrasuli

BMA Building
(City Hall)

Wat
Thepthidaram

Wat
Sunthon

Golden
Mount

Rommaninat
Park

SLEEPING	(pp193–7)
Baan Sabai	62 B3
Bhiman Inn	63 C2
Boworn BB	64 E3
Buddy Lodge	65 D3
Chai's House	66 B3
KC Guest House	67 C2
Lamphu House	68 C3
Mango Lagoon	69 B3
New World House Apartments &	
Guest House	70 D2
Old Bangkok Inn	71 F4
Prakorp's House	72 C3
Prasuri Guest House	73 E4
Rajata Hotel	74 D2
Royal Hotel	75 C4
Thai Cozy House	76 D3
Thai Hotel	77 F2
Viengtai Hotel	78 C3
Villa Guest House	79 D2

INFORMATION	
Bangkok Bank	80 D1
Bangkok Tourist Division (BTD)	81 A3
Banglamphu Post Office	82 D3
Chana Songkhram Police Station	83 C3
Post Office	84 D4
Siam Commercial Bank	85 D2
TAT Information Compound	86 G3
Tourist Information Booth	87 C3

287

KO RATANAKOSIN

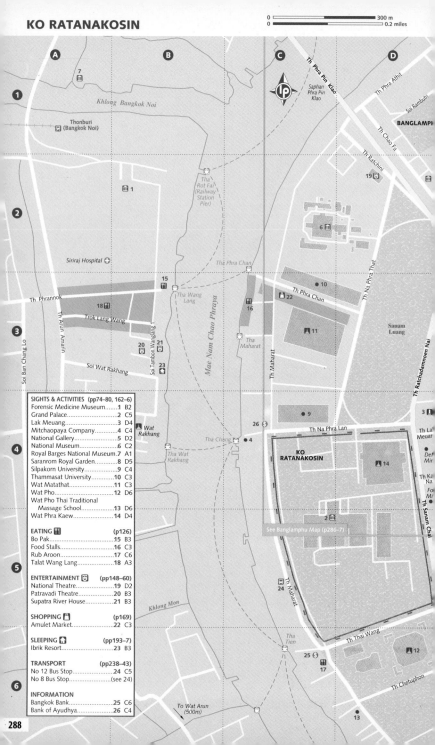

0 — 300 m
0 — 0.2 miles

Khlong Bangkok Noi

Thonburi (Bangkok Noi)

Siriraj Hospital

Th Phrannok

Th Arun Amarin

Trok Lang Wang

Soi Ban Chang Lo

Soi Tambon Wanglang

Soi Wat Rakhang

Wat Rakhang

Tha Wat Rakhang

Khlong Mon

To Wat Arun (500m)

Mae Nam Chao Phraya

Tha Phra Chan

Tha Wang Lang

Tha Maharat

Tha Chang

Tha Tien

Tha Rot Fai (Railway Station Pier)

Saphan Phra Pin Klao

Th Phra Pin Klao

BANGLAMPI

Th Phra Athit

Soi Rambuti

Th Chao Fa

Th Ratchini

Th Na Phra That

Sanam Luang

Th Ratchadamnoen Nai

Th Phra Chan

Th Maharat

Th Na Phra Lan

KO RATANAKOSIN

Th La Meuar

Def Mir

Th Ka Na Fo Mi

Th Sanam Chai

Th Maharat

Th Thai Wang

Th Chetuphon

See Banglamphu Map (286–7)

A **B** **C** **D**

1

Tha Krom Chao
(Harbour Department
Pier)

Th Charoen Krung

Th Maha Phrutharam

Soi Phra Nakhare

Soi Kaeo Fa

Th Si Phra

2

Mae Nam Chao Phraya

Th Yotha

55

See Chinatown Map (pp284–5)

3

69

25

Tha Si Phraya

40

Soi 30

19

Soi 43 (Soi Saphan Yao)

BANG RAK

32

Communications
Authority of
Thailand Office

Soi 32

81

29

Manohra
Hotel

20

Th Charoen Krung

Soi 34

Wat Muang
Khae

65

21

Soi 26

Tha Muang
Khae

9

Mahesak
Hospital

Haroon
Mosque

80

53

Soi 32

Central
Department
Store

Soi 30

Soi 28

Th Silc

76

4

Soi 36

59

Th Mahesak

67

Soi 38 (Soi Oriental)

Soi 40

56

31

Soi 19

1

Tha
Oriental

10

Soi 34

Phayathai – Bangkok Expwy

Soi 36

Th Surasak

5

Wat Suan
Phlu

28

77

Soi 42

34

Soi Wat Suan Phlu

70

Soi Si Wiang

15

68

51

62

16

6

Th Krung Thonburi

Th Krung Thonburi

Th Charoen Krung

Th Charat Wiang

Surasak

Saphan Taksin

Saphan Taksin

Tha Sathon
(Central Pier)

LUMPHINI & SATHON

See Siam Square, Pratunam &
Ploenchit Map (pp294–5)

10

38

16
13

Th Sarasin

Soi Lang Suan

8

1

2

Skytrain

Th Ratchadamri

Chulalongkorn
Hospital

Silom

17   28

18

34

25

Th Silom

21

Silom
Complex

Th Sala Daeng

Soi Sala Daeng 2

23

Soi Yommarat

Th Sala Daeng

Soi Sala Daeng 2

Soi Sala Daeng 1

31

3

44

Th Withayu (Wireless Rd)

So

43

Lumphini
Park

39

Th Phra Ram IV

Lumphini

6

1

41

32

3

37

Christ
Church

Th Sathon Neua (North)

14   27   24

40

9

Soi 1 (Atakamphasit)

Soi C

Th Convent

Th Sathon Tai (South)

35

4

36

15

26

7

See West Silom & Surawong
Map (pp296–1)

Soi 7 (Soi Phra Phinij)

SATHON

Soi Suanphlu 1

Soi Nantha

5

42

Soi Suan Phlu

Soi Ngam Duphli

SIGHTS & ACTIVITIES	(pp107–10, 162–6)
Banyan Tree Spa	(see 24)
Central Sports Club Tennis Court	1 D4
Lumphini Stadium	2 E4
Surapon Gallery	3 B4

EATING 🍴	(pp135–40)
Baan Khanitha	4 A4
Colonnade Restaurant	(see 32)
C'yan & Glow	(see 27)
Duck-Noodle Shop	5 B6
Lunchtime Market	6 D3
Mali Restaurant	7 D5
Ngwan Lee Lang Suan	8 C1
Ratsstube	9 D4
Sara-Jane's	10 D1
Soi Polo Fried Chicken	11 E1

DRINKING 🍸	(pp149–52)
Moon Bar at Vertigo	(see 24)
Wong's Place	12 E5

ENTERTAINMENT 🎭	(pp148–60)
70's Bar	13 C1
Alliance Française Bangkok	14 B4
Babylon Bangkok	15 D5
Brown Sugar	16 C1
DJ Station	17 A2
Freeman	18 A2
Goethe Institut	19 D4
Joe Louis Puppet Theatre	20 E3

SHOPPING 🛍	(pp185–6)
Bookazine	21 A3
Suan Lum Night Bazaar	22 E3

SLEEPING 🛏	(pp201–4)
Bangkok Christian Guest House	23 A3
Banyan Tree Hotel	24 C4
Dusit Thani	25 A2
Malaysia Hotel	26 D5
Metropolitan	27 B4
Pan Pacific	28 A2
Penguin House	29 F6
Sala Thai Daily Mansion	30 F6
Siri Sathorn Executive Residence	31 B4
Sukhothai Hotel	32 C4

TRANSPORT	(pp238–43)
Garuda Indonesia	33 F4
KLM Royal Dutch Airlines	(see 24)
Singapore Airlines	34 A2

INFORMATION	
Australian Embassy	35 B4
Austrian Embassy	36 D5
BNH Hospital	37 A4
Cambodian Embassy	38 B1
Canadian Embassy	39 B3
Danish Embassy	40 D4
French Consulate	(see 14)
German Embassy	41 C4
Immigration Office	42 B6
Police	43 D2
South African Embassy	(see 13)
Tourist Police	44 A2

See Th Sukhumvit Map (p296–7)

Benjakiti Park

Bon Kai Market

Khlong Toei

Th Phra Ram IV

Port-Din Daeng Expwy

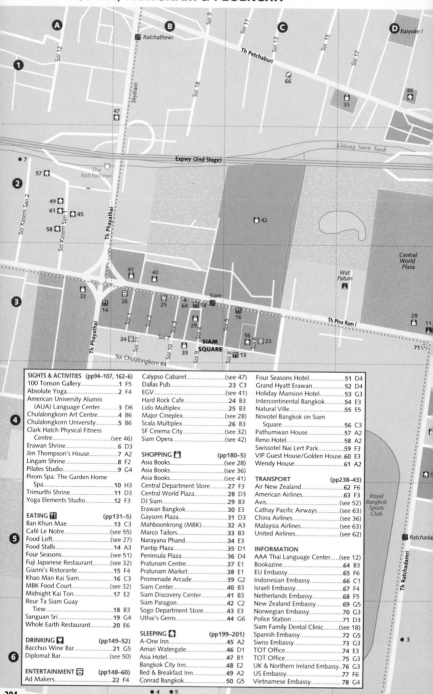

SIGHTS & ACTIVITIES (pp94–107, 162–6)
100 Tonson Gallery....................1 F5
Absolute Yoga...........................2 F4
American University Alumni
(AUA) Language Center............3 D6
Chulalongkorn Art Centre...........4 B6
Chulalongkorn University............5 B6
Clark Hatch Physical Fitness
Centre...............................(see 46)
Erawan Shrine..........................6 D3
Jim Thompson's House.................7 A2
Lingam Shrine..........................8 F2
Pilates Studio...........................9 G4
Pirom Spa: The Garden Home
Spa.................................10 H3
Trimurthi Shrine.......................11 D3
Yoga Elements Studio.................12 F3

EATING (pp131–5)
Ban Khun Mae.........................13 C3
Café Le Notre.......................(see 55)
Food Loft............................(see 27)
Food Stalls...........................14 A3
Four Seasons........................(see 51)
Fuji Japanese Restaurant.........(see 32)
Gianni's Ristorante...................15 F4
Khao Man Kai Siam..................16 C3
MBK Food Court....................(see 32)
Midnight Kai Ton.....................17 E2
Reur Ta Siam Guay
Tiew................................18 B3
Sanguan Sri..........................19 G4
Whole Earth Restaurant.............20 E6

DRINKING (pp149–52)
Bacchus Wine Bar....................21 G5
Diplomat Bar.......................(see 50)

ENTERTAINMENT (pp148–60)
Ad Makers...........................22 F4

Calypso Cabaret....................(see 47)
Dallas Pub............................23 C3
EGV................................(see 41)
Hard Rock Cafe.......................24 B3
Lido Multiplex........................25 B3
Major Cineplex.....................(see 28)
Scala Multiplex.......................26 B3
SF Cinema City....................(see 32)
Siam Opera.........................(see 42)

SHOPPING (pp180–5)
Asia Books..........................(see 28)
Asia Books..........................(see 36)
Asia Books..........................(see 41)
Central Department Store...........27 F3
Central World Plaza...................28 D3
DJ Siam..............................29 B3
Erawan Bangkok.......................30 E3
Gaysorn Plaza........................31 D3
Mahboonkrong (MBK)...............32 A3
Marco Tailors.........................33 B3
Narayana Phand......................34 E3
Pantip Plaza..........................35 D1
Peninsula Plaza......................36 D4
Pratunam Centre......................37 E1
Pratunam Market.....................38 E1
Promenade Arcade....................39 G2
Siam Center..........................40 B3
Siam Discovery Center................41 B3
Siam Paragon.........................42 C2
Sogo Department Store...............43 E3
Uthai's Gems.........................44 G6

SLEEPING (pp199–201)
A-One Inn...........................45 A2
Amari Watergate......................46 D1
Asia Hotel............................47 B1
Bangkok City Inn......................48 E2
Bed & Breakfast Inn..................49 A2
Conrad Bangkok.......................50 G5

Four Seasons Hotel....................51 D4
Grand Hyatt Erawan..................52 D4
Holiday Mansion Hotel................53 G3
Intercontinental Bangkok.............54 E3
Natural Ville.........................55 E5
Novotel Bangkok on Siam
Square..............................56 C3
Pathumwan House.....................57 A2
Reno Hotel...........................58 A2
Swissotel Nai Lert Park................59 F3
VIP Guest House/Golden House.....60 E3
Wendy House..........................61 A2

TRANSPORT (pp238–43)
Air New Zealand......................62 F6
American Airlines......................63 F6
Avis................................(see 52)
Cathay Pacific Airways.............(see 63)
China Airlines......................(see 36)
Malaysia Airlines...................(see 63)
United Airlines.....................(see 62)

INFORMATION
AAA Thai Language Center.....(see 12)
Bookazine............................64 B3
EU Embassy..........................65 C1
Indonesian Embassy..................66 C1
Israeli Embassy.......................67 F4
Netherlands Embassy..................68 F5
New Zealand Embassy.................69 G5
Norwegian Embassy...................70 G3
Police Station.........................71 D1
Siam Family Dental Clinic.........(see 18)
Spanish Embassy......................72 G5
Swiss Embassy........................73 G3
TOT Office...........................74 E3
TOT Office...........................75 G3
UK & Northern Ireland Embassy....76 G3
US Embassy..........................77 F6
Vietnamese Embassy..................78 G4

294

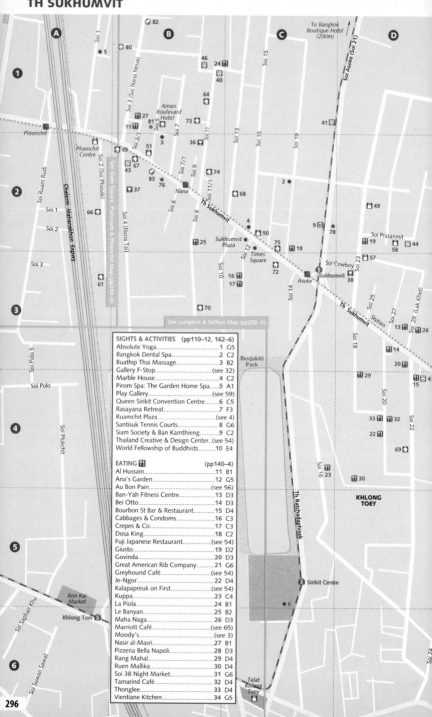

SIGHTS & ACTIVITIES (pp110–12, 162–6)

Absolute Yoga	1 G5
Bangkok Dental Spa	2 C2
Buathip Thai Massage	3 B2
Gallery F-Stop	(see 32)
Marble House	4 C2
Pirom Spa: The Garden Home Spa	5 A1
Play Gallery	(see 59)
Queen Sirikit Convention Centre	6 C5
Rasayana Retreat	7 F3
Ruamchit Plaza	(see 4)
Santisuk Tennis Courts	8 G6
Siam Society & Ban Kamthieng	9 C2
Thailand Creative & Design Center	(see 54)
World Fellowship of Buddhists	10 E4

EATING 🍴 (pp140–4)

Al Hussain	11 B1
Ana's Garden	12 G5
Au Bon Pain	(see 56)
Ban-Yah Fitness Centre	13 D3
Bei Otto	14 D3
Bourbon St Bar & Restaurant	15 D4
Cabbages & Condoms	16 C3
Crepes & Co	17 C3
Dosa King	18 C2
Fuji Japanese Restaurant	(see 54)
Giusto	19 D2
Govinda	20 D3
Great American Rib Company	21 G6
Greyhound Café	(see 54)
Je-Ngor	22 D4
Kalapapreuk on First	(see 54)
Kuppa	23 C4
La Piola	24 B1
Le Banyan	25 B2
Maha Naga	26 D3
Marriott Café	(see 65)
Moody's	(see 3)
Nasir al-Masri	27 B1
Pizzeria Bella Napoli	28 D3
Rang Mahal	29 D4
Ruen Mallika	30 D4
Soi 38 Night Market	31 G6
Tamarind Café	32 D4
Thonglee	33 D4
Vientiane Kitchen	34 G5

Benjakiti Park

KHLONG TOEY

🚇 Sirikit Centre

Bon Kai Market

Khlong Toei 🚇

Talat Khlong Toey

0 | 300 m
0 | 0.2 miles

Th Petchaburi Tat Mai

Dutchess Plaza

Soi 8

Dental Hospital

Soi 49

Soi 55 (Thong Lor)

Samitivej Hospital

To Zantika (300m)

Soi Prommit

Prommit Hospital

Phrom Phong

Soi 37 (Soi Phrohnchai)

Soi 39 (Phrompong)

Th Sukhumvit

Soi 41

Soi 43

Soi 45

Soi 24

Soi 26

Soi 28

Soi 30

Soi 32

Soi 34

Soi 36

Soi 38

Soi 49

Soi 51

Soi 53

Soi 55 (Thong Lor)

Soi Thong Lor 3

Soi Thong Lor 1

Thong Lor

Soi 57

Soi 59

Soi 61

Soi 2

Sukhumvit Soi 63 (Ekamai)

Ekamai

แผนที่เส้นทางรถไฟฟ้า บีทีเอส
BTS SkyTrain Route Map

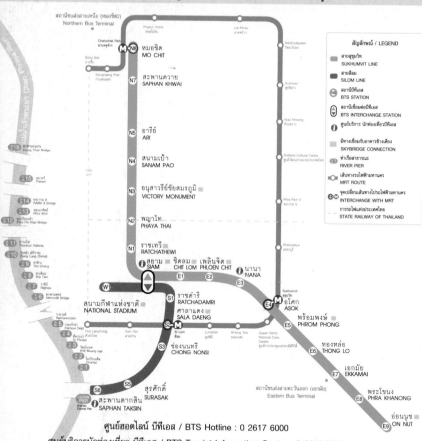

สัญลักษณ์ / LEGEND

สายสุขุมวิท SUKHUMVIT LINE

สายสีลม SILOM LINE

สถานีบีทีเอส BTS STATION

สถานีเชื่อมต่อบีทีเอส BTS INTERCHANGE STATION

ศูนย์บริการ นักท่องเที่ยวบีทีเอส

มีทางเชื่อมกับอาคารข้างเคียง SKYBRIDGE CONNECTION

ท่าเรือสายธารณะ RIVER PIER

เส้นทางรถไฟฟ้ามหานคร MRT ROUTE

จุดเปลี่ยนเส้นทางรถไฟฟ้ามหานคร INTERCHANGE WITH MRT

การไฟฟ้าประเทศไทย STATE RAILWAY OF THAILAND

ศูนย์ฮอตไลน์ บีทีเอส / BTS Hotline : 0 2617 6000

ศูนย์บริการนักท่องเที่ยว บีทีเอส / BTS Tourist Information Center : 0 2617 7340

เปิดให้บริการ / Service Hours : 06.00 - 24.00 hrs.

www.bts.co.th